THE BHUT

T0049023

Owen Bennett-Jones has reported for the BBC from over sixty countries. He is the author of *Pakistan: Eye of the Storm*. Bennett-Jones has won journalism prizes and written for the *Financial Times*, the *Guardian* and the *London Review of Books*.

Further praise for *The Bhutto Dynasty*:

'An excellent study that is far more than a chronicle of the Bhutto family, although that history is fascinating enough. ... *The Bhutto Dynasty* is essential reading for any historian of Pakistan as well as for any scholar interested in civil-military relations in South Asia.' R. Gerald Hughes and Ryan Shaffer, *Intelligence and National Security*

'[Bennett-Jones's] new book tells the necessary and important story of how a new political party, the Pakistan People's Party, emerged in the late 1960s to displace a military dictatorship in Pakistan and gradually transmogrified itself into a dynastic order rooted in the feudal roots of its founder Zulfikar Ali Bhutto. It is a riveting tale based on deep reportage and sleuthing.' Shuja Nawaz, *The Friday Times*

'Blending the Bhutto family's eventful history with that of the broader political developments, Bennett-Jones's exploration is riveting and thought-provoking in equal measure.' Sarah Ansari, author of *Boundaries of Belonging*

THE BHUTTO DYNASTY

THE STRUGGLE FOR POWER IN PAKISTAN

OWEN
BENNETT-JONES

YALE UNIVERSITY PRESS
NEW HAVEN AND LONDON

For information about this and other Yale University Press publications, please contact:
U.S. Office: sales.press@yale.edu   yalebooks.com
Europe Office: sales@yaleup.co.uk   yalebooks.co.uk

All reasonable efforts have been made to provide accurate sources for all images that appear in this book. Any discrepancies or omissions will be rectified in future editions.

Set in Adobe Garamond Pro by IDSUK (DataConnection) Ltd
Printed in Great Britain by Clays Ltd, Elcograf S.p.A

Library of Congress Control Number: 2020942571

ISBN 978-0-300-24667-4 (hbk)
ISBN 978-0-300-26473-9 (pbk)

A catalogue record for this book is available from the British Library.

10 9 8 7 6 5 4 3 2 1

CONTENTS

ILLUSTRATIONS

1. A British colonial certificate praising the loyalty of Doda Khan Bhutto, 1877. Owen Bennett-Jones.
2. Mir Ghulam Murtaza Bhutto. By permission of Sanam Bhutto.
3. Sir Shahnawaz Bhutto. By permission of Sanam Bhutto.
4. Benazir Bhutto as a schoolgirl. By permission of Sanam Bhutto.
5. Zulfikar, Sanam and Shahnawaz Bhutto in Karachi. Keystone Press/Alamy.
6. Zulfikar Ali and Begum Nusrat Bhutto, Paris, 1969. © Guy Le Querrec/ Magnum Photos.
7. Afrasia, 'Yesterday's Bhutto, Today's Bhutto: Exclusive', 31 March 1978. Cartoonist Mazhar.
8. *Zulfikar Ali Bhutto: The Martyr of Democracy*, magazine special edition, published by Mohammed Rafiq Mogul.
9. General Zia ul-Haq. White Star.
10. Shahnawaz and Murtaza Bhutto, London, 1978/9. By permission of Sanam Bhutto.
11. Benazir Bhutto's return to Lahore, 1986. White Star.
12. Al Zulfikar.
13. Benazir Bhutto being sworn in as Pakistan's prime minister, Islamabad, 1988. Reuters/Muzammil Pasha/Files.
14. Benazir Bhutto reads to her eldest son Bilawal. By permission of Bashir Riaz.
15. Poster of Benazir Bhutto during her electoral campaign, 1988. © A. Abbas/Magnum Photos.
16. Electoral poster featuring Zulfikar Ali Bhutto and Benazir Bhutto, 1988. © A. Abbas/Magnum Photos.

17. Portrait of Zulfikar Ali Bhutto and Benazir Bhutto. Pakistan People's Party.
18. Murtaza Bhutto. Pakistan People's Party.
19. Immediate aftermath of the shooting of Murtaza Bhutto. Ziad Zafar.
20. Fatima Bhutto, Karachi, 2008. Reuters/Zahid Hussein.
21. Rockwood House. Andrew Hasson/Alamy.
22. Bilawal Bhutto Zardari at Oxford University, 2008. Reuters/Toby Melville.
23. Mourners gather at the Bhutto family mausoleum, 2007. Shutterstock.
24. Bakhtawar and Aseefa pray at Benazir Bhutto's grave, 2007. Reuters/Zahid Hussein.
25. Shrine to Benazir Bhutto. Shutterstock.
26. Benazir Bhutto's political will. Ziad Zafar.
27. President Asif Ali Zardari holds up a picture of Benazir Bhutto at the 63rd United Nations General Assembly, New York, 25 September 2008. Reuters/Eric Thayer.
28. Bilawal Bhutto Zardari out campaigning, 2018. Reuters/Akhtar Soomro.

ACKNOWLEDGEMENTS

While this is not an authorised history of the Bhutto dynasty, many members of the family were good enough to talk to me and I would like to thank, in particular, Sanam Bhutto and Tariq Islam, who both gave me time whenever I asked for it. I also benefited from the advice of Ali Bhutto, who is doing impressive research on the family's early history in Sindh. Ashiq Bhutto was very helpful on Zulfikar Ali Bhutto's early days, with his memories of nights out in London back in the 1940s. Ghinwa Bhutto welcomed me to 70 Clifton, although sadly I was unable to see or use the library there. Thanks too to Muslim Bhutto for his help. Before writing this book, I presented a podcast series on the assassination of Benazir Bhutto. Both Asif Zardari and Bilawal Bhutto granted interviews for those podcasts.

Film-maker and journalist Ziad Zafar could not have been more generous with his remarkable knowledge and subtle understanding of the Bhutto family: we all look forward to his film on Zulfikar Ali Bhutto. Thanks also to Hassan Abbas, Paaras Abbas, Safdar Abbasi, Zehra Abid, Peter Acland, Aitzaz Ahsan, Kamal Alam, Kamal Azfar, Farhatullah Babar, Jeffrey Balkind, Shyam Bhatia, Linda Francke, Peter Galbraith, Ihsan Ghani, Ejaz ul-Haq, Husain Haqqani, Talat Hussain, Yasmin Islam, Akram Kaimkhani, Secunder Kermani, Naheed Khan, Roedad Khan, Malik Hammad Lang, Mushtaq Lasharie, Shafqat Mahmood, Rehman Malik, Hamid Mir, Pervez Musharraf, Aftab Nabi, Abbas Nasir, Shuja Nawaz, Yousuf Nazar, Rosanna Nissen, Amna Paracha, Nadeem F. Paracha, Raza Rabbani, Adil Rashdi, Bashir Riaz, Ameena Saiyid, Richard Saran, Victoria Schofield, Masood Sharif, Mark Siegel, Shoaib Suddle, Ron Suskind, Bushra Taskeen, Salma Waheed, Samiya Waheed, Rabia Zia, Usman Zahid and Najib Zaffar.

ACKNOWLEDGEMENTS

Farzana Shaikh, who always gives good advice, kindly agreed to read the manuscript and made lots of helpful comments. Heather McCallum at Yale University Press was an enthusiastic supporter of the project from the outset.

I also owe thanks to staff at The National Archives of the UK in Kew and the British Library in central London. It never ceases to amaze me that one can have original documents, however obscure, on one's desk within ninety minutes of asking for them. I also benefited from material kept at Pakistan's National Archive – technically known as the National Documentation Centre. Partly because of its location in the cabinet secretariat, access is not easy and a lot of sensitive subjects are clearly still considered off limits, but, once one has got in, there is more declassified material available there than many appreciate. In Karachi, Shahzeb Jillani helped me work out what the Sindh Archives have on the colonial period. Pakistan's leading newspaper, *Dawn*, has a beautifully preserved collection of not only its own back copies since 1947 but also cuttings from all of Pakistan's English media arranged by topic. The paper also has a very impressive collection of historical images. Pakistan is lucky to have a media house so committed to preserving the country's history, one that does so with greater passion and transparency than many of the state bodies charged with the task. I am very grateful to Hameed Haroon and Zaffar Abbas for making it so easy to use the newspaper's rich resources.

The Bhuttos are still active in politics and many interlocutors requested anonymity, especially when it came to describing recent times and presidencies. Thanks, too, to these contributors.

I am grateful to Tariq Islam, Ali Bhutto, Fakir Aijazuddin, Riaz Ujjan and Javed Jabbar all of whom made suggestions to improve this edition.

INTRODUCTION

At around 1 a.m. on 27 December 2007 Benazir Bhutto was told someone would try to kill her that day. The warning came from no lesser a source than the director general of Pakistan's main intelligence agency, the Inter-Services Intelligence (ISI). Despite the late hour, Lieutenant General Nadeem Taj, the second most powerful man in the country after the army chief, was so sure of his information that he travelled to her home in Islamabad to deliver the message in person. General Taj told her that suicide bombers would target her before, during or after an election rally she would be addressing in Rawalpindi. Suspicious that he was trying to trick her into cancelling the event, Benazir[1] told Taj that, if he knew about some suicide bombers, he should arrest them. That was impossible, Taj replied, because it would expose his sources. 'Giving me security is the responsibility of the state,' Benazir insisted. 'You beef up security and make sure that I'm fully protected. Not only I'm protected, but my people who are there, they're fully protected.' Taj said he would do his best.[2]

As General Taj and Benazir were speaking, her assassins were making their final preparations. A Taliban handler, Nasrullah, had arrived in Rawalpindi shortly after midnight, bringing with him two fifteen-year-old boys, Bilal and Ikramullah. According to the rituals they had learnt in the suicide bomb facility where they had been trained, the boys had to bathe to ensure they were clean for when they entered paradise. As they prepared for martyrdom, two more handlers, named in the eventual trial as Husnain Gul and Rafaqat Hussain, went to Rawalpindi's Liaquat Park, where the Pakistan People's Party (PPP) rally was due to be held, to check nothing would upset their plans. The police were already setting up metal detectors at each of the three gates to the park, but since the plan was to attack her as she left the rally, that didn't matter. Satisfied that they could do it, the two young men returned and gave a pistol

1

with live rounds to Bilal and a hand grenade to Ikramullah. As Bilal put his suicide jacket on, he took off a shawl and cap, which he left at Husnain Gul's house. Although the state would later ignore the evidence, the clothes and the DNA left on them would provide what could be considered irrefutable proof about the identities of the conspirators. Husnain then advised Bilal to wear something other than training shoes, as the security forces had the idea that jihadis wore trainers and might pick him up. He put on some sandals and left his trainers behind as well. After some prayers, Husnain took Bilal to the exit gate they thought Benazir would use, while Rafaqat took Ikramullah to another gate in case she used a different route.

Shortly after she got up, Benazir phoned her family in Dubai. 'Your voice is going hoarse,' her son Bilawal told her. 'You have to make sure you drink your lemon and honey.' She then spoke to her husband Asif Zardari. 'I told her not to go out . . . She said, you know, some things I have to do,'[3] he later recalled. It was the last time she would speak to either of them. Her attitude was in part a reflection of her fatalism. 'I believe that the time is written and when it comes it will come,' she once said. 'I used to be scared of death but after my father's death I was no longer scared . . . The body is just the clothing and it is the soul that is important and the soul is free and with God and not under 6 feet of earth.'[4]

Next, she went to a meeting with the Afghan leader Hamid Karzai in an Islamabad hotel. It has often been reported that he warned her that she was about to be attacked, but in fact, he says, they just discussed the threat she faced in general terms. Benazir's convoy set off for Rawalpindi at around midday. She reached the park and was rushed up onto the stage. In front of her were 10,000 people, and she spoke for around half an hour, proclaiming her attachment to dynastic politics. Referring to herself twice as 'the daughter of Zulfikar', she invoked her father's name no fewer than seventeen times. Zulfikar Ali Bhutto, she told the crowd, found his greatness struggling against military dictators. By founding the PPP, he had placed his trust in the Pakistani people and had thereby been empowered to build the nuclear bomb and make Pakistan a great nation. And despite all these achievements he had been hanged. 'Long live Benazir!' the crowd roared back. 'Benazir, Prime Minister!'

The speeches over, she got into her bulletproof Toyota. As normal, her supporters surrounded it, and by the time the vehicle moved onto the road just outside the park it was almost at a standstill. Two of Benazir's guards climbed onto the rear bumper, while others went to the front and the sides. 'I should stand up,' Benazir said. As normal, she stood on the back seat, her head and shoulders sticking out of the emergency hatch above the roof. It was ten past five in the afternoon. Having waited all day, Bilal saw that his moment had come. He moved first to the front of the car and then to the side where there were fewer people, took out his pistol and pointed it at Benazir's head. One of the guards clawed at the young man but, although he touched his arm, he was slightly too far away to get a firm grip. Bilal fired three shots in less than a second. As the second shot rang out, Benazir's headscarf, or *dupatta*, moved away from her face. After the third, she fell like a stone, through the escape hatch, into the vehicle. As she did so, Bilal set off his suicide bomb.

'I turned my face and she was on my lap,' recalled Naheed Khan, who had been sitting on the car's back seat, beside Benazir. 'And her blood was oozing like I can't explain to you. I have no words to say. Her blood was oozing. My hands, my – she was soaked in blood. My whole clothes were soaked in blood.' Naheed Khan's medically trained husband, Dr Safdar Abbasi, was also in the vehicle. 'You know, I was trying to see her pulse and I was finding it very difficult, you know, to get to her pulse. But naturally, we had to take her to hospital. By that time, you know, the Jeep was all alone. There was no police car. There was no backup car.'[5]

There was no backup car because, inexplicably, Benazir's security chief, Rehman Malik, had driven away. He later gave a bewildering number of different accounts of his actions in those moments. In a TV interview shortly after the blast he said his car had been just 4 feet away from Benazir's vehicle when Bilal had blown himself up. He claimed he then led Benazir's car to the hospital and remained there. In a different interview shortly afterwards, he said that his car was moving in front of Benazir's and that immediately after the bomb went off they accelerated, fearing another attack. Initially Benazir followed, but, after some time, they saw that Benazir's car was no longer behind them; so they did a U-turn and returned. Both accounts – and other versions he gave – were completely untrue. In fact, Rehman Malik, together with others who were sharing his car, had simply left the scene and headed for Islamabad. A decade later, when asked why he had done this, Malik said he had been following police instructions. Another occupant of the car, Benazir's longstanding and famously loyal spokesman, Farhatullah Babar, gave a similar account, although he added that allowing himself to be driven away that day was the greatest regret of his life.[6]

Having been abandoned by some of her closest advisers, Benazir's driver had to deal with the situation himself. The bomb had blown out the Toyota's tyres, so, as he tried to speed away on the metal rims, he soon became stuck. Naheed Khan and Safdar Abbasi found themselves in the extraordinary situation of trying to hail a taxi to get Benazir to the hospital. The police had vanished. 'When we were waiting for a taxi,' Naheed recalled, 'then another Jeep came within two, three minutes. And we took her to the hospital in that car.' The vehicle belonged to Benazir's spokeswoman, Sherry Rehman. Records show they reached the hospital about twenty-five minutes after the attack. Benazir was put on a stretcher in the parking lot, then carried inside. She had no pulse and was not breathing. Her pupils were fixed, dilated and didn't react to light. Blood dribbled from a wound to her head, and doctors saw whitish material, which, they said, looked like brain matter. Despite the evidence that she was already dead, the doctors tried to revive her. Within a minute, they had cleared her throat and put tubes in her. They pumped her with fluids and adrenaline. There was no response. Blood began to trickle from her ears and nose. They moved her to the operating theatre and just before six o'clock, almost fifty minutes after the attack, opened her chest and began to massage her heart by hand. Again, there was no response. They tried drugs and a defibrillator. Nothing. At 6:16 p.m., a little over an hour after the attack, Benazir was declared dead, and all men were asked to leave the operating room. Women began to clean her body and dress the wound on her head. They removed her blood-soaked dress and replaced it with surgical clothes. Then they filled in her death certificate, number 202877. Under cause of death, it was written: 'To be ascertained by autopsy.'

When the announcement of her death was made outside the hospital, a deep, guttural groan came from a crowd appalled, but perhaps not that surprised, that yet another Bhutto had met a violent death. They all knew the history: the family's story was part of Pakistan's national fabric. Benazir's charismatic father had filled the hearts of Pakistan's toiling masses with hope before the army hanged him; her brothers, sworn to avenge their father's death, had been poisoned and shot. The Bhuttos may have enjoyed power, but they paid a heavy price. And as with her siblings, the question as to who killed Benazir, and why, has never been resolved. Many assumed that the army had asked the jihadis to murder her, but others rushed to blame Benazir's own family. And as soon as the speculation began in homes all over Pakistan and on the satellite TV channels, the cover-up was well underway. Before Benazir was even declared dead, the local police had asked the fire department to hose down the crime scene, washing away all the evidence scattered on the road.

As officials tried pre-emptively to frustrate any investigation, all over the country young men took to the streets setting up checkpoints, destroying cars and trains and looting banks. Realising that they would be seen as representatives of a state many blamed for her murder, the police stayed at home, leaving it to the army to restore order.

The Bhuttos, then and now, divide opinion. Indeed, the family is so controversial that writing about them carries obvious hazards: supporters and detractors alike judge anything said about the family not against a yardstick of truth but rather on the basis of whether or not the account they are reacting to is favourable to the family or not. Some dismiss well-grounded criticism as hearsay while others consider well-deserved praise as suggestive of a hidden Western or anti-military agenda. The various views on the Bhuttos and the many issues surrounding the family are, more often than not, irreconcilable. Take the killing of Benazir Bhutto's brother, Murtaza Bhutto, on the streets of Karachi on 20 September 1996. Some people jumped to the belief that Benazir, possibly with some collusion by her husband, ordered Murtaza's death. Zardari has always denied that, and, indeed, at the end of a long-running trial relating to the death he was acquitted. Others believe the killing was nothing more than a bungled attempt to arrest, or maybe just disarm, some of Murtaza's bodyguards. It is impossible to settle the matter. While some have suggested that there was growing hostility between Murtaza and Zardari in the period before Murtaza's death, they cannot produce any document or contemporaneous eyewitness to indicate that any order or encouragement to kill him was made. Nor can the other side provide convincing evidence of orders having been given for an arrest that went wrong. Yet each camp doggedly hangs on to its view and shows no sign of ever being willing to change its opinion. Even if irrefutable evidence emerged, many would probably still hold on to the version in which they believe. It's much the same when it comes to Murtaza's father, Zulfikar. 'Murdered by the army he challenged', say his supporters. 'Undone by his lust for power', counter the critics.

The family itself says that it has repeatedly made sacrifices for the good of Pakistan and that the Bhuttos' commitment to democracy and the country's poor is so deep that they are willing to soak the nation's soil with their blood to challenge the status quo. There is truth to this version – both Zulfikar and his daughter Benazir walked willingly and bravely towards their deaths. If Zulfikar had accepted the coup that threw him out of power and gone into exile, he could have escaped the gallows. Had Benazir remained abroad in 2007 rather than returning to fight an election, she could have looked forward to a long and comfortable retirement. Both said no to the easy life. And yet this only tells part of the story. By the time he was ousted from power, Zulfikar had become so convinced of his own greatness and indispensability that he did not believe the generals would dare hang him. As I shall describe, there is good reason to believe that he only came to realise that he would actually be hanged a few hours before it happened. As for Benazir, her continued engagement in politics was not just a case of giving up the comforts of Dubai and New York so that she could fight for her ideals. Her political comeback in 2007 also enabled her to get all the legal cases against her overturned. The amnesty she secured from General Musharraf scuppered a Swiss trial in which there was a very high chance she would have been convicted of, among other things, using money from bribes to buy a necklace worth $175,000.

The Bhuttos' story is so full of passion, talent, suffering, courage, violence and money that it never lacks a strong narrative thrust. And the family story provides a good vehicle for telling the history of Pakistan as a whole – from before the time the country was created up to the present day. The first major figure in the dynasty, Sir Shahnawaz Bhutto, like many Indian aristocrats, readily accepted the authority of his colonial masters, working closely with them and even aping their habits. His son Zulfikar articulated Pakistan's aspiration to be a successful country independent of the West, leading the Islamic world and matching Indian power, both conventional and nuclear. And then his daughter Benazir framed the national debate as one between the military usurpers and the forces of democracy. Many of the political and national questions asked by successive generations of Pakistanis were asked first and most loudly by a Bhutto. And many of the ideas and trends the family has grappled with, such as colonialism, democracy, religion, military power, inequality and nuclear technology, are the issues that have been at the heart of Pakistan's political and social development.

The phenomenon of dynastic power raises a question which political scientists seem to have largely ignored: do dynasts perform better or worse than less privileged politicians? Hopefully this book gives some of the raw data needed to answer that question. And with Bhuttos and Gandhis still seeking power, it is a question of some importance: there is, after all, at least a possibility that following his great-grandfather, grandfather, mother and father, Bilawal Bhutto will become the fifth in his family to run a state. But that raises another question: to what extent is each generation influenced by what came before? Do dynasties hold true to certain values and political positions?

From colonial days onwards, the question of how the Bhutto family positioned itself in relation to the West has been a defining issue for successive generations. Sir Shahnawaz was as pro-British as it was possible for a Sindhi landlord to be – hence his knighthood. It was a stance that worked in the corridors of power in Bombay but was also a factor in his surprise election defeat in Larkana in 1937. Zulfikar was not as consistently pro-Chinese and anti-Western as many say, and the claim that his nuclear policies led the US to conspire to kill him is, as I shall argue, not supported by evidence, although he was probably right to believe that his perceived anti-Americanism contributed to his losing his job as foreign minister. For her part, Benazir's pro-Americanism was cited by those in the Taliban who ordered her assassination as one of the reasons she deserved to die, although whether that was the real reason is discussed in Chapter 8. As well as defining themselves in relation to the West, the post-Pakistan Bhuttos have had to face the question of military power. Both Zulfikar and his daughter tried to find a way of living with the army. The story of the Bhutto dynasty since Pakistan was created has been, to a significant extent, the story of the conflict between it and the army and of the Bhuttos' failed attempts to reach a compromise with the generals. The family story, then, illustrates key themes of Pakistani political history. The dilemmas faced by Bhuttos – how to think about the West and how to manage the military – are the issues that preoccupy Pakistan as a whole.

1
THE BHUTTOS AND THE COLONIALISTS

Among the many documents hidden away in the Bhutto family library in 70 Clifton, Karachi, is a family tree commissioned over fifty years ago by the dynasty's most famous son, Zulfikar Ali Bhutto.[1] It traces twelve generations of Bhuttos, but the dynastic story really goes back twelve centuries to a time when the Bhuttos' ancestors were Rajputs, a warrior caste that became the most important Hindu ally of successive Moghul emperors, providing them with military forces. The Rajputs were composed of tight-knit, disputatious clans, and it is from Rajput culture that the Bhuttos inherited some enduring traits, such as a willingness to embrace confrontation in defence of personal honour, placing a high degree of value on owning land and, until the advent of Benazir Bhutto, the practice of keeping the family women covered and secluded.

Occasional references to the Bhuttos' ancestors in various seventeenth- and eighteenth-century Rajasthani chronicles confirm their Rajput heritage. But details are scarce, and the story is complicated by confusions between Bootas, Bhuttas, Bhuttos and Bhattis, and some inter-marriages between them. The latest research suggests that the Bhattis (and many Punjabis still bear that name) are a distinct genealogical line, while the Bhuttas and Bootas are the ancestors of the Bhuttos of Pakistan:[2] in many cases an 'a' at the end of family names changed to 'o' as part of the process of colonial anglicisation. Over the centuries, however, many Rajasthani and Western historians, and even family members, have conflated these different groups, making it hard to disentangle who was doing what, where and when. Lieutenant Colonel James Tod in his 1920 *Annals and Antiquities of Rajasthan* described a ninth-century Bhatti prince who ruled an area around Tanot, now an Indian town near the Pakistan border. The prince arranged for his son to marry the daughter of the chief of the Bootas. In the first of many colourful tales about the family's internecine competitiveness, bold strokes and ambition, Deoraj, the son of the Bhatti/ Boota union, asked the Boota chief for a village in which to settle down. The chief offered some remote desert land, the size of which was described by the area that could be encompassed by thongs cut from a single buffalo's hide. When Deoraj built not just a home but a castle on the site, the Boota chief sent a force of 120 men to destroy it. However, Deoraj tricked the assailants, inviting them in groups of ten into his castle before murdering them.[3]

Deoraj's action is the first recorded episode of the Bhuttos' unceasingly dramatic dynastic story, although that's not to say that a direct line can be traced between him and the Bhuttos of Pakistan. But from time to time Bhutto ancestors appear in various Rajasthani histories, and often in prominent roles. According to the *Gazetteer of the Bahawalpur State 1904*, for example,[4] the Bahawalpur town of Bhuttavahana was named after the Bhuttos when they won control of it around 900 AD. The earliest known artefacts relating to the family are two stone pillars engraved in Sanskrit which to this day can been seen standing in the open near the Indian city of Jaisalmer in Rajasthan.[5] The oldest, over 2 metres high, was erected in 1148 under the instruction of a queen, Naikadevi, who is described in the carving as having been born a Bhutta and married to a Bhatti. A second pillar dated 1173 also mentions 'the renowned Naikadevi', whom it describes as a pious devotee of a Sarva, a belligerent god who killed with arrows. Naikadevi, the inscription says, worshipped the arrow, and, although there is no evidence that he was aware of the precedent, nearly 800 years later Benazir Bhutto used the symbol for the Pakistan People's Party.

That Naikadevi married a Bhatti indicates that at that time – the twelfth century – the Bhuttos were still Hindu. It's not clear when they converted, but family folklore suggests it was during the seventeenth century – much the same time as the branch that went on to govern Pakistan moved from Rajasthan to Sindh. According to one of the present-day elders of the Bhutto family, Ashiq Bhutto, some of the Bhutto homes still contain remnants of the family's Hindu heritage, such as traditional Hindu wedding clothes, although they are now in tatters. 'Even when I got married some aspects of the ceremony were what the Hindus do, Hindu tradition,' he said.[6]

Why the Bhuttos moved is unclear. One family story talks about a feud between different branches of the family. Another has the Bhuttos' forebears aligned to Dara Shikoh, the Sufi-minded brother and rival of the Moghul emperor Aurungzeb. According to this version, passed down orally through the Bhutto generations, a branch of the family had picked the wrong side, and when Aurungzeb had Dara Shikoh executed in 1659 they were forced into exile and moved to Sindh. Despite being Hindus, the Bhuttos had started taking an interest in Sufi Islam – which is suggestive of a link to Shikoh – and began visiting shrines, thereby starting a process that led eventually to their conversion.[7] The man who appears to have led these geographic and spiritual shifts was Sehto Bhutto, who settled near the village of Ratodero, close to Larkana in what is now the Pakistani province of Sindh. It was an area in which vast hunting grounds afforded space for newcomers to settle and prosper, and it may be that political disruption in the area meant that the existing occupants had been forced to move.[8] However they got hold of the land, Bhuttos have been there ever since.

As he settled in Sindh, Sehto Bhutto would quickly have become aware that there were three groups who mattered in his new home area: the tribes, the religious leaders and the landowners. His most pressing priority was to build good relationships with Sindh's tribal rulers. At the time, as Moghul power declined, Sindh was undergoing a period of some turbulence, and various groups tried to fill the vacuum. Eventually the Kalhoras, described by an early British colonial historian as 'a tribe of fighting fanatics',[9] became dominant but in 1783 they were toppled by another tribe, the Talpurs, who held sway until 1843 when they were defeated by the British. Sehto and his descendants had to pick their way through these significant political changes.

While staying on the right side of the most powerful tribal leaders was crucial, the Bhuttos also needed to be mindful of the power of Sindh's religious leadership. Although the eighth-century Arab conquest of Sindh had established Muslim rule, the conversion of Sindhis was a slow process: over a millennium later, at the time of Pakistan's independence in 1947, around a third of Sindhis were still Hindu. But most Sindhis did convert, and by the time the Bhuttos arrived, Muslims were not only in the majority but the practice of their faith was a prominent part of daily life. As one British visitor observed, 'no land in Asia can boast of a like number of ecclesiastical establishments'.[10] And those establishments – mainly shrines to saints – nurtured a distinctive branch of Islam. Most Sindhi Muslims, and some Hindus too, followed a chosen spiritual leader, or *pir*, who was normally the descendant of the saint buried at the shrine he controlled. These men gave the impression of being unworldly ascetics, but since their followers were passed down from one generation to the next, the leading religious families gradually became politically important. Anyone in power in Sindh needed the support of the pirs, and the deal was simple enough: pirs who kept their followers in line, loyal to whoever was in power, became jaghirdars, which is to say they were rewarded by the state with land rights.[11]

Alongside the tribes and the pirs, farmers were becoming an emerging force as increasing numbers of people gave up a nomadic lifestyle, albeit retaining a strong clan identity. The Bhuttos themselves became a good example of this strand of Sindhi society, and they might well have felt that securing ownership of a large estate put them on the right side of history. While James McMurdo, an English army officer who roamed around Sindh in the 1830s, described the tribes as 'jealous, proud, knavish and mean', he thought those who followed trade or agriculture were 'as industrious as the former are indolent'.[12] It wasn't just a matter of their work ethic: improved irrigation systems enabled many settled Sindhis to cultivate their land and get rich.

The best single source for the early history of the Bhutto family in Sindh is a personal memoir written in the twentieth century by Sir Shahnawaz Bhutto, who lived from 1888 to 1957 and whose son Zulfikar and granddaughter Benazir went on to great heights. According to Zulfikar Ali Bhutto's biographer, Stanley Wolpert, at the time when he was writing his book there was a copy of the memoir, perhaps the only one in existence, in the 70 Clifton library.[13] Wolpert recorded that the memoir began with the phrase: 'This is not an autobiography'. The current occupant of 70 Clifton, Ghinwa Bhutto – of whom more later – says she has never heard of the book,[14] and it seems Wolpert is one of the few historians ever to have seen it. On the basis of the memoir, Wolpert described how the Bhuttos did not advance into the first rank of Sindhi landowners until the nineteenth century, when Sehto's grandson Pir Bakhsh Khan Bhutto fought many battles in Larkana but swore allegiance to the ruling Talpurs, who, in return, recognised the Bhuttos' land holdings. It was a mutually advantageous relationship, but one that was not free of anxiety and suspicion. Wolpert reports the Shahnawaz memoir as saying that in 1821 the Talpurs 'invited' Pir Bakhsh Khan Bhutto to send a son to their base in

Khairpur, where he was kept for five years as 'an honourable hostage'.[15] It was an early case of 'trust and verify'.

The Bhuttos' story has been affected to a significant degree by their relationship with the West, first Britain and later the US. By the time the Bhuttos reached Sindh, the British already had some experience of the area. The first Englishman known to have set foot in Sindh, Anthony Starkey, arrived in 1612, many decades before Sehto Bhutto. Starkey, the steward of the ship *The Dragon*, landed in the Sindhi city of Thatta, east of Karachi, having been asked by his captain to return overland to England carrying some letters. Like many of the early English arrivals, he was not welcome: he died in Thatta, possibly poisoned by two Portuguese traders who were already there and did not want any competition.[16] There followed a series of failed attempts by Englishmen to establish a trading relationship. In 1640 the East India Company dispatched a chief factor to set up a trading post, but a combination of natural disaster, disease and the suspicions of Sindh's elite meant that business was disappointing, and by 1662 Sindh had been declared too poor and hostile to justify the expense of an East India Company official living there.[17] A century later, the East India Company tried again and encountered similar problems, with successive English traders being expelled. The hostility they experienced flowed from the concerns of many Sindhis about British intentions. And, as events subsequently proved, those concerns were well founded. In 1830, a British officer, Colonel Henry Pottinger, navigated the Indus as far as the Sindhi capital, Hyderabad. British power and technology were making it impossible for the Sindhis to hold back the British, and in 1838 the Talpurs, seeing no alternative, signed a treaty with Pottinger allowing a permanent British presence in Hyderabad. Four years later their worst fears were realised when Sir Charles Napier dispensed with the diplomatic and legal niceties and launched a military attack. After a bloody battle in 1843 in which thousands of Sindhis were killed, the Talpurs were defeated and Sindh belonged to the British.

From the Bhuttos' point of view, the removal of the Talpurs opened up new opportunities. The family was by this time in the hands of a man, Doda Khan Bhutto, who proved more than equal to the task of managing the transition to British rule. As his great-great-great-great-granddaughter, the writer Fatima Bhutto, has pointed out, this involved not just diplomatic skill but also a capacity, if necessary, to use force. She has written that Doda rounded up

Bhuttos from around Sindh and told them to settle land and cultivate it. Conflict between Bhuttos and Baloch tribesmen led to many casualties, and, often enough, the Bhuttos prevailed.[18] But Doda Khan Bhutto did not rely on force alone: he had brains as well as brawn. General Napier had offered Sindhi landowners much the same deal as his tribal predecessors: if members of the local rural elite remained loyal and kept good order, Britain would reward them with land rights, titles and access to power. Certainly, there was no way of avoiding the British presence, even in remote rural areas. Just months after Napier's conquest, for example, the British set up the Scinde Camel Corps near the Bhuttos in Larkana.[19] Next came surveyors. As the *Evening Mail* recorded in March 1847: 'A survey of a canal extending miles from the Sutlej into the Bhutto's country is now in progress and active operations will in all likelihood follow the survey.'[20] And when they reached the land occupied by members of what was described as the Bhutto tribe, the British were impressed by what had become of the village by which they had settled, observing in a parliamentary report: 'Ruttah Deera about 20 miles from Larkhanah is the only other town of importance: it has a good bazaar and fort.'[21]

A few landowners resisted cooperating with the colonialists. But Doda Khan Bhutto was among the majority who tried to work with the new administration and see what he could get in return. It is a remarkable fact that when India's First War of Independence, or Mutiny, came in 1857, just fourteen years after Napier's conquest, it took only a couple of hundred British soldiers to maintain peace in the whole of Sindh. The area was so biddable in part because the main concern for Doda Khan Bhutto and others with similar amounts of wealth was to keep their property intact. The British top priority was to ensure the landowners remained loyal. Just how important this was to the British became clear with the Sind Encumbered Estates Act of 1876. Under the Talpurs, Sindhi Hindus had been forbidden from owning land. That's not to say they were not commercially active. In fact, Sindh's Hindus had a long tradition of business success. The British imperialist Richard Burton wrote that 'throughout Sindh the Hindu element preponderates in the cities and towns, the Moslem in the country: the former everywhere represents capital, the latter labour'.[22] It was the Hindus who collected taxes, lent money and managed trade. Nevertheless, a British decision to allow Sindh's Hindus to own land tilted things in their favour, and with many Muslims heavily indebted to Hindu financiers, some ended up losing their land to Hindu moneylenders. In 1896, a survey of villages in Sindh found that Hindus held 28 per cent of the land; fifty years earlier they had owned virtually none. The British were concerned. The Sindh commissioner Evan James complained that when Hindus obtained other people's land through usury, the former owners were reduced to a state of abject dependence. 'The feeling of injustice engendered by this tyranny strikes at the foundations of our rule,' he said.[23] The British worried that if the big estates were broken up, a crucial pillar of support in Sindh would be lost. Under the Sind Encumbered Estates Act a British manager could take over a bankrupt estate and declare many of its debts null and void. For the landowner there was a downside – the manager would take over ownership of the land until such time as the estate was solvent again – but once the books were balanced and the estate returned to profitability, it was given back to the landowner.

Doda Khan Bhutto, sharp as well as forceful, was quick to exploit the Act. While some landowners held back, either to preserve their dignity or because they did not trust the British, Doda knew a good thing when he saw it and ensured that his estate was one of the first to be taken over. A manager, appointed in 1876, went through the books and confirmed Doda Khan was heavily in debt. Then, declaring that much of what Doda Khan owed was the result of exorbitant interest rates charged by Hindu moneylenders, the manager wrote off over half of his liabilities. At a stroke, Doda Khan's situation was transformed. The remaining debts were dealt with by a government loan that the manager repaid from estate income over a five-year period. By 1884, Doda Khan's finances were back in order and the land was restored to him. Throughout this process, Doda Khan had pushed his luck. British officials complained about the 'persistently dishonest behaviour' of Doda Khan and his sons, who somehow managed to ramp up the estate debts even when it was meant to be under the manager's control. And at the start of the process, the Bhuttos had also significantly underestimated their income, giving the manager a false impression of how much help they needed. Doda Khan Bhutto told the British that he and his two sons had an income of 20,000 rupees and debts of 134,644 rupees. When the manager took over and did the sums, he reckoned that Doda's income, without that of his two sons, was in fact 52,798 rupees.[24] But these tactics worked well for Doda Khan. The year after he regained control of his estate, he was busy investing in the construction of a canal across some of his land.[25] Doda Khan may have cooked the books, but he was loyal, and, for the British, that was all that mattered. A document that is kept in one of the Bhutto homes in Karachi and dated 1 January 1877 reveals the British thinking: 'By command of his Excellency the Viceroy and Governor General, this certificate is presented in the name of her Most Gracious Majesty Victoria, Empress of India, to Doda Khan Bhoota in recognition of his loyalty and good service as a landholder' (Plate 1).

The British may have prided themselves on bringing the rule of law to Sindh, but they also taught the big families how to bend the law to their purpose and how to get away with infractions. Having said that, to think of all of the Bhuttos in the colonial period as nothing more than cynical operators subserviently expressing pro-British sentiment for private gain would be unfair. A few, as we shall see, clashed with the colonialists, albeit on personal rather than ideological grounds.

Uncertainty within the family about what attitude to take towards the West remains a live issue to this day. The 1877 document praising Doda has been kept for posterity, but the Bhutto family member who currently possesses it, Ashiq Bhutto, once said he was so embarrassed by the British praise of Doda's loyalty that he kept the document hidden away,[26] although now it is on public display in his house. Then and now, the Bhuttos had conflicting impulses. The maintenance of personal honour was, no doubt, highly prized, and yet most managed to swallow their pride and live under British rule. Few Bhuttos saw much point in futile gestures of defiance. Some in later generations, such as Sir Shahnawaz Bhutto, could even be accused of having fawned to the British, gladly accepting their compliments and titles while keeping any resentments well hidden. In more recent times there have been similarly confused attitudes regarding the Americans. Zulfikar Ali Bhutto was simultaneously impressed by and hostile to American power. When he went to California as a student, his social superiority in Sindh counted for nothing and he faced racial discrimination. Some of his antipathy to the West was firmly rooted in the history of colonial exploitation. In one article, he cited a series of Western studies which had tried to quantify just how much Britain had extracted from the subcontinent, concluding: 'The effects of the wholesale destruction of the Indian manufacturing industries on the economy of the country can be imagined. In England the ruin of the old handloom weavers was accompanied by the growth of the new machine industry. But in India the ruin of the millions of artisans and craftsmen was not accompanied by any alternative growth of new forms of industry.'[27] His book *The Myth of Independence*[28] highlighted Western hypocrisy in its pursuit of economic domination, but, at the same time, he respected power and he wanted all his children educated in British and American universities. While Zulfikar had conflicted attitudes his daughter Benazir Bhutto was so pro-American that those in the Taliban who ordered her assassination cited that as one of the reasons to kill her.

Admiration and respect for the West, mixed with cynicism about its double standards, has been a running theme of the Bhutto dynasty for many generations. In turn, Western attitudes to the Bhuttos determined the fortunes of the family. Whether the family flourished or floundered has been to a significant degree a function of Western policy, as developed first by the British colonialists and later by the Americans.

By the end of the nineteenth century the Bhuttos were major landowners, but just how much they owned is disputed. When it suited him, Zulfikar could describe his holdings in modest terms. In December 1971, he told President Nixon that if he failed to win power he would 'go back to his small ranch in Sindh'.[29] But for all his socialist ideals, Zulfikar also used to insist with pride that his forebears were in the first rank of the Sindhi aristocracy. In his prison cell before he was hanged, he wrote: 'My family has owned not thousands of acres but hundreds of thousands, for generations'.[30] And he delighted in telling this story:

Sir Charles Napier toured many parts of Sindh after its annexation by the British in 1843. It is said that every day after covering a considerable distance, Napier would ask his Sindhi guide, 'Who owns this land?' and every time the answer would be 'The Bhuttos'. At one stage he told the man, 'I'm tired and want to sleep. When we come to the place where the Bhutto lands finish, wake me up.' The guide didn't have to do so, and as Napier got up from a long spell of sleep he was amazed to learn that they were still in 'Bhutto territory'.[31]

Zulfikar Ali Bhutto's claims were, in fact, somewhat exaggerated. In the first place, like many other estates, the family's tracts of land were not contiguous –

Napier would have been moving in and out of Bhutto land as he travelled through northern Sindh. Secondly, even taken together, the Bhutto lands could in fact be measured in the tens, not hundreds, of thousands of acres. In the 1880s, Doda Khan had 30,000 acres in Upper Sindh, 6,709 acres in Ratodero, 21,026 acres in Jacobabad, 2,749 acres in Naushahro Abro and 919 acres in Larkana.[32] That said, Zulfikar's claim about hundreds of thousands of acres might have referred to the pre-British period. In his memoir about Zulfikar Ali Bhutto, Chakar Ali Junejo wrote – without explanation – that 'the legend goes that the 250,000 acres of Bhutto land had shrunk 50,000 acres after the British rule began in Sindh'.[33] Nonetheless, having 30,000 acres in Upper Sindh put Doda Khan Bhutto in the first rank of farmers. In 1888 the British recorded that there were forty-four large landowners in the Upper Sindh town of Jacobabad, with an average holding of just 2,384 acres. And there was something else. The Bhuttos owned their land. As we shall see, that didn't mean they could afford to alienate the British, but it did put them at something of an advantage compared to some of their peers who were more dependent on the colonialists' largesse.

From the 1850s, the British continued the practice they inherited from the previous tribal leadership whereby the central government granted land rights to important, loyal citizens who thereby became jaghirdars. In fact, the British not only continued the system, they refined it, creating four distinct classes of jaghirdar. The first-class jaghirdars – just fourteen individuals in total – mainly consisted of the heads of the old tribes of Sindh, many of them Baloch. The biggest of them, Ghaibi Khan Chandio, received a land grant of 148,024 acres or 230 square miles – more of a small state than an estate, and all of it on old tribal land.[34] As the head of the Chandio tribe on the border with Balochistan, the British considered it vital he remain loyal. Jaghirdars – particularly the fourteen first-class ones – enjoyed great prestige, but they also had a problem: should they display disloyalty or should the family become less influential, they could have their land taken back by the British authorities. This most often happened when the existing jaghirdar died and the British judged the next generation insufficiently politically important to merit continued support. In general terms, the British wanted to reduce the number of jaghirdars so that they had to give out less land. Because they owned their land, the Bhuttos never had to worry about these issues.

At some point, most dynasties must survive a generation that loses interest in the creation and retention of wealth. In the Bhuttos' case, that generation came in the late 1800s. Doda Khan Bhutto's son, Khuda Bakhsh Khan Bhutto, was, like his father, determined to hold on to the family fortunes. But his son, Ghulam Murtaza Bhutto, had other priorities. The few shreds of evidence we have about Ghulam Murtaza suggest he was arrogant, contemptuous of the law and driven above all else by the values of honour and reputation. Ghulam Murtaza, whose portrait shows a man with a somewhat cocky smile (Plate 2), did as he pleased, not endearing himself to local opinion – for instance, turning up to the death anniversary of a local Sufi saint adorned with gold, even though it was an occasion that demanded modest clothes of mourning.[35] The British records show that Ghulam Murtaza clashed with a British official, Colonel Alfred Hercules Mayhew, whose hostility to the Bhuttos became intense. As the Collector in Shikarpur between 1885 and 1898, Mayhew was the most senior British official in the Bhuttos' area. Mayhew came under the authority of the Sindh commissioner in Karachi but, in an era of poor communications, he enjoyed a large degree of discretion and broad powers as he went about running the northern third of Sindh. Mayhew was a diehard colonialist who had headed out east in 1861 and stayed nearly four decades.

The Bhuttos have recounted various different versions of the clashes between Mayhew and Ghulam Murtaza. The most detailed is in Sir Shahnawaz's memoir, which claimed that Ghulam Murtaza fell for Colonel Mayhew's Sindhi mistress. The suspicious colonel laid a trap, ostentatiously pretending to leave his Sukkur residence but in fact concealing himself to await developments. When Ghulam Murtaza rushed to his Sindhi lover, the colonel burst in and, finding them naked, lashed Ghulam Murtaza with a horsewhip. Ghulam Murtaza, unable to tolerate the insult, knocked Mayhew to the ground, grabbed the whip and lashed him back. As Mayhew nursed his wounds, Ghulam Murtaza left the scene, deposited his lover with her parents, and returned home. Ghulam Murtaza's father, Khuda Bakhsh Khan Bhutto, advised his son to flee. He went first to the princely state of Bahawalpur, but when Mayhew established that he was there, he moved to Kabul, beyond British reach. According to the Shahnawaz memoir, Mayhew then induced some men to ambush Ghulam Murtaza's father as he returned from inspecting some land in Jacobabad. The seventy-five-year-old man was thrown from his horse and died of his injuries. The death enabled Mayhew to declare that, since Ghulam Murtaza was an absconder, he had no right to inherit. In 1896, having auctioned off all the valuables he could find, he ordered that the Bhutto family house be burnt to the ground. No doubt Mayhew felt that British prestige had to be restored, but it was an extraordinary thing to do. Shahnawaz, who was just eight years old at the time, recorded the experience. 'We saw the fire ablaze at night,' he wrote. 'In the morning we saw the ashes.'[36]

Shahnawaz's account of how his father recovered from these setbacks is implausibly romantic. Having travelled in disguise from Kabul, Ghulam Murtaza pretended to be a labourer and, using the influence of an old feudal friend, got himself employed on a British building project of H.E.M. James, the most senior British official in Sindh. When James toured the construction site, Ghulam Murtaza stepped forward and said: 'I have a story to tell and I want you to do justice by hearing me.' Ghulam Murtaza was taken into custody and gave his version of his dispute with Mayhew. Subsequent members of the Bhutto family have come up with their own versions of these events. Zulfikar Ali Bhutto added a layer of political meaning by telling his children that the mistress was not Sindhi but English. And as he fled, Ghulam Murtaza worried that, should the British recapture the woman, he would suffer a loss of face, and so, with his honour at stake, ordered his men to kill her.[37] On Fatima Bhutto's account the woman was not just English (or maybe Anglo-Indian, she writes) but, in fact, the wife of the British official.[38]

Clearly these contradictory accounts cannot all be true: if there was a mistress, she could not simultaneously have been Sindhi, English and Anglo-Indian. The British archives are unsurprisingly silent on such a scandal, but it is safe to say that had she indeed been English, or even Anglo-Indian, the story would have attracted a lot more press attention. And it is likely that in the retelling of these various versions, politically helpful details have been added. Was Khuda Bakhsh Khan really thrown from his horse because of a British plot? Or did the old man just have an accident? The latter seems more likely.

While Bhutto family lore leaves many open questions, the British archives do at least confirm the tension between Mayhew and Ghulam Murtaza and detail various legal cases which Mayhew brought against the young Bhutto. In one, eyewitnesses claimed to have seen Ghulam Murtaza murder Rao Jeramdas, a revenue officer in Ratodero. According to the eyewitness testimony preserved in the Sindh archives, Ghulam Murtaza had been to see Jeramdas the day before the murder to discuss a report about the Bhuttos' affairs that Jeramdas was writing for Mayhew. But rather than see him immediately, Jeramdas kept Ghulam Murtaza waiting for an hour and then only met with him briefly. Ghulam Murtaza, feeling his honour had been impugned, left complaining that Jeramdas had disrespected him and would 'see' him.[39] That evening, Jeramdas set off for a nearby village where he was due to survey some crops. The next morning, he was found dead in his bed covered in blood. At much the same time as the body was found, Ghulam Murtaza, possibly attempting to give himself an alibi, walked into the chief constable's office in Larkana to declare that he had lost a horse. The case against Ghulam Murtaza was considered weighty enough to justify two bail applications being turned down.[40] The murder of a revenue official was a grave crime, and Mayhew was determined to bring the Bhuttos to heel, accusing them of having carried out thirteen murders without ever being caught, writing: 'the legendary Doda Khan Bhutto and the family one and all have for years been notorious for their influence for Evil'.[41] But he directed most of his anger at Ghulam Murtaza who, he believed, had murdered an honest and praiseworthy official whose intention had been 'to bring this man Ghulam Murtaza Khuda Bux Bhutto to his senses and to make him end his wicked ways and to give up evil practices which are dishonest and criminal'.[42] As these events faded into history, Mayhew's dislike of the Bhuttos lost none of its intensity. In 1901, retired and back in London, he wrote to the secretary of state at the India Office, Lord George Hamilton, complaining that the governor of Bombay had prostituted himself by awarding one of the Bhuttos – Doda's grandson Rasool Bakhsh Bhutto – a sword of honour in public *durbar* (a meeting or assembly). The letter, sent from Mayhew's club, is so difficult to read that it is possible he was drunk when he wrote it, but it is clear that he thought the Bhutto awarded the sword of honour a 'notorious bad character . . . and harbourer of thieves'.[43]

Sir Shahnawaz's account assumes that all the legal cases brought against Ghulam Murtaza were blatantly false. In fact, the court records suggest that Ghulam Murtaza had a strong case to answer, but that the Bhuttos hired top lawyers and achieved repeated acquittals on various charges. Unable to accept defeat, Mayhew secured a retrial in Bombay, where Ghulam Murtaza was again acquitted and his property restored to him. But it was a Pyrrhic victory. Within a month of getting back home to Larkana, he had been poisoned to death: Sir Shahnawaz suspected local landowners who had earlier given evidence against his father and feared his taking revenge.[44]

Ghulam Murtaza's experience entrenched the Bhuttos' view that there was always a way around legal cases. It is a view that has recurred across the generations. By working within the legal system to secure acquittals, the Bhuttos were taking advantage of what many colonial administrators saw as a weakness in their judicial arrangements. If a British official such as Mayhew made accusations against someone such as Ghulam Murtaza and the court found him innocent, then Mayhew's authority was undermined. From the point of view of the Bhuttos, however, the system meant they could behave in their locality much as they always had and then work on securing exoneration in the courts. Some landowners tried to reject the British system altogether. The Bhuttos played a subtler game of securing their objectives by working within it. For over a century now, many Bhuttos, from Ghulam Murtaza through to Bilawal, seem to have believed that making legal accusations against them is a political tool wielded by opponents. Sir Shahnawaz thought that of the cases against his father, and Bilawal Bhutto believes it of the cases against his father, Asif Zardari, today. As for Zulfikar Ali Bhutto, it is widely accepted that, whatever the merits of the case against him, he went on trial only because General Zia wanted to neutralise an opponent whom he feared. The family routinely describes his death as judicial murder and the courtroom where he was tried as a crime scene. Zulfikar's conviction was unusual for a Bhutto: the family normally secures acquittals, and cases faced by Bhuttos not only in Pakistan but also in European jurisdictions have been subject to attempts at political pressure. But, of course, it's a big step to believe, as the family seems to, that no Bhutto can ever be justly accused.

The case of Shahnawaz's cousin, Wahid Bakhsh Bhutto, an elected member of the Central Legislative Assembly of India, illustrates the point. In January 1929 he was arrested at his home in Larkana on the charge of abetting the kidnapping and murder of Khanzadi, a Hindu woman described by the *Sunday Times* as 'unusually pretty'.[45] Eighteen others, including his servant and a chauffeur, were also charged. The allegation was that Khanzadi's husband had given information to the authorities which resulted in some of Wahid Bakhsh's staff being jailed. Bhutto's men then raped Khanzadi, and, after she became pregnant, tried to force an abortion, which resulted in her death. As ever, the Bhuttos argued that the case was politically motivated, this time by Hindus who were determined to bring down an upstanding member of the Muslim community. Understanding that one of the ways to defeat a case is to control the process, Wahid Bakhsh Bhutto moved petitions to get the proceedings held outside Sindh; he offered to pay for all the witnesses to be transported to Bombay; and he suggested setting up a committee of inquiry to look into the case. When all those efforts were rebuffed, the family resorted to political pressure, eventually managing to persuade the British authorities to instruct the public prosecutor to withdraw the case.[46] The scandal that ensued resulted in the first mention of a Bhutto in the British Parliament: when a backbencher asked the secretary of state for India why the case had been withdrawn, he was fobbed off with the reply that, since the process of withdrawing the case was not finalised, the matter was *sub judice* and could not be discussed.[47]

The Bhuttos' long-standing ability to remain influential has depended not only on their management of legal cases but also on keeping their land holdings. This was achieved in large part by the practice of Bhutto men marrying female relatives, who were prohibited from marrying non-Bhuttos so as to avoid anyone who did not bear the family name inheriting Bhutto land. But there was another factor that often affected inheritance issues: the tendency of Bhutto men to die young. As a boy, Ghulam Murtaza's son, Shahnawaz, looked set to become a relatively obscure member of the Bhutto family. Doda Khan Bhutto died in the early 1890s and his estate was divided between his sons; for reasons unknown, Shahnawaz's branch of the family did not do very well, inheriting a relatively small acreage.[48] Worse still, from Shahnawaz's point of view, there was a good chance that even that land would not pass down to him because his father, Ghulam Murtaza, had at that point lost his right to own property. There were many other Bhuttos who looked set to inherit far more than Shahnawaz.

Despite this unpromising start, Shahnawaz ended up with enough property to support his political career, although it took some surprising dynastic plot twists to get him there. As we have seen, his grandfather Khuda Bakhsh Khan died after falling off his horse. With Ghulam Murtaza in Afghan exile, Shahnawaz's great-uncle Elahi Bakhsh took over his land. When Ghulam Murtaza won his court case in Karachi, he re-established his right to own and bequeath property, but when he was poisoned weeks later, the schoolboy Shahnawaz lost his father but inherited the land; his half-brother Ali Gohar Khan missed out because he was a single day younger than Shahnawaz. Elahi Bakhsh remained the far wealthier man, however. Having finished his schooling in 1908, Shahnawaz went to stay with Elahi Bakhsh in Upper Sindh. They had an evening meal together but never shared breakfast: the next morning the twenty-eight-year-old Elahi Bakhsh was found dead in his bathroom. The death was never explained. But even to this day, some members of the family whisper their dark suspicions about the possible involvement of Shahnawaz, citing as a motive his desire to increase his estates. Such grim accusations were not unusual within the family. Sayid Ghulam Mustafa Shah, a family friend from Upper Sindh, remarked that the Bhutto habit of nursing hereditary animosities meant 'there was something ominous in the whole lot of them as they were constantly engaged in internecine intrigues, troubles and fights. Every Bhutto was enemy of every other Bhutto.'[49]

The Bhutto tendency to harbour grudges is well illustrated by another, probably apocryphal, family story. Benazir recalled how, having had four sons, Doda Khan married for the second time and produced a fifth, to whom he became very attached. He had already handed over his land in equal shares to his first four children, and now asked for the land to be given back so that he could redistribute it to include his youngest, and now favourite, son. Three agreed, but the eldest insisted that his share of the land was now his, that his youngest brother had no right to it and that he didn't have to give it back. When Doda Khan refused to withdraw his request for the return of the land, the eldest son sold it overnight at a cheap price, saying he could do whatever he wanted with it. For Doda Khan, this breached the cardinal principle of feudal culture: that you never sell land. He disowned his son and said that if he died he would not weep but would drink a glass of milk – a sign of joy. Some years later the son did predecease Doda Khan, who duly ordered a glass of milk and was about to drink it when his second wife rushed over and threw it away. Only then did Doda Khan break down in tears to mourn his son.[50] While there is no way to verify this tale, it nonetheless helps illustrate the kind of issues that Bhuttos discuss and worry about. To this day, fathers cut off sons who irritate them and one branch of the family will refuse to attend the marriage of Bhuttos in another branch. The most high-profile row of recent years was between Benazir Bhutto and her brother Murtaza, but there are other examples, such as Mumtaz Bhutto, who has bad relations with some of his family.

Shahnawaz was in a better position than other Bhuttos to take advantage of his wealth. His upbringing had given him more schooling than any previous member of the family. He started out in the Larkana Madrasah Middle School, an institution created for the children of wealthy local landlords and devoted to regular prayers, daily sport and the learning of English.[51] He was thus prepared for his second school, the Sindh Madrassatul Islam in Karachi, which, a few years before Shahnawaz arrived, had educated the boy who went on to found Pakistan, Mohammad Ali Jinnah. Shahnawaz was given two rooms in the bungalow of the British principal, Mr Vines. The word *madrasah* today is associated with extreme religiosity and even Taliban-style militancy. But the British-funded Sindh Madrassatul Islam was part of a very different tradition: it was established in 1895 by followers of the educationalist Sir Syed Ahmad Khan, who had pioneered modern education for Indian Muslims in the more famous Aligargh Muslim University. The English-medium Karachi madrasah was designed to equip pupils to operate in the colonial administration. Shahnawaz was also influenced by a British official, H.C. Mules, who had taken over from Colonel Mayhew as the Collector for Sindh. A less tempestuous man than his predecessor, Mules took care of Shahnawaz. Like Vines, he was probably motivated in part by a desire to inculcate pro-British attitudes in a member of one of the elite families. If so, it worked. One of Shahnawaz's friends, Hussain Shah Rashdi, later described how from a young age Shahnawaz 'changed his lifestyle and was one of the first persons to switch over to the Western way of life'. As an adult he wore archetypically British clothing: suits, bow ties and, when occasion demanded, full ceremonial dress replete with medals and a sword. And he also developed a British attitude to punctuality: the Sindhi nationalist G.M. Syed, who worked with Shahnawaz in the 1920s and 1930s, recalled him embracing, as he put it, a modern way of life: 'he followed strict timings for everything that he did'.[52]

Photographs of Shahnawaz show a man whose ample moustache and straight back gave him natural presence and bearing. He has been described as staid,[53] but that does not quite capture someone who enjoyed the occasional vice. There is a tape recording in the British Library in which a retired Inspector

General of Police in Sindh, Walter Pryde, described a chance encounter with Shahnawaz at Sukkur railway station:

> Shahnawaz was a man who used to drink far too much. He was a clever man but a very honest man . . . He loved the women and he loved drink. He had the money and he spent it. I remember early one morning I was at Sukkur and I was going off to Karachi. I was going to catch the Quetta Mail, which was passing through Sukkur. I was waiting at the station and Shahnawaz, drunken fellow, was there. And he was tight then and it was 6 o'clock in the morning.[54]

A soft-spoken man who insisted on his dignity, Shahnawaz would not have enjoyed that description, although his ingrained aristocratic nature might have led him to dismiss Pryde as having an overly bourgeois sensibility. When he described himself, Shahnawaz portrayed a patrician fulfilling his duty to dispense beneficence to those less fortunate than himself. 'I was courteous to the common man and rarely did I lose my temper,' he wrote in the personal memoir seen by Wolpert, adding, as only a grandee could, 'I spared no efforts to cultivate and befriend the masses.' Shahnawaz was a stickler for codes of rank, dress and decorum. A friend, Syed Mir Mohammad Shah, recalled a horse and cattle show in Jacobabad in which the members of the Bombay Legislative Council were placed in the second row, behind the British officials. Shahnawaz was so outraged that he led a boycott of the event and fired off a letter of complaint to the governor of Bombay.[55]

Many a man in Shahnawaz's position might have devoted himself to the two traditional activities of Sindhi aristocrats: maintaining family honour and hunting. But it was a time of change in India, and Shahnawaz had greater ambitions. As the century progressed, the British introduced reforms that enabled Indians to seek election to advisory bodies. Their powers were limited, but it opened up the possibility of political careers, and Shahnawaz took his chance. He began in 1910 with membership of the District Local Board in Larkana and in 1920 became its president, a post that would give him considerable authority in northern Sindh for over a decade. Shahnawaz's tactics for maintaining control involved an unabashed use of patronage politics. He also introduced a process whereby he would make a decision and then send it to the

Board for subsequent ratification. Tiring of this, another local landowner, Ayub Khuhro, publicly objected, saying that if all the Board was going to do was support decisions that had already been taken, there was little point in its meeting. Ayub Khuhro's daughter recalled how Shahnawaz reacted to this challenge:

> Bhutto was very alarmed at this sign of rebellion and realised that if allowed to go further this could mean more trouble from the members and an end to his dominance. He asked Khuhro to come and see him and explained in a fatherly way that it was dangerous to air his views or protest publicly in this hot headed youthful way and that he should understand that if there was open debate he would not be able to keep control over the Board and all kinds of elements would raise their voices. So, if Khuhro wanted anything in the way of scholarships or employment for his protégés or any other benefits Khuhro should come and see him and all would be settled in a gentlemanly manner with no fuss.[56]

By 1921 Sir Shahnawaz was sitting on the Bombay Legislative Council, and in 1925 he became president of the Sind Mohammedan Association – one of his obituarists claimed that he had become 'the acknowledged leader of the Muslims'.[57] But Sindh's Muslims were by no means unified around one leader or one political stance. The Sindh Mohammedan Association had been founded in 1884 to ensure that Muslims got a greater share of the benefits on offer from the British colonialists and, in particular, representation on elected bodies at local and district level. But it was an organisation that espoused gradualism, and some of Sindh's Muslims, particularly younger, urban ones, found it rather tame: they were more interested in political campaigns to protect Muslims from a resurgent Hindu nationalism.

In the 1920s an issue emerged on which most of Sindh's Muslims could agree: the separation of Sindh from the Bombay Presidency. It was a question with a long history. For a four-year period after Napier's 1843 conquest, Sindh had been run as a separate entity before being brought under the control of British officials in Bombay. Many Sindhis – initially both Hindu and Muslim – came to resent this arrangement and demanded that Sindh should have more say in its own affairs, free of Bombay's influence. They presented their arguments in terms of the distinct nature of Sindhi culture, but as time passed the issue took on a sectarian dimension, with Hindus coming to fear that separation could enable the Muslims to get the upper hand over Sindh's minority Hindu community. Separation was eventually achieved in 1936, and Shahnawaz was among its most enthusiastic champions: 'Sindh is free,' he declared. 'The first of April 1936 is the biggest day in modern times for Sindh, a fateful day. On this memorable day of the formal constitution of Sindh as a separate province we get a distinct and definite individuality, a sense of nationhood'.[58] And it was fateful: the fact that Sindh was its own unit meant that, in 1943, Muslims in the Sindh Assembly easily passed a resolution backing the creation of Pakistan. In that way, separation made a crucial contribution to the establishment of Pakistan.

To this day, many credit Shahnawaz with having spearheaded the campaign to achieve separation, and Wolpert described it as the 'crowning political achievement of Shahnawaz's life'.[59] In fact, Sir Shahnawaz was one of the last major Muslim politicians in Sindh to back separation. In 1928 he served as chair of a Bombay Legislative Council subcommittee known as the Bombay Provincial Committee, which was charged with preparing recommendations on the working of the Indian constitution. Advocates of separation submitted evidence to press their case:

The Province of Sindh has absolutely nothing in common with the Bombay Presidency. The union is based neither on ethnographic, geographic, linguistic, agricultural nor any other sound considerations. A mere accident that it was the army of the Bombay presidency that conquered Sindh is responsible for this un-natural arrangement. Our Province has suffered very much on this account. Educationally, economically, politically and socially we are far behind the Presidency . . . this Association strongly urges that the Province of Sindh should be separated from Bombay Presidency and given its own executive and legislative machinery.[60]

When it came to the vote, separation was rejected, with Shahnawaz declaring it impractical.[61] Another Muslim on the six-member committee dissented, issuing a minority report backing separation.[62] Given his pro-British history it was reasonable to draw the conclusion that Shahnawaz was simply backing colonial officials who worried that Sindh was too economically weak to support itself, although others have wondered if his view was partly based on personal factors: separation would bring an end to his living in Bombay – something he enjoyed.[63]

As political sentiment in India changed, Shahnawaz started to shift his position on a number of issues, including separation, which, by the time of the 1931 Round Table Conference in London, he came to support partly because he considered it the best way of confronting growing Hindu power in Sindh. His politics were often driven by sectarianism. As early as 1913, when he was just twenty-five, Shahnawaz had been a vocal defender of Muslim interests in the face of what he saw as Hindu encroachment. Muslim landowners, he said, 'had to be saved from the Hindu money lender' and the 'creeping conquest of the Hindus into the rural heartland of Sind'.[64] That same year his first public political act was to attend a meeting in Hyderabad in which landowners discussed the threat posed by Hindus buying land. Although Shahnawaz often spoke about intercommunal harmony, and, as we shall see, married a Hindu convert, his suspicion of the Hindu community remained with him throughout his life. His attitude was a reaction to the Hindus' growing self-confidence under British rule. When Shahnawaz had been a boy, for example, Hindus in Sindh were second-class citizens to such an extent that there were areas they dared not even ride a horse for fear that it would cause offence to a Muslim grandee.[65] By the time Shahnawaz was becoming an active politician, they had a far greater sense of their rights and demanded more equal treatment. He and many others resented it. As part of his work for the Bombay Provincial Committee, Sir Shahnawaz questioned a delegation from the All-Sind Hindu Association and took the opportunity to complain that Hindus were becoming more prosperous than Muslims and over-represented in the bureaucracy. When his Hindu interlocutor responded that that was because Hindus were more enterprising and better educated, Shahnawaz complained: 'Since the British raj came I think about 22 lakhs [i.e., 2.2 million] of acres of land have passed to the Hindus, that is in the last 80 years, while they only had a few thousand acres before.'[66]

There are other examples of Sir Shahnawaz's support for the status quo. The *London Times* reported in 1930 that as opposition to the British Raj grew, he had 'been taking active part in opposing the civil disobedience movement'.[67] And the *Daily Mail* approvingly cited his warning that 'the next phase in the present agitation will be Bolshevism in its naked form'.[68] In a letter to *The Times* in December 1930, Shahnawaz laid out his position on the big issues of the day. 'Like every sober minded Indian,' he wrote, 'I stand for the British connexion'.[69] His loyalty was amply rewarded. In time he became Sir Shahnawaz Khan CIE, OBE, OBI, that is to say he was made not only a knight – that came in 1930 – but also a Companion of the Most Eminent Order of the Indian Empire, and an Officer of the Order of the British Empire, and an Officer of the Order of British India.

Because Sir Shahnawaz had eventually put himself on the winning side of the separation issue, he was well placed to be the premier or chief minister of the new Sindh administration. Ahead of the first elections to the Sindh Legislative Assembly in 1937, he had been involved in the foundation of the Sindh United Party. According to its rhetoric, the party was meant to promote inter-communal harmony. In reality, however, while it did have a few Hindu members, it became a vehicle to advance the interests of elite Muslim politicians.[70] And it did well, winning twenty-one of the twenty-eight seats it contested. But, on one of the rare occasions when the Larkana electorate rejected a Bhutto candidate, Shahnawaz failed to get elected to the Assembly. It was a shock, and there are various explanations for his defeat.

Sir Shahnawaz's opponent, Shaikh Abdul Majeed, was not even from Larkana, but he campaigned well, portraying Sir Shahnawaz as British and even Christian, suggesting he might be planning to impose a beard tax on Muslims.[71] Sir Shahnawaz never took such claims seriously and was accused of overconfidence – he only turned up in his constituency a week before the vote and assumed that the normal tactic of paying voters for their support would work. Instead, as one of Sir Shahnawaz's political associates put it: 'Voters got the money from Sir Shahnawaz but voted for Shaikh Abdul Majeed.'[72] The British *Observer* newspaper reported that the result was due to devious campaign tactics by his opponent: 'Sir Shah Nawaz Bhutto, who was everywhere regarded as the future Premier, was defeated by a converted Hindu owing to the circulation of leaflets containing an alleged message from Ambedkar, one of the leaders of the "Untouchables", saying that if the convert were successful, 30,000 "Untouchables" would embrace Islam. This roused the greatest excitement amongst the Muslim public and produced a heavy poll in the hope of securing the mass conversion.'[73]

Zulfikar Ali Bhutto offered another explanation for Sir Shahnawaz's election defeat: he is quoted as having told another Larkana landowner, 'You know why my father lost the elections? It was because he was very pleasure loving and he was having an affair with Mrs. Parpia at the time which is why he delayed coming to Sind to organize his elections.'[74] If that account is true – or even if it isn't – then, just as in the Ghulam Murtaza saga, a Bhutto was taking pride in the male prowess involved in conducting an affair. The Parpia family was mentioned by Zulfikar's sister Munawar ul-Islam when she recounted a story about how, as a boy, Zulfikar got lost in the grounds of the Parpias' Bombay house.[75] Whatever the cause of his defeat, Shahnawaz reacted to it by, at the age of forty-nine, giving up on elected politics, despite offers from some of his party colleagues to vacate their seats in the Sindh Assembly so that he could take their place. Instead he moved back to Bombay, where, as chairman of the Sindh Public Service Commission for a decade, he continued to mix with the elite in an official rather than political capacity. One admirer explained how Shahnawaz now 'devoted himself to the task of getting as many Muslims employed in the then province of Sind as could not get a chance before his appointment'.[76]

As partition approached, Shahnawaz had one more public duty to perform. It concerned the question of what would become of one of the princely states. Because of the way the British had governed India, significant amounts of territory had remained, in theory, independent states, albeit under de facto British control. With the British leaving, the rulers of these states could supposedly make their own decisions about their future. While a few, such as the ruler of the fantastically wealthy Hyderabad, made unsuccessful bids for independence, the majority accepted the prevailing geopolitical reality and joined either Pakistan or India. In some places, however, there were difficulties. Kashmir, for example, had a Hindu ruler of a Muslim-majority population. The decision of that ruler, Raja Hari Singh, to opt for India led to violent conflict that continues to this day. The state of Junagadh on India's west coast was in a diametrically opposed situation: there was a Muslim ruler of a Hindu-majority population. The Indian leadership believed that the *nawab*, or ruler, of Junagadh would opt for India, not Pakistan. The *dewan*, or prime minister, of the princely state had indicated that that would be the case, but in May 1947, just three months before independence, he had to go abroad for medical treatment and Sir

Shahnawaz filled his place. Still confident that it had Junagadh in the bag, the Indian government sent an Instrument of Accession to the nawab for signature. But to India's dismay, on 15 August, the very day the British withdrawal from the subcontinent was formally completed, the government of Junagadh announced it was acceding to Pakistan. The new Indian government, which accused Shahnawaz of having deliberately deceived it, only found out what had happened by reading press reports published on 17 August.

Sir Shahnawaz received much praise in Pakistan for persuading the nawab of Junagadh to switch from a pro-India position to a pro-Pakistan one. Less has been said about what happened next. On 13 September Pakistan announced that it had accepted Junagadh's accession. The new government in Delhi, however, ordered Indian troops to surround the princely state. On 19 September, V.P. Menon, the Indian minister charged with corralling recalcitrant princely states to join India, travelled to meet Sir Shahnawaz. In fact, he wanted to see the nawab, but Sir Shahnawaz insisted that that would be impossible: the nawab was ill and his son was also indisposed as he was playing cricket. Instead, the two men spoke with each other and, according to Menon, it was a conversation in which Sir Shahnawaz gave a lot of ground: he agreed he had made a mistake in not making more approaches to the government of India before finally announcing the accession of Junagadh to Pakistan; he admitted that there was no doubt that most people in the Hindu-majority state wanted to join India, and said he was in favour of the issue being decided by means of a referendum. But, he added, if his private opinion became known, his position in Junagadh would become untenable.

With the troops around Junagadh enforcing a blockade, the state was effectively under siege. Food became scarce and, while Pakistan tried to help, it was unable to do so on a scale that made a material difference. Realising that his days were numbered, the nawab fled for Karachi, taking with him as much portable wealth and as many of his pet dogs as he could, leaving Sir Shahnawaz to write a letter to Mohammad Ali Jinnah in which he said that Junagadh's principal sources of revenue had dried up and that food was in short supply. He urged Jinnah to discuss the state's future with India. Meanwhile, the nawab sent Sir Shahnawaz a telegram from Karachi asking him to use his 'judicious discrimination as the situation demanded'. On 5 November the Junagadh State Council decided that 'the position arising out of the economic blockade, inter-stately complications, external agitation and internal administrative difficulties make it necessary to have a complete reorientation of the State policy and a readjustment of relations with the two Dominions even if it involves a reversal of the earlier decision to accede to Pakistan'. Thus authorised, Sir Shahnawaz wrote a letter capitulating to the Indian government: 'The Junagadh Government have requested that in order to avoid bloodshed, hardship, loss of life and property and to preserve the dynasty, you should be approached to give your assistance to the administration.' Two days later the Indian troops marched in.[77]

With Pakistan unable to defend Junagadh, Sir Shahnawaz accepted an Indian takeover. Far more powerful princely states such as Hyderabad had also been unable to resist Indian might, and Sir Shahnawaz's suggestion of a referendum was not as disadvantageous to Pakistan as it might have first appeared. True, the Hindus of Junagadh were bound to opt for India. But by holding a plebiscite – it eventually occurred in April 1948 – the Indian government had created a precedent for the same thing to happen in Kashmir. There are fringe voices on the internet who, to this day, describe Sir Shahnawaz as a traitor for his conduct in Junagadh, but they fail to take into account his limited options and discount too easily how he created a basis for a central element of Pakistan's longstanding Kashmir policy: the demand for a popular vote there.

Always keen to burnish the Bhutto dynasty's image, in 1998 Benazir Bhutto organised a 'national seminar' on Sir Shahnawaz Bhutto, in which successive speakers heaped praise on her grandfather. But there was one aspect of his life that no one mentioned: his marriages. His first marriage was an entirely conventional union with a cousin, Amir Bano, entered into in order to preserve land holdings in the family. Nusrat Bhutto recalled that Shahnawaz's first wife 'was a conservative lady and a religious person. I accompanied her to Ziaraat to Najaf e Ashraf, Karbala, Baghdad. She used to wear a burka and asked me to wear it whenever I visited Larkana.'[78] Shahnawaz had three sons and four daughters from the first marriage. In the normal course of events the sons would have inherited Shahnawaz's vast estate, but, once again, the limited life expectancy of Bhutto males affected events. The oldest son, Mir Sikander Ali, died of pneumonia at the age of seven. The next in line, Imdad, succumbed to cirrhosis of the liver in 1950 when he was thirty-six. The third son, also called

Mir Sikander Ali, who defied Shahnawaz by wearing his hair long and insisting he was an artist,[79] also died before he reached fifty. It was said he died of pneumonia, but many suggested that, like Imdad, he succumbed to a high-living, playboy lifestyle.

If Shahnawaz's first marriage was conventional, the same cannot be said of his second. According to Nusrat Bhutto, 'Sir Shah Nawaz's first wife was very old and he wanted to marry again,'[80] and he selected a younger woman: the generally accepted story is that, at the age of thirty-seven, he wed Lakhi Bai, an eighteen-year-old Hindu 'dancing girl', a phrase often used in South Asia as a euphemism for a courtesan – and while family members are loath to confirm her history, they don't deny it either. When she converted, Lakhi Bai took the name Khurshid, and she lived with Sir Shahnawaz until his death. But that could not protect Zulfikar from the insults hurled at him as a result of his parentage. A political rival, the nawab of Kalabagh, for example, called his mother's status into question.[81] And the fact that she was a Hindu, poor and not related meant many Bhuttos considered the marriage scandalous. For all three reasons, she was ostracised within the family. Salmaan Taseer, whose biography of Zulfikar Ali Bhutto relied on briefings from the man himself, recorded:

In 1924 Shahnawaz had fallen in love with, and married, an attractive Hindu girl who, before marriage, converted to Islam, changing her name to Khurshid. The 'nikah' was held in Quetta at the residence of the Nawab Bahadur Aazam Jan of Kalat. Khurshid's humble origins were anathema to the feudal Bhuttos, and for a considerable period they remained adamantly opposed to the union. Even as a young boy, Zulfikar was aware of this clan hostility towards his mother and her anguish made a deep impression upon him. He never forgot his mother's mortification at her treatment by the clan. 'Poverty was her only crime' he once said and even attributed his own equalitarian attitudes to his mother's talk of the inequities of the feudal system.[82]

The remark about his mother's poverty was something Zulfikar returned to in his death cell, writing to his daughter Benazir: 'Your grand-father taught me the politics of pride, your grand-mother taught me the politics of poverty.'[83] But there was in fact another aspect of Khurshid's story. One of Zulfikar's fellow feudals in Sindh described helping Shahnawaz secretly book a train in Karachi that took him and his fiancée to their wedding in Quetta. According to Khuhro, she was in a burka and carrying a baby daughter in her arms.[84] And there was another issue regarding the family tree that was a deep source of anxiety to Zulfikar throughout his life. Zulfikar believed that his mother was the offspring of, at best, a 'temporary marriage' between her mother and a well-known Sindhi landowner, Sir Ghulam Hussain Hidayatullah. Throughout his life, Zulfikar would refer to Sir Ghulam's descendants as his cousins.[85] When she recalled her grandmother, Benazir said: 'my grandmother was the offspring of the first marriage of her father. We don't know much about her family except that when he remarried she was not well treated and was shipped off to look after aunts rather than being looked after.'[86] One relative recalled that as a student in Oxford Zulfikar lay on his bed bemoaning the fact that 'people say I am not a real Bhutto',[87] by which he meant that, unlike his relatives, he was not the product of successive generations of marriages within the family. The issue was so important to Zulfikar that one night when he was a student in London he raised it with his cousin Mumtaz. 'You people in the family look down on my mother,' Zulfikar said. When Mumtaz argued back, the two came to blows and had to be separated. But Zulfikar was right to believe that some of his relatives rejected his mother: when she died, some members of the Bhutto family said she should not be buried in the family graveyard.[88] 'His mother's background had a damaging effect on him,' Mumtaz later recalled. 'He had a deep complex about that which made him more aggressive and intolerant. It affected his character quite adversely.'[89] Another close relative and admirer of Zulfikar agrees. 'His arrogance came out against his own class. I know from Sindhi landlords that when he was prime minister and these feudals would visit him, even if only to present an invitation to a child's wedding, he would keep them waiting in the sun for hours to humiliate them completely. This was his way of fighting back for the way they treated his mother.'[90]

Zulfikar Ali Bhutto was very close to his mother, so much so that she accompanied him on his honeymoon with Nusrat – and more than that, on the first night of his honeymoon in a hotel in Turkey, Zulfikar, anxious about his mother's unfamiliarity with travelling, shared a room with her rather than his new wife.[91] But his concern that he had shakier genetic antecedents than all his cousins left him with a sense of inferiority that he was always fighting. His energy and personal drive arose partly out of his need to prove himself. And his mother affected him in another way. Traditionally, the Bhuttos had quite sectarian attitudes. Two of Zulfikar Ali Bhutto's forebears had been accused of murdering Hindus, and his father Shahnawaz had railed against Hindu financiers. But even if, as we shall see, Zulfikar later failed the Ahmadi minority, in general terms he led the family to become much less sectarian, and Pakistan's non-Muslim communities looked to it for protection. When they were in power, Benazir Bhutto and, perhaps more surprisingly, her husband, Asif Zardari, adopted pro-minority positions, at least to the extent that the political context in which they operated allowed them to. Dynasties are about attitudes passed down the generations, but successful ones are also able to change with the times and adopt new political values.

2
ZULFIKAR'S ASCENT

Zulfikar Ali Bhutto's courage as he awaited death and his refusal to beg for mercy have been so thoroughly documented and widely admired that it is difficult to imagine him ever having been scared. But at the age of four, when Sir Shahnawaz Bhutto was away in London for the Round Table Conference, Zulfikar and his five-year-old elder sister Munawar were left behind in Larkana. By day, the servants thrilled the children with tales of a daring bandit who roamed the locality. At night, fearing the outlaw might break into their home, the two siblings retreated to beds on a rooftop courtyard and from time to time called out servants' names to make sure they were still in earshot.[1] Like many boys, Zulfikar enjoyed riding bikes, roaming the countryside and chasing rabbits. But he was also exposed, while being raised in Bombay, to the great and the good of colonial India, absorbing their political conversations and broad horizons. He was growing up in a time of political change in which traditionalists, reformists, democrats, revolutionaries, colonialists and Islamists jostled for control of the future. He was also taught – as were the offspring of all the big Sindhi landowners – that for all the internecine struggles between rival relatives, the family was always the reference point around which the rest of the world revolved. Nothing else mattered quite as much.

Throughout his career Sir Shahnawaz had to deal with better-educated Indian and British counterparts, and he was determined that his son would not face the same handicap. In 1934, when Zulfikar was six, he was sent to a convent kindergarten in Karachi. There was then a period of some disruption as Sir Shahnawaz's political responsibilities obliged him to move to Bombay, and then, with the separation of Sindh, back to Karachi, followed by the 1937 election defeat and a return to Bombay. After that, things settled down and Zulfikar was sent to the Bombay Cathedral School, which, having boys from

British, Hindu, Parsi and Anglo-Indian families, added depth to his cultural influences. While it did not try to convert its pupils to Christianity, the school nonetheless inculcated British attitudes, and the teachers – many of them British nationals – inevitably became role models for their young Indian charges. Indeed, the Cathedral School and others like it existed largely because, as imperialist theorist and mid-nineteenth-century politician Lord Macaulay put it, Britain wanted to produce 'a class of persons Indian in blood and colour, but English in taste, in opinions, in morals and in intellect'.[2] In the case of Sir Shahnawaz, the British had achieved exactly that. But by the time the next generation was put through the system, some of the more independent-minded pupils, such as Zulfikar, railed against the attempt to inculcate pro-British sentiments. Zulfikar may have turned up each day dressed as an English boy scout, with shorts, a blazer and garters to hold up his socks, but he had ideas of his own. 'There are many conflicts in me,' he later reflected, 'I'm aware of that. I try to reconcile them, overcome them, but I don't succeed and I remain this strange mixture of Asia and Europe. I have a layman's education and a Muslim's upbringing. My mind is Western and my soul Eastern.'[3]

One schoolboy experience in particular brought home those contradictions. At the age of twelve Zulfikar became engaged to Shirin, a twenty-two-year-old first cousin and the daughter of Zulfikar's uncle, Khan Bahadur Ahmed Khan Bhutto. Zulfikar later remembered objecting to the idea: 'I didn't even know what it meant to have a wife and when they tried to explain it to me I went out of my mind with rage. With fury. I didn't want a wife, I wanted to play cricket.'[4] Sir Shahnawaz only managed to make his son go through with it with the promise of a cricket kit from England. Like his father before him, Zulfikar's first marriage was not for love, but for land: because of the alliance, Zulfikar later inherited a third of Khan Bahadur Ahmed Khan Bhutto's estate. Shahnawaz may have had something else in mind when he arranged the marriage. Since Zulfikar's mother was still not accepted by some Bhuttos as worthy of the family name, tying Zulfikar to another branch of the family removed any doubts about his status as a Bhutto. Shirin's marriage with Zulfikar was an entirely pragmatic arrangement, but it was still a marriage and as such required the twelve-year-old Zulfikar to manage a marital relationship. It's difficult to avoid the thought that his sometimes shallow relationships with women later in life had their origins in the schoolboy Zulfikar trying to prove himself to a woman ten years older than him with whom he can hardly have been expected to have any significant emotional bond. They lived together for a short period while Zulfikar was still at school in Bombay. She later described how he would sit in his bedroom practising his cricket. 'He had also tied a ball in his room with the ceiling fan and used to hit it with the bat to practice,' she recalled.[5] After Bombay, Shirin spent the remainder of her life in purdah, hidden away in Larkana while her schoolboy husband pursued more normal romantic attachments, including flirting with one of India's best-known stars at the time, Nargis. One friend recalled, 'I remember him driving up and down Marine Drive to get a glimpse of her',[6] and Nargis herself thought he had a teenage crush on her. She remembered him as 'very charming and likable' but always reeking of gin and perfume: 'Bhutto as I knew him was the feudal landlord with princely pleasures: drinks, shikar (hunting) and a new girl every night.'[7] While Nargis was a passing infatuation, in his final year of school he fell for a girl, Suraiya Currimbhoy, so thoroughly that he tried to marry her – a proposal that was resisted by her parents, who eventually married her off to a cousin instead.[8]

Zulfikar's access to the rich and powerful in Bombay helped him in another area of life which increasingly interested him: politics. While still in his teens he sought meetings with the big names of Indian public life. His sister recalled how Jawaharlal Nehru, who went on to become the first Indian prime minister, used to stay in a neighbouring house in Bombay:

> Zulfi was determined to meet Pandit Nehru. Not that this was difficult. Across the low dividing-wall we saw the garden and pathway crowded with people in the Gandhi dress. Zulfi walked through the open door. He was a young student not in the white Congress dress. Panditji noticed him and called him near. Panditji asked Zulfi his name and then his views on Pakistan. Zulfi was an enthusiastic Pakistani. Panditji told him that youth was always emotional but India was a large country which would soon become great and India needed young people like him to serve it.[9]

Zulfikar was keener still to meet Nehru's great rival, the man campaigning for Pakistan, Mohammad Ali Jinnah, whose ideas he fully accepted and would hold on to for the rest of his life. 'In abandoning his advocacy of Hindu–Muslim unity,' Zulfikar later wrote, 'the founder of Pakistan left a lesson, which has, with the passage of time, become clearer in its relevance. The fact that the Hindus and Muslims of the sub-continent constituted two separate nationalities formed the foundation of the edifice of Pakistan.'[10]

The schoolboy Zulfikar from time to time used to go to Jinnah's house in Bombay hoping he might be there. When that strategy failed, he instead tagged along with his father to tea parties attended by senior Muslim leaders, including Jinnah. In 1945, at the age of seventeen, Zulfikar wrote to Jinnah saying that the time would come when he would sacrifice his life for Pakistan. 'The Musalmans should realize that the Hindus can never unite, will never unite with us, they are the deadliest enemies of our Kuran and our Prophet. We should realize that you are our Leader. You, Sir, have brought us under one platform and one flag and the cry of every Musalman should be "onward to Pakistan". Our destiny is Pakistan, our aim is Pakistan.'[11] The next year Zulfikar was invited as part of a small group of Muslim students to discuss launching a direct-action campaign in Bombay. According to Zulfikar, he suggested organising a strike in Elphinstone College and Jinnah told him to go ahead.[12]

Educated by the British, mixing with people of many faiths and inspired by Jinnah, Zulfikar's upbringing had been cosmopolitan. But his next move took him onto a whole new level of worldly experience. Overriding his mother's objections, Zulfikar headed for the US. It was the beginning of a volatile relationship with a country and culture that he both admired and reviled. His positive feeling towards the US was apparent in his first week in New York, where he wrote about the 'unrestricted and unfettered right of the individual to live free and unmolested'.[13] By this time, he had developed the rather grandiose habit of associating himself personally with great trends in human society. When he saw the Statue of Liberty, for example, he recorded that he took pride in it. On a later trip to Manhattan he identified his own ambitions and drives as being intertwined with those of humanity, as represented by the Americans who had created the skyscrapers: 'knowing full well that I had made them, they were a source of pride to me, a reminder of my progress and ingenuity. From caves to skyscrapers, from darkness to glowing neon lights, these were my accomplishments. I was pleased; I was proud.'[14]

While Zulfikar was proud of New York, the city of Los Angeles, home of the University of Southern California, taught him about another aspect of the

US: racial discrimination. A man with a deeply ingrained sense of entitlement, it must have come as a huge shock to reach USC and be barred from the university's elite fraternities. It is a mark of his determination to succeed in the US that he did not pack his bags and go straight back home. On the contrary, he threw himself into LA life, both intellectually and socially. On the academic side, at USC and later for a year at Berkeley in San Francisco, Zulfikar absorbed ideas to which he would return throughout his career. His courses covered Western philosophy from the ancient Greeks up to contemporary thinking on democracy and greater national equality in international relations. After the Second World War the creation of the United Nations was supposed to guarantee the status and independence of small countries. For a young Pakistani, nothing could have been more relevant, but Zulfikar soon developed a well-founded scepticism about the UN: 'the entire set-up is a race for supremacy between the two omnipotent nations while the rest of the world stands back in disgrace and helplessness to witness this titanic struggle'.[15] Socially, Zulfikar embraced the multiracial milieu in which he found himself obliged to live. And he had a series of relationships with women, some intense, some casual, but all brief. One of his partners, Mary Ellen, was a single mother in her early thirties with two small girls. Another, an eighteen-year-old Iranian, was caught by surprise when he proposed to her despite their never having had any physical intimacy. He was fired, she later thought, by a 'fervor of pan-Islamism'. He wanted to turn Islamic nations into a bloc which could take on the great powers and was, she said, fanatical about it.[16] There is no record of Zulfikar ever having attended a mosque in California. Much like Jinnah, Zulfikar had a Muslim identity primarily grounded in cultural solidarity.

Zulfikar spent some of his university holidays back in Karachi, and it was on one such break in 1949 that he first met the woman who would become his second wife, Nusrat Sabunchi Isphahani. While Shirin was hidden away in Larkana, Nusrat had joined the Pakistan Women's National Guard, become a captain and learnt how to drive and do drill. He proposed two days after their first encounter. He was due to return to study in California in just two weeks' time and, unable to persuade Nusrat that he was serious, the matter was left unresolved. Back in the US, Zulfikar continued dating women, and it was two years before he returned to Karachi. But he had not forgotten Nusrat and repeated his proposal. Again, time was short as he was due to return to his studies, this time in Oxford. Nusrat later recalled saying: '"I thought you were joking." He got mad and said: "dammit I am serious! I'll have to go back to study and I want to finish it off now."'[17] Faced with this second, insistent declaration, Nusrat told her father, a Karachi-based Kurdish Iranian soap manufacturer, what had happened. He objected, as did Sir Shahnawaz, who complained that Nusrat was not Sindhi and was also too modern. But already Zulfikar was in the habit of getting what he wanted, and both families relented, although Nusrat's father told her that if she had troubles she should not come back asking for help. And she did face difficulties – after the wedding she was only permitted to visit her own family once a week, and trips out with friends were forbidden by the conservative Bhuttos.[18]

At the wedding on 8 September 1951, Zulfikar decided not to wear the traditional costume of a Pakistani groom but instead opted for a Western suit. The newly married couple reached Oxford in time for the academic year to begin. Zulfikar and Nusrat's relationship has often been described as a love match, and the two did go on to offer each other great mutual support in times of trial and tribulation. But even after he married Nusrat, Zulfikar was still pining for Suraiya Currimbhoy. When he reached the UK, Zulfikar wrote to a friend in Bombay, reminiscing about his first love, who by this time had accepted an arranged marriage with a cousin, Asif Currimbhoy: 'I am now married to a fine girl but . . . Suraiya will remain deep within me always. But I gave up hopes as I told you, at Berkeley when I saw the picture of her beside Asif Currimbhoy a good friend of mine . . . They were engaged . . . I have cried at Berkeley a number of times but then my pride and arrogance came and helped me.'[19]

Nusrat and Zulfikar's relationship was not without turbulence, and even early on there was a significant source of tension: he had omitted to tell his new wife that he was already married. When she found out she complained, 'You are a married man. You cheated me. Why didn't you tell me before you were already married?'[20] Zulfikar explained that the first marriage was just about land and she should think nothing of it. But that wasn't the end of the matter, because he also hadn't told Shirin that he was marrying Nusrat. 'My father,' Shirin later said, 'asked if Zulfikar told me about his marriage. I replied in negative. Then my father apprised me about Bhutto's engagement with an Iranian girl.'[21] It must have been a huge shock, but Shirin seemed to think that her lack of schooling meant she was not equipped to support her husband in his political work. 'He needed educated life partner who may go accompany him everywhere. In our family girls were not allowed to go to school. We got only Quranic education.' Zulfikar did express sympathy for Shirin's situation, telling the Italian journalist Oriana Fallaci: 'Her whole life has been ruined by this absurd marriage to a boy, by the absurd custom in which we've been raised.'[22] For all that, he kept seeing her on his trips to Larkana, particularly at Eid, leaving her resentful that his visits were in secret, presumably to avoid Nusrat's ire. 'Why should I lie?' she later said. 'I fought with him sometimes. I used to tell him, "You have come clandestinely to me." He would reply, "You are my wife, don't fight with me." '[23]

At Oxford Zulfikar declared that he wanted to finish his master's degree in jurisprudence in two years, not the usual three. His college adviser, the historian Hugh Trevor-Roper, having first rebuked him for not wearing a gown,[24] told him that two years was out of the question as Zulfikar did not have any Latin, without which he was bound to fail. And then the Oxford academic said: 'You know, even the best brains of our own boys would not be able to do it in two years.'[25] Trevor-Roper probably forgot the remark as soon as he made it, but Zulfikar dedicated the next two years of his life to proving that he was not just equal to but better than the best brains of Britain's boys. He crammed Latin with such intensity that his young wife found herself endlessly administering vocabulary tests. For Nusrat, Oxford was difficult. She was installed in a hotel – and English hotels in the post-war period were famed for their rudimentary facilities – while Zulfikar fulfilled his residency obligation to live in college. Used to a world in which women were secluded, the arrangement might not have seemed too strange to Zulfikar. But for Nusrat, after a life of moving in the most glamorous social circles in Bombay and Karachi, it was a strain, and after three months she returned to Karachi to live with Zulfikar's parents in Larkana. It was far from an ideal situation, and after another few months she returned to the UK, became pregnant and again went back to Pakistan. Right at the start of her marriage Nusrat learnt that being married to one of Pakistan's most brilliant and ambitious men came at the expense of a regular domestic life.

While Nusrat gave up on the UK, Zulfikar kept up his work rate. In 1952 he secured his Oxford degree with distinction and in 1953 was called to the bar at Lincoln's Inn, where Jinnah had been before him. In London he mixed with other elite Pakistanis who had come to the UK for university or professional qualifications, such as Chakar Ali Junejo, a fellow Sindhi at Lincoln's Inn who would become a lifelong associate. Junejo later recorded how Zulfikar was still highly conscious of the status of Pakistanis vis-à-vis the British: 'He often used to laugh about Englishmen who occupied important posts in united India but when they retired and came back home they had to be content with insignificant jobs in shops or small establishments. "In one of the department stores I met a man here working as salesman," he said. "Do you know what he was in India? He was Superintendent of Police in Larkana or Sukkur." '26

Back in Larkana, Nusrat delivered their baby – Benazir Bhutto – and must have hoped that Zulfikar would now return to be with her. But again he delayed, this time to take up a post as an associate lecturer at Southampton University. He only planned to do a single term there, but, in the event, his parents asked him to return, citing Sir Shahnawaz's bad health. In the days before he left, Zulfikar got together with his cousins Mumtaz and Ashiq and visited old haunts in Soho, such as the fashionable Gargoyle Club, where the bar was so well stocked that the barman would give a free drink to anyone who could name an alcoholic beverage he didn't have. There, Zulfikar told his cousins that back home he was going to try his hand at politics and that he expected to succeed: he would be prime minister, he said, in ten years.27 'This guy was going places,' Mumtaz later recalled, 'he had no blood in his veins, only politics.'28

On 30 September 1953, the twenty-five-year-old boarded a ship in Southampton and travelled first class to Bombay. As he set sail, what did Zulfikar Ali Bhutto's politics consist of? Having helped out on a congressional campaign in California, he understood some of the realities of politics. He had no embarrassment about saying 'one has to live by a profitable absence of scruples if we are to be successful politicians. We have to do what others do to us, but we must do it before the others.'29 In terms of his beliefs, he was strongly anti-imperialist. As his sister Munawar observed, it was all very different from their father's approach. 'Father's love of reading and wide travels made him much more liberal than the other feudals, nevertheless he was of the old school of thought. Zulfi had socialist ideas. He believed in the power of the people. He envisaged a future of social justice and equal opportunities.'30 Sir Shahnawaz had negotiated the corridors of colonial power step by cautious step, moving from district to regional – and, for a brief period at the London Round Table Conferences, international – politics. Zulfikar had a different approach. From the outset he operated on the broadest possible historical and intellectual plane. He started to call himself a socialist in California, reading everything from *The Communist Manifesto* to more contemporary socialist works, including the writings of Jawaharlal Nehru. His most impressive piece of early writing was a defence of Islam through the ages, delivered as a lecture on 1 April 1948 to the University of Southern California. There was no new research in his lecture, nor any insights that had not been described before, but for a twenty-year-old undergraduate he displayed a very impressive range of knowledge, revealing a significant amount of reading.[31]

By the time Zulfikar left the UK the key contours of his personality had been formed. He was, to an extreme degree, talented, driven, simultaneously self-confident and anxious about criticism, politically engaged, emotionally immature and, perhaps most importantly, resentful of any suggestion that he, or Pakistan, was not being taken seriously. When he returned to Karachi in 1953, he began work as a lawyer for a Hindu-run law firm that looked after the interests of many of the Sindhi upper class. One of his colleagues there subsequently provided a vivid description of Zulfikar at the time:

Duck cotton trousers. Royal blue blazer with brushed brass buttons. Oxford University necktie. A key chain with outer end clung to the trousers loop and the other running down and disappearing in the trousers pocket. All this sat pretty on his solid sporty frame of approximately 5' 10". His classic features were dominated by his broad forehead. Jet black hair meticulously brushed back caused symmetrical waves which naturally delineated his forehead so neatly that it suggested of hairdresser's charisma.[32]

Zulfikar's handling of his first case for the firm gives a sense of the man as he embarked on his career. The question at stake was whether he could persuade a judge to allow an appeal of an earlier judgment. Two days before the hearing, Zulfikar paid the judge a courtesy call as a colleague waited outside:

It was about half an hour that he was inside the chambers when he came out he looked quite excited. He came closer and whispered in my ear:

44

'Abbasi, damn it, we are going to win the appeal.'

I was none the wiser. 'What happened?' I asked.

He said: 'You know, I introduced myself as an Oxonian and all the while rubbed in the fact that Christ Church was my college at Oxford. This college is more prestigious than all other colleges in the entire university and hardly any Asian is given admission there. The judge himself was from Queens, not so famous as Christ Church. So, he damn well was highly impressed.'[33]

To avoid being at anyone's beck and call, Zulfikar soon set up his own legal practice. It was a time when he had to work to make contacts. Having been brought up in Bombay, followed by seven years abroad, he hardly knew anyone in Karachi. But soon enough Zulfikar and glamorous Nusrat were being invited to all the best social events. Richard Nixon met Nusrat at a banquet held in Karachi at this time, later saying to Henry Kissinger, 'have you ever met his wife? Boy, she is one of the most beautiful women in the world.'[34] After the death of his eldest brother, Imdad, in 1950, and with another brother, Sikander, too dissolute to take an interest, Zulfikar also took over the management of the family estates, which provided him with more opportunities to make contacts: the family had some of the best hunting grounds in the country, and Pakistan's leading politicians, civil servants and military officers often accepted invitations. His guest list – no doubt helped by Sir Shahnawaz's contacts – included Prince Philip, the husband of Queen Elizabeth, who shot no fewer than 143 ducks in 5 hours.[35]

While Zulfikar's British royal visitors must have made other Sindhi feudals envious, the most important guest in terms of his political career was Pakistan's president, Iskander Mirza, who shot at Larkana every year from 1954 to 1958. It may be that Zulfikar had Nusrat to thank for this social connection – she was friendly with Iskander Mirza's wife, who was also Iranian. Impressed by Zulfikar's intellectual capacity, the president asked him to write some speeches and position papers. He liked what he saw and in 1957 sent Zulfikar to represent Pakistan at the UN. Zulfikar's education had prepared him perfectly for such a forum: he had the intelligence and the drive to do his own research and the ability to deliver his material well. In 1958 the army chief Ayub Khan, who had also been a regular guest at the Larkana shoots, mounted a coup and became prime minister, with Iskander Mirza initially staying on as president. The two men wanted fresh faces for what they hoped would be a technocratic cabinet, and, at the age of thirty-one, Zulfikar was made the commerce minister. His sister recalled: 'Zulfi came to know of his appointment in Iskander Mirza's cabinet when he and Nusrat were in Rex Cinema. On the screen they read that Zulfikar Ali Bhutto's presence was desired at Government House. I presume his whereabouts was given by 70 Clifton. It was then he learnt that he was to become commerce minister.'[36]

Given that Zulfikar was later overthrown by a coup, it is hardly surprising that the Bhutto dynasty has become associated with ardent anti-militarism. But as he climbed the greasy pole he was quite prepared to make common cause with the army, an impulse that stayed with him throughout his career. It wasn't just that he joined Ayub's military government: in line with the army's thinking, Zulfikar argued that democracy had failed due to the failures of the politicians. 'May I ask who was responsible for the collapse of democracy? Is the present government responsible for it or are the misdeeds of the past responsible for the death of democracy? Though there was democracy in name yet the most brutal, ruthless and selfish form of dictatorship of a coterie ran the country.'[37] As for the military ruler, Zulfikar praised Ayub in extravagant terms. 'In President Muhammad Ayub Khan we have a dauntless leader. I can assure the people that never has a cause had a man with greater purity of purpose,' Zulfikar told a rally in Balochistan.[38] He advised Ayub Khan to promote himself from general to field marshal, although he later stated that he only did this cynically. 'I told him that it was essential for him to be head and shoulders above the others. It would be better if he elevated his own rank from that of a general to that of a field marshal. He thought it to be a brilliant idea.'[39] Later, in March 1969 when Yahya Khan announced another period of martial law, Zulfikar said the decision was wise and in keeping with the yearnings and requirements of the times.[40] It is striking that Zulfikar used to refer to Ayub Khan as 'Daddy'[41] and, in turn, Ayub involved himself in Zulfikar's business in a sometimes paternalistic way. An incident in 1962 revealed something of the relationship between the two men. The year before, Zulfikar had fallen for a married woman in Dhaka by the name of Husna Sheikh. The affair led to rows with Nusrat, and on one occasion Zulfikar threw his wife out of their home. When Ayub came to hear about it, he told Zulfikar to take Nusrat back, failing which he would have to leave the cabinet. Zulfikar backed down but didn't give up on Husna, who divorced her husband and moved to Karachi. The affair became so well known that Nusrat was humiliated, and when rumours spread that Zulfikar had actually married Husna, Nusrat took an overdose, after which she left Pakistan for some months. She lived with her family in Iran before returning to Pakistan, after which she had to accept that her husband would see other women.[42]

Overlooking Zulfikar's turbulent domestic life, the army focused on governance, seeing him as usefully influential abroad. In 1965, when Indian forces were approaching Lahore, the army asked him to go to the UN in New York. Again in 1971, despite being just a private citizen at the time with no official position, he was called back from holiday in Egypt and told to go to Beijing to ask for Chinese help. Such cooperation only existed because Zulfikar was careful not to alienate the army. In the early Ayub years one fellow cabinet minister recalled how, on one occasion, he and Zulfikar both disagreed with one of Ayub Khan's proposals. While Zulfikar made his real views clear in private, in cabinet he supported Ayub, later explaining that men in his family died young and he had to do whatever it took to get to the top as soon as possible.[43] His willingness to flatter extended to Mirza too; he preposterously told the president, 'when the history of our country is written by objective historians your name will be placed even before that of Mr. Jinnah'.[44]

No doubt Ayub Khan was influenced by the obsequiousness, but he also saw Zulfikar's energy and talent and made little secret of his view that one day Zulfikar would succeed him.[45] Zulfikar's self-confidence dazzled his colleagues: which other minister, for example, would dare walk behind the all-powerful, dignified Ayub, mimicking his gait? The young Sindhi was quite plainly more impressive than anyone else at the top of Pakistani politics. And, especially when it came to foreign affairs, he had policies he wanted to implement. In December 1958 he told Foreign Minister Manzur Qadir that 'in the event of a war with India, the US is not going to come to our help militarily. Therefore, we should not extend our American connection too much.'[46] In 1960, eighteen months after being appointed to the Ministry of Commerce, Zulfikar was switched to the Ministry of Information and National Reconstruction. Three months later he was given the extra responsibilities of Kashmir Affairs and the Ministry of Fuel, Power and Natural Resources, a job which took him to

Moscow, where he set about negotiating a draft treaty with the Soviet Union under which it would provide soft loans for oil exploration. Many cabinet members strongly opposed the move, but Ayub went along with it, perhaps feeling that there was benefit in showing Washington he should not be taken for granted. When Zulfikar had returned to Pakistan from Oxford, he had joined an informal group of up-and-coming businessmen, civil servants and aspiring politicians, who met regularly in a Karachi coffee house. After becoming a minister Zulfikar still attended the sessions, albeit less frequently, but his friends found he had become something of a bore. Jamsheed Marker, who later became the Pakistani ambassador to the US and a critic of Benazir Bhutto, recounted how, after his trip to the Soviet Union, Zulfikar would boast about the deal he had done with Moscow, acidly recalling: 'Of course, at our Coffee House sessions we were regaled ad nauseam with the details of this monumental achievement.'[47]

Increasingly, Ayub Khan relied on Bhutto to help him with sensitive political tasks, including management of the effort to give the military government a democratic veneer. Zulfikar was becoming ever more important – and he knew it. With Zulfikar's help, Ayub set up a system of so-called 'basic democracy', which relied on indirect elections to produce loyal politicians. Ayub also needed a tame political party to support him and decided to create his own faction of the Muslim League under the name Pakistan Muslim League (PML). Persuading senior politicians to join the new party involved the sort of horse-trading and threats that are so central to Pakistani politics, providing Zulfikar with valuable lessons in the business of party management. In 1962 he was rewarded by being made secretary general of the new party. His praise of Ayub Khan became ever more extravagant. 'He is our Ataturk, for, like the great Turkish leader, he has restored the nation's dignity and self-respect in the comity of nations, and, above all a Salahuddin, for, like that great Ghazi of Islam, this heir to the noble heritage has regained a hundred million people's pride and confidence'.[48] The admiration was mutual, and Zulfikar was made foreign minister in 1963. Western journalists lapped up a fresh face on the international political scene. As the *New York Times* put it in 1963, 'Zulfikar Ali Bhutto, the 35-year-old Foreign Minister of Pakistan, displays the informality of an American student, the assurance of a British barrister and the prosperity of a Pakistani aristocrat.'[49] One of Zulfikar's first trips as foreign minister was to the US, where he made an immediate impression on President Kennedy in an encounter that gave rise to one of his more celebrated quotes. There are various versions of exactly what was said, but the pithiest has Kennedy saying: 'Mr Bhutto, if you were an American you would be in my cabinet.' To which Zulfikar replied: 'Mr Kennedy, if I were an American, you would be in mine.' The people of Pakistan were thrilled to have a leader with such self-assurance, charm and wit that he could sit at the top table of global politics and hold his own.

Some of Zulfikar's policy positions troubled Western leaders, especially when it came to China, about which, as his friend Chakar Ali Junejo pointed out, he had been expressing strong views ever since living in the UK.[50] Now foreign minister, Zulfikar could act on those ideas. In 1962 China had thrust itself onto the international agenda when it went to war with India over a border dispute in Kashmir. When the West responded by arming India, Zulfikar could not help wondering how it could be that Pakistan's main ally, the US, was arming its main enemy, India. He saw Beijing as a potential alternative that could give Pakistan support in the face of Indian hostility and Western indifference. He calculated that India would be more nervous of China coming to the aid of Pakistan in the event of hostilities than it would be about possible US intervention. China, as he put it, was a 'plus factor'.[51] And, looked at from the other side, the US desire to limit Pakistan's relationship with China might lead it to scale back its support for India. In 1963 Pakistan and China signed a trade agreement, and two months later Zulfikar signed a deal recognising Chinese sovereignty over a part of Indian-held Kashmir. In return, China backed Pakistani calls for a plebiscite in Kashmir. The agreement meant that, should India and Pakistan come to blows in Kashmir, China could get drawn in, fighting India to defend the territory that Pakistan had just given it.[52] With both sides having an interest in supporting each other, particularly vis-à-vis India, the Chinese prime minister Chou En Lai went on a state visit to Pakistan in 1964. As Farzana Shaikh has pointed out, Zulfikar's ideas about China developed into a belief that an 'Asian Asia' along similar lines to the idea of a European Europe could emerge as a global power bloc.[53] Asia, he believed, shared not just geography but also economic deprivation largely as a result of colonial oppression. Always keen to challenge Western power, he also began to advocate Afro-Asian unity.

As it observed these shifts in regional politics, the US calculated that its support for India vis-à-vis China gave it an opportunity to pressure Delhi to settle the Kashmir issue. A reluctant Nehru was told that if he would not countenance international mediation, then, if he wanted continued US aid, he should be willing to hold direct talks with Pakistan. The first round took place in Rawalpindi in December 1962, followed by four more in Delhi, Karachi (twice) and Calcutta. The dialogue would ultimately fail but nonetheless revealed that Zulfikar was capable of being more flexible than might have been expected. The young foreign minister indicated that Pakistan might be willing to settle for some adjustments to the ceasefire line and to accept that the issue at the heart of the dispute, the status of the Kashmir Valley, could be blurred either by soft borders or through it being internationalised in some way.[54]

In taking this line, Zulfikar was in part trying to establish himself as a politician the international community could work with. But that turned out to be more difficult than he anticipated. The assassination of President Kennedy meant Zulfikar needed to impress the new occupant of the White House, Lyndon Johnson – which he signally failed to do. Zulfikar's policy on China had raised Johnson's hackles. Zulfikar then compounded the problem by his conduct at Kennedy's funeral. Sent to represent Pakistan, he had been granted a meeting with Johnson, at which he told the president he would need a second meeting to deliver a personal and extremely important message from President Ayub – subsequently revealed to be 'No government led by me [Ayub] will enter into an alignment with the Communists or otherwise undermine existing alliance relationships.'[55] Although he already had a very hectic schedule, an irritated Johnson reluctantly agreed to a second meeting,[56] but was confounded by Zulfikar who, for some reason – presumably relating to his disagreement with Ayub's position – decided not to pass on the message, instead telling Johnson that Ayub sent his warmest wishes. Annoyed at his time being wasted, Johnson proceeded to give Zulfikar what insiders called a 'dressing down'. He told Zulfikar that there would be a problem if Pakistan built up its public relations with China and that it was increasingly difficult for the US when Pakistan invited the Chinese communists for state visits.[57] When Zulfikar later told the US ambassador to Pakistan about the incident, American analysts concluded that Zulfikar could have passed on Ayub's message but decided not to.[58] Certainly it was an encounter that US officials didn't forget: asked about the clash, Johnson's national security adviser, McGeorge Bundy, described Zulfikar as 'the biggest four letter word in international politics'.[59]

As Zulfikar tried to manage both Beijing and Washington, he was also pursuing his agenda in Kashmir. In December 1963 a rumour, later confirmed as true, spread through the Kashmir Valley that a religious relic, a hair from the Prophet's beard, had been stolen from a shrine near Srinagar, provoking a wave of social unrest. It made Zulfikar wonder if it was time to act on Kashmir, where he claimed the people were 'unmistakably in revolt'.[60] He was influenced in part by his idea, expressed in a 1964 speech in Washington, that the death of Nehru in May 1964 'released in that country centrifugal forces on an unprecedented scale'.[61] Pakistani intelligence reports seemed to confirm that the levels of discontent in Kashmir had reached new heights. If Pakistan could show the Kashmiris that removing the Indians was a real possibility, Zulfikar believed, they would readily join an anti-Indian uprising. Zulfikar was in a good position to push for a more active policy because he was the chair of a 'Kashmir cell', formally titled the Kashmir Publicity Committee, that had been established by Ayub in 1964 to keep the situation in the former princely state under constant review. The cell brought together senior Foreign Office bureaucrats and military officers, and was, under Zulfikar's guidance, soon developing options to defreeze Kashmir. That's not to say he was the only hawk pushing for a more robust policy, but he was the only one who had a good chance of selling such an approach to Ayub. Other members of the Kashmir cell believed that offensive action by Pakistan was problematic. The commander-in-chief of the army, General Musa, has claimed he expressed his doubts in a memo which he sent Ayub, who sent it back saying he concurred and that he would not take aggressive action in Kashmir.[62]

Despite Musa's reservations, many of his fellow officers agreed with the Kashmir cell's call for a more hardline policy, and by late 1964 the Pakistan Army had developed plans for Operations GIBRALTAR and GRANDSLAM. In GIBRALTAR, armed militants, having crossed into Indian-controlled Kashmir, would instigate a general revolt. Should that prove insufficient to force the Indians out of Kashmir, it would be followed by GRANDSLAM, in which Pakistani troops would be deployed with the same objective, all the while avoiding an escalation to full-scale war. The two codenames said a lot about the Pakistan Army. 'Gibraltar' played to its exaggerated sense of its power: it was the place in which the Muslims began their conquest of Spain. 'Grandslam', meanwhile, reflected the rather more bourgeois concerns of some officers: the general who came up with it was a keen bridge player.

The idea of winning Kashmir is intoxicating for any Pakistani leader. Increasingly excited, Ayub came to think his foreign minister might be right. He was partly encouraged by Pakistan's success in a clash with the Indian military on another piece of disputed territory located on the India–Pakistan border south of Hyderabad, the Rann of Kutch. As one of his advisers, Altaf Gauhar, recorded, Pakistan's minor win in the Rann of Kutch influenced Ayub's thinking: 'For all his realism and prudence, Ayub's judgement did get impaired by the Rann of Kutch in one respect: his old prejudice that "the Hindu had no stomach for a fight" turned into belief, if not a military doctrine'.[63] UN resolutions and bilateral talks over Kashmir had both failed. There was a chance China would intervene on Pakistan's side and there was a time factor: ever since Delhi's conflict with China in 1962, the Western powers had been pouring arms into India. On 12 May 1965, Zulfikar wrote to Ayub about the 'relative superiority of the military forces of Pakistan in terms of quality and equipment' and warned that India's capacity was increasing with every passing day.[64] The military balance, in other words, was bound to tilt ever further in Delhi's favour. Zulfikar also insisted that after its defeat by China in 1962 the Indian military was demoralised and in no position to open a general war against Pakistan – any military action would be restricted to Kashmir.[65] It was now or never.

In July 1965, Ayub decided to act. Bhutto had advocated it, but Ayub decided to do it. The infiltration of Kashmir outlined in Operation GIBRALTAR began, and, on 10 August, a body that no Kashmiri had previously heard of, the Revolutionary Council, called on the people to rise up against their Indian occupiers. However, when the militants contacted supposedly sympathetic clerics, they found that most were reluctant to help.[66] From Pakistan's point of view, the initial results of Operation GIBRALTAR were disappointing. But they were about to get a lot worse: the Indian prime minister, Lal Bahadur Shastri, launched an offensive crossing the 1947 ceasefire line in Kashmir, preventing further infiltration and cutting off the militants' supply lines. Zulfikar urged Ayub to carry on fighting, arguing that failure to do so 'would amount to a debacle which could threaten the existence of Pakistan'.[67] His anti-Indian rhetoric reached new heights:

Sometimes Pakistan is called a truncated State. I have never looked upon Pakistan as a truncated State. I have seen Pakistan as two mighty pillars, pushing against a predatory aggressor and a reactionary, ruthless country, these mighty pillars sandwiching an evil force. That is what Pakistan is. Two mighty pillars, not separated by a thousand miles of Indian territory as the Anglo-Saxon jargon describes Pakistan, but two mighty Islamic pillars of peace pressing their weight against a feeble, flippant society, a decadent society.[68]

GIBRALTAR was followed inexorably by GRANDSLAM. Initially the Pakistani Army offensive went well, but the military leadership in Rawalpindi was relying on its extraordinarily complacent assumption that India would not extend the fighting beyond Kashmir. But that is exactly what India did, opening up a 50-mile-wide front near Lahore, launching an offensive in Sindh and making a drive for the Pakistani city of Sialkot. Ludicrously, Pakistan's planners were taken by surprise. In a matter of hours all thoughts of offence were abandoned as the priority became saving Lahore. Zulfikar came under fire in top-level meetings as he was reminded of his repeated statements that India would not cross the international borders.[69] 'We are getting ready for a desperate fight,' Ayub Khan told the American ambassador.[70] After halting the Indian advances, Ayub Khan visited Beijing, Zulfikar in tow, to see whether China was prepared to go beyond supportive statements and launch an offensive against India. Beijing offered moral support but not much more. Ayub's last card had been played. By the time he returned to Pakistan he was determined to agree a ceasefire. India, which had achieved its objective of preventing the loss of Kashmir, was likeminded. The fighting stopped on 23 September 1965. The Pakistan government's information managers tried to portray the outcome as a victory or at worst a draw. But the reality was that the country's military planners stood exposed as highly incompetent: not for the last time they had started something they were never in a position to finish. Their goal of winning control of Srinagar seemed even more distant than before the conflict began.

Salmaan Taseer's biography of Zulfikar recorded an interesting exchange in which, as Zulfikar looked back, he tried to shift responsibility for the failure of 1965 onto the military planners, complaining they had sent Pakistani soldiers across the line of control rather than militants from Pakistani-held Kashmir (Azad Kashmir), who would have had, he believed, greater potential to drum up support because they would have found it easier to operate in Kashmir.

Bhutto: They sent in regulars whereas I wanted guerrillas. You know the fish in water theory. I wanted Azad Kashmiris.

Taseer: But sir, guerrillas of the same racial type are not enough. They must be indigenous people from the same village. Even if they are from a nearby village they can be clearly identified as outsiders.

Bhutto: Well, maybe. Anyway, they fucked it up.[71]

Since Ayub Khan had been the ultimate decision-maker, it was natural he would have to accept responsibility for the failure to fight for more than sixteen days. But Zulfikar too was vulnerable. He had been a leading hardliner on Kashmir, urging Ayub first to launch a military action, then to escalate it and later not to back down in the face of international pressure for a ceasefire. Speaking afterwards in private to a British diplomat who put it to him that the action in Kashmir had been his idea all along, Zulfikar made no effort to contradict him: 'Mr. Bhutto smiled and did not deny that he had initiated the affair.' Bhutto added that the British high commissioner at the time, Sir Morrice James, had played a leading role in getting the two sides to agree a ceasefire. ' "I could have killed him," Mr. Bhutto said smilingly.'[72] Sir Morrice later gave his take on the affair. 'Bhutto felt angered and personally affronted by the ceasefire. He thought he had built up significant support from Muslim countries and China which has shown a willingness to deploy some forces on India's northern border – but only if Ayub gave them a face to face guarantee that Pakistan was prepared to fight to the end. He thought Ayub had been weak.'[73]

With Pakistan having failed to make any headway, Zulfikar now needed to extricate himself from a politically dangerous situation. His chance came when Ayub Khan dispatched him to the UN to plead Pakistan's case. He did so with verve, not only vowing to fight a thousand years for Kashmir, but also likening the Indians to dogs, Nazis and bloodthirsty barbarians. Many of those listening to him in New York were shocked. But Zulfikar had a different audience in mind. Back in Pakistan, millions were thrilled to hear one of their politicians on the world stage, giving voice to their feelings. Far from being a defeat for Zulfikar, 1965 was the moment when he captured the hearts of many of his countrymen. But his performance before, during and after 1965 did lead to a setback: the US administration had come to view him as unreliable and disruptive, and when Ayub went to Washington in late 1965 Johnson advised him to sack his foreign minister. Johnson later recalled the conversation: 'I just said to him – now Mr. President, I know you rely on Bhutto just like I rely on Dean Rusk and like Eisenhower relied on Dulles but you cannot rely on him in that way and I am not entering your internal affairs but this man is damn dangerous as far as you are concerned'.[74]

If Johnson had severe doubts about Zulfikar, so too did the British. 'Bhutto's declared opinions seldom reveal his inner thoughts,' one official wrote. 'Trained as an advocate, he plays with words and attitudes, taking pleasure in being all things to all men. In this he expresses his basic lack of principles: he probably adheres to nothing except self-interest. Thus he is neither anti British, nor for us: not even basically anti Indian.'[75] Perhaps guided in part by such briefings, Prime Minister Harold Wilson said in late 1965: 'I am convinced Bhutto is a crook. Have we any views on the Tunku's allegation?'[76] 'The Tunku' was the Malaysian prime minister, Abdul Rahman, who had told Wilson that China had paid Bhutto a million dollars[77] in return for his diplomatic outreach. Officials told Wilson they had no evidence of illicit Chinese payments but said: 'we agree that Bhutto is a thoroughly untrustworthy person. He has considerable ability, is amusing and cultivated, but he uses these advantages without compunction in order to deceive, and he is skilful at adapting his attitudes to the audience of the moment . . . he is in fact, a self-seeking intriguer who is convinced his interests lie in promoting entente with China and a hard line towards India.'[78]

In fact, it was not fair to call Zulfikar an intriguer. Ever since his student days he had been talking about the importance of reducing Pakistan's reliance on the West and of looking for friends elsewhere. It was a principled and consistently held position, and it was part of a global trend: Zulfikar was the most articulate of a number of postcolonial and leftist leaders in the developing world who were searching for a way to develop independent policies. British hostility to him reflected concerns that Zulfikar represented a new trend in global politics which would result in the West having to cede power and resources to the developing world. But if Zulfikar could write off British concerns as the hurt pride of a colonial master scorned, alienating the US was a rather different matter. The fact that his having annoyed Johnson ended up with his being fired cemented his idea that power in Pakistan depended on having friends in Washington. As we shall see, Zulfikar was subsequently assiduous in cultivating President Nixon and Henry Kissinger. And it was an attitude he bequeathed to his daughter Benazir, who always believed that if she wanted to become prime minister, she needed US backing.

Even though they had agreed a ceasefire, India and Pakistan came under increasing pressure to talk. In January 1966 they did so in Tashkent, where the two sides agreed to go back to their pre-war positions. For the Pakistani public it was a shocking and disappointing outcome. Even after the ceasefire, the official media in Pakistan had given the impression that India had suffered a humiliating defeat: it was now perfectly clear to everyone that the true result was closer to a draw. The joint statement made at Tashkent hardly even noted the existence of the Kashmir dispute and certainly offered no realistic prospect of its resolution. The story behind the Tashkent talks shows, once again, how Zulfikar was the least willing to compromise with India. At the final stages of the talks, Ayub Khan agreed to an undertaking that Pakistan would never try to resolve its disputes with India by force. The original text said: 'The two sides will settle their disputes through peaceful means'. Zulfikar favoured: 'The two sides will try to settle their disputes through peaceful means'. The final text talked of a 'firm resolve' to use peaceful means.[79] The clause was only changed after a last-minute rearguard action by Zulfikar. But away from the fine detail in the smoke-filled negotiating rooms, there was a larger truth: the exaggerated hopes that Ayub's regime had encouraged, and the subsequent letdown at Tashkent, began the process that eventually forced the field marshal to relinquish power. The deterioration of the relationship was well illustrated by a story that did the rounds in the weeks after Tashkent. Shortly after the deal was done, Indian Prime Minister Lal Bahadur Shastri died of a heart attack in the early hours of the morning. Zulfikar was roused by an Ayub aide saying, 'Wake up! Wake up! The bastard is dead.' To which Zulfikar is supposed to have replied: 'Which one? Ours or theirs?'

Ayub's and Zulfikar's distinct approaches to foreign policy now came out into the open. Ayub's close relationship with the US had never been only about aid: it also reflected his ingrained suspicion of communism. In 1959 he had said, 'A Russian Chinese drive to the Indian Ocean is a major aim in the communist drive for world domination', and he had even flirted with the idea of using a shared fear of Sino-Russian strategic cooperation to find common ground with Delhi, hoping that that might nudge India towards a resolution of the Kashmir dispute.[80] For a brief period Zulfikar's pro-Chinese orientation had made sense to Ayub. But now the Sandhurst-educated Ayub reverted to his pro-Western orientation. Ayub had come to think that Zulfikar had advised him badly and regarded his foreign minister as 'most dangerous: a Maoist as well as a madman'.[81] In June 1966 he announced that Zulfikar was ill and needed time at home to convalesce.[82]

After his sacking, a depressed Zulfikar took a calculated decision to travel back home by train and was gratified to see crowds gathering to meet him.[83] Many Pakistanis, it seemed, were responding to his defiance over Tashkent but also to a sense that Ayub's regime was running out of ideas and that it was time for political change. Nervous about Zulfikar's growing popularity, Ayub ordered ever more personal attacks on his former protégé, who found that he was having to defend himself against one allegation in particular that would dog him for the rest of his life: that after 1947 he had claimed Indian citizenship and only renounced it when he became a minister in 1958. An official in the Ministry of Refugees, Ali Raza, subsequently explained what had happened.[84] Shortly after partition, India and Pakistan signed a treaty on evacuee property, prompting Zulfikar to try to recover the value of one of the family's Bombay homes which had been in his name. Sir Shahnawaz had sold the home and, following the correct procedure at the time, deposited the funds with the Bombay courts because Zulfikar was a minor. Partition meant the money had become stuck in India. As well as pursuing the matter through the Pakistani ministry, however, Zulfikar tried a parallel approach, arguing that since he had travelled to university in California on a British Indian passport he should not have been declared an evacuee by the Indian authorities. In support of this argument he said he was not sure where he would settle down after finishing his studies, implying that he might choose to live in India. He also said he was thinking of settling permanently in England. Eventually, when he became a minister, he accepted that he was resident in Karachi and withdrew his case from the Indian Supreme Court,[85] and worked to recover the funds instead only through the Pakistani ministry. In time, the Indian authorities handed over the value of the house to the Pakistan government, which passed it on to the Bhuttos.

It's generally believed that Zulfikar was not corrupt. He was a man of significant means who, it is often said, was more motivated by power than money. Against that, there are still whispers among those close to the family about how Colonel Gaddafi was particularly generous. And people close to Gaddafi say that his enthusiasm for Pakistan's nuclear project led him to provide Zulfikar with tens of millions of dollars.[86] Some British documents also raise questions. One tells the story of the Danish consul in Karachi, who was renting one of the Bhutto houses. When he asked to extend his lease, Nusrat said he would need to pay a higher rent to take inflation into account. He agreed and observed that a new lease should be drawn up to reflect the new figure. But Nusrat then said the family would rather not have a new lease as taxes were very heavy: would it not be possible to pay the enhanced rent on the old lease?[87] More tellingly, a 1968 internal British High Commission document claims Mr Bhutto was 'certainly not above taking money' and went on to recount the experience of a British businessman who had been trying to sell an atomic reactor in Rawalpindi. This was a period when the big powers were encouraging the developing world to use nuclear technology to generate electricity. The British company Mothercat failed to win a contract despite bidding 40 per cent less than the next bid. Mothercat approached Zulfikar and said it was willing to hand over the lion's share of 7 to 8 million rupees (nearly £800,000 in 1968 prices) if he secured the contract for Mothercat – something he tried but failed to do, but he did not turn down the offer of the commission.[88]

Such allegations were not made at the time, and Ayub's attempts to damage Zulfikar's reputation were no match for Zulfikar's growing political momentum as he fleshed out the ideas that would propel him to power. The idea of founding a new party had taken some time to form in Zulfikar's mind: he told a friend that creating a party takes a hundred years and he was in too much of a hurry. And anyway, he reasoned, as a Sindhi he would not be able to set up a party that could appeal to the youth of Punjab.[89] Initially he contemplated joining up with a faction of the Muslim League or the opposition National Awami Party. But both had established leaderships who saw no reason to give up their positions in favour of Zulfikar. It was then that Zulfikar began receiving letters from J.A. Rahim, a communist intellectual and Pakistani diplomat who was at the time ambassador in Paris and witness to the leftist movement there. Rahim advised him that the ideas of the left were not only in the ascendant but also provided a framework through which to analyse Pakistani society.[90] In November 1967, at a meeting in Lahore, Zulfikar acted on these ideas, establishing the vehicle that would carry him to power: the Pakistan People's Party, or PPP. With its famous slogan, 'bread, clothing, shelter', the PPP pledged to work towards a classless society through the nationalisation of all major industries, including banks and insurance companies. Neocolonialist powers would be denied permission to station military personnel on Pakistani soil and no military overflights would be allowed. Fearing that socialism would be portrayed as a Western idea, Zulfikar always took care to talk about 'Islamic socialism'. In a speech shortly after the creation of the PPP he said: 'I'll give my life and blood to strengthen this country and establish Islamic socialism according to the wishes of Quaid e Azam.'[91] It was a clear acknowledgement of Pakistani sensibilitics, in spite of which the PPP's first manifesto was remarkable for the contempt with which it treated the country's religious establishment: 'It can be shown from the history of Muslim peoples that their civilizations declined into intellectual sterility because dogmatic fanaticism obtained ascendancy . . . Our governments have too readily yielded to the blackmail of ignorant bigots.'[92] Zulfikar directly rejected the religious parties' powerful slogan, 'Islam is in danger': 'I respect the ulema [religious scholars] but those who give fatwas after receiving money have served the kafirs [infidels or non-believers]. Islam is not in danger, those who are in danger are the landlords and their puppets who cannot sleep at night.'[93]

The clerics, including most notably those in the conservative Islamist party Jamaat-e-Islami, always saw Zulfikar for the rationalist and secularist that he was and did their best to undermine him. At least at this stage of his career, he hit back without apology or equivocation. Famously, when accused of liking wine and women, he replied that yes, he was fond of women: as men were supposed to be. And as regards drinking, well, he may drink alcohol but at least he did not drink the blood of the poor, and anyway, he drank less than Ayub Khan and Yahya Khan.[94] A generation later such political rhetoric was impossible for a mainstream Pakistani politician, but in 1967 Zulfikar thought he had the future in his grasp and, as his manifesto made clear, he believed he was up against irrational fanatics: 'We, on the other hand, appeal to reason, to the accumulated wealth of human knowledge, to the methods and techniques devised by human ingenuity through the centuries, to show the way out of our national misery towards life worthy of a great people. The real problems that confront the nation are political and economic, but not religious, since both exploiters and exploited profess the same faith – both are Muslims.'[95]

With such ideas being openly discussed in Pakistan for the first time, the PPP's inaugural meeting was an exciting although not very well-attended event: only half the hoped-for number of delegates turned up.[96] Perhaps the most significant moment came right at the end of proceedings: when the question of who should be chairman of the party arose, Zulfikar was proclaimed leader by acclamation and no other officeholders were elected. Leftists such as J.A. Rahim and Mubashir Hasan may have thought they were using Zulfikar to advance their ideals, but in fact, it turned out, Zulfikar was using them. The party was, from the outset, unambiguously a vehicle for Zulfikar alone: he shared power with no one and all party posts were in his gift. As he once said: 'I am the PPP.'[97] Although there have been non-Bhutto officeholders, there were no internal party elections until they became a legal requirement, and, even then, the family controlled the process, and PPP officials have always been expected to do nothing more than implement the ideas of the Bhutto family member in charge at the time.

As Zulfikar held rallies throughout the country, his speeches became more strident. Even as a schoolboy he had been good at public speaking. As one childhood friend recalled, 'he was wonderful at twisting and turning the opposition'. His geography teacher had a rather grumpier reaction: 'Less of your flowery language,' he said, 'I know you can make a stone water but you cannot make me water.'[98] As he campaigned, Zulfikar moved on from the erudite debating style he had picked up in Bombay, California and Oxford, but he had not yet slipped into the boorishness of some of the speeches towards the end of his life. He was, in the late 1960s, at the height of his rhetorical powers, and he taunted Ayub Khan, portraying him as a coward unable to face the wrath of the people. In a series of mesmerising performances, he mixed high-flown political ideology with crude, earthy language. Some of the footage of him from this period shows crowds of tens of thousands. He shed his Western suit, donned Pakistani clothes and performed on stage with ever more extravagant gestures, sometimes speaking with such passion that he knocked over the microphones in front of him. Pakistanis had never seen anything like it. He revelled in his relationship with the crowds, confident that he fully understood them. To take just one example of how he handled himself at this time, when asked how he, a major landowner, could promise land reform if he was not prepared to give up his own land straight away, he took off his jacket and threw it to the crowd. As people fought to grab it, the jacket was torn to shreds. Then Bhutto spoke: if he gave away his land straight away, that is what would happen and no one would get any. But when there were laws and systems in place, he would happily give up his land for redistribution.[99]

Zulfikar's timing was good. Pakistani students, inspired by the street protests in Paris, echoed their French counterparts' rebelliousness and swung behind the PPP. Ayub Khan, though, finally lost patience and in November 1968 placed Zulfikar under house arrest on the grounds that he was a danger to public peace. Predictably enough, it backfired. Zulfikar used his arrest, and the subsequent legal wranglings, as a platform from which he could deliver his message. And he was heartened that his incarceration led to agitation on the streets, as supporters demanded his release. The Bhuttos have always made the idea of martyrdom a key part of their pitch. Both Zulfikar and Benazir went on to lay down their lives for the cause. Benazir's husband Asif Zardari spent years in prison, all the while portraying himself as the victim of a vendetta by his political opponents. Party activists also willingly accepted arrest and imprisonment to further PPP goals. It was an aspect of PPP politics that for many years gave the party a significant advantage over rivals who were not prepared to make such sacrifices. It would be decades before some other key politicians, such as those from the Sharif family, understood the power of political martyrdom to inspire support among the Pakistani electorate.

The army could see what was happening and, after a decade of military rule, decided that the only way of coping with an increasingly difficult political situation was to change military leader and hold elections, which were duly promised by Ayub's successor, Yahya Khan. The campaign lasted almost the entire year of 1970. Zulfikar decided there was no point in contesting in East Pakistan where the Bengali leader Mujibur Rahman's Awami League was dominant. And he paid little attention to Balochistan, where tribal politics had their own dynamic. But in Punjab and Sindh in particular, he ran an electrifying campaign, enthusing his excited audiences with promises of radical change.

Yahya Khan had vowed not to interfere in the electoral process, and he was as good as his word: when the elections came in 1970, they were among the fairest that Pakistan has ever held.

In West Pakistan Zulfikar won a striking victory with 81 out of 138 seats. His party had only existed for three years and the results exceeded the predictions of the country's intelligence agency, the ISI, which was also surprised by the scale of Mujib's win in East Pakistan; with no fewer than 160 out of the 162 directly elected constituencies, he effectively created a one-party state in East Pakistan and had enough National Assembly members to form a government for the country as a whole. To be fair to the ISI, it wasn't alone in failing to predict the election outcome. The morning after the results were announced, Mujibur Rahman told one of his aides, 'this is more than I had expected'.[100]

But if Mujib was the winner, Zulfikar also had a lot to celebrate. By tapping into the desire for change among trade unionists, students and urban voters, the PPP had rewritten the rules. Detailed analysis of the result revealed some unexpected sources of support. Despite Zulfikar's repeated denunciations of Ayub, he polled well in areas of Punjab near the border and in places with a large number of voters from the Pakistan Army. People living near India, it seemed, like those from the army, appreciated Bhutto's strong anti-India stance.[101] It was a remarkable personal achievement and led Zulfikar to believe he was on the threshold of real power. After the elections a senior minister told Yahya that if Bhutto did not become prime minister within a year, he would literally go mad.[102]

In the event he did come to power but only after half of Pakistan had broken away. The issues that led to Bangladesh's independence had been apparent ever since 1947. East Pakistan wanted its numerical majority to be reflected in the national parliament, but West Pakistan was reluctant to give up control. Under the 1956 constitution, the two wings were each given 150 representatives in a unicameral parliament, a manifestly unfair solution which alienated East Pakistani opinion. The arrival of Ayub Khan's military government meant Bengali nationalists were silenced by diktat, making matters worse. With West Pakistan showing no sign of accommodating East Pakistan's concerns, Mujibur Rahman formulated his demands in his famous 'Six Points': he wanted a federation in which the central government would control only defence and foreign affairs. The two wings of Pakistan would have separate currencies and distinct fiscal arrangements. For many in West Pakistan – especially in the army – this was too much, but by the time Yahya Khan took over power from Ayub, in March 1969, there were almost continual protests in Dhaka.

Yahya wanted to keep the two wings of Pakistan within a single country and was prepared to make significant compromises to achieve that outcome. But there were limits: he believed the Six Points would leave the centre with so little authority that a united Pakistan could not survive. He may also have calculated that the longer he drew the issue out, the greater his chance of weakening Mujib's mandate. But the 1970 election result forced the pace of events. As Pakistanis in both wings absorbed the results, Yahya went to Dhaka in January 1971 and told reporters the obvious: Sheikh Mujibur Rahman would be the next prime minister. He did not add what he at the time surely believed: that he himself would stay on as president. Yahya hoped the prospect of actually taking office might encourage Mujib to show greater flexibility on the Six Points. In fact, the election result gave Mujib little choice but to stick to the demands on which he had fought the campaign; as Ayub Khan put it in his diaries as he watched these events unfold, Mujib was 'the prisoner of his vast support'.[103] Having previously expressed a willingness to discuss the Six Points, he now said they must be implemented in their entirety. It was at this stage that Zulfikar played a significant role in the unfolding events. At a duck shoot in Larkana, Zulfikar complained to Yahya that he had named Mujib as prime minister without first consulting him. Yahya not unreasonably replied that Mujib would be prime minister not because Yahya had named him but because so many people had voted for the Awami League.[104] But Zulfikar insisted on a share of power, saying the PPP was 'not prepared to occupy the opposition benches in the Assembly'.[105] From Mujib's point of view, the Larkana meeting reinforced his feeling that he was up against a hostile West Pakistani elite hobnobbing with each other and determined to deny him his victory. And there was a sense in which, for all his self-interested scheming, Zulfikar was speaking for the West Pakistan establishment as a whole: as the situation deteriorated, Zulfikar seemed to get closer to the army.[106]

Shortly after the Larkana meeting, Zulfikar went to Dhaka to meet Mujib. Yahya had asked him to prevail upon the Bengali leader to be flexible about the Six Points, but, partly because he had no official role in the negotiations with Mujib, Zulfikar had a different agenda. As one of the Awami League negotiators put it, 'He showed no interest in the basic constitutional issues. He spent all his time discussing his share of power and the allocation of portfolios',[107] infuriating Mujib. While Yahya, Mujib and Zulfikar circled around each other, the question of when the National Assembly would be convened became an ever more pressing issue. Mujib wanted it to begin as soon as possible, suggesting mid-February. Zulfikar, unsure he could get into government, wanted it delayed until the end of March. Yahya split the difference and announced it would take place on 3 March. Zulfikar then made his most significant contribution to the dismemberment of Pakistan. Frustrated that the Awami League was offering him no guarantees about his future role and fearing that Mujib might be able to split the PPP, he told a mass rally in Lahore that the party would not attend the National Assembly's opening session. If any PPP members did attend, Zulfikar said, he would see to it that their legs would be broken.[108]

Increasingly, it seemed that Zulfikar wanted to create a situation in which he was supreme in West Pakistan and Mujib was supreme in East Pakistan. He hardly helped dispel that perception by reportedly saying at one rally, 'udhar tum, idhar hum', literally, 'you there, we here'. Many took that to mean he envisaged two countries, although Zulfikar and his supporters insist to this day that he was only making the less controversial point that Mujib had a majority in the east and he had one in the west. Others claim he never said it at all,[109] although that has been contradicted by one eyewitness, who insisted that he did say it but that the remark was taken out of context.[110] As attitudes hardened, Zulfikar could now see that his route to power once again was through the military. If Mujib stuck to the Six Points, the military would be left with only one democratically elected leader whom they could consider acceptable: Zulfikar himself. In other words, he could rely on the military to propel him to power. Unwilling to have a National Assembly with the PPP absent, Yahya decided to postpone the session. Many of his advisers thought it was a mistake and predicted a ferocious backlash in East Pakistan – which did indeed come to pass. On 2 March the US Consulate General in Dhaka reported on the popular reaction in East Pakistan: 'It would be impossible to over-estimate sense of anger, shock and frustration which has gripped people of east wing. They cannot but interpret postponement as act of collusion between Yahya and Bhutto to deny fruit of electoral victory to Bengali majority.'[111] Yahya, however, believed that a whiff of grapeshot would bring the East Pakistanis back into line,[112] a view which showed how little he understood of the state of public opinion there.

Had he won an overall majority, Zulfikar would not have hesitated to form a government. But he considered Mujibur Rahman's insistence that he be allowed to do just that 'intolerably rigid'. As Yahya failed to find a way to reconcile the two politicians, military action became ever more likely. Zulfikar could not be sure what the military would do and feared that the army might try to put together an alliance of religious and right-wing parties and tempt some PPP National Assembly members to join them. As for East Pakistan, he predicted that since the Awami League was a bourgeois party, it would be quite incapable of launching a guerrilla struggle.[113] It was a remark that echoed Ayub's claim that Hindus never had the stomach for a fight. On 26 March, General Yahya addressed the disintegrating Pakistani nation. Negotiations, he said, had failed: Mujib was an obstinate, obdurate traitor, and his party, the Awami League, was banned. 'I should have taken action against Sheikh Mujibur Rahman and his collaborators weeks ago,' Yahya declared.[114] It was war.

When discussing Zulfikar's role in 1971, his supporters make a number of good points in his defence. While none say he was blameless, they argue that he was never in a position to save Pakistan single-handed. Attending the National Assembly would never have produced a solution: if a deal between the PPP and the Awami League were to have been reached, it could only have happened as a result of closed, back-room negotiations. If Mujib wanted the two wings to be largely separate, then it was inevitable that Zulfikar would be in charge in the west, and he could hardly be blamed for trying to secure that outcome. And when it came to the Six Points, Zulfikar had tried to reach a compromise, saying he accepted most of them. The army, by contrast, was rigid in its almost total rejection of them. The difficulty was that if West Pakistan did not agree to all the Six Points – which the army would never accept – then a clash with Mujib was unavoidable. One of Zulfikar's closest advisers, Rafi Raza, makes another point. Like many others in 1971, the PPP leader didn't realise how high the stakes were. He believed that, ultimately, the army would prevent East Pakistan's secession. Consequently, he was reactive rather than proactive as the crisis unfolded, seeing his main task as safeguarding West Pakistan's – and his own – interests. If he made a mistake, Rafi argues, it was more by the way of a miscalculation. He did not do enough to save a united Pakistan because he didn't realise the extent of the jeopardy it was in. 'Events proved that he over-estimated military power, under-estimated Bengali nationalism, and, most surprisingly, did not properly anticipate India's determination to seize this opportunity to break Pakistan.'[115] Another indication that Zulfikar failed to grasp the gravity of the situation is that even after he took over he believed it might be possible to maintain some links between East and West Pakistan. On 20 December he told US Ambassador Farland that he still hoped to keep the two wings together in some loose federation. Pakistan, he said, had a real reason for coming into being, and that same reason justified its survival.[116] That India had to use military force to achieve its objectives in East Pakistan showed there was still considerable pro-Pakistan sentiment there.[117]

Shortly after Yahya launched military action, Zulfikar showed he did not fully understand what was happening in East Pakistan. 'By the grace of God, Pakistan has been saved,' he said, whereas in fact Pakistan was already beyond saving. The next day he accused Sheikh Mujib of wanting to set up 'an independent, fascist and racist state in East Pakistan' and declared that whatever military steps had been taken by Yahya Khan 'were in the interests of the country'.[118] His reluctance to criticise the army action was motivated in part by his fear that, having launched a military campaign in the east, Yahya could also use his soldiers in the west to establish another prolonged period of military rule there. In the event, the military reached out to Zulfikar: he was reinstated as foreign minister and sent to the UN in New York. But even as he told the Security Council that he would fight to the bitter end, he knew the war was being lost. Deciding to make the best of a bad job and strengthen his own political position back home, he opted for a dramatic gesture to capture the headlines: he would storm out of the Security Council. The night before he did it, his daughter Benazir, who had come down from Harvard, was with him. Not realising that the element of surprise was vital, she was telling a friend what her father planned to do when an official overheard her and snatched the phone from her hand.[119] Zulfikar's performance, when it came, did not disappoint. With tears streaming down his face, and while ripping up his notes, he told the Security Council that he would never address them again:

I have not come here to accept abject surrender. If the Security Council wants me to be a party of the legalisation of abject surrender, then I say that under no circumstances, shall it be so ... I am leaving your Security Council. I find it disgraceful to my person and to my country to remain here a moment longer than necessary. I am not boycotting. Impose any decision, have a treaty worse than the Treaty of Versailles, legalise aggression, legalise occupation, legalise everything that has been illegal up to December 15, 1971. I will not be a party to it. We will fight. We will go back and fight. My country beckons me. Why should I be a party to the ignominious surrender of a part of my country? You can take your Security Council. Here you are. I am going.

It was a repeat of 1965. Once again, he captured the imagination of the Pakistani people, thereby obscuring his personal role in a national defeat. As protestors took to the streets, the exhausted and increasingly isolated Yahya sent a message to New York telling Zulfikar to come back home. Not 100 per cent sure of Yahya's intentions, Zulfikar first checked with General Chief of Staff Gul Hassan, with whom he had built a relationship of trust, that it was safe for him to return.[120] Gul Hassan had spent the days after the surrender gauging the opinions of junior officers, an exercise that left him convinced that Yahya should give up the idea of staying on as a figurehead president.[121] Although it would be an overstatement to describe what happened as a sort of reverse coup installing a civilian leader, it was nonetheless the case that pressure from junior officers was a significant factor in securing the transition from a military ruler to a politician.

Before he left the US, Zulfikar fixed a meeting with President Nixon, at which he assured the American leader that he was not the 'Yankee Hater' that some Americans considered him to be and that he was determined to improve Pakistan–US relations.[122] Nixon was no fan of Zulfikar: just a few days earlier he had described him as a son of a bitch, a bad man and a terrible bastard.[123] On another occasion Nixon explained that he held Zulfikar in such low regard because Ayub Khan had been strongly critical of his former protégé: 'Ayub Khan gave me a rundown on him, and he's a pretty good judge of men, and he said this fellow is just bad news.' He also described him as a demagogue, but despite these views, Nixon was friendly at the meeting, saying he wished Zulfikar and Pakistan well, and Zulfikar headed home with the US's blessings.

At the age of just forty-two, Zulfikar had fulfilled his ambition. But many continued to discuss his role in the break-up of Pakistan. There was a lot of blame to go around, and much of it has been directed at Zulfikar, not least for his decision not to attend the National Assembly. But even if he did contribute to the break-up of Pakistan, he was by no means solely responsible. As the election results sank in, Mujibur Rahman saw that he had no reason to hold back from demanding what many East Pakistanis wanted. And Yahya too was not without fault, not least because of his misunderstanding of the strength of East Pakistani opinion and, many argued, his lack of military competence too. In June 1972, US National Security Adviser Henry Kissinger, as part of his diplomatic outreach to Beijing, discussed what had happened with Chinese Prime Minister Chou En Lai. Yahya, the Chinese leader said, 'was a general who did not know how to fight a war. He was not only useless in war, he did things that worsened the situation.' Kissinger concurred. 'Yahya was a decent man, but not very intelligent and, it turned out, not a very good general.'[124] Yahya had a different take. In 1978, just two years before his death, he submitted a secret affidavit to the Lahore High Court in which he gave his views. The document has never been published in Pakistan but strangely was put into the public domain by the *Bangladesh Defence Journal* in 2009. No doubt Mujib was a liar, Yahya said in his narrative account, 'but Mr. Z A Bhutto was a clever and venomous toad'. He went on: 'As for fall of Dacca responsibility lies both on Mujib and Bhutto but Bhutto was far more responsible than Mujib.' Yahya based that view on a detailed account of what had happened, in which he highlighted Zulfikar's role in refusing to accept that Mujib had a right to govern and his willingness to accept separation if it meant he secured power.[125]

As for Zulfikar, he knew full well that many in the army blamed him for what had happened and tried to answer his critics in a short book, *The Great Tragedy*, in which he wrote: 'It was maliciously suggested by my opponents that, as I could not expect to be Prime Minister of one Pakistan because of Mujibur Rahman's absolute majority, I was scheming to be the Prime Minister of West Pakistan.' He dismissed the charge out of hand, instead blaming Mujib, Yahya and even Ayub Khan for the disaster. And as for that crucial decision to boycott the Assembly, the best he could come up with was that he needed more time to prepare West Pakistani public opinion for greater East Pakistani autonomy. 'We had not completed our consultations and we had not gone to the people of the West Wing for their approval for a Constitution based on far-reaching concessions. We thus found it impossible to attend the National Assembly session on the 3rd of March.'[126] With his deep reading and confident prose, Zulfikar was generally a highly persuasive writer. *The Great Tragedy* is one of his least convincing pieces of work.

The key sentence in *The Great Tragedy* contained a piece of advice that Mujib gave Zulfikar when the two met in Dhaka. 'He cautioned me against the military and told me not to trust them: if they destroyed him first they would also destroy me. I replied that I would much rather be destroyed by the military than by history.' Seven years later, as Zulfikar awaited his hanging, Mujib's analysis and Zulfikar's breezy reply both looked prescient. The military did destroy Zulfikar, and as he awaited death he did try to secure his place in history, spending his time in the prison cell writing a series of articles and essays for posterity. But there was something else. Mujib's remark came in the context of an appeal he made to Zulfikar, suggesting that they work together to make Pakistan, East and West, a decentralised people's democracy in which the army would have less say. Zulfikar was later extraordinarily rude about Mujib, describing him as a 'congenital liar' with a 'sick mind'.[127] But Mujib's suggestion was in fact one that should have interested Zulfikar. It might be that the disintegrationist forces in Pakistan were so strong, West Pakistani arrogance so ingrained and Indian policy so hostile, that the two leaders were powerless to change the outcome. But it is also possible that, had Pakistan's two most legitimate politicians combined forces to limit the power of the army, the history of the country could have taken a different course, and one that would have been entirely in line with Zulfikar's stated ideological principles. Mujib said he was ready to do it. But for once Zulfikar did not see the big picture, and he let the moment pass. It was a missed opportunity.

3
ZULFIKAR IN POWER

Zulfikar's espousal of Islamic socialism and land reform, his disdain for obscurantist clerics and his moments of anti-Americanism have led many to view him as leftist and a liberal. His reading habits suggested something else. His fascination with Napoleon is well known. But, as Oriana Fallaci pointed out after she saw his library in 70 Clifton, there were also volumes on Mussolini and Hitler, which were not only in pride of place but also sumptuously bound in silver. Their provenance is unknown, but even if they were gifts rather than purchases, Zulfikar felt no embarrassment in displaying them prominently. When he was detained by the army in 1977, his mind turned to Hitler. He asked for some of his books on the German leader to be brought to him so that he could figure out 'how Hitler was able to control his generals and I was not'.[1] Zulfikar perceived his impending death as a personal failure: he had set out to dominate Pakistani society and to build a nation, but had fallen short. It is possible that as a student he had even wondered whether he could lead a pan-Islamic movement, but, if so, that too had failed to materialise. As for Zulfikar's ideology, he was always aware that some people considered him to have fascistic tendencies, not only because he was a strong leader who wanted his party to control Pakistan's power structures but also because he seemed to embrace some symbols of fascistic rule, such as the uniform he designed for PPP officials, complete with piping of various colours to denote rank.[2] But he brushed aside such suggestions, partly on the grounds that while Hitler was *petit bourgeois* and of the right, he was an aristocrat and of the left. And he was never remotely interested in the kinds of violence Hitler inflicted on the world. Nevertheless, Rafi Raza recorded that Zulfikar did have a 'penchant for comparisons with Hitler: he would urge Kausar Niazi as Information Minister to outdo Joseph Goebbels, Mumtaz Bhutto in Sindh to be a Heinrich Himmler, and myself as Production Minister to be another Albert Speer.' What he meant by this was that he wanted his ministers to be as driven and impactful as those of Hitler. And that went for him too. Zulfikar wondered, 'if a small Bavarian could master the Prussian Army, what could prevent ZAB [Zulfikar Ali Bhutto] from doing the same with the Punjabi Army'.[3]

As for Napoleon, Zulfikar freely conceded that he was an 'exploiter' fighting a war of domination,[4] but he also said, 'Napoleon was a giant. There was no man more complete than him.' He would say to his children: 'Napoleon conquered the world and I have not.'[5] And he declared, 'His military brilliancy was only one facet of his many-sided genius. His Napoleonic code remains the basic law of many countries. Napoleon was an outstanding administrator, a scholar and a romanticist'.[6] In other words, more than virtually any other man in history, Napoleon, because of his personal qualities, had left his mark on the world. Zulfikar wanted to do the same. When he was in prison in 1968, he gave his daughter Benazir a reading list. Urging her to read more literature and history, his specific suggestions concentrated on the latter; she should learn more about the great men of history he wanted to emulate: Genghis Khan, Alexander the Great, Bonaparte, Bismarck, Lenin, Atatürk, Lincoln and Mao.[7] Another hero was closer to home. As one of the most influential men of his age, Jawaharlal Nehru was an easy qualifier for Zulfikar's pantheon of great men of history. Zulfikar admired the Indian leader for exercising 'compulsive power over the crowds', which he could drug into submission.[8] That he saw parallels with himself was clear. Zulfikar often described himself as a bridge between East and West, and he saw the well-born, Cambridge-educated Nehru in the same terms: the Indian leader was to some extent a role model. And it is striking to note that, while praising Nehru, Zulfikar also registered his view that the Indian leader's commitment to democracy was in fact nothing more than a political contrivance.[9]

Zulfikar could produce purple prose about democracy. In the affidavit submitted to the court when he was arrested by Ayub in 1968, he wrote that democracy is 'like a breath of fresh air, like the fragrance of a spring flower. It is a melody of liberty, richer in sensation than tangible touch.' Maybe, but there were limits to Zulfikar's democratic instincts. S.J. Burki claims that in 1962 Bhutto wrote a long memorandum to Ayub, outlining his idea for a one-party state in which the roles of the judiciary and the legislative branches of government were to be completely subservient to the all-powerful central authority. The party would have cells down to village level that would even undertake functions such as health and education provision. Eventually, the civil service, the judiciary and even the armed forces would recruit personnel from party cadres. China and the Soviet Union were to be the models. When Ayub rejected the idea, Bhutto thought him timid.[10] He kept thinking about alternatives to democracy. Shortly after his election win in 1970, Zulfikar told American diplomats that he questioned the suitability of parliamentary democracy in Pakistan and thought there should be a constitutional role for the military. He wanted, he said, to govern as a strong man within the Turkish model, with the army in the wings.[11] After the Islamic Summit in Lahore, he said to a PPP Central Executive Committee meeting: 'Why don't we wrap this up and establish a one party state like Nasser's in Egypt? After all, the people of Pakistan are behind me and so is the army.' He only backed down when he faced strong objections from the PPP secretary general, Mubashir Hassan.[12]

He also expressed doubts about the democratic system to foreign interlocutors including, in 1972, *Le Monde*:

> You can't run a democracy by putting paint on your nails. I am not a blockhead running the country. We have to be firm. People have a right to speak. They have a right to make speeches. They have a right to go out and express their point of view ... But when they say that they will overthrow this Government, break down the walls of the President's House, well, that is something you can't do democratically. That you can only do undemocratically. And if these people then expect that under the cover of democracy they can violate each and every law of the land and get away with it, they are wrong.[13]

Such views were not just off-the-cuff remarks to justify moments of repression. He also articulated a theoretical basis for his doubts about, as he would see it, democratic excess. While Ayub Khan had spoken of 'controlled democracy' and 'guided democracy', Zulfikar came up with the phrase 'disciplined democracy' to describe how to govern. He wrote in 1967:

> With all its admitted virtues, Western institutional democracy is also responsible for considerable confusion and dislocation in Asia and Africa. John Lock [*sic*] and Stuart Mill with all their acknowledged contributions

were born neither in Lahore nor in Jakarta. Our leaders who came out of Oxford and Cambridge, and even Sandhurst, were imbued with Western democratic ideals. They grasped the concept and sought to apply it to our conditions. What we really had to do was to begin with a clean slate and evolve a system from the foundation of our conditions instead of applying anything from above.[14]

To the end, Zulfikar insisted that the charge on which he was eventually convicted – ordering the murder of a political rival – was false. But there was no hiding the fact that he had used force to project his power. As always in Pakistan, the use of violence was influenced by class considerations. Striking workers, Baloch tribal insurgents and the relatively few violent jihadists who existed at the time all ran the risk of being killed by the security forces. But the very top strata that governed Pakistan, the generals and politicians who ruled from GHQ, Prime Minister's House and the presidency, were subject to different rules, always allowed to fight another day. The eventual hanging of Zulfikar was so shocking and remains so controversial in part because it was the only occasion when a Pakistani leader had a fellow leader killed. Bhutto's use of violence was not exceptional by Pakistani standards, but he was unusually forgiving of mass murderers. That Mao and Stalin killed so many he found excusable. 'To build a country,' Zulfikar told Oriana Fallaci, 'Stalin was obliged to use force and kill. Mao Tse-tung was obliged to use force and kill . . . My respect for Stalin has always been deep, a gut feeling I'd say'. Not only that, Zulfikar deplored the man who dismantled Stalin's system of mass murder, Nikita Khrushchev. 'You may understand me better when I say I never liked Khrushchev, that I always thought him a braggart. Always swaggering, yelling, pointing his finger at ambassadors, drinking . . . And always ready to give in to the Americans. He did a lot of harm to Asia, Khrushchev.'[15] It seems inexplicable that Zulfikar would favour a genocidist over a communist reformer – until one considers, first, that Stalin was a more consequential leader than Khrushchev, and, probably just as importantly, that Khrushchev once rebuked Zulfikar. During his 1964 trip to Moscow, the Soviet leader had said to him:

Tell me Mr. Bhutto, it is so difficult to understand. Will you tell me something? You are such a fine young man, handsome, well educated, intelligent, clever and competent; your President has such a fine personality. He is handsome at his age and carries himself so well; but may I ask, with all this, why do you take such dirty decisions which land you in trouble and bring you a bad name. Can't you have a policy and be on your own. Your dependence on others will bring you disaster and ruin you.[16]

The harangue reportedly left Zulfikar 'embarrassed and confused'.[17] As Zulfikar's childhood friends knew all too well, he could not let something like that go. Piloo Modi once said, 'You know this Zulfi has always been a strange chap. If a cricket ball hit him as a child he would say: I'll fix you.'[18]

His reflex to hit back at anyone who crossed him was apparent as soon as he took over. A British High Commission document from January 1972 described how a senior retired Pakistani officer, Lieutenant General Habibullah, who in retirement ran the National Press Trust, had previously taken Bhutto to task for behaving inappropriately at one of Yahya's dinner parties in Karachi. 'There were as usual ladies present and Bhutto was misbehaving with one of them when Habibullah told him sharply to desist. Bhutto asked Habibullah who he was to reprimand him in this way, to which Habibullah replied he had been a general before Bhutto was born. This led to a dreadful scene in which Habibullah pulled no punches in insulting Bhutto. There is no doubt that Bhutto's ancestry was dragged in.'[19] When Zulfikar took over power, his first acts were to address the nation, to appoint Gul Hassan to run the army, to meet the US and Chinese ambassadors and . . . to fire General Habibullah.[20] There are many such stories, but one in particular brings home just how sensitive Zulfikar was. At a press conference in Lahore, Zulfikar once stated, 'I say this beyond the shadow of a ghost'. One of his quick-witted advisers, Khalid Hasan, chipped in. 'Excuse me, Mr. Bhutto, but I would like to remind you that ghosts don't have shadows.' Everyone laughed, including Zulfikar, but he didn't forget the incident and complained about it in a written memo to the minister of information.[21] These stories can be dismissed as criticisms by less powerful and less impressive former colleagues, but there are too many of them to disregard the overall picture: Zulfikar was vengeful, just as his feudal background had taught him to be.

Zulfikar's attitude to protocol was another early indicator of how things would develop. Finance Minister Mubashir Hassan, a man who respected Zulfikar to the end, recalled that on his first meeting with Zulfikar after he became president, he saw him sitting behind his desk at the far end of the room and moved towards him. As he did so an aide-de-camp announced: 'Mr. President, Dr. Mubashir Hassan'. Zulfikar was irritated and later told his close friend and colleague that he should have waited for the formal introduction before approaching him.[22] This trait was not just a personal matter, it also had political significance. Keen that Zulfikar should secure his political base in Sindh, Rafi Raza once suggested that he should reach out to the pre-eminent Sindhi landlord and spiritual leader Pir Pigara. 'Why should I call him?' said Zulfikar, who was reluctant to be seen as a supplicant of a fellow feudal and wanted Pir Pigara to make the first move. 'You're the President,' said Raza. 'You are not asking for anything so you can call him.' But Zulfikar refused and even went on the offensive, arranging for charges to be brought against Pir Pigara. It was a mistake: Pir Pigara would later become a senior member of the opposition alliance that brought Zulfikar down.[23]

Most Pakistani leaders have succumbed to the flattery of sycophants. Zulfikar was perhaps particularly vulnerable because, especially towards the end, he really was surrounded by people with less talent than him. But his ego knew few bounds. In his speeches he spoke a lot about himself, repeatedly claiming he was willing to sacrifice himself for the nation and often describing himself in the third person. Ayub, he said, wanted to capture him, 'but I am a better hunter. He could trap others but failed to trap Zulfikar Ali.'[24] And on another occasion, 'I am the same Bhutto whose name makes the imperialists and the Indian expansionists sweat.'[25] This self-regard was coupled with an intolerance of criticism which set in even before he came to power. In December 1971 – just three days before he took over from Yahya – Zulfikar addressed a group of Pakistanis in New York and was asked, among other things, why his enthusiasm for land reform had not led him to give up all his own land voluntarily. Someone at the meeting described what happened next: 'At this point Mr. Bhutto got very excited and proceeded to explain how he was gradually selling his lands in order to meet the campaign expenses of his party. But this failed to satisfy the questioner who insisted on his point. Mr. Bhutto then lost his cool and said, "Shut up, you stupid man . . . how can you talk to me like that, I am your leader"'.[26]

In 1971, however, Zulfikar's overwhelming self-confidence was just what Pakistan needed. The loss of East Pakistan raised fundamental questions: had partition been justified? Why had Islam failed to hold the country together? Was the army guilty of genocide in its own land? Having been sworn in, Zulfikar addressed the nation. His adviser Rafi Raza asked if he wanted help with the speech, but Zulfikar declined: he would write the speech alone. 'This is my moment,' he said.[27] And he set about trying to answer the big questions. The two-nation theory was valid: the creation of Bangladesh did not alter the fact that Muslims and Hindus could not live together – it just meant there were two Muslim nations instead of one. The task was to pick up the pieces – the very small pieces, he said – and build a new Pakistan. As he not unreasonably told the American ambassador in his first meeting after coming to power, 'we are in one hell of a mess'.[28] It is only in hindsight that we know that the disintegration of Pakistan was not to progress further. There was talk of provinces in West Pakistan breaking away too. These were times when, perhaps, a great man could make a difference. The public's anger was raw and sharp. Zulfikar immediately assumed almost total power. Initially, he was in the highly irregular position of being a civilian chief martial law administrator while also having assumed the posts of president and defence, foreign and interior minister. After its defeat, the army was powerless to resist him. In May 1972 Zulfikar acknowledged that, for the moment, he had the upper hand: 'Looking into the future, if we messed it up, if we didn't make the parliamentary system work, if our constitution breaks down, then that's a possibility of the army stepping in again. But for the moment neither are they physically in a position nor mentally is the army interested.'[29] It was a fair assessment, and the army's decision to step in again five years later was indeed partly a result of Zulfikar's failure to make the parliamentary system work.

It has often been said that it is too soon to write a definitive account of Zulfikar's historical significance. But forty years after his death some things are becoming clearer. Like many other Pakistani civilian leaders, he quite understandably became consumed by the risk of the army snatching power away from him. It distracted him from his purpose and led him to concentrate on accumulating more power. But, as he discovered, however hard he tried, that risk could never be eliminated. When Zulfikar came to power he had a great opportunity to create a new political reality: the army was in disarray, he had an overall majority in the parliament and his charisma had given him a deep well of political capital. A democratic experiment was in his hands, and his five and a half years in office were to be revelatory, exposing the hard boundaries which even the most powerful, driven and capable civilian leader could not breach. So what did the Zulfikar years reveal about the nature of Pakistani politics and society? What did Pakistanis learn from his administration about just how far a leader could go before the military blocked his way? As well as the army, Zulfikar challenged a series of other power centres, including the feudals, the business elite, the Islamists, the Americans, the provinces, the press, the bureaucracy and India: their various reactions helped subsequent civilian politicians understand the limits to their power.

Some of Zulfikar's targets were in no position to resist him. For example, his campaign against the press largely succeeded and has set precedents which many subsequent governments have followed. Zulfikar actually began by lifting restrictions on the press, but it only took a few weeks in office for him to realise he didn't much enjoy journalistic criticism. In February 1972 he jailed Altaf Gauhar, the editor of the main English-language paper, *Dawn*. Gauhar's offence had been to respond to a speech Bhutto gave in Lahore in which he said that if any attempt were made to overthrow his government, 'the Himalayas would cry'. Gauhar's rejoinder, in the form of an editorial, was entitled 'Mountains Don't Cry'.[30] Even though the arrest could be explained by a personal rivalry going back to the days of the Ayub government when Gauhar had been close to Ayub and critical of Zulfikar, the incarceration of such a senior journalist sent a strong message to the rest of the press: if the editor of *Dawn* could go to jail, anyone could. In the days that followed, the still extant martial law regulations were used to ban some newspapers and detain recalcitrant editors. While civil servants in the law and information ministries used legal measures to control what journalists wrote, there were also less formal techniques, such as restricting state entities' advertising in critical newspapers. In opposition, the PPP had demanded the dissolution of the National Press Trust, a government body that gave Ayub power over a significant proportion of Pakistan's newspapers. In power, Zulfikar, rather than abolish the body, appointed loyalists to the board.[31] Asked by officials which 'holy cows' he wanted protected from journalistic criticism, Zulfikar replied, 'I am the only holy cow'.[32] Zulfikar justified his restrictions on the press on the grounds that journalists were guilty of 'filthy abuses' by writing against the head of state and other elected politicians. 'No country,' he said, 'no society, no decent people would tolerate that kind of thing and let this pass as journalism.'[33] And on another occasion he complained: 'People once again have gone on a verbal rampage without any regards for each other's rights and feelings. They justify this as freedom of expression. They want to disregard all laws, from treason to perjury, and call it freedom of the press. The point is that when we pick up the political pieces, then these elements make atrocious charges, unbecoming charges, unbecoming of them and of a free nation.'[34] From the point of the view of the press, Zulfikar's legacy is disappointing.

While Zulfikar used tough tactics to control journalists, he tried, at least initially, to demonstrate more empathy when dealing with the people on whose behalf the PPP said it was struggling: the workers and peasants of Pakistan. In his election campaign, Zulfikar had raised expectations. In power, he celebrated 'the spirit of the Paris Commune' and declared May Day a holiday. But the workers weren't demanding time off – above all else they needed increased pay. It is difficult to appreciate the extent of poverty in Pakistan at the time: life expectancy for men was just fifty-two years.[35] Zulfikar did apply pressure on businesses to increase wages and even to recompense workers for earnings lost during illegal strikes, but such gains were soon wiped out by inflation. Aware of the economic dislocation caused by the 1971 defeat, Zulfikar repeatedly appealed for people to understand the country's parlous situation and to get back to work. 'We have a marginal economy,' he said, 'and within this marginal economy I have really gone to the brink, and I can't take even a single step further because it may, at the present stage, mean complete collapse. But with greater production and hard work when the base expands our policy will always be tilted in favor of the proletariat.'[36] When Zulfikar's exhortations to work harder were ignored, he fell back on more coercive measures. In June 1972, during two days of running clashes, police shot down thirty – or, by some estimates, fifty – workers in the streets of Karachi.[37] In October another twelve workers were killed in the Landhi industrial area. In early 1973 strikes almost halted industrial activity in Karachi, in response to which Zulfikar ordered another crackdown, with militant union leaders arrested. And the workers, it turned out, were too weak to offer significant resistance to the Bhutto government. It was much the same in rural areas: after agitation in the remote area of Dir, Zulfikar deployed 10,000 troops, who killed 600 people as they successfully overpowered unrest there. So, far from keeping the army out of politics, even in the early years of his administration, Zulfikar frequently called on the army to impose his writ.

Such tough actions raised questions about what motivated Zulfikar and the degree to which he was committed to socialist principles. When speaking later to his biographer Salmaan Taseer, Zulfikar said: 'We do not advocate the communist kind of socialism . . . We stand for a socialism which is compatible with our own conditions.'[38] These attitudes contrasted sharply with what he had said four years before when he was running for power: 'The establishment of socialism is not possible until all the sources of production and resources of wealth, all the fields and factories are nationalized by snatching them from the feudal lords and the capitalists. Nevertheless, I announce that if the nation required my wealth I would place all my property at the disposal of the nation.'[39] His cousin Mumtaz – who knew Zulfikar's politics as well as anyone – believed that even if he tried to deliver on some of his socialist promises he was, at heart, 'always a conservative'.[40] Zulfikar's old friend Piloo Mody was far from convinced by Zulfikar's socialism: 'He is irritated when I tell him that somehow or the other he stumbled into becoming a socialist! He indignantly maintains that his commitment to socialism is an old one which found its origins in the grotesque poverty of Sindh, that it is a commitment that stems from human values and from human reactions to the realities of life.'[41] For all that, however, even before the elections Zulfikar was describing the leftists in his party as a problem that he needed to manage.[42]

At a rally in November 1968, he argued that 'in the socio-economic sector there is no difference between Islam and socialism; had these two systems been in conflict with each other, I would have given up socialism.'[43] Speaking in 1976, he explained that view more fully:

We reject Marx on the ground that it denies the existence of God. Marx said that there is no God and that there is no world hereafter. We believe that there is a God and that there is a world hereafter. We reject Marx's concept of a stateless society. We believe that structures of states are part and parcel of the scheme of things. We reject Marx even to the extent that there can be a complete withering away of what are called the upper classes.

We think there will always be groups of people who are better endowed, with some talent or the other, than others. And this will result in class differences, but what we do not want is that there should be a distinct class of exploiters or a permanent class of exploited people.[44]

In an interview as early as 1972, he was asked about the pressure he was getting from 'extreme left wing elements in your party, which is urging you to take more and more steps'. Zulfikar's reply was unequivocal: 'I have made it quite clear. I was not going to be at their mercy.'[45] It is also striking that in his early writings, even when complaining about the big powers and especially the US, he did not use the anti-imperialistic language of socialism or the left. That remained true even when, as foreign minister, he reached out towards communist China. His writings and speeches suggest he saw that policy not as an act of solidarity with Chinese comrades but as the best thing to do from a Pakistani nationalist's geostrategic point of view. After the 1971 elections the PPP's leftists were immediately emboldened, and they claimed that landowners had no need to wait for new laws: they should immediately redistribute their land or face being kicked out of the party. But, as an American diplomat pointed out, the landowners did not seem to have any intention of giving up anything: Zulfikar's right-hand man Mustafa Khar, for example, asked the diplomat to a shoot in the next year's season, showing no sign of being worried that he would have lost possession of his estates.

Although the PPP was to all intents and purposes a Bhutto possession, its activists – at least those who trusted each other to be discreet – discussed all these issues throughout Zulfikar's time in power. There were three main factions. The secularist, leftist wing advocated Chinese-style communism and revolutionary change and was hostile, if not to Islam, then at least to any hint of Islamism. A second group, the centrists, warned that too close an association with global communism would risk being perceived as godless and urged mixing socialist ideas with Islamic language. Some of these Islamic socialists looked for inspiration from Middle Eastern Baathist movements. A third, pragmatic tendency was not ideologically rooted at all.[46]

It didn't take long for disillusionment among the leftists to set in. Just six months after Zulfikar assumed power, a leftist magazine wrote that the famous PPP slogan, 'Islam is our religion; socialism is our economy; democracy is our politics', should be changed to 'radicalism is our rhetoric; confusion is our tactic; oppression is our profession'.[47] And it wasn't just the intellectuals. Interviews with grassroots party activists in Lahore in early 1971 revealed enthusiasm for the party's socialist ideology. Interviewed again in July 1974, the same activists were disappointed and pessimistic: the PPP, they believed, had been infiltrated by corrupt individuals and factionalised by ministers and National Assembly members trying to rally their respective bands of followers.[48] As for Zulfikar, he was variously a feudal who wanted to dispossess landlords, a socialist who admired Hitler, a civilian politician and chief martial law administrator and, fittingly, a man who said coherence is the virtue of a small mind. But there was one constant besides his desire for power: his nationalism. It was an issue on which Zulfikar and the army were as one. Zulfikar thrilled Pakistani audiences, soldiers included, not only when he railed against India but also when he denounced the great powers. When, in 1971, he insulted the Soviet ambassador to the UN to his face, likening him to a czar, he gave Pakistanis a sense that they were a country that had already become strong enough to exchange blows with even the mightiest. A strong supporter of the idea of Pakistan from childhood, Zulfikar consistently adopted hawkish positions. In the run-up to the 1965 conflict, he urged Ayub to fight for Kashmir, he opposed the ceasefire and afterwards, despite a speech or two in which he toed the line over Tashkent because he was still in the Ayub government, he denounced the peace treaty, declaring it to have given too much to Delhi.

The 1972 Simla agreement with Indira Gandhi after the loss of East Pakistan is generally seen as one of Zulfikar's great achievements. India was holding some 90,000 Pakistanis, mostly soldiers, as well as territory in West Pakistan. By way of a bargaining chip, Pakistan had captured just 600 Indian soldiers and a small pocket of Indian territory. At Simla, Zulfikar regained the territory, and, as he predicted, the prisoners of war were later released. But there was another aspect to Simla which for some reason is not much discussed. From the outset, Indira Gandhi's main objective was to secure agreement that the ceasefire line in Kashmir established in 1947, which was monitored by the UN, be changed into a line of control managed by India and Pakistan bilaterally. Pakistan, always keen to internationalise the Kashmir dispute, resisted this demand. When the talks were about to fail, Zulfikar shifted on this point. One of his advisers suggested accepting the term 'line of control' but adding a phrase: 'without prejudice to Pakistan's internationally recognised positions'. Zulfikar watered that down to 'Pakistan's recognised positions' – a formulation Indira Gandhi agreed to.[49] Zulfikar thought he had slipped in wording that preserved Pakistan's right to involve the international community, but India saw it differently, and ever since has cited Simla as the reason why the Kashmir dispute should be resolved bilaterally. The international community, unwilling to upset a major trade partner, has subsequently tended to favour India's interpretation. Simla also showed Zulfikar at his petty worst. In the run-up to the talks, Indira Gandhi had granted an interview to Oriana Fallaci in which she described Bhutto as 'not a very balanced man'. Bhutto characteristically hit back by asking Fallaci to interview him, at which point he described Indira Gandhi as an unintelligent, 'diligent drudge of a school girl'. His remarks – which his advisers insisted had been off the record[50] – nearly derailed the talks, and Fallaci found herself being chased around the world by Pakistani officials trying to persuade her to say that she had misquoted their leader. She refused, and eventually the two sides had to agree to overlook her interviews.[51]

While Zulfikar was able to take on the press, the workers, the PPP and even India, the civil service proved to be a more difficult proposition. 'I am opposed to our bureaucracy,' he said shortly after assuming power, 'since I have the people in the mass by my side, our bureaucracy will not be able to obstruct my way.'[52] Zulfikar declared that he wanted to transform the administrative system inherited from the British because the senior civil servants were self-interested, unaccountable elitists with generalist backgrounds which rendered them unable to cope with the demands of administration in a technological age. In March 1972 he dismissed 1,300 civil servants, whom he described as parasites sucking the blood of the people. The process was chaotic: in one case a civil servant whom Zulfikar had met and approved was sacked two days later on the grounds that he was irredeemably corrupt.[53] In their place, so-called 'Bhuttocrats' were appointed. Appointment on merit assessed by public examinations gave way to selection for displaying loyalty to the leader. Zulfikar went on to abolish the elite 320-strong Civil Service of Pakistan (CSP), complaining: 'It has created a class of Brahmins or mandarins unrivalled in its snobbery and arrogance, insulated from the life of the people and incapable of identifying itself with them.'[54] He had a point: the CSP had indeed become very powerful and was quite capable of not only blocking his policies but also becoming a centre of opposition to him personally and the leftists in general. Nevertheless, the CSP consisted of a cadre of highly educated senior civil servants whom Zulfikar later needed to implement policy. As early as August 1972, Zulfikar was complaining about a 'growing implementation gap'.[55] As the files in the Pakistani national archive reveal, even the simplest issues got snarled up in the increasingly incompetent bureaucracy for months and even years.

British Prime Minister Lloyd George once told the parliament in London that the civil service in India was the 'steel frame' which had held everything together. Even if Zulfikar could legitimately argue that he should have a civil service committed to implementing his policies, his actions resulted in civil servants fearful that if they gave critical advice, they would be denounced as traitors. To give just one example of the risks they ran, Zulfikar objected when the commissioner of Sargodha arrested some PPP activists for public disorder. When Zulfikar asked that they be released, the commissioner said that under the law he was powerless to do that. 'Don't teach me the law,' Bhutto replied, and ordered that the commissioner be sacked.[56] Zulfikar could always dress up these actions in the language of revolutionary politics, but the Pakistan state was weak enough without his firing and undermining its most capable officials and replacing them with party hacks. His increasingly autocratic conduct made it impossible for civil servants to do their job. On his 'meet the people' trips he would sanction health, education, water and housing projects so often that an administrative unit had to be set up in the prime minister's secretariat to handle these directives, thereby disrupting the work of the body supposed to allocate such resources, the Planning Commission.[57]

Zulfikar's campaign against the bureaucracy was both successful and self-defeating. His most rapid retreat was in the face of the feudals. Before he espoused socialism and founded the PPP, he had expressed sympathy for the feudals. 'I belong to this privileged class,' he had told the National Assembly in 1962, 'therefore, I do admit the advantages of the system.'[58] But by the time of his first PPP manifesto, he had a different view: 'The breaking up of the large estates to destroy the power of the feudal landowners is a national necessity.'[59] Even before that document was put to the people, however, the backsliding had begun. In the run-up to the 1970 elections, Zulfikar had faced a dilemma familiar to Pakistani party leaders before and after him. To win seats, the PPP needed candidates with strong personal vote banks in their constituencies. Some feudals were so strong locally that they would be likely to win their seat whichever party they stood for. Zulfikar felt that, to win in 1970, he needed some of the 'electables' to join the PPP. His first success was to persuade the leading family in the Sindhi town of Hala to stand. Makhdoom Muhammad Zaman not only had vast land holdings but was also a hereditary saint, or *pir*, who provided spiritual solace to the local people. He had a total grip on the constituency, and when he said he would stand for the PPP, Zulfikar could be all but certain the PPP had just secured a seat in the National Assembly. With Makhdoom Muhammad Zaman on board, others followed, and, particularly in Sindh, Zulfikar attracted considerable feudal support.

By having these candidates Zulfikar was accepting, even before he held power, that there were limits to what he could do. While he publicly insisted that these feudals accepted the PPP's values, privately he assured them that, if he won power, their interests would not be damaged.[60] And the land reform package, when it came, gave the feudals plenty of leeway. True, Zulfikar imposed tighter limits on the number of acres someone could own, but plenty of loopholes remained, including the biggest of all, which allowed land to be transferred to relatives and peasants, who were sometimes told by their feudal master to put their thumbprint on ownership documents which they were unable to read. Tellingly, there was also a get-out clause for military officers, whose land holdings were exempt.[61] The fact that land reform was more thoroughly implemented in the North-West Frontier Province (NWFP) than elsewhere suggests it was used, in part, as a political tool to bolster PPP support in areas of the country in which it was weak. By using a measure of productivity rather than acreage, landowners in less fertile Sindh were favoured over their Punjabi counterparts. 'Agriculture should continue to be an attractive and profitable vocation,' Zulfikar said. This was the land reform of a landowner, and it remains the case that Pakistan has never managed to tackle big landowners as effectively as India. A committee set up to investigate land reform after the fall of the Bhutto government concluded that, out of all the country's cultivated land, only 3.06 per cent had been affected.[62] But it wasn't just a question of Zulfikar lacking the political will to force through more radical change in all parts of Pakistan. The landlords were past masters at evading whatever rules were introduced, not least because they could buy off or intimidate local officials responsible for implementing some of the land reform measures. The extent to which the Bhutto family itself was affected by land reform is unclear. In 1968, shortly after he set up the PPP, Zulfikar claimed that under Ayub's reforms the family had given up 40,000 acres.[63] Asked about his own reforms, he said that he had personally given up 6,000 to 7,000 acres and that the family as a whole lost 45,000.[64] He told one reporter that when he heard that one of his sons was going to have to give up more than the other, he decided that the family would accept more substantial cuts in acreage.[65] 'I've felt no fear of giving up what I own,' he said, 'ever since the day I read Marx. I can even tell you the time and place: Bombay, 1945.'[66]

While there were signs from the outset that Zulfikar was not committed to far-reaching land reform, it seemed his campaign against the 'fat industrialists',[67] as he called them, was more serious. Pakistan's industrial power was highly concentrated. According to one famous study, just twenty-two families owned 66 per cent of the industrial capital, 80 per cent of banking and 97 per cent of insurance businesses.[68] In his election campaign, Zulfikar had repeatedly raised the issue of the wealth of the twenty-two families, and he set about confronting the industrialists soon after he took over. He and his advisers knew that the almost complete lack of opposition to him when he first came to power could not last for long. They were consequently in a hurry to get as much done as quickly as possible. In its opening gambit, the government issued the Economic Reforms Order of 3 January 1972, thereby taking over iron and steel plants; heavy engineering; the assembly and manufacture of automobiles, trucks and tractors; cement; public utilities like gas and electricity; oil refineries; petrochemicals; and heavy and basic chemicals. The government controlled some 20 per cent of the large-scale manufacturing industry.[69] In theory, it was a limited nationalisation, in that the government only took over the management and not ownership of the companies. 'If we had gone about it the other way,' Zulfikar explained, 'we would have had to pay fantastic compensation and we don't have the money to pay the compensation.'[70] In practice, the companies were nationalised without compensation. He took care to avoid disputes with foreign governments by not taking over any company with substantial foreign investment.

The policy was bitterly resisted, and its implementation involved some very tough tactics. Industrialists were arrested, had their passports seized and were paraded in handcuffs on national television. It was undisguised populist politics, and the industrialists did not take it lying down. While some of their money ended up in the treasury, far more of it left the country, as businesses calculated that, if they wanted to keep their assets, it would be best to move them as far from Pakistan as possible. Others fought back in different ways. One of the families affected was the little-known Sharif family, who were persuaded by the loss of their steel foundry that, to continue doing business, they would have to get into politics. Zulfikar thereby unwittingly laid the basis of a dynasty that would go on to challenge his own. Faced by this resistance, Zulfikar was left flailing around as he told his finance minister to threaten to hang businessmen who did not bring back foreign exchange. But as Mubashir Hassan pointed out, the government had left 'no way for the industrialists to cooperate with us . . . we neither got their money nor their cooperation'.[71] It wasn't long before Zulfikar realised that he needed the industrialists, fat or otherwise, and set about trying to reassure them. In November 1972 he said: 'For the next five years we don't intend to nationalize any further or take any other steps that might be considered against them. 80% of industry is still in their hands. We are prepared to give them encouragements and other inducements and incentives within the framework of our objectives. Now they should settle down and start contributing to the economy.'[72] He even appointed some of them to run loss-making state companies, such as the national airline, PIA.[73]

Alongside these attempts to reassure the business community, however, he also wanted to press on with a key aspect of the nationalisation policy package: taking over the banks. There was good reason for this. There was strong evidence that the banks were playing an important role in helping the big families maintain their grip on the economy. A 1970 State Bank report had found that just eighty-eight accounts had access to 25 per cent of the total credit in the country.[74] India had already nationalised fourteen of its major banks in 1969, but in Pakistan the banks had been left out of the initial 1972 round of nationalisations. Zulfikar was determined not to flunk it a second time. He ordered the takeover of shipping companies and petroleum distribution at the same time. If the takeover of the banks was the most successful element of the nationalisation, the third round, which came in 1976, was politically disastrous. In an attempt to cut out the middleman in the agricultural sector, Zulfikar announced that thousands of cotton, ginning and rice-husking units would be taken over by the state. It was an attempt to reach out to the socialists in the PPP who had abandoned him, but it led to widespread public resentment. The degree to which the nationalisations were a success depended on how one saw their purpose. Certainly, the stated aim to, as he put it, 'eliminate, once and for all, poverty and discrimination'[75] remained a dream. Some nationalisations did reduce the power of families that controlled industrial assets, although, as the Sharifs showed, many went on to thrive. But any gains have to be judged along-side the economic problems that arose. Political, rather than economic, factors came to influence decisions on where plants were opened. Loss-making firms were not declared bankrupt for fear of the political impact of job losses. And the numbers employed in the state-owned companies skyrocketed as politicians handed out jobs as gifts to constituents. No Pakistani leader since Zulfikar has tried to emulate his nationalisation programme.

While the feudals and the industrialists were formidable opponents, neither could match the street power of the Islamists. Throughout his time in power, Zulfikar grappled with the difficult issue of what role Islam should play in Pakistani society. His basic orientation of campaigning for social justice became wrapped up with his advocacy of Muslim causes. Omar Kureshi, a schoolfriend from the Bombay Cathedral School and fellow student at the University of Southern California, recalled that 'if there was one issue about which he would really get worked up, it was Israel. He would sit in the student union cafeteria and he would be scathing about Israel. About America's support to Israel, he would say: "not the United States but the Jewnited States of America." '[76] His April 1948 lecture on 'The Islamic Heritage' to fellow students at the University of Southern California had summarised most of his views as a young man. He began by assuring his American audience that he was not coming at the subject from a religious point of view. 'I do not say my prayers regularly; I do not keep all the fasts. I have not been on a pilgrimage to Mecca. Therefore, religiously speaking, I am a poor Muslim. However, my interest is soaked in the political, economic and cultural heritage of Islam.' As he developed his theme, Zulfikar ranged over the history of the faith from its inception to the current day, insisting that when Islam was properly interpreted, it was committed to tolerance and, in particular, the protection of Christians and Jews. He highlighted the intellectual and artistic achievements of past Muslim kingdoms and railed against the current state of the Muslim world and the way it was perceived: 'We are not barbarians. Instead we opened the doors of civilization and pride.' He referred repeatedly to the British socialist writer Arnold Toynbee, highlighting his observation that 'Pan-Islamism is dormant – yet we have to reckon with the possibility that the sleeper may awake, if ever the cosmopolitan proletariat of a "westernized" world revolts against western domination and cries out for anti-western leadership. That call might have incalculable psychological effects in evoking the militant spirit of Islam – even if it has slumbered as long as the Seven Sleepers – because it might awaken echoes of a heroic age.'[77] Maybe it was Toynbee who set Zulfikar thinking about the potential of pan-Islamism, which he tried to marry with his liberalism. 'This is the time when the younger generation of Muslims, who will be the leaders of a new force of an order based on justice, want the end of exploitation.' An international association of Muslims would give the world 'a blueprint of the brotherhood of mankind'. He ended with a peroration, the rhetorical structure of which pre-figured some of his later speeches. 'Destiny demands an Islamic association; political reality justifies it, posterity awaits it and, by God, we will have it. Courage is in our blood: we are the children of a rich heritage. We shall succeed.'

One thing that he did not say to his Los Angeles audience was just how much contempt he had for the clerical classes. After all, while the clerics had been studying the Koran in the gloom of decrepit, hidebound madrasahs, teaching children to learn it by rote without even understanding the Arabic, Zulfikar had been studying at the world's best universities and engaging with the world's leading scholars. Like many in the army, Zulfikar consistently underestimated the strength of the clerics. Even if the gap between Zulfikar and the clerics was wide, there was one policy area on which they converged. The Pakistan state's support for some violent jihadists and its use of them in advancing foreign policy goals is generally associated with the army and the ISI, which ran campaigns against the Soviets and later NATO forces in Afghanistan. In fact, it began right at the start under Jinnah, when tribesmen from the north-west headed for Kashmir. Zulfikar also used proxies, all the while assuming – wrongly – that once the state had used them, they could easily enough be disbanded. As early as May 1972 he was talking about making a Mujahid Force comprising in part paramilitary organisations loyal to political parties that he wanted to disband.[78] By late 1974 he was increasingly concerned by Afghan support for the Pashtunistan movement. Rather than using the armed forces to deal with the issue, he backed Islamists to oppose the Afghan government and even opened training camps in North and South Waziristan to attract recruits from the groups of Islamists fleeing repression in Afghanistan. Between 1973 and 1977 Pakistan's Frontier Corps trained 5,000 Afghan Islamists opposed to their government.[79] The trainees included some individuals who would go on to become major players in Afghanistan's civil strife, including Gulbuddin Hekmatyar, Burhanuddin Rabbani and Ahmed Shah Masood. The colonel who headed up this effort later recorded that 'the first phase of the Afghan war was now on'.[80]

Zulfikar's attitude to Islam became highly relevant during the debate about his efforts to introduce a new constitution. In the run-up to the promulgation of the 1956 constitution, the Islamic-based parties pressed for a document that would establish Pakistan as an ideological state committed to the faith. Some even asked whether a constitution was necessary. The Koran and Sunna, they maintained, set down all the rules necessary for life, and there was no need for mere men to create political institutions that could only distort Allah's word. In the event, the politicians charged with writing the first Pakistani constitution came down on the side of the modernists. While Pakistan was named as an Islamic Republic and a clause in the preamble recognised Allah's sovereignty over the universe, the document made clear that, in practice, the people of Pakistan would be sovereign. When Ayub came up with another constitution in 1962 to cement his military rule, he tried to avoid describing the country as an Islamic Republic but had to back down on the issue.

Zulfikar took a similar line – he had no desire for Pakistan to become a theocracy: when in 1972 his most prominent religious minister, Kausar Niazi, spoke of making all laws in the country come into line with Islamic laws, Zulfikar slapped him down in cabinet, telling him to be more 'circumspect in making such statements'.[81] And yet, as Zulfikar set about writing a new 'permanent' constitution (following his interim one of 1972), he accepted stronger Islamic provisions than either the 1956 or 1962 documents. Islam was declared the state religion of Pakistan, and the constitution stated that teaching

Arabic would be encouraged and that *Islamiyat* (Islamic studies) would be a compulsory subject for students. As a lawyer who took a close interest in constitutional issues, Zulfikar knew full well that such detailed educational policy issues were hardly matters for the country's most fundamental document. But Zulfikar knew that to get the constitution through he would have to make significant concessions to the religious right and those who wanted greater provincial autonomy.

Even if he could justify his compromises with clerics as pragmatic necessities, however, it seems that Zulfikar was blinded by his contempt for clerics, most of whom he viewed as uneducated, venal and regressive. His disdain meant he did not fully appreciate the clerics' strength. What he saw as tactical retreats which he would later reverse, the clerics saw as strategic gains. And they were right. But Zulfikar ploughed on, thinking he had to pick his battles: he had an eye on what were for him more important constitutional clauses relating to the extent of his authority and how the prime minister could be removed. When it came to his powers, he secured the right to appoint provincial governors and to declare a state of emergency. As for his being safe in office, he attempted to secure a provision that for the next fifteen years the prime minister could only be sacked by a two-thirds majority of the National Assembly. When the opposition successfully argued against that measure, Zulfikar came up with a more convoluted clause that achieved much the same thing: for the next ten years the prime minister could only fall in a motion of no confidence if a majority of his own party voted for it. As long as he had the support of half of the PPP, he was safe.

Despite these issues, many consider the 1973 constitution to have been Zulfikar's greatest achievement and credit it with holding West Pakistan together as a single country. It was, by any standards, extraordinary that Zulfikar managed to push it through with no one in the National Assembly voting against it. Mubashir Hassan described how the final hold-out – a cleric – was persuaded to vote in favour with a payoff: 'The amount was settled and Bhutto described the scene to me how when the fellow came to President's House to collect the money, Bhutto threw a packet of notes on the floor and ordered him to pick it up. There the man was, moving over the carpet on all fours, picking a bundle from here and a bundle from there. Bhutto was mightily amused.'[82] By using all his political skills – bribery included – Zulfikar had made a significant contribution to Pakistan's national story. 'The country owes him everything,' said Hafeez Pirzada, the man who worked on the constitution for Zulfikar, 'even its continuance as a sovereign country. He was not the founder, but the saviour of the country.'[83] It's a fair point – 1971 was as big a disaster as could be imagined, and Zulfikar dealt with it in a way that it is hard to imagine any other civilian or military leader in the country's history having been able to do.

There was a moment in Zulfikar's presidency when it seemed that his ideas about pan-Islamism might become relevant and operable: the steep rise in oil prices in 1973 opened up new possibilities. 'With the recent dramatic improvement,' he said with his usual perspicacity, 'in the terms of trade of the oil-producing countries, which will lead to a rapid increase in their financial resources, an unprecedented shift will occur in the global monetary and financial balance of power.'[84] He was right, and having already led initiatives to improve relations with the Soviet Union and China, Zulfikar now turned his attention to the Arab states, stating that Pakistan's armed forces were available to them. He offered to send skilled and semi-skilled workers, engineers, teachers and military experts and started building relationships with King Faisal of Saudi Arabia, Muammar Gaddafi of Libya, the Palestinian leader Yasser Arafat, and Syria's Hafiz al-Assad.[85] These initiatives climaxed with the Lahore Islamic Summit of 1974, a sumptuous event that created a feel-good factor throughout Pakistan. It marked a high point of Zulfikar's political career, bringing together many of the themes that defined his politics: it was an event on a grand scale and played on Zulfikar's desires to have Pakistan respected and to build alternative postcolonial global power structures. It also placed him where he liked to be: at the centre of attention. Just three years after the disaster of 1971, the country was hosting six kings, twelve presidents and six prime ministers: perhaps there was a role for Pakistan on the world stage after all. Back in 1956 the then Pakistani prime minister H.S. Suhrawardy had said there was little point in Muslim majority countries joining forces because they were just too weak. 'Zero plus zero plus zero is, after all, equal to zero. We have, therefore, to go farther afield rather than get all the zeros together because they will never be able to produce anything which is substantial.'[86] Now it was different, or, at least, it looked as if it might be. And in a political masterstroke Zulfikar used the event to announce, as he realised he had to at some point, Pakistan's recognition of Bangladesh. It was a clever way of getting the nation to swallow a bitter pill. His ideas about pan-Islamism may not have led to the broad Muslim revival in world affairs he hoped for but, for Pakistan, they did bring some immediate material benefits in the form of aid from OPEC countries.

All this international activity, however, could not hide the opposition Zulfikar faced from Islamists at home. In the 1970 election campaign he was frequently under attack from clerics who denounced his secular lifestyle. Zulfikar came to realise that, while people in his own social milieu habitually treated clerics with contempt, when he expressed such attitudes in public it put off some voters. The concessions Zulfikar made to the Islamists in the 1973 constitution showed how seriously he took the issue of trying not to alienate the religious parties. Seeing that street power was a vital protection vis-à-vis the army, Zulfikar realised that when it came to mobilising mass rallies, the religious parties were the PPP's only rival. That concern helps explain why in June 1974 he made a decision that has stained his reputation ever since. It concerned the Ahmadis, a sect that follows the teachings of Mirza Ghulam Ahmed, a nineteenth-century Punjabi theologian. Ahmed said he had revelations direct from Allah. Even though Ahmed considered himself subservient to Mohammed, his claim clashed with the basic Islamic tenet that Mohammed was the last and final prophet. In 1953, long before Bhutto came to power, radical Islamists had demanded that the Ahmadis be declared non-Muslims, and the issue had led to rioting throughout Punjab. Many Ahmadis had had their properties looted and burnt, and some of the riots had become so violent that Ahmadis had been murdered. Faced with this outburst, the central government, after some prevarication, had called on the army to restore law and order in Lahore.

A major inquiry into the riots produced one of the most thoughtful official documents ever published in Pakistan. The Munir Commission set about interviewing senior clerics and asking them how one could determine if someone was a Muslim or not. The question immediately brought sectarian issues to the fore, as no two clerics could agree on a definition of a Muslim. Zulfikar was well aware of the fundamental issues the Munir Commission touched on. In the run-up to the 1970 election he had criticised General Yahya for having attempted to include the phrase 'Islamic Ideology' in his Legal Framework Order, on the grounds that with so many different Muslim sects it was unclear 'who will determine what is in conformity with the concept of Islam and according to which will it be decided?'[87] Now he had not only put that phrase into the 1973 constitution but was also supporting a constitutional amendment which defined who was and who wasn't in conformity with Islam. There is reason to believe that Zulfikar realised that the measure was regressive and damaging. He told Pakistan's Nobel Prize-winning scientist Abdus Salam, an Ahmadi, that: 'This is all politics ... give me time and I will change it.'[88] But rather than thanking him, the hardliners increased the pressure for more measures: Ahmadi organisations should be banned, they now demanded, and Ahmadis should be removed from key positions in the government. His minister, Kausar Niazi, recorded Zulfikar's frustration: ' "The maulvis [Islamic clerics] are claiming all credit for the Amendment," he complained'.[89]

As the years passed, Zulfikar increasingly needed the support of the PPP's machine. But the party was not what it used to be and even its capacity for organising mass rallies was diminished. In his first full year in power – 1972 – Zulfikar addressed thirteen such rallies, some of which he described as people's courts, which he would consult over major decisions. The next year there were just six such meetings, and in 1974 just one, after which he avoided mass audiences and addressed smaller groups.[90] There was a sense of the PPP atrophying. In 1974 Zulfikar clashed with the leading PPP ideologue who had encouraged Zulfikar to set up the party in the first place, J.A. Rahim. Initially the two men communicated very directly with each other. Shortly after the publication of the manifesto in 1967, Rahim wrote to Zulfikar urging him, in quite stark terms, to adhere to its principles: 'When dealing with politicians who will come to you to bargain for themselves, please do not compromise on the doctrines. Without the Doctrine the Movement is nothing.'[91] After the 1970 elections, Rahim was Zulfikar's closest adviser. Not only did Zulfikar delay his swearing-in ceremony so Rahim could be present, he also insisted that every paper that reached his desk should first be seen by Rahim. But as time passed the relationship deteriorated, and Rahim became disaffected from both PPP policies and Zulfikar's increasingly imperious manner. Matters came to a head in 1974 when Zulfikar was hosting a dinner for some 300 people but, not untypically, didn't turn up, leaving them all waiting, as protocol demanded that they not eat until he arrived. 'You bloody flunkies can wait as long as you like for the Maharaja of Larkana, I'm going home!' Rahim said. He later left a written account of what ensued, the details of which have been confirmed by his son, who was also present.[92] Inevitably, Zulfikar was told what Rahim had said. Having returned home after the non-dinner, Rahim then heard a knock on the door in the night. Security personnel rushed into his house, beat him and imprisoned him. Given how close the two men had been, it was an incident that revealed the extent to which Zulfikar had lost touch with normal human relationships. As Rafi Raza observed, within less than three years of the establishment of the PPP government, all Zulfikar's key allies, including Rahim, Finance Minister Mubashir Hassan, Mustafa Khar and his cousin Mumtaz Bhutto, had left him. 'In each case,' Raza wrote, 'ZAB was largely responsible. The camaraderie, a main feature of the early PPP years, ceased. Mir Afzal Khan and I both warned of the danger of this state of affairs, pointing out that he was isolating himself, replacing the affection his colleagues had felt for him with awe, if not fear.'[93]

In the early years the PPP had performed an important political function. As an overtly political organisation with a structure reaching down to towns and even villages, it at least gave people hope that their voices might count for something in exerting political control over a haughty and uncaring bureaucracy. But the 1977 manifesto showed how much the PPP had changed. The promises of radical reform made in 1970 had transmogrified into vague statements about consolidating gains. The document claimed that the PPP had already 'brought an end to feudalism in Pakistan and ushered in a new era of progress and prosperity for our rural society'. These were boasts no one believed. All talk about socialism had disappeared. Even 'Islamic socialism' was dropped and replaced with Musawat-i-Muhammadi (Islamic Egalitarianism).[94] Now, the PPP proclaimed, it would 'hold high the banner of Islam'. Jamaat-e-Islami's Maulana Maududi knew he had prevailed and didn't hesitate to say so. 'They found out that their socialism cannot dance naked . . . After realizing this they started calling socialism Islamic . . . If it is really based on the Quran and the Sunnah then what is the need for calling it socialism? . . . Now when they can see that this does not work they have started calling it Muhammadi Muswat. The object is the same, pure socialism.'[95]

There is one other policy area to assess. As a strong leader at the centre, Zulfikar had little regard for alternative provincial power brokers. His attitude led to two major crises, both of which further exposed the limits to his power. The first concerned the Urdu-speaking Mohajirs. As a result of partition,

Pakistan received 8 million Muslim refugees, or Mohajirs, who had previously been living in areas that remained in India. Many of the Mohajirs were urban intellectuals who had been at the forefront of the campaign for Pakistan. They arrived in areas in which the indigenous population was largely rural and uneducated. From the outset, the Mohajirs wielded disproportionate influence, dominating the early governments. As a Sindhi landlord, Zulfikar was an archetypal representative of the indigenous groups that increasingly resented Mohajir influence and power. And he acted accordingly. In 1972, Zulfikar's cousin Mumtaz, in his capacity as Sindh chief minister, made Sindhi an official language. The measure had a direct impact on the employability of Urdu speakers, who, to keep their government jobs, faced the prospect of having to learn Sindhi, a language that many Mohajirs considered beneath them. And many had government jobs. The Mohajirs had flourished in Pakistan: by 1973 they held 33.5 per cent of posts in the civilian bureaucracy despite comprising only 8 per cent of the population. Sindhis, twice as populous, held just 2.7 per cent of bureaucratic posts.[96] Another rule introduced in 1973 meant 40 per cent of government jobs and educational places were allocated to people living in urban areas, but 60 per cent went to rural areas, where the native Sindhis tended to live. The Mohajirs thought they were being singled out for hostile treatment: there were no similar bills in other provinces. And they pointed out that since many Mohajirs had set up businesses, Zulfikar's nationalisations had hit their community disproportionally hard as well.

Zulfikar was warned that the bill would cause trouble but pressed on regardless. The day the new language laws were passed there were massive pro-Urdu demonstrations in Karachi. The police tear-gassed the protestors and announced a dusk-to-dawn curfew. The next morning the Urdu daily *Jang* – showing that the press still had some fight in it – bordered the whole of its front page with thick black lines. The banner headline ran: 'This is the funeral procession for Urdu: let it go out with a fanfare.'[97] Fired up, the Mohajirs returned to the streets. This time the police fired directly into the demonstrators, killing twelve people, including a ten-year-old boy. The Mohajir movement had its first martyrs, and the protestors responded with fury, burning down buildings throughout Karachi. Students from Karachi University targeted the Sindhi department, setting all its records alight. On 9 July ten more people were killed. Calm was restored only when Bhutto passed an ordinance under which Urdu was also given official status.[98] He had learnt, once again, that there were limits to how far he could go.

Although he was a champion of Sindhi rights, Zulfikar remained a firm advocate of centralised power. This was in part due to his acute awareness that, after the disaster in East Pakistan, he could not risk the loss of another province, a development that would have meant the total defeat of the idea of Pakistan. The danger was most acute in Balochistan, where many people had always been reluctant Pakistanis. In October 1958, Baloch resistance took violent form as tribesmen opposed the incorporation of their province into West Pakistan under the 'One Unit' programme. The Pakistan Army prevailed, defeating a tribal force of around 1,000 men, but the Baloch didn't give up. There were confrontations involving hundreds of men on both sides in 1964 and 1965, with the fighting continuing sporadically until 1970. All of these uprisings, however, paled into insignificance compared to that of 1973.

Even though the Baloch had longstanding grievances, the crisis of 1973 was to a large extent of Zulfikar's own making. When he came to power in 1971, he reached out to two parties with support in Balochistan: the leftist National Awami Party (NAP) and the religiously minded Jamiat ul-Ulema (JUI). He not only conceded the right of a NAP–JUI coalition to form a government in Balochistan and NWFP but also let it propose governors of the two provinces. This was not quite as generous as it seemed: he was at the time trying to persuade the NAP to back his interim constitution, and from the outset Zulfikar tried to limit the amount of authority he had to give up. In an April 1972 letter to the Baloch governor Mir Ghaus Bakhsh Bizenjo, for example, Zulfikar said that by forbearing from appointing a PPP leader or a non-party figure he was acting in the interests of national unity and asked that the gesture be reciprocated: that there should be no political victimisation or unfair treatment of non-locals; that law and order should be maintained; that the provincial government should not assume jurisdiction in strictly federal subjects; that the loyalty of the armed forces should not be subverted; and that fissiparous tendencies and movements, however nebulous, should be put down firmly. Mir Ghaus Bakhsh Bizenjo replied the next day, assuring Zulfikar that he accepted these conditions.

It didn't take long for Zulfikar to tire of the arrangement and to press for PPP governments in NWFP and Balochistan. He removed Governor Bizenjo, accusing him of not having adhered to his assurances. To help justify the move, Bhutto announced the discovery of a cache of 350 Soviet submachine guns and 100,000 rounds of ammunition in the house of the Iraqi political attaché in Islamabad. Bhutto claimed the weapons were destined for Baloch separatists and would be used by fighters seeking independence. Writing to President Richard Nixon, he claimed that the discovery showed that 'powers inimical to us are not content with the severance of Pakistan's eastern part; their aim is the dismemberment of Pakistan itself'.[99] The Americans thought it more likely the arms were intended for Baloch fighters in Iran.[100] The suggestion that the whole affair was concocted was hardly assuaged by the government's decision to take the arms cache on tour, displaying it in various parts of the country.

It is striking that the 15 February proclamation in which Zulfikar dismissed the Baloch government read very much like the proclamation issued by successive Pakistani military leaders whenever they launched a coup. Citing the 'national interest', he declared that he would 'assume . . . all functions and powers of the Government of that Province'.[101] Some of those close to Zulfikar, such as Mubashir Hassan, have tried to shift the blame for what happened onto the military, arguing that no civilian leader in Pakistan can ever ignore military advice, which is almost always to shoot first and think about the politics later.[102] But in this case Zulfikar had precipitated the political crisis, thereby creating a situation in which military advice was needed. It was a disastrous situation. Baloch fighters mounted actions against the Pakistani Army, which, in turn, responded with force. With Zulfikar describing the Baloch rebels as 'miscreants',[103] causing many to draw parallels with what had happened in East Pakistan, the army was given a free hand to restore control. The fighting was to last four years, and the central government had to deploy tens of thousands of troops to suppress an insurgency of 55,000 rebels.[104] The army operation ended only after the 1977 coup, when General Zia declared victory and ordered a withdrawal. Even though the fighting in Balochistan might well have been avoided, the conflict nonetheless carried yet another warning for Zulfikar: there were significant elements of Pakistani society that would not bend to his will. But the press, the industrialists, the workers, the Mohajirs, the PPP, the Baloch and even the Americans were all second-order opponents when compared to the real centre of power that Zulfikar faced: the army.

4
ZULFIKAR'S DOWNFALL

There was one area of policy in which Zulfikar and the military worked together over a sustained period. Despite the sheer implausibility of a country as poor as Pakistan, and with such low education levels, mastering the technology required to build a nuclear bomb, Zulfikar famously said as early as 1965: 'If India builds the bomb, we will eat grass or leaves, even go hungry, but we will get one of our own. We have no alternative.' On 20 January 1972, just a month after assuming power, he called a meeting of scientists in Multan and told them he wanted 'fission in three years'. 'We can do it,' came back the enthusiastic response, 'you will have the bomb!'[1]

Zulfikar wasn't only thinking about India. He hoped that, should Pakistan get the bomb, its status in international diplomacy would be on an altogether new level. And in terms of the Muslim world, it would bolster his efforts to help Pakistan assume a leadership position. But building one was easier said than done. After India tested in 1974, international concerns about nuclear proliferation intensified. Pakistan complained bitterly that it should not be punished for India's test, but it was. Canada was worried that a nuclear reactor it was building in Pakistan to create electricity now posed a significant proliferation risk. It cut off all supplies of nuclear fuel to the plant. Bhutto appealed to the French for help, but Paris eventually succumbed to pressure from Washington and, in 1977, stopped its nuclear cooperation with Pakistan. But Zulfikar had already explored an alternative. In 1974 a Pakistani nuclear scientist, A.Q. Khan, who had access to a uranium enrichment facility in the Netherlands, had written to Zulfikar saying that he would also be glad to return to Pakistan. In December the two men met in Karachi and Khan explained what he could do. Two years later he had set up the Kahuta laboratory near Islamabad and started work. Building the bomb was a consistent effort by many parts of the Pakistani state over a period of decades. But none of the subsequent contributors to Pakistan's nuclear project could deny that, without Zulfikar's vision and determination to match the Indian programme, it would never have got off the ground.

For all their various collaborations over the years, however, Zulfikar and the army never fully trusted each other. Indeed, once in power, Zulfikar's tussles with the press, the bureaucrats, the PPP and other institutions he wanted to control were all dwarfed by his struggle with the army. It was never the case that Zulfikar wanted to weaken the military's fighting capability – his nationalism and his sense of history persuaded him that Pakistan needed a force capable of defending against Indian attack. From the outset the PPP had contended that the only answer to an armed India was an armed Pakistan, and in 1972 Zulfikar promised to outspend the Ayub and Yahya regimes in defence so as to create the finest fighting machine in Asia. Zulfikar's finance ministry met every request that came in from the military for funds and equipment.[2] During his tenure, despite the army having lost East Pakistan and consequently having far less territory to defend, military expenditure went from 3.2 billion rupees in 1971 to 8.1 billion rupees in 1976. While he wanted a strong and effective army, he also wanted control of it. He strived continuously for that goal, and his failure to achieve it would cost him his life.

Anxious from the outset that the army was the main threat to his holding on to power, Zulfikar moved fast. As soon as he took over, he put Yahya Khan under house arrest and asked a man he trusted, General Gul Hassan, to run the army. He then set about sacking forty-four senior officers from the army, navy and air force, going so far as to describe them as 'fat and flabby'[3] and as having 'Bonapartic tendencies'. The loss of East Pakistan had put the army on the back foot and Zulfikar exploited its self-doubt. Challenged on his remark that 'by the grace of God, Pakistan has been saved', which endorsed the army action in East Pakistan, he replied: 'Yes, I did support military action but only to curb the secessionists and restore law and order and to stop indiscriminate mob killings of non-Bengalis. I did not endorse the orgy of military violence against the populace of East Pakistan.'[4] He then sanctioned a PTV broadcast of a documentary which showed the Pakistani forces surrendering to the Indians. It was a deliberate humiliation of the army, and at a dinner with some senior officers Zulfikar was faced with demands that the programme not be repeated and quickly backed down.[5]

Zulfikar's agreement not to broadcast it again was the first example of his giving in to the military. There would be many more. Later, he would also agree not to publish the findings of the Hamoodur Rehman Commission Report into the events of 1971 and the loss of East Pakistan. At the time, many thought he kept the report under lock and key because it had been critical of Zulfikar himself. But when it was eventually published in the Pakistani press in 2000, it turned out that Hamoodur Rehman had used his strongest language to describe the failures of the military. The report, for example, accused the most senior officer in East Pakistan, General Niazi, of having relations with two prostitutes: 'he came to acquire a stinking reputation owing to his association with women of bad repute and his nocturnal visits to places also frequented by several junior officers under his command'.[6] But even if Zulfikar tried to please the army by withholding the TV broadcast and the Hamoodur Rehman Commission Report, there were many other areas of tension. Within weeks of taking over, Zulfikar asked Gul Hassan to deploy troops in Karachi to quell some labour unrest. The army chief declined, telling Zulfikar to use the police instead. Zulfikar also wanted some PPP youths who were imprisoned for deserting the National Cadet Corps to be released; he wanted to visit military units with Gul Hassan; and he wanted soldiers to break police strikes in Peshawar and Lahore.[7] When all of these and other requests were turned down by Gul Hassan, Zulfikar concluded, just three months after appointing him, that he needed an army chief more willing to accept civilian control.

The extent of Zulfikar's anxiety that the army would not accept the removal of Gul Hassan can be gauged from the precautions he took when firing him. Rather than risk a stenographer informing the army, the resignation letter Gul Hassan would have to sign was ham-fistedly typed by Zulfikar's most senior aides.[8] Then, after the sacking, he not only placed the general in protective custody but even had his most senior and trusted colleague, Mustafa Khar, the governor of Punjab, accompany Gul Hassan on a journey to Lahore, effectively holding him incommunicado while a successor was appointed. Other senior officers who might have rallied to the defence of Gul Hassan were called to a fake meeting and kept waiting until the general's resignation was obtained. Police were deployed at the radio and TV stations,[9] and the PPP also organised a mass rally in Rawalpindi just in case their president needed some street power.[10] Zulfikar explained the sackings in terms of the military top brass having been insufficiently deferential: 'since they had been ruling for many years, they found it difficult to take orders.' Asked specifically about whether Gul Hassan had been planning a coup, Zulfikar gave a deliberately unclear reply: 'There was no concerted plan for a coup, just light remarks.'[11] Gul Hassan's successor, General Tikka Khan, was chosen as someone who would not pose a threat. 'He is a professional soldier and there is not an iota of Bonapartism in him . . . If a general is not bitten by the bug of politics, and is a first class professional soldier, then I cannot muck around the armed forces.'[12] And just to reinforce the point about who was boss, Tikka Khan was given the title of chief of army staff, while Zulfikar declared that from now on he would be the commander-in-chief.

Although Zulfikar was comfortable with Tikka Khan, he was still unsure if the army could be relied upon to do his bidding, and he moved to tighten his control, for example by securing agreement that he could – as he had wanted from the outset – sit on promotion boards for officers above the rank of briga-dier general. His method of selecting who should be promoted was simple enough – he tried to choose officers who he thought would not be able to attract loyalty and support from senior colleagues. For example, Mohajirs, being somewhat marginalised in the army, were preferable to Pashtuns.[13] Zulfikar also tried to bend the ISI to his purpose, placing increasing reliance on an ISI internal political cell initially set up by Ayub but used by Zulfikar to monitor ministers' private lives and bug their phones. He told the Intelligence Bureau to set up a parallel cell watching the ISI, but it did not gather much information and, when it came to the crunch in 1977, it failed to get wind of the coup that was to bring Zulfikar down.[14] Realising that he would never get complete control of the army, Zulfikar thought he needed another security force that he could be sure would obey his orders. Even if his motivation in setting up the Federal Security Force (FSF) was understandable, it was to become a highly controversial and somewhat notorious arm of state power, used to target Zulfikar's enemies. When opposition members of the National Assembly complained that FSF personnel were PPP 'storm troopers', they had a point. And it packed a considerable punch. By 1976 it consisted of 18,875 men with heavy weapons and hundreds of vehicles.[15] From the outset, the army resented the attempt to undermine its monopoly on violence, refusing, for example, to provide the FSF with any training facilities. In turn, Zulfikar's pressure on the army didn't let up. The 1973 constitution for the first time gave the military a clearly defined role to 'defend Pakistan against external aggression or threat of war, and subject to law, act in aid of civil power when called upon to do so'. The document also specified an oath for members of the armed forces, which stated: 'I will not engage myself in any political activities whatsoever.' Three years later in a White Paper on Defence Organisation, Zulfikar re-emphasised his view that 'The evolution of national defence policy and its administration requires political control at the top'.[16] Ultimate responsibility for national defence, the White Paper said, lay with the prime minister.

Zulfikar's worries about a coup were not fanciful. From the first months of his government, some mid-ranking army and air force officers had been discussing what to do about their complaints against both Zulfikar and the army leadership. When General Tikka Khan become aware of the plot, he had the officers arrested and put on trial.[17] The proceedings were significant in themselves – a clear message was being sent that breaches in discipline would be punished. But they were important for another reason too. The man chosen to manage the trial was a brigadier by the name of Zia ul-Haq, who in the course of his duties reported frequently to Zulfikar himself. Zia, apparently keen to make a good impression, sentenced twenty-four officers to heavier-than-expected sentences, including two who were imprisoned for life.[18] Zia always made the most of any interactions he had with Zulfikar. On one occasion he presented Zulfikar with a sword in recognition of his services to the country and its armed forces. Similarly, Zia made Zulfikar honorary commander-in-chief of the Armoured Corps and had a special uniform made up for him. 'All I can say,' Zia oozed, 'is that perhaps one day by the Grace of God while you are still President, this Pakistan army can show you all the attention and affection that it received from you did not go to waste.'[19] When Zulfikar visited Multan, Zia, who was stationed there as corps commander at the time, organised the wives and children of officers to give him a rousing ovation.[20] Had Zulfikar been more self-aware, he might have reflected that there was an echo in all this of his own flattery of Ayub Khan. Instead, he seems to have drawn the conclusion that Zia was pliant – which, when it came to choosing a new army chief, was just the kind of man he wanted. When General Tikka Khan retired on 1 March 1976, it fell to Zulfikar to pick his successor. His one concern was to choose whoever was least likely to challenge him. Tikka Khan provided him with a list of seven potential candidates, in which Zia was not named on the grounds that he was the most recently appointed lieutenant general and consequently lacked sufficient experience. Despite that, or perhaps in part because of it, Zulfikar chose him.

Zia had been born to a modest middle-class family, and it never occurred to Zulfikar that he would think himself as equal, never mind superior, to the aristocratic Bhutto. Indeed, Zia was so devout and so different to his, in many cases, rather swashbuckling colleagues that he seemed to have few friends at the top of the army, again suggesting he would not be a threat. He simply did not look or behave like the type of man to mount a coup. Zulfikar never took him seriously: he even used to be disparaging about the poor state of his teeth.[21] A story – possibly apocryphal – did the rounds that on one occasion Zia was smoking when he was surprised by Zulfikar entering the room. Afraid that having a cigarette in front of the prime minister would be seen as disrespectful, he thrust the cigarette into his pocket, which then began to smoulder, with acrid smoke filling the air. How, Zulfikar thought, could such a man lead a country?

Misjudging Zia's Uriah Heep-style humbleness was Zulfikar's first mistake. His second was to rely too often on the army to control society. It might have seemed to Zulfikar that, with so many challenges, Pakistan could not afford to forgo the services of the best-resourced organisation in the country. But by giving the army so many responsibilities, he allowed officers to overcome their sense of failure after 1971 and to once again start thinking that they were so indispensable they had the right to overrule elected politicians. The most striking use of military power was in Balochistan, where Zulfikar deployed no fewer than 70,000 troops in the long-running campaign to suppress the tribal insurgency. Some of Zulfikar's colleagues tried to warn him against it. For example, Rao Rashid, who worked at the prime minister's secretariat, advised that sending the army into Balochistan to confront tribal leaders carried risks: 'It is time that the experiment of gradual withdrawal of the army from law enforcement is given a trial. The impression amongst the junior army officials that the army is the panacea for all ills, which had received a severe blow after the debacle in East Pakistan, is again gaining ground.'[22] By the time he was in his death cell, Zulfikar understood his mistake. 'The pollution of the armed forces by its involvement in politics had not conveyed any message,' he wrote. 'The catastrophe of East Pakistan and the surrender of 90,000 prisoners of war did not teach a single elementary lesson.'[23] The problem was that, when in power, Zulfikar felt he needed the army.

The Balochistan campaign helped rebuild the army's self-confidence. But that in itself was not enough to bring about the coup that threw Zulfikar out of power. The final stage of his journey to the gallows began when he called for elections to be held on 7 March 1977. Even though the realities of governing had meant that Zulfikar had not been able to keep all his manifesto promises, he was still a towering figure and was widely expected to win. But the campaign did not go according to plan. Realising that disunity was ruining their chances, Zulfikar's various opponents pulled together a rather implausible alliance, the Pakistan National Alliance, or PNA, ranging from Jamaat-e-Islami at one end to the socialist/liberal and nationalist party, the NAP, at the other. The PNA touched a nerve and found it could attract significant crowds. And given the success of the PNA campaign, the actual election result, when it came, was, to many Pakistanis, unbelievable: the PPP won 155 of 200 seats of the National Assembly, while the PNA got only 36. In the 1970 elections, when the PPP was at the height of its popularity, it had secured 39 per cent of the popular vote. Now it had 55 per cent. As for the opposition, despite being able to run some very large campaign rallies, its share of the vote went down. Zulfikar's information minister Kausar Niazi subsequently recounted a conversation held shortly after the results came through:

> Mr. Bhutto was sitting in the PM House with Hafiz Pirzada, Rafi Raza and a couple of other friends. Looking towards Pirzada, he said,
>
> 'Hafiz, how many seats must have been rigged?'
>
> 'Sir . . . Around 30 to 40,' was his brief reply.
>
> 'Can't we ask the PNA to have their candidates elected against these seats and assure them that we'll not contest them?'[24]

A year later the military government published the results of its trawl through official files for anything that would incriminate Zulfikar. By far the longest of these series of documents – over 1,000 pages – was the *White Paper on the Conduct of the General Elections of 1977*.[25] Perhaps because election rigging is not generally an exercise committed to paper, a significant number of the government memos reproduced in the White Paper failed to land fatal blows. But there were enough that were sufficiently damning to indicate the elections were indeed subject to widespread manipulation. One of the most difficult documents for PPP supporters was a secret memo signed by the prime minister – 'eyes only', it said – in which he wrote: 'I have prepared a scheme for the elections both central and provincial of the District of Larkana. This scheme might be of some assistance to you in the preparation of arrangements we have to work out on a scientific basis for the whole country'.[26] The scheme described how committees of reliable local notables – some of them on government salaries – would form committees to organise the movement of voters to the polls and to 'ensure that the votes are cast in favour of the right candidate'.[27] Rafi Raza later claimed that the White Paper made far too much of the so-called 'Larkana Plan'. Many such documents, he said, came across his desk and were filed away only to be forgotten. But Rafi Raza could not deny that Zulfikar had also wanted to run unopposed in Larkana, something Rafi Raza had unsuccessfully advised against. Zulfikar's main opponent – a PNA candidate from Jamaat-e-Islami – was offered another seat, which PPP managers said they would allow him to win unopposed. When he turned that down, he was kidnapped to prevent him filing his papers to register as an official candidate in Larkana. Journalists were then prevailed upon to file false affidavits saying that, far from being detained, the opposition candidate had been out and about in the constituency giving news conferences.[28] As even the diehard loyalist Hafiz Pirzada later conceded: 'He wanted to be elected unopposed in Larkana. It started from there.'[29] Rafi Raza's objection was that, if the prime minister was seen to have a clear run, other senior party members would want to burnish their prestige by following his example. 'ZAB said that I was an idealist, but "our politics are not ideal".'[30] But Raza was right: when it came to election day, no fewer than eighteen senior PPP leaders ensured that no one was standing against them.[31] It gave the opposition a stick with which they could beat the PPP and undermined the legitimacy of the election as a whole.

Some documents in the White Paper showed Zulfikar in a good light: when his information minister suggested organising fake, surrogate opposition candidates to use up the opposition's allocated time on radio and TV, the prime minister annotated the document with the remark: 'We will have to give the leaders some time. Some reasonable time.'[32] Against that, when one of his officials discussed organising surrogate candidates to stand for the Assembly, 'to generate apparent but controlled heat in the elections to make it appear well contested', Zulfikar remarked: 'please proceed on these lines'.[33] The document went on to suggest that the surrogate candidates could afterwards be 'rewarded in some way . . . a few of them may even be allowed to win'.[34] There was also a proposal for a list of sensitive constituencies 'and of persons who must not be allowed to be elected'.[35]

The White Paper, however, was published months after the election, and in the meantime Bhutto continued to insist that the elections were free and fair – a stance which provoked the PNA to launch a civil disobedience campaign. A protest strike on 11 March 1977 brought Karachi to a halt. When more protests were announced, the government reacted with curfews, and Amnesty International reported that thousands of opposition activists were arrested, most of them under preventative detention laws.[36] But the PNA had no reason to back down. Many of its leaders believed that this would be their last chance to oppose Zulfikar. If he hung on after such a rigged election, he could be in power indefinitely. The PNA also drew strength from all the groups Zulfikar had confronted, not least the industrialists, who now helped fund the opposition rallies, and the Islamists, who provided much of the street power.

Zulfikar tried to use every lever to hang on. The salaries of a million civil servants and half a million armed forces personnel were increased by an average of 25 per cent, with the lowest paid getting 50 per cent.[37] He offered the suspension of land reforms and assured the industrialists that no further nationalisation was contemplated for five years.[38] He also tried to appease the religious parties, which were demanding he ban alcohol and gambling. As he contemplated the issue, he had a one-to-one conversation with Rafi Raza on the sumptuous lawn of Governor's House in Lahore. Zulfikar said that he did not want to go down in history as someone who compromised on his core beliefs. It was axiomatic to his thinking that he did not want to mix religion with the state. And he knew that if he made concessions Jamaat-e-Islami would simply ask for more. Baring his anguish in an unprecedented way, he even asked Rafi Raza if he should resign. Given all this, Rafi Raza was shocked to learn the next day that Zulfikar had given in to Jamaat's demands.[39] He even went cap in hand to the mosque of his most vehement opponent, the founder of Jamaat-e-Islami, Maulana Maududi, who barely bothered with niceties and simply told him to resign. Bhutto's tilt to Islam convinced nobody.[40] He was always behind the curve, offering too little, too late. As power slipped away, he kept in close touch with the army leadership, needing their power to keep order on the streets but also nervous they could move against him. At one point he considered a referendum on his leadership but then learnt that the army didn't like the idea and would prefer new elections.

As the anti-government agitation became more violent, the army came to think that it alone could hold the line. The man who eventually organised the mechanics of the coup, Lieutenant General Faiz Ali Chishti, described how the army watched Zulfikar try and fail to maintain law and order. 'Initially they used their own party workers . . . They failed. Then they used the police . . . The police could not control. They then asked the FSF . . . FSF could not do it. Then they called in the army in aid of civil power.'[41] But the army was hesitant. When Zulfikar asked for plans to be drawn up for the imposition of so-called partial martial law in selected cities, it advised against it, saying that the agitation would simply be moved to other cities, but Zulfikar decided to go ahead regardless.[42] Soldiers were now required to go on the streets to defend a government some of them believed to be illegitimate. At one protest in Lahore, soldiers had apparently obeyed an order to fire on protestors but, it later transpired, had fired above their heads. Three brigadiers in Lahore openly refused to obey an order to fire on demonstrators. For the army leadership, that was a serious moment – it could not afford divisions opening up in the ranks. General Tikka Khan, who having retired as army chief was working directly for Zulfikar, suggested a display of force to deter further protests. 'Kill more and the situation will come under control,' he is quoted as saying.[43] But his former colleagues were not convinced. The army's confidence in Zulfikar was also shaken by his frequently consulting them on how to extricate himself from the political impasse with the PNA. One of Zulfikar's mistakes was to allow the corps commanders to become an integral part of the negotiations – it was an admission of weakness. Doubtless Zulfikar saw this as a way of co-opting the army, but the senior officers perceived it rather differently: to them the prime minister seemed weak and unable to govern.

The pressure was building, and the army made it clear to Zulfikar that he needed to reach a deal with the PNA: if that involved holding a fresh election then so be it. The two sides did talk and came close. According to Hafiz Pirzada,

Zulfikar did eventually accept that there would have to be fresh elections, and the offer was put to the PNA, whose negotiators initially accepted it.[44] But, presumably because the PNA leaders calculated that by blocking a deal they could provoke military action, the opposition alliance ultimately refused to sign up to the terms Zulfikar offered. It was the final straw. 'The government and the PNA have agreed to disagree,' General Zia told his inner circle. 'There is no light at the end of the negotiating tunnel. The corps commanders agree with my assessment.'[45] The coup was on, and Zulfikar had no idea it was coming. One of his advisers, Raja Anwar, witnessed the last meeting between Zulfikar and Zia before the coup, after which Zulfikar remarked to General Tikka Khan, 'Well General do you recall how you opposed Zia being promoted chief of staff? You will now have to concede I made the correct choice. Had it been another army chief he would have long since grabbed power, taking advantage of the law and order situation.' Seven hours later Zia was in charge.[46]

As soon as he was sure his military takeover had been successful and all key installations were in army hands, Zia spoke to Zulfikar on the phone. There are various accounts of the call, but they generally agree that Zia said the military takeover was temporary and elections would be held. According to Zulfikar's close adviser Kausar Niazi, the conversation was surprisingly polite.

He asked the operator to get Gen. Zia-ul-Haq in GHQ. After a long wait, Gen. Zia-ul-Haq attended the call.

'What's happening?' asked Mr. Bhutto, 'I hear the army is on the move, is that correct?'

'What you've heard is correct, Sir,' answered Gen. Zia-ul-Haq, most calmly, 'I'm sorry there was no other way out of this.'

Taking some time to explain the situation, Gen. Zia-ul-Haq asked Mr. Bhutto, 'Sir, where would you like to go, Murree, Larkana or Karachi?'

'Murree,' said Bhutto . . .

'Right, Sir,' said Gen. Zia-ul-Haq, 'you'll be conveyed to Murree in the morning after breakfast.'[47]

Technically, Zulfikar had not been arrested – rather he was in protective custody – and ten days later the two men met at the government's Murree guesthouse. In his memoir, the man who had been in command of the troops who mounted the coup, General Faiz Ali Chishti, gave his eyewitness account of the encounter, in which the two men continued to observe the courtesies, with Zia saluting Zulfikar, who in turn said that the army takeover had perhaps been inevitable but that the question was what would happen next. He said that he was available to help and guide General Zia, with whom he could run the country jointly and smoothly, and that Zia could be assured he would not be vindictive. In reply, Zia said that the army would remain neutral and hold elections as promised.[48] Two weeks later Zulfikar and all the other politicians were released so that they could participate in the election campaign, which Zulfikar did, aggressively. As his rhetoric intensified, it was increasingly clear that, if Zulfikar won, Zia would face real danger. The phrase 'one grave, two bodies' started circulating.

General Chishti believes that Zia decided he would not allow Zulfikar back into power the day he heard that the PPP leader had vowed that, if he did win the elections, he would hang the generals. The master politician had made an elementary miscalculation. In reality, no prime minister in Pakistan could ever hang a general – it was simultaneously an idle threat and one that Zia could not be expected to tolerate. A journalist, Inam Aziz, was in the right place at the right time to witness some of the deterioration in the relationship. Aziz interviewed Zulfikar on 10 August 1977, just over a month after the coup and thirty-three days before his arrest. Shortly after the interview began, Zulfikar took a call, after which he said, 'It was Zia and he threatened to kill me. I have told him that if I survive, I will have him and 35 of his generals hanged for treason. This is the first time he has been impertinent with me. When he came to see me in Murree, he could not stop "sirring" me. Today there was arrogance in his voice.'[49] General Chishti also noticed the change when he saw Zulfikar and Zia meet a couple of weeks later. 'General Zia was not warm. He was rather frigid.'[50] It was increasingly clear that the two men were on a collision course. A number of issues were playing on Zia's mind. Zulfikar was defiant – more so than Zia expected – and relying on his favourite theme, political martyrdom. He was drawing big crowds: there was a real chance he would be returned to power and that a respectable vote for the PPP would amount to a rejection of the coup.

And as the two men circled each other, the press was enjoying its newfound freedom to dig up some hitherto hidden scandals and criticise the record of the

Bhutto administration. One story that found its way into the papers was about a case in the Lahore High Court concerning the death of Nawab Mohammad Ahmed Khan Kasuri, the head of the former ruling family in the princely state of Kasur. Shortly after midnight on 11 November 1974, after attending a wedding in Lahore, Kasuri and his son, Ahmed Raza Kasuri, who was a member of the National Assembly, were heading home. There was an ambush. With machine-gun fire slicing through the car, Ahmed Raza Kasuri sped away thinking he had survived another assassination plot: there had already been previous attempts on his life. But his father, in the front seat of the car, was not so lucky. Hit by some bullets, he slumped onto his son's shoulder and a few hours later died in hospital. Within hours, Ahmed Raza Kasuri went to a police station and filed a first information report in which he named Zulfikar as the person suspected of having commissioned the murder. His suspicion reflected the fact that he and Zulfikar had a very volatile relationship. Having initially been a PPP National Assembly member, elected in 1970, Kasuri had fallen out with the prime minister because, on a couple of issues, he had displayed a high degree of independence. He was one of a handful who expressed any reservation about the 1973 constitution, a stance which led to a verbal exchange on the floor of the Assembly in which Zulfikar ended up saying: 'You keep quiet. I have had enough of you. Absolute poison.'[51]

With Zulfikar in power, the first information report was never going to be acted on, and Kasuri's allegation made very little impact. Perhaps realising that continued opposition to Zulfikar was unlikely to yield many benefits, Kasuri tried to reconcile with him, sending him some sycophantic letters.[52] His attempts to make up with Zulfikar were doomed to fail: the prime minister displayed his usual attitude to those who had crossed him: 'he must repent and he must crawl before me. He has been a dirty dog'.[53] But the coup changed everything. Immediately after it, Mohammad Ahmed Khan Kasuri's widow asked that the case concerning her husband's murder be heard before the Lahore High Court, and within just a few weeks it was moving through the system with unusual speed: the initial stage, in the sessions court, was dropped and the proceedings went straight to the High Court, meaning that, when the process was over, Zulfikar had been granted one right to appeal fewer than he should have. Many believed that this legal shortcut could only have happened if Zia had given his approval.

Legal cases of senior politicians in Pakistan are famous for the length of time they can take – which sometimes runs to decades. Zulfikar's case wasn't like that. The trial started on 11 October 1977, with the prosecution relying on Masood Mahmood, the man who had run Zulfikar's FSF. In return for his evidence against Zulfikar, he secured a pardon, which inevitably calls into question the validity of his testimony. He told the court Zulfikar had ordered him to organise the killing of Mr Kasuri, which he reluctantly agreed to do. The guilty verdict came on 18 March 1978. The proceedings were highly controversial for a number of reasons. The head of the panel of five judges who heard the case, Maulvi Mushtaq Hussain, was well known to be hostile to Zulfikar. The two men had first clashed back in 1968 when Mushtaq presided over the trial that followed Zulfikar's falling-out with Ayub Khan. Then, when Zulfikar was in power, he twice overlooked Mushtaq for promotion, favouring judges junior to him.[54] Now Mushtaq had Zulfikar where he wanted him, and he made little secret of his animosity – some of it quite petty. When Zulfikar, for example, showed his unhappiness at being made to sit in a specially constructed dock in the courtroom, Mushtaq reportedly said with heavy sarcasm: 'we all know that you are used to a very comfortable life. I am providing you with a chair behind the dock instead of a bench.'[55] More importantly, when the time came for Zulfikar to give his defence, he was shocked to find that, overnight, the judges had decided that from that point on the case would be heard *in camera* – no reporters would be able to hear Zulfikar's side of the story. 'You call this a trial? You call this justice?' Zulfikar railed. But no one was listening – except the judges.[56] At one point Zulfikar boycotted the proceedings – a tactical error which meant the defence witnesses were not heard.

As soon as the guilty verdict was announced Zulfikar appealed it, thereby starting a stage in the proceedings that ran until February 1979, when the Supreme Court, by a majority verdict of four to three, confirmed the High Court conviction and sentence. In devising its appeal strategy, Bhutto's legal team went on the offensive. The Lahore Court's unanimous guilty verdict, it argued, should be overturned because that panel of judges had been trying to achieve the political and physical elimination of the accused: the Lahore judges, in other words, were trying to have the defendant killed. The appeal stage was marked by two of the judges dropping out, one on grounds of ill health, while the other retired. The other notable aspect of the appeal stage was Zulfikar's four-day speech in his defence. Unlike the Lahore High Court, the Supreme Court let him be heard by the public, and his speech was widely reported all over the world. 'Pakistan is today in a very precarious and critical condition. You may say "This is a very vain man, a boastful man." But don't you see the void in the country? It is a barren void. There is no direction.'[57] As for the allegation against him, Zulfikar said Kasuri was too insignificant to be worth murdering. 'My level of political antagonists is much higher,' he said.[58] And anyway, he argued, if he wanted to murder someone – which being a modern man he would never do – he would not have asked the FSF to do it but would have relied instead on some of his loyal villagers. The Supreme Court was unmoved and confirmed the Lahore High Court's verdict and sentence.

The final stage of the proceedings took the form of a review petition. The most compelling argument made by Zulfikar's legal team was that the whole case depended on the evidence of Masood Mahmood, who by becoming a witness for the prosecution had saved his own skin. Without him, there was nothing to link Zulfikar with the shooting. The defence also had a series of subsidiary points. Never before had a death sentence been handed down in a conspiracy to murder case, and it was the first time the Supreme Court had failed to reach a unanimous judgment on both the sentence and the guilt of the accused: the narrow margin of the split verdict should lead to at least a commutation of the death sentence. Legal precedents were also cited to cast doubt on a murder conviction when the accused had not been at the scene of the crime. The review petition, however, was rejected unanimously on the grounds that no arguments had been presented which suggested that the previous stage had suffered from an error in law.

There was one last chink of light for the Bhutto family: the judges said that even if the review petition arguments were not sufficiently strong to overturn the verdict, they might be relevant in considering whether clemency should be granted. The only remaining issue, then, was whether General Zia would show mercy. Many world leaders, including President Brezhnev of the Soviet Union, Chairman Hua Guofeng of China and King Khalid of Saudi Arabia, asked him to commute the death sentence. The UK's prime minister James Callaghan wrote three letters, one of which ended with the remark: 'As a soldier yourself you will, I know, remember the truth of the old saying that the grass grows swiftly over a battlefield but never over a scaffold.'[59] But Zia's mind was made up. Such appeals, he said, were nothing more than a formality and he would not interfere with the decision of the courts. 'I would also take it as trade union activity,' a British diplomat quoted Zia as saying, 'because all politicians are asking to save a politician. Not very many non-politicians have asked me for clemency . . . All have respect for independence of judiciary but on humanitarian grounds they appeal to save his life which is no argument.'[60] As for Zulfikar, he was adamant that neither he nor his family should ask for clemency: it would not only be humiliating but was also unlikely to make any difference. Although Zia did not need to receive a petition to show mercy, the family worried that the lack of one could give him a means of blaming the Bhuttos for Zulfikar's fate. Consequently, it was arranged for Zulfikar's politically inactive sister, Shaharbano Imtiaz, to submit an appeal. But it was no great surprise that late in the evening on 1 April 1970 Zia wrote three words on the documents she had submitted: 'Petition is rejected.'[61]

The hanging of Zulfikar left a wound on Pakistan's body politic that is still raw forty years later. Some have tried to shift the blame onto external actors. Benazir Bhutto repeatedly stated that she heard Henry Kissinger, the US's most famous exponent of realpolitik, directly threatening her father that if he did not delay the nuclear programme, he would risk being made into a 'horrible example'.[62] To this day PPP activists and some Bhutto family members believe the US was behind Zulfikar's death. There is, however, no convincing evidence to back that up, and the US record contains not even a hint that that was the case. The clash between Zia and Zulfikar was so momentous precisely because it was a Pakistani, not an international, affair. The sheer drama of Zulfikar's own appointee having him killed has enduring power of its own. But the PPP has also done its best to keep what it portrays as Zulfikar's martyrdom fresh in the public memory. To this day some in the military use derogatory language about Zulfikar, but there are many Pakistanis who think back to his execution and see it as a cruel act by an unelected military leader. And people still talk about exactly what happened in his final hours and the precise circumstances of his death.

The final countdown began when Nusrat and Benazir were released from house arrest to visit him. Since it was not their regular day, the women asked the prison authorities why the meeting was being allowed: would it be their last meeting? Yes, they were told, he was being executed that night. In the months leading up to the Supreme Court's rejection of his review petition, Zulfikar had had access to a corridor and eight prison cells that led off it, four on each side. Now he was restricted to one cell, and despite their request to be let into it, Nusrat and Benazir, sitting on two chairs, had to talk to him through the iron bars.[63] 'I pleaded with the jailers,' Benazir said, 'I begged them to open the cell door, so that I could embrace him, and say a proper goodbye. But they refused.'[64] When Nusrat and Benazir told him he was to be hanged, Zulfikar called for the prison superintendent, Yar Mohammed, and asked if that was true. Another official in the prison subsequently interviewed Yar Mohammed for an account of what happened.

> Mr. Bhutto asked Yar Mohammed to come even closer to him . . . When Yar Mohammed had moved closer Mr. Bhutto moved his hand across his throat as if it were being cut. Then he moved his head inquisitively to get confirmation whether lethal action was to be taken against him. Yar Mohammed said plainly, 'Yes sir, it is true.' Mr. Bhutto made the same enquiring signal again and Yar Mohammed confirmed it again.[65]

Benazir later recalled that this last meeting with her father influenced the course of her life. Her father said: 'You are so young. You just finished university. You came back. You had your whole life and look at the terror under which we have lived. I set you free. Why don't you go and live in London or Paris or Switzerland or Washington . . .' Benazir reached through the bars and grabbed his hands: 'No, papa, I will continue the struggle that you began for democracy.'[66]

After four hours Nusrat and Benazir left. 'When I left him, I couldn't look back,' Benazir later wrote, 'I knew that I couldn't control myself. I'm not even sure how I managed to walk down that corridor, past the soldiers and past the guards. All I could think of was my head. "Keep it high," I told myself. "They are all watching." '[67]

Zulfikar had managed to put a brave face on things while his wife and daughter were there and even afterwards was keen to keep up appearances, asking for a shaving kit, saying, 'I do not want to die like a bearded mullah.'[68] Through his period of imprisonment Zulfikar had repeatedly told his wife and daughter that he had accepted his fate. 'They are going to kill me. It doesn't matter what evidence you or anyone comes up with. They are going to murder me for a murder I didn't commit.'[69] But some of those who were close to the family, as well as some of the staff in the prison, believe that, at heart, Zulfikar did not believe that Zia would do it. Hafiz Pirzada, for example, has recorded his view that neither Benazir nor Zulfikar thought the military would be able to execute him.[70] But now, with just hours to go, the reality sank in, and as the evening wore on, his confidence wavered. At around 8 p.m. he started writing things on notepaper and repeatedly reordering the limited number of items he had in his cell. It was a couple of hours before he regained his composure, at which point he burnt the notes he had just written and lay down on his bed to smoke a cigar. The authorities had thought that he had been writing his will, but now all they had was ashes. When it was suggested that he dictate his will, Zulfikar replied that he had been too disturbed to complete the task. 'My will shall now be written in history.'[71]

When the time came to move him from the cell he was largely unresponsive, so the prison authorities put him on a stretcher and four men carried him, handcuffed, to the gallows. Getting to the noose involved climbing some steps, but Zulfikar was still lying prone and was heard to say, 'It's a pity that Nusrat will be left alone.'[72] The jail's assistant superintendent, Majeed Quereshi, who believed that in the previous weeks he had won Zulfikar's confidence, leant over the former prime minister and urged him to walk to the gallows. 'Sir, history is being written and so create a place for yourself in its pages. Please, now get up.' On hearing these words Zulfikar jerked up. 'He walked up to gallows, fully awake, and stood at the white mark,' Majeed Quereshi recalled.[73] The hangman put a hood over Bhutto's head, completely covering his face, and a rope around his neck. 'God help me, for I am innocent,' Zulfikar mumbled.[74] And then, true to his feudal nature, his last words were a command: 'Finish it!' he said.[75] The lever was pulled and his frail body plunged downwards through the trap door. It was left hanging for half an hour before the prison doctor declared him dead.[76]

The fight for Zulfikar's legacy had begun even before he died. At one level, Zulfikar wrote impassioned defences of his time in power, the most notable of which was published under the title *If I Am Assassinated*. Outside the prison there was a more pressing and urgent battle for public opinion. When the initial guilty verdict and death sentence had been announced by the Lahore High Court there had been widespread disturbances throughout the country.

The PPP hoped the actual hanging would produce an even bigger reaction. Before the execution was carried out, Benazir had been asked what would happen if her father was hanged. 'Civil war, the breakup of Pakistan, a massive and total outburst from the people,' she replied.[77] But in the event, next to nothing happened. That was partly because potential protestors knew that an open display of defiance would have invited severe punishment. But there was more to it than that. The lack of reaction was a sign that Zia had achieved his objective. With Zulfikar dead, the PPP lacked leadership – with the symbol of hope gone, what was the point of protesting?

Despite the muted response to the hanging, the decades after it have revealed an enduring well of support for Zulfikar's ideals. That's not to say his legacy isn't contested – for some, Zulfikar remains a flawed civilian despot, while for others he is a martyr and the stuff of myth. Besides these polarised perspectives, there are the glaring paradoxes: the feudal loved by the dispossessed, the democrat who began his career working with the army, the bully who was vulnerable to the slightest criticism, the nationalist who failed to prevent the break-up of the country, the civilian who became chief martial law administrator and the man who railed against the mullahs before giving in to their demands. And then there was the sense of a great man brought low by fatal flaws. As his first army chief put it: 'He was the most charismatic personality on our political scene . . . he could, or rather should, have left his mark on the history of Pakistan. Nevertheless, the fact is that he did not. He became a victim of his own vanity, egocentrism, and extreme arrogance'.[78] One of the reasons he still elicits strong reactions is because of what came after him. To be negative about Zulfikar can be taken in Pakistani political discourse as a signal of support for General Zia – which only those in religious and right-wing military circles want to exhibit. And Bhutto's ghost haunted Zia, who repeatedly had to postpone elections for fear of a PPP victory largely built on sympathy for what had happened to Zulfikar. So, for many, while Zia was a disaster, Zulfikar remains a symbol of something better. But to view his contribution to Pakistan through the prism of Zia's dictatorship sells him short. Zulfikar Ali Bhutto was one of Pakistan's most significant political figures and deserves to be judged on the basis of his own performance, not his successor's.

One of the most quoted remarks about Zulfikar was made by the former British ambassador Sir Morrice James, who with remarkable perspicacity wrote in 1965 that he was a 'man born to be hanged'. While praising his drive, charm, intelligence, energy and sense of humour, he added something else: 'there was – how shall I put it? – the rank odour of hellfire about him. It was a case of corruptio optimi pessima [the corruption of the best is worst of all]. He was a Lucifer, a flawed angel. I believe that at heart he lacked a sense of the dignity and value of other people; his own self-worth was what counted.'[79] Or, as another Foreign Office official rather pithily put it: 'A man of great gifts of the head and great defects of the heart.'[80] Another memo – this time to Prime Minister Edward Heath – caught a further aspect of people's fascination with Zulfikar: 'stimulating company if you can keep up with him, equally at home in the Senior Common Room at Christ Church and among a crowd of half a million in the stadium in Lahore.'[81] Zulfikar was always a man that people wanted to comment about.

Taking a step back, Zulfikar's life and death exposed deeper tensions and fissures in Pakistani society. Some of these divisions reflected ethnic and religious difference: just like every other Pakistani leader, Zulfikar grappled with, but never controlled, the forces of provincialism and sectarianism. What was unusual about his time in power was what it revealed about Pakistani society. By championing socialist ideas, Zulfikar was tapping into something new for the country. His most obvious pitch was to the urban and rural poor. But in the 1970 election he was able to create a coalition which also took in middle-class intellectual leftists who believed in liberal and sometimes secular values. To this day the PPP has held on to some of the rural poor. For them, the party is still on their side. The class that was always suspicious of him consisted of the traders and shopkeepers, often very devout, whose conservatism made them suspicious of his radicalism.[82] General Zia was himself part of this group and spoke for it when he said how much he despised Zulfikar's hedonistic lifestyle.[83]

Zulfikar Ali Bhutto enthused millions of Pakistanis with a vision that still inspires many to this day. He raised the consciousness of the oppressed masses. Even if he could not solve poverty, at least he recognised that it existed and gave voice to the dispossessed, and, after his hanging, the downtrodden felt empowered to make political demands in a way that they had not dared to before Zulfikar showed them what was possible. But, for all that, by the end of his time in power Zulfikar relied more on the rural elite – the feudals – than their vassals. There is some evidence that Zulfikar was aware of this paradox. Mubashir Hassan described a moving scene in 1974 when, in a one-on-one encounter, he told Zulfikar his power was weakening.

'What do you want me to do?' Bhutto said.

'I have come to suggest you rebuild your power base among the people.'

He paused for a while and then said, 'Doctor, what you want me to do, I do not have the power to do'.[84]

Hasan was shattered. Zulfikar, after all, was not a man to admit his power-lessness. As he looked back at his career and at how he might have done things differently, Zulfikar could take some satisfaction from having done the big things well. He realised earlier than virtually anyone else in international politics that China would have a major role to play in global affairs: his quick appreciation of this worked to Pakistan's benefit. And however much Pakistan's nuclear programme is deplored in the West, it is, for most Pakistanis, the greatest aspect of his legacy. It is difficult to imagine either Ayub or Zia having had the vision to have initiated the nuclear programme: it was something that could only have been started by a man of Zulfikar's strategic insights and soaring self-confidence. Less often discussed, the tricky issue of recognising Bangladesh was also well handled. Within a few weeks of taking over, Zulfikar realised that East Pakistan was never going to come back and that he would have to recognise Bangladesh. But with public opinion hostile to such a move, he had to take care. The first task, which he successfully achieved, was to persuade the US and others not to announce recognition before Pakistan: he wanted to avoid being forced into recognition by global opinion. Zulfikar then used the cover of the 1974 Lahore Islamic Summit to slip recognition through: Mujibur Rahman came to the summit, got his recognition and for good measure agreed that there would be no war crimes trials of West Pakistani officers too. No wonder Henry Kissinger once said, 'I am reluctant to negotiate anything with Prime Minister Bhutto. I always lose my shirt.'[85]

Zulfikar's handling of Mujibur Rahman showed his broad vision in another way. Had the army remained in power after 1971, it is possible that Mujibur Rahman would have been executed. Mujib himself believed that an order for his execution had been a real possibility and that Zulfikar thwarted it.[86] Zulfikar confirmed the story: Yahya, while relinquishing power, had said that it had been a mistake not to kill Mujib and offered to have him hanged before handing over power. 'But I told him no,' Bhutto recalled. 'I wouldn't accept that. But that got me a little suspicious and by way of abundant caution when I took over I passed an order and I said I wanted to see Mujibur Rahman safely brought to Pindi immediately. Helicopter was sent and he was brought and kept in the custody of our people.'[87] But perhaps more impressive was Zulfikar's decision to accept the political realities and to release Mujib from custody without getting any quid pro quo: when he had no cards to play, he realised it. Needing political cover for such a move, he called for an impromptu vote at a mass rally. Zulfikar asked the crowd if he should release Mujib, before interpreting its response as the 'yes' he was looking for. He had sought and obtained 'people's permission'.[88]

There were also domestic accomplishments. Previous Pakistani leaders had found the process of constitution-making next to impossible. Within eighteen months of assuming power, Zulfikar had not only secured agreement on an interim constitution but also shepherded the 1973 constitution through the National Assembly with no one voting against it. His strategy was clever: in addition to mastering the usual dark arts that drive Pakistani politics and offering the provinces a significant shift in resources from the centre,[89] he traded in his position of chief martial law administrator to secure agreement on the interim constitution and then gave up on his desire for a presidential system to win support for the 1973 constitution. Decades later the 1973 constitution is still held up by liberals in Pakistan as a document that survived a couple of coups and which expresses their democratic ideals. And yet Zulfikar failed to build democratic institutions, despite having had an opportunity to do so: when he took over, the military lay powerless before him. Maybe no Pakistani politician could ever prevail over the military, but Zulfikar had a better chance than any other. And it is impossible to avoid the conclusion that some of the factors behind his failure were of his own making. The reality was that he could not tolerate opposition from either his own or other parties. He banned and jailed opponents, suppressed critical press coverage and more generally focused on the consolidation of his power above all other considerations. As his generally sympathetic biographer Salmaan Taseer put it: 'He ruled his own party with an iron fist and proved pathologically incapable of sharing power in any form'.[90] Had he governed at a time when institutions to constrain him already existed, it might have been a different story. But it fell to Zulfikar to create institutions, and he didn't. As he acknowledged in his death cell, he had not made the mark on history that he once dreamt of.

Perhaps aware of his regret, Benazir tried to confer on her father the accolade of adding an 'ism' to his name. What she meant by Bhuttoism, though, was unclear. In October 1986 Benazir posited that it consisted of four principles: Islam, democracy, socialism and the people, rapidly adding that the socialism she had in mind was unlike that of China or the Soviet Union.[91] On another occasion she said Bhuttoism stood for a constitutional government, a federal government, human rights, an independent judiciary and a free press.[92] These various ideas were too nebulous to stick, and anyway, others saw it differently. The same year, a *Los Angeles Times* correspondent defined Bhuttoism as a cult of personality that lent itself to repression and intimidation.[93]

For all his radicalism, Zulfikar left Pakistan under a military government. He failed to build institutions that could make democracy function and he failed to resist military power. He had shown that he could control his party, dent press criticism and dominate the civil service. But he had also discovered that the feudals and the industrialists could adapt and survive, that the Islamists could never be satisfied and, most importantly of all, that the army was more powerful than any civilian leader ever could be. He confronted but failed to resolve key issues that, as his daughter later discovered, continued to lie at the heart of Pakistani politics.

1. A certificate issued by the British colonial authorities in 1877 praising the loyalty of Benazir Bhutto's great-great-great-grandfather Doda Khan Bhutto, who expanded the family's landholdings in Sindh but had to be bailed out by the British.

2. Mir Ghulam Murtaza Bhutto, great-grandfather of Benazir Bhutto. Accused of murder, he fled the British colonial authorities, returned and cleared his name before being poisoned to death in 1899 at the age of thirty.

3. Sir Shahnawaz Bhutto, grandfather of Benazir, who worked closely with the British colonialists, and was one of the few in the male line to have a natural death in old age.

4. Benazir Bhutto as a schoolgirl.

5. Zulfikar in Karachi, relaxing with Sanam and Shahnawaz Bhutto.

6. Zulfikar Ali Bhutto with his wife Begum Nusrat Bhutto in Paris in 1969.

7. Zulfikar Ali Bhutto's changing attitude to the international media. In 1977, he admonishes the BBC saying, 'Stop interfering.' In 1978, he pleads, 'Please save us.'

8. A silhouette of Zulfikar Ali Bhutto juxtaposed with a dismembered body representing the people of Pakistan – mutilated, beheaded and crucified.

9. General Zia ul-Haq, the man who launched a coup against Zulfikar Ali Bhutto and in 1979 had him hanged.

10. Shahnawaz and Murtaza protest in an attempt to save their father's life in London, 1978/9.

11. Massive crowds welcome Benazir Bhutto on her return to Lahore in 1986.

THE SON FIGHTING FOR HIS FATHER

Bhuttoism

SHAH NAWAZ . . . " We were taught to be tough."

12. After Zulfikar Ali Bhutto died his two sons decided to avenge his death by setting up the Kabul-based militant group, Al Zulfikar.

13. Benazir Bhutto listens to the Pakistan national anthem as a member of the honour guard salutes, before she is sworn in as Pakistan's prime minister in Islamabad in 1988.

14. Benazir reads to her eldest son Bilawal.

15. The 1988 election campaign: Benazir Bhutto depicted as a Bollywood star.

16. The 1988 election campaign: Benazir Bhutto and her father depicted as warriors.

17. Dynastic claims: a portrait of Zulfikar Ali Bhutto and Benazir Bhutto.

18. Murtaza Bhutto poses in front of the portrait – with his sister Benazir removed.

19. Police stand by doing nothing in the minutes after Murtaza Bhutto's convoy was attacked in Karachi. He died of blood loss as a result of his gunshot wounds.

20. Fatima Bhutto, daughter of Murtaza and niece of Benazir Bhutto, holding her father's picture in Karachi, 2008.

21. Rockwood House, or, as the Pakistani press dubbed it, Surrey Palace. A British judge found it had likely been purchased with the fruits of corruption.

22. Bilawal Bhutto Zardari at Oxford University in 2008, where his mother and grandfather had studied before him.

23. Mourners gather at the family mausoleum in Garhi Khuda Bakhsh in Sindh in 2007. It was built by Benazir Bhutto between 1993 and 1997. It contains her grave and that of her father Zulfikar Ali Bhutto.

24. Benazir Bhutto's two daughters, Bakhtawar (right) and Aseefa, pray at their mother's grave, 29 December 2007.

25. A shrine to Benazir Bhutto.

26. Benazir Bhutto's political will, which hangs on the wall of the family home in Dubai. The text reads: 'To the officials and members of Pakistan Peoples Party I say that I was honoured to lead you. No leader could be as proud of their party, their dedication, devotion and discipline to the mission of Quaid-a-Awam Zulfikar Ali Bhutto for a Federal Democratic and Egalitarian Pakistan as I have been proud of you. I salute your courage and your sense of honour. I salute you for standing by your sister through two military dictatorships. I fear for the future of Pakistan. Please continue the fight against extremism, dictatorship, poverty and ignorance. I would like my husband Asif Ali Zardari to lead in this interim period until you and he decide what is best. I say this because he is a man of courage and honour. He spent 11½ years in prison without bending despite torture. He has the political stature to keep our party united. I wish all of you success in fulfilling the manifesto of our party and in serving the downtrodden, discriminated and oppressed people of Pakistan. Dedicate yourselves to freeing them from poverty and backwardness as you have done in the past.'

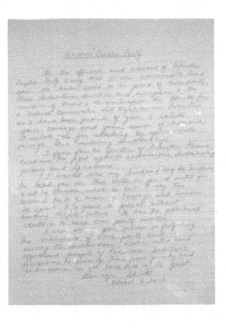

27. Pakistan's president Asif Ali Zardari holds up a picture of his late wife Benazir Bhutto before addressing the 63rd United Nations General Assembly at the UN headquarters in New York, 25 September 2008.

28. The next generation: Bilawal Bhutto Zardari out campaigning.

5

THE BHUTTOS RESIST

Benazir's lifelong respect for the US – a stance that would cause her significant political problems – can be traced back to her having gone to university in Boston at the age of just sixteen and staying for four years. Benazir later said that her Harvard (or Radcliffe[1]) years were the happiest of her life, partly because she made her friends there before her father became so famous.[2] But, initially, she found the US difficult. As her father had experienced before her, it came as something of a shock not to have servants providing food, clean clothing and chauffeuring services. She was so protected that in Larkana she had never been to a shop, for example – the traders would come to the Bhutto house to offer their wares. As she later put it, 'I grew up as a pampered child of privileged family with political and social dominance.'[3] And that privilege extended to having a father who could contact Harvard's best-known professor at the time, the economist J.K. Galbraith, to help secure her a place. Once she got to Harvard, though, she was an also-ran. As Anne Fadiman, who had the next room to her in her first year, pointed out in a *Life* profile, there were many other students with parents more famous than a former foreign minister of a developing country. Benazir cried for much of the first semester.[4]

Since most of her schooling had been in convents, Harvard was not her first taste of Western culture. As a young father, Zulfikar encouraged Benazir to avoid comic books on the grounds that they lead to idle minds and would instead test her on more improving material, such as the Ladybird history books on figures such as Alfred the Great and Joan of Arc. When Zulfikar became a minister, he shifted the family to Islamabad, moving Benazir to a convent in Rawalpindi and then in 1964, as a boarder, to the Convent of Jesus and Mary in Murree, where Benazir lived from the ages of eleven to thirteen. The convents, a hangover from the colonial period, were used by many in the

121

elite as a way of ensuring a high-quality education with a broad curriculum and strictly enforced rules: to instil discipline, the nuns beat the girls with hairbrushes. 'Her father thought that convent discipline is very important for children,' Benazir's childhood friend Samiya Waheed later recalled. 'He said just because you're born with a silver spoon in your mouth doesn't mean you shouldn't know how to make your bed.'[5] Benazir later acknowledged the impact that the convent had on her: 'I think the two powerful influences in my life in my childhood were my father and my teacher in the Convent of Jesus and Mary, Mother Eugene.' In the days of the Raj the convents had emphasised Christian values, but by the 1960s that was changing: the nuns, for example, started teaching Indian as well as British history and replaced the daily recital of the Lord's Prayer with a rendition of the Pakistani national anthem. The teaching of Islam was considered a family matter and was mostly conducted at home, and, like many of their peers, Benazir and her younger sister Sanam had a female religious instructor who would come to their house to help them read the Koran. When Zulfikar resigned as foreign minister in 1966, he moved back to Karachi, taking Benazir out of Murree Convent and eventually sending her to the Karachi Grammar School to complete her A levels. It was a difficult time. With her father now opposing the military regime, many elite Karachiites, ever sensitive to the prevailing political atmosphere, no longer wanted any contact with the Bhutto family.

It also marked the start of Benazir's activism. When Zulfikar was arrested by the Ayub Khan regime, Benazir printed off some pictures of him behind bars, and, with some of her fellow pupils, stood outside a cinema to demand his release. 'We were politicized right from the beginning,' Samiya Waheed recalled.[6] Perhaps it was because of the increasingly tense political atmosphere that Zulfikar decided, despite her being only sixteen years old, to pull her out of the grammar school after just one term and send her instead to Harvard, where she started in the autumn of 1969. At first, she found university life shocking and was horrified, for example, that when she went to the bathroom she might encounter men in the corridor. She also found it hard to believe that the university facilitated the availability of birth control pills for students and she thought there was too much sexual liberation.[7] But once she had settled there, Benazir threw herself into campus life: even if she could never quite escape the hubris that came with her aristocratic upbringing, she wasn't so grand that she wouldn't join in college activities, such as being one of the Crimson Key tour guides, delivering a potted history of the campus to new students. It is difficult to imagine Zulfikar having volunteered for such a mundane task when he was at the University of Southern California. While Zulfikar had dated women, engaged in political debate and generally made a mark, Benazir was content to make friends, enjoy life and fit in. 'She does not smoke, drink, use drugs or eat pork,' one of her fellow students wrote, 'but she doesn't blink when her friends pass joints around.'[8] Benazir herself said that at Harvard she lost the habit of prayer – something she picked up again later in life.[9]

It was a time of change in the US, and Benazir soon found herself caught up in liberal activism. 'It was a time of student power,' she later said. 'It was a time of war. American forces were engaged in Vietnam. There was an anti-war movement on campus. As an Asian at Harvard, I felt strongly about the war in Vietnam. I joined other students to protest it. It was a time of white minority rule in parts of Africa. The fight against apartheid shaped my commitment to stand up for the principle of equality between men irrespective of race or colour.'[10] She also became interested in the women's movement, although there were limits to her embrace of feminism: she thought, for example, that 'unwomanly' conduct was undesirable.[11] If her first year at Harvard was for adjustment and the second for becoming politically aware, Benazir's third year thrust her to prominence. It wasn't just that back home Zulfikar won power: he also became associated with the army's use of overwhelming violence in East Pakistan. Benazir was used to having a father who basked in the adulation of mass rallies of fervent supporters. At Harvard she found she had a father against whom many of her fellow liberals were protesting. By all accounts she defended him passionately. In her fourth and final year Benazir moved on to broader horizons. Having asked her to join him at the UN in New York, where she witnessed him haranguing the Security Council, Zulfikar then took Benazir to Simla for the summit with Indira Gandhi. Benazir was now becoming an international figure, photographed and gossiped about in newspapers all over the world. And, according to her roommate, she liked the attention.[12]

In 1989, by which time she was prime minister, Benazir returned to give the Harvard commencement address. Having picked up a good understanding of what Americans like to hear, she said Harvard had been the 'cradle of her liberty'.[13] Maybe, but Harvard had given her more than a soundbite. She left a confident, academically grounded, liberal woman with a world of opportunity in front of her. Benazir and her father wrangled over her future. She wanted to stay in the US; he said she should go to Oxford; and, inevitably, he got his way. She started at the university in 1973. In her autobiography she recorded how he had repeatedly drummed home to the children that he wanted them to study there,[14] and Benazir opted for a second undergraduate degree in PPE, Oxford's famous course which covered philosophy, politics and economics and often prepared members of Britain's elite for a career in government. Having secured a second-class degree, Benazir stayed on for an extra year of postgraduate studies at St Catherine's College, at which time she stood for the presidency of the prestigious nursery of British politicians, the Oxford Union Debating Society, which she had joined, she freely admitted, to please her father. As an undergraduate she had already tried and failed to secure election to become its president. Now she tried again, and this time she won. The achievement became part of her political pitch, which she regularly referred to in speeches: 'I had been told that as a foreigner, I could not win and should not run. I had been told that as a woman, I could not win, and should not run. I knew I could win, and I did.'[15] For her father it was a dream come true. She had entered the heart of the British establishment and come out on top. 'Overjoyed at your election as President of the Oxford Union,' he cabled, 'congratulations on your great success. Papa.'[16]

Zulfikar was now so well known that there was no chance of Benazir repeating the experience of her first two years at Harvard, when she had been able to enjoy a normal student life. But even if her time at Oxford was high profile, she nonetheless managed to avoid too many constraints, even if she did find it 'colder and more formal' than Harvard. She wore clothes – such as jeans and the Rolling Stones tongue T-shirt – that would not have gone down well in Pakistan, dated men and, famously, roared around in a yellow sports car. When she later looked back at her time in Oxford she remembered laughter-filled garden parties, strawberry-and-cream picnics, punting on the Cherwell, cobbled streets and college spires.[17] Oxford also had a lot to offer by way of connections, and she was a formidable networker: one of her more notable social interventions was to introduce a history undergraduate, Philip May, to a geographer and future British prime minister, Theresa Brasier. She also encountered another future prime minister of Pakistan who was there at the same time as her: Imran Khan. Benazir did not restrict her political activity to the Oxford Union. Always keen to please her father, she campaigned to secure him a prize she knew he would like – an Oxford honorary degree. Zulfikar's former tutor Hugh Trevor-Roper supported the idea, but it ran into problems with students and faculty who complained about Zulfikar's support for the Pakistan Army in 1971. The issue went to a vote, and Zulfikar was denied. As Zulfikar's adviser Rafi Raza later recorded, the rejection upset him: 'His was a love–hate relationship with Britain, scornful yet admiring many qualities of her people. He prided himself on his Oxford past and derived immense pleasure from the fact that his two older children followed in his footsteps, valuing their Oxford careers much more than their earlier American education. He was consequently deeply hurt when, on 7 February 1975, the Oxford University Congregation denied him an Honorary Doctorate.'[18]

The second child at Oxford referred to by Rafi Raza was Benazir's brother Murtaza. Zulfikar's two oldest children had very different characters. While Benazir was always the responsible one, bossing around her siblings to keep everything in good order, Murtaza thought of himself as something of a rebel, at one point taking to the garden of 70 Clifton where he lived in a tent, reading Marx and other leftist writers – until, that is, his father ordered him back into the house. As he grew into his late teens – he was seventeen when his father became president – he took to the town, partying at night. To his father's irritation, his work at the Karachi Grammar School was not a high priority, and, despairing of his son's progress, Zulfikar decided to send him to join his sister at Harvard. Sanam later went there too. Murtaza was one year below Benazir in the US and also at Oxford, inevitably leading to feelings that he was to some extent trailing in her wake. Meanwhile, the youngest child, Shahnawaz, was left at home. By all accounts, he was far from happy as a teenager, and after a spell at the American School in Islamabad he was packed off to a school in Switzerland known for its strict discipline. Even the ever-loyal PPP spokesman Bashir Riaz hinted that this was unlikely to benefit an emotionally vulnerable child.[19]

Benazir's student days ended on 25 June 1977 when she flew back to Pakistan with Murtaza, who was on summer break. She was about to start her professional life and planned, along with her friend Samiya Waheed, to put in an application that autumn to join the foreign ministry. In the meantime,

Benazir started working for her father in an office in the prime minister's secretariat. It wasn't an easy experience. When she followed her father's instruction to summarise some policy papers, he was unimpressed: 'This is rubbish,' she later recalled him saying. 'This is like a high school graduate. It is not like a college student who had graduated from Harvard or Oxford.'[20] In any event, the arrangement did not last long: Zia's coup took place just ten days after she got back. Having been deposed, Zulfikar's first priority was to secure his political base. He did not expect Zia to honour his promise to hold elections within ninety days, but, as a precaution, he sent Murtaza to Larkana to prepare the constituency. As for Benazir, she was put straight to use in the public sphere: there had been some floods in Punjab, and Zulfikar instructed his daughter to go to Lahore to show solidarity with those who had lost their homes. Her life as a politician had begun, and for the next decade Benazir experienced a very tough political apprenticeship, with long periods in detention. Zia treated her harshly, but there were limits to what he could do. Military rulers in Pakistan have tended to enjoy initial popularity followed by a long period of decline in which they struggle for legitimacy. Even if General Zia was, by a considerable margin, Pakistan's most repressive military ruler, he could not escape these pressures. During his eleven years in power he always felt the need to at least pretend he was committed to restoring democracy. And detentions were, from the military's point of view, of limited efficacy because the greater the Bhuttos' suffering, the more public sympathy for them grew. For their part, both Nusrat and Benazir proved well capable of organising protests demanding Zulfikar's release. According to one PPP activist, Nusrat at this time also flirted with the idea of increasing the pressure for her husband's release with a violent campaign, going as far as paying for a consignment of weapons, which were intercepted by police in Lahore.[21] That setback was enough to persuade her to put such plans on hold, but, as we shall see, there is evidence that she had mixed feelings about using both political and violent tactics.

As soon as he felt sure elections would not happen, Zulfikar wanted Murtaza out of the country. A trusted member of his staff, Dost Mohammed, later described Zulfikar giving him the following instructions from a prison cell.

He asked me to listen to him very carefully and carry his message to Begum Sahiba [Nusrat Bhutto]. Mir [Murtaza] should be sent to London without wasting a single day. I asked if Mir Murtaza went away who would look after the elections in his Larkana constituency. 'Which elections? There shall not be any elections. This country will see what it has never seen in its entire history.' He was irritated. 'Why don't you listen to what I am telling you to do? Tell Begum Sahiba that Mir has not completed his education, and by tomorrow I should know that he has left the country. Benazir knows what she has to do. She has completed her education. It will be good if she goes away too, because if she stays here she will have to face unimaginable hardships. But she is free to decide for herself. Now you go and give this message very carefully to Begum Sahiba. Mir must leave'.[22]

Benazir, brushing away her father's concerns, opted to stay in Pakistan while the boys headed for the UK and Switzerland. But given their father's situation, the brothers found it impossible to study and soon became full-time campaigners for his release. And so, a pattern was established. While Nusrat and Benazir stayed at home soaking up Zia's punishments, thereby steadily increasing their standing in Pakistan, the boys would do their best to publicise what was happening from abroad, establishing themselves in London where they set up the Save Bhutto Committee, organising marches on the British parliament and publishing the PPP newspaper *Musawat*. The tensions between Benazir and Murtaza began at this time. In a letter Benazir sent to Murtaza in London, for example, she relayed guidance, gleaned from visits to her father's prison cell, that Murtaza should be seen to live less lavishly and avoid giving interviews to Indian newspapers. 'I hated writing Mir such a seemingly bossy letter,' she later recalled.[23] No doubt he hated reading it too. There were also issues within the family. At this stage Benazir was not thinking in terms of leading the party herself. 'I thought my mother would be prime minister and that I'd work for her to be the prime minister,' she later wrote.[24] But afterwards she gave the impression that around this time her father had chosen her over Murtaza as his successor. In reality it was never that clear-cut, but it is certainly the case that in the period from 1977 to 1979 Zulfikar grew to be very impressed by his daughter's dogged campaigning and willingness to face down the regime. It wasn't that he dismissed Murtaza as a successor but rather that he increasingly came to realise that Benazir was tough and had the potential to lead.

Perhaps because Benazir's widely read autobiography inevitably focused on her activities rather than those of her mother, and because she eventually won power, most commentary on the resistance to General Zia has dwelt on the role of the daughter rather than the mother. In the immediate aftermath of the coup, however, Benazir was a youngster fresh out of university, and only Nusrat could unite the party. When Zulfikar was imprisoned, his deputy, the leftist Sheikh Rashid, told the PPP Central Executive Committee that, in the past, Zulfikar had told him he should lead the party in his absence. Rather than accept that, the committee decided to refer the matter to Zulfikar. But there was no need to do so. Before the meeting was even completed a message arrived from Zulfikar saying that his wife would be the acting chairman.[25] He wrote to his wife saying that as acting chairman she would have his authority and support to take whatever measures she deemed fit to discipline anyone in the party. And she really did take over, directing PPP tactics in both formal and real terms. 'Do not worry if your father is in jail,' she declared, 'you have the mother who is still free.'[26] The leftists in particular backed her, believing that no one else in the party leadership could be trusted not to backslide in the face of military power. And they were right. Nusrat constantly urged party leaders to be more confrontational, but many senior figures in the party wanted an easy life and favoured a more measured approach.

Benazir took to the road, with a plan for a rolling programme of speeches in different cities. It was a challenge: one journalist who attended her first speech described her as slim and awkward-looking and her speech as brief, hesitant and delivered in 'frankly terrible' Urdu.[27] She was on her third stop when she was subjected to her debut incarceration: a few days of gentle house arrest. Nusrat, exploiting her daughter's detention, immediately homed in on two key Bhutto themes, glamour and martyrdom, telling a crowd in Karachi, 'My daughter is used to wearing jewelry. Now she will be proud to wear the chains of imprisonment.'[28] Even if some senior, and patronising, PPP leaders believed that the Bhutto women had a limited knowledge of politics, they couldn't deny that they knew how to get headlines. In December 1977, for example, they attended a large public gathering, which, they calculated, Zia would be unable to disrupt: a cricket match in Lahore's Gaddafi stadium. But when some pre-placed PPP activists started to chant anti-government slogans, police waded in, firing off tear gas and beating Nusrat Bhutto, causing a gash in her scalp which she did not hesitate to display to the press. Nusrat was brave, radical and charismatic and she fired up young activists. For months the Bhutto women were alternately arrested and released. Sometimes, but not always, they were in detention at the same time. And whenever they got out, they went back to campaigning. It was a period in which Benazir would find out who her true friends were, and the women who stuck with her at this time would go on to form a protective ring around her for the rest of her life. It was also a time when Benazir became increasingly comfortable addressing large rallies. Now the discussion in the PPP was not about the possibility of having a non-Bhutto leader but rather concerned the pace of the two women's campaign – should they press on relentlessly or, from time to time, pause, reducing the chances of arrest and giving the PPP time to organise bigger crowds for their speeches?

When Zulfikar's legal process reached its conclusion and he was finally hanged, everything changed. No longer were his wife and daughter seeking his release: now they were struggling for power. And as General Zia contemplated his options after the hanging, he realised he would be greatly advantaged if the PPP was not led by a Bhutto. Even if a new leader would continue to oppose military rule, someone from outside the family would almost certainly be more open to compromise and deal-making. Attempting to cut Nusrat and Benazir off from their party, the regime began detaining them for increasingly long periods of time at a stretch. In late 1979 and early 1980 both were held for a straight six months. When they were released in the spring of 1980, Nusrat asked her daughter to undertake a role that took her away from party affairs: she suggested Benazir go to Larkana to look over the somewhat neglected Bhutto estate. There are various possible explanations for this request. At one level it was a sensible, practical move. If Benazir kept a lower political profile, it would mean she could take over running the party in the event of Nusrat being arrested. But having Benazir out of the way may also have enabled Nusrat to exert control over the party without having to worry about her increasingly high-profile and ambitious daughter.

When she reached Larkana, Benazir, a single woman in her twenties, soon found that villagers wanted her to perform the classic role of a feudal in Pakistani rural society: adjudicating in legal and other disputes. Benazir was thereby interacting with farmers and elders at a time when some of her female cousins were still in purdah, never seen in public. But even if Benazir's stay in Larkana signalled the changing nature of the family, as a political tactic it didn't work. When the next arrests came, both mother and daughter were detained. With the two Bhutto women locked up, left-wingers in the PPP wanted to intensify the party's struggle against the military regime. Moderates proposed either a less confrontational approach or, in some cases, an accommodation with the army and even a willingness to participate in elections held on a non-party basis. Nusrat, still running the PPP, was faced with difficult choices. The moderates, many of whom had strong followings in their constituencies, were the greater force within the party. They included feudals, Punjabi business interests and retired military officers, including Zulfikar's favourite general, Tikka Khan. Some of them were so anxious about protecting their business and property interests that they wanted the Bhutto women to give up the leadership altogether and move into exile. The leftists, meanwhile, offered Nusrat the morally clearer path of open opposition to Zia. Having been sidelined by Zulfikar since 1973, they were keen to reassert themselves. Some, such as former Zulfikar confidant Sheikh Rashid, were favoured by Nusrat because they had shown great loyalty to Zulfikar during the campaign for his life. And they were not without political assets: the leftists had a genuine popular base among trade unions, students' organisations and impoverished rural voters who remembered with gratitude how Zulfikar had lifted their aspirations.

There was another issue with which Nusrat had to grapple. Since General Zia had started to move against civilian politicians from all parties, and not just the PPP, there was a growing opportunity for the opposition to unite. The difficulty was that a multi-party alliance would require the PPP to cooperate with politicians who had helped bring Zulfikar down in 1977. For Benazir it was a step too far: she could not stomach working with people she held partially responsible for her father's death. This was the time of her most radical convictions, and she also worried that the right-wing opposition parties would block the PPP's agenda for deep change in Pakistani society. Nusrat was also reluctant but, showing herself to be more focused on the task of opposing Zia, insisted that the PPP explore contacts with opposition figures. She called a secret meeting of the PPP Central Executive Committee, and for once there was a genuine policy debate within the party. Benazir, biting her lip, swung behind her mother's point of view, and the idea of reaching out to other parts of the opposition prevailed. It was a crucial moment in the formation of the opposition alliance, the Movement for the Restoration of Democracy (MRD).[29]

While Nusrat and Benazir were concentrating on politics, Murtaza and Shahnawaz reacted to their father's death in a markedly different way. In the hours after the hanging, Shahnawaz vented his frustration by phoning in a bomb threat to the Pakistan High Commission. The police soon traced the call and, confronting Shahnawaz, scared him sufficiently to force a confession, after which the matter was discreetly dropped. But it turned out that such threats were not entirely idle: the two brothers soon committed themselves to violent resistance against the Zia regime. What drove them to do so is controversial. According to Fatima Bhutto, shortly before his death, Zulfikar wrote her father, Murtaza, a letter in which he instructed him and Shahnawaz to move from London to Afghanistan so that they could do what Sindhi feudals were meant to do: settle the score. 'If you do not avenge my murder,' the letter read, 'you are not my sons.' The significance of the claim is largely to do with timing. In *If I Am Assassinated* Zulfikar had written that 'My sons will not be my sons if they do not drink the blood of those who dare to shed my blood.'[30] While that could be seen as rhetoric, a private letter from prison would be more of an instruction. The source of the information about the letter was Murtaza's girlfriend at the time, Della Roufogalis, who apparently remembered reading such a letter many times on the day Murtaza received it.[31] But Zulfikar's nephew, Tariq Islam, has insisted the letter never existed. 'This is nothing more than a fictionalised history,' he told *Dawn* after Fatima Bhutto's account was published in a book. 'I don't want to get into a family feud, and Fatima is my niece so I love her. But unfortunately, this book is full of faults.'[32] A week later, Sanam Bhutto backed up Tariq Islam. 'I challenge anyone to produce that letter. Because there is none! . . . My father never told any of us, his sons or his daughters, to start a terrorist wing'.[33] Tariq Islam's certainty on the matter derived from his own involvement in the last days of Zulfikar's life. His memory is that it was Murtaza who raised the issue of a violent campaign and who wanted his father's blessing. Tariq Islam visited Zulfikar twice in his death cell. During the first visit, ten days before the hanging, he conveyed Murtaza's desire to go to Kabul to fight. 'ZAB flew into a rage. His words . . . were: "Did I send Mir to Harvard and to Oxford to learn about all this stuff? Already they are calling me a murderer . . . next they will be calling me a terrorist. Tell him that I forbid him to go to Kabul. No matter what happens to me, he should concentrate on his studies and complete his course at Oxford." ' Tariq Islam says that when he relayed this message back to Murtaza, he was 'extremely distraught and disappointed' and asked him to try and meet Zulfikar again. 'You have to convince my father. You must do it for my sake. I don't care how you do it, but please don't come back empty-handed.' Tariq Islam managed to get permission to meet Zulfikar once more on 30 March – just four days before his execution.

> The reaction was the same, but I persisted. Time was running out. In sheer frustration, ZAB remarked with great prescience:
>
> I think Mir has boxed himself into a corner. He has made some commitments to the Afghans and is finding it difficult to back out now. Tell him to go if he wishes but I am not at all happy. The Afghans are too shrewd; they have fooled two superpowers for so many years. They are master diplomats and schemers and they will manipulate Mir for their own reasons . . . and sell him down the river when it suits them. He must be very careful in what he does and says. I leave him in God's hands. But ask him to complete his studies at Oxford.

The father may have realised that his boys were not cut out for violence, and certainly others had their doubts. The author Tehmina Durrani, who together with her husband Mustafa Khar hosted the brothers in London, later described Murtaza as 'a spirited youngster playing at terror' and Shahnawaz, generally described as the more hot-headed and aggressive of the two, as having soft eyes into which he could not force the steely-cold look of a terrorist.[34]

This is not to say that Murtaza didn't do some traditional peaceful lobbying. Since the US was courting General Zia, he could not meet President Carter, but he was granted time with his mother, Lillian Carter. He also put the case for Zulfikar's life to Henry Kissinger, Colonel Gaddafi, Sheikh Zayed of the UAE and Greek Prime Minister Konstantinos Karamanlis. But these meetings could not hide the fact that he had been contemplating a violent campaign for some time. In April 1978, a year before his father's death, he had flown to Beirut to investigate what might be possible. He reached out in particular to Yasser Arafat, the leader of what at the time was considered the world's most powerful militant outfit, the Palestine Liberation Organisation. These initial contacts were just exploratory, and it wasn't until after the hanging that Murtaza decided to act. At the time it did not seem too outlandish a notion. During the 1980s various groups seeking change in the Middle East and Europe were exploring the efficacy of violence, and in particular hijackings, to advance their agendas. Also, there was a strong moral case. General Zia, who himself used the gun to grab and hold on to power, was a military ruler who had mounted an illegal coup and who offered no democratic route to his removal. There was every prospect that he would rule for life – which, in the event, he did. After the hanging, Arafat provided the young Bhutto with a cache of weapons, and Murtaza also secured funding from another of Zulfikar's old allies, the Libyan leader Colonel Gaddafi. Meanwhile, Shahnawaz headed for Lebanon with a small group for some training with Palestinian fighters. Colonel Gaddafi also set up a training camp near Tripoli, staffed again by Palestinians, to train early recruits.[35] With the preparations well underway, Murtaza decided to base himself in Kabul, where the Soviet-backed regime was all too happy to host an organisation committed to overthrowing General Zia. Having imbibed the writings of Mao and Che Guevara, Murtaza hoped he was joining their ranks. With a nod to his sponsors, he put portraits of Yasser Arafat, Colonel Gaddafi and Syrian President Hafiz al-Assad in his Kabul office[36] and named his organisation the People's Liberation Army. In a late 1979 communique, Murtaza described the People's Liberation Army as Marxist and dedicated to overthrowing 'the usurper Zia'. In 1981 he changed the name to the Al Zulfikar Organisation (AZO) and organised for volunteers from Pakistan to join him.

The most remarkable of these recruits was a young man from Karachi, Salamullah Tipu, who made an impact as soon as he reached Afghanistan in late 1980. He was powerful, resourceful and soon came to the attention of Murtaza and Shahnawaz, who discussed possible actions with him, including the idea of a hijack. Tipu slipped back into Pakistan, where he mixed with radical underground circles, while two young Punjabi Al Zulfikar members were shifted to Karachi to act as his helpers in the proposed hijack.[37] Murtaza, meanwhile, appealed in a press statement to Pakistanis not to fly on the national airline PIA, which he said was a legitimate target.[38] These plans, however, came at a difficult time for Al Zulfikar. Their hosts in Kabul were increasingly dissatisfied with the organisation, leaving the brothers unsure whether they should stay there. In January 1981 the brothers decided to move on and started packing up their equipment. And with such flux at headquarters, Murtaza decided the hijack would have to be called off. He called a Bhutto family member in London and asked for the message 'stop doing that which you were going to do' to be relayed to Tipu.[39] The two Punjabis who were going to help him were sent back to their homes and left Karachi.[40]

Tipu was, by general consent, a hothead, and even if the hijack was off, it wasn't long before he was in the thick of it. In February 1981 he became caught up in a gun battle at Karachi University, in the course of which he killed a Jamaat-e-Islami activist. The police were now after him and he needed to leave the country; a hijack seemed as good a way to get out as any. Needing replacement hijackers, he found a young activist, Nasir Jamal, and persuaded him to join him. Realising they needed another person, the pair persuaded a cousin of Nasir Jamal, Arshad Tegi, to accompany them to the airport. The trio then boarded a PIA domestic flight to Peshawar, and shortly before it was due to land, seized the plane, forced the passengers to the back, diverted it to Kabul and demanded that General Zia release ninety-two prisoners. At first Zia refused. So Tipu increased the pressure. Having seized the victims' wallets and purses he knew that one of them, Major Tariq Rahim, was a former Pakistani military officer who had transferred to the Foreign Office. Ironically, the major had previously been an aide-de-camp to Zulfikar, a position which meant he had very close contact with the prime minister for several hours a day over a two-year period. But that did not count in his favour: the kidnappers accused him of having helped the army convict the PPP leader, an allegation for which there is no evidence whatsoever. On 6 March 1981, with Zia not backing down, the major was taken to the front of the plane, beaten, shot and thrown out of the fuselage onto the tarmac. Al Zulfikar now had everyone's attention. The hijacking was resolved only after the plane had moved from Kabul to Damascus and Tipu threatened to kill five American hostages, at which point Zia relented and released fifty-four prisoners from Pakistani prisons. To that extent, the hijacking was a success for Al Zulfikar: the organisation now not only found it easier to get publicity but also attracted more Pakistani recruits.

The PPP, however, paid a heavy price. General Zia arrested opposition activists including Nusrat and Benazir. Fifty-four people may have been released, but around a thousand were taken into custody. It was a genuinely frightening time for Benazir. She faced ten months in solitary confinement, a time in which she became so emaciated that the government worried she had cancer. Friends of Benazir say that most accounts of her life tend to overlook the impact the periods of incarceration had on her. Senior political prisoners in Pakistan are sometimes given better facilities than most prisoners. Zia did not treat Benazir like that. Particularly in Sukkur prison in 1981 the conditions were very bad indeed. She wrote in 1993:

Even now, though so many years have passed, I shudder when I think of it. It was like being buried alive in a grave. You live, yet you don't live. The days turn into months. You grow older, but there's no measure – nothing is a landmark. I'll never forget how hot the desert was. There seemed to be a constant dust storm swirling inside my cell. I was always sticky from sweat, and often coated with grit. My skin cracked open from the dryness, and the sweat felt like acid as it cut into my skin. My entire body changed: I couldn't eat, yet I always felt bloated – my stomach seemed to expand. I discovered later that I'd become anorexic, and, as though that were not enough, my teeth began to rot, and my hair fell out.[41]

Zulfikar had said in his death cell that Benazir was made from pure Damascene steel. Maybe he saw her potential before others, but it was solitary confinement that tempered her. After all, when she heard, while in captivity, that the military was preparing a legal case against her in which she would be charged with helping run Al Zulfikar, she had good reason to wonder if she was going to suffer the same fate as her father.[42] She later said that at this time she found a deepening faith that gave her greater resilience. 'When I was in prison I became very devout. I'm not a fundamentalist but I am very devout and I believe God places a burden on one's shoulder that he feels you can bear. So when the burden grows heavy I turn to God and say, "God, don't let it be so heavy that I cannot put up with it." So I would say that in solitary confinement'.[43] After Sukkur the world held no fear for her: she had survived, defiant, imperious and alone. To the delight of her Western friends, she did not lose her pleasure in going out for ice creams and gossiping, but underneath her sociable veneer there was now an inner strength, or, as her adviser Iqbal Akhund put it, 'an aura of loneliness. An elemental kind of inner loneliness.'[44]

In a sense Murtaza was telling the truth when he later told the BBC that the hijacking was carried out by Al Zulfikar members without his authorisation – he had, after all, tried to call it off. Fatima Bhutto has written that when Tipu first arrived in Kabul he suggested a hijack, but that her father turned him down.[45] In saying this, she was following the BBC interview in which Murtaza said that he had not known about the hijacking in advance and that it had come as a 'complete surprise'.[46] But when it happened, he felt he had to accept ownership of it. 'Once it had taken place we couldn't stop it. It was like a giant ball rolling.'[47] In any event, Murtaza acknowledged that his men had carried out the hijacking. He could hardly say anything else. Speaking in 2019, a former senior Al Zulfikar operative who ran the cell Tipu was a member of said that Murtaza gave the order to kill but that it was Shahnawaz who provided the hijackers with a submachine gun, which hostages noticed came onto the plane in Kabul.[48] Others have suggested that the weapon came from the head of Afghan intelligence Mohammed Najibullah. Some of Murtaza's supporters have tried to play down or deny his role in the killing of the major by making a generalised claim that the blame lay entirely with Tipu, who, they argue, defied Murtaza's order that none of the hostages should be killed.[49] Fatima wrote that when her father, disguised as an airport employee, spoke with Tipu on the tarmac near the plane, he urged his young activist not to use violence.[50] In an interview a decade later in Damascus, Murtaza added a detail: Major Rahim had been shot, he said, because he tried to overpower the commandos.[51] That last claim certainly was not true. Hostages who witnessed the murder of Major Tariq at close quarters all agree that, having been led down the aisle to be killed, the major simply pleaded for his life. Just before he shot Major Rahim, Tipu accused him of having betrayed Zulfikar – a statement with two significant implications. A street activist not familiar with high-level politics and appointments, it is likely that Tipu would not have known that Major Rahim had been Zulfikar's aide-de-camp unless someone – presumably Murtaza – had told him so. Secondly, it scotched a rumour that later did the rounds that the hijackers made a mistake because they had misidentified Major Rahim as the son of another general with same name.

Denouncing the brothers as terrorists, the only question for Zia was whether Nusrat and Benazir were involved as well. The historian Malik Hammad Ahmad has suggested that the distinction between the PPP and Al Zulfikar was not as clear-cut as the Bhuttos liked to make out.[52] He argues that the family had a dual strategy, using both democratic methods and a campaign of violence, and that, as is often the case in organisations that use such tactics, each side denied being involved with the other. For example, in one of their messages from the cockpit, the hijackers stated, 'we are freedom fighters of the Al Zulfikar Organization, which is not connected to the Pakistan People's Party'.[53] The question is whether that division was as clear as the hijackers claimed.

Al Zulfikar's own publications indicated that, as it discussed how best to resist the Zia regime, the PPP had considered using violence. In December 1981 a newspaper produced by Al Zulfikar in Kabul said that the PPP had a meeting in the Netherlands in which the issue of setting up a guerrilla organisation in London was discussed.[54] The CIA believed that there was collusion between the PPP and Al Zulfikar and that while moderate and feudal elements of the PPP opposed Al Zulfikar, leftists in the party thought it might help bring Zia down.[55] The CIA even reported that some in the PPP leadership believed Nusrat had known in advance that Major Tariq Rahim would be killed.[56] Some insiders said much the same thing. The fullest account of Al Zulfikar, *The Terrorist Prince*, was written by Raja Anwar, a former radical student activist turned youth adviser to Zulfikar who subsequently joined the brothers in Kabul. His version of events is controversial because he wrote it after spending three years in an Afghan prison on the basis of Murtaza's accusation that he was a Zia agent. Having been a diehard Bhuttoist, Anwar became a vehement critic of the family and eventually went into mainstream politics on behalf of the PPP's opponents, the Muslim League. Some of the events he described occurred when he was in prison, and for that material he relied on second-hand accounts, including the version put to him by Tipu, who by that point had also fallen out with Murtaza. The validity of some of his statements, in short, is questioned. On the question of the PPP's relationship with Al Zulfikar, Anwar claimed that PPP officials became involved in passing on messages from Nusrat to potential Al Zulfikar recruits, encouraging them to go to Kabul.[57] Other go-betweens carried messages from Kabul to Karachi.[58] So too did family members. The former senior Al Zulfikar member who ran Tipu's cell, for example, recalls that Nusrat once asked him to go to Rawalpindi and Peshawar but when he reached Rawalpindi he found that the man he was supposed to meet had been arrested after the authorities found weapons in his house.[59] At times even non-political relatives got drawn in: Raja Anwar describes how, in June 1979, Nusrat Bhutto used her sister in London to inform Murtaza of important operational information: that one of his operatives had been arrested in Peshawar and that he should not send any more volunteers over the border.[60]

One former member of Al Zulfikar, Muhammad Agha Waseem, has said that the Bhutto women were aware of the hijacking plan. Anxious that it was about to happen just as the opposition alliance was being pieced together, Benazir, he said, sent a coded message to Murtaza that 'winter has come to its end, so we do not need blankets anymore' – or, in other words, do not go ahead with the hijacking plan.[61] These claims are contradicted by others, such as Mushtaq Lasharie, a PIA employee and leftist activist close to the family. He believes that initially Benazir had sympathy for her brothers' campaign, saying she understood why people fought the Zia regime. 'She was similar age, her politics was very radical so yes, she was sympathetic to the movement against Zia ul-Haq on every level.' She helped organise the distribution of underground publications, some of which supported Al Zulfikar. But that did not extend, he believes, to planning the hijack, about which she was unaware and after which she became resolute in her opposition to the use of violence.[62]

In the immediate aftermath of the Al Zulfikar hijacking, Benazir said: 'All hijacking is bad, whether it is a plane or a nation'.[63] After her release from prison in 1984, she told an Indian journalist that she had not had the chance to discuss the use of violence with her brothers: 'We were not consulted in this matter. For a long time when they were based in London, we kept in touch with them. But after 1979 when they moved, we didn't know what had happened to them. We thought they had gone somewhere to get over their grief. We used to get reports of various actions.' And she didn't hold back from voicing criticism of their actions: 'We have always wondered if violence once inducted into society would not be difficult to eradicate.'[64] Nonetheless, there were areas of ambiguity. Benazir did show some sympathy for detained Al Zulfikar members, repeatedly demanding their release. One of her first prominent campaigns from London was on behalf of Naseer Baloch, a bus driver who had been recruited by Tipu as a helper prior to the hijack. Benazir insisted that the allegations that he was involved in Al Zulfikar were false – but former members were clear he had indeed been involved, and given that he had been a regular visitor to 70 Clifton and had gone to Afghanistan, it is difficult to believe that she had heard no word of this. In any event, there was no doubt whatsoever that she understood what she was doing when, on a number of occasions, she honoured the memory of Ayaz Sammu, an Al Zulfikar militant who was hanged for murdering four people in Karachi in 1982.[65] Even as late as April 1986 she visited the home of Idrees Baig, an Al Zulfikar activist who had been hanged for his work with the organisation. 'I am here to condole the death of Idrees Baig on humanitarian grounds and not because of his association with Al Zulfikar,' she told the press – which everyone understood to mean the opposite.[66]

It is tempting when discussing the Bhutto women to assume that they always acted in concert. In fact, they may have had slightly different views on the use of force. Even before Zulfikar was hanged, Nusrat had been approached by people willing to use direct action. There are credible accounts that on one of her visits to Zulfikar in prison, Nusrat asked him whether he wanted to take up an offer to use Palestinian fighters to break him out. Zulfikar turned down the suggestion, saying he did not want to seek refuge abroad.[67] After her husband's death Nusrat never condemned Al Zulfikar and she never criticised the hijacking.[68] Her line was that she and Benazir were doing one thing while Murtaza and Shahnawaz were doing another. 'My sons are not young boys anymore,' she said in January 1983. 'They are grown up. They know what they are doing. As far as I and the Pakistan People's Party are concerned, we believe completely in democracy and democratic methods.'[69]

The issue of how much Nusrat and Benazir knew about Al Zulfikar's activities will remain controversial. But no one can doubt that Al Zulfikar both was emboldened by the hijack and failed to take advantage of it. Other spectacular attacks were planned but, to varying degrees, they went wrong. Three in particular were notable. In 1982 two Al Zulfikar members twice tried to launch a heat-seeking missile beneath the flight path used by General Zia's plane as it took off from Rawalpindi. On the first occasion the missile didn't fire and on the second it narrowly missed its target.[70] Al Zulfikar also tried to kill Justice Maulvi Mushtaq, the man who had sentenced Zulfikar in the Lahore High Court, but they botched it and ended up killing a colleague instead. Murtaza told the BBC he took responsibility for the attack, describing it as a legitimate action against a pillar of a terroristic state: Al Zulfikar were not terrorists, he said, but counter-terrorists.[71] The statement caused some anguish to Benazir, who was in prison at the time: 'Mir Murtaza didn't help when, the day after the assassination, he took credit for it in a BBC interview in the name of Al-Zulfikar,' she later wrote.[72] The third action was meant to be on a huge scale. A group of Al Zulfikar militants were moved to Vienna with a view to capturing some Westerners and trading them for prisoners. But the operation was so haphazardly organised that it never came close to success, and most of the militants were arrested. According to one press report the operation went wrong when the Al Zulfikar men entered a five-star hotel with a plan to seize some Ford car company executives who were having a reception. Things unravelled when they followed signs to 'Reception', ending up at the check-in desk, where no executives were to be found.[73]

The mix-up in Vienna was emblematic of an organisation in decline. With the government in Kabul ever more doubtful about the benefits of hosting Al Zulfikar, the Bhutto brothers decided in September 1982 that they should move on,[74] leaving behind some members under the leadership of Tipu.[75] Murtaza was now highly mobile, living for spells in Delhi, Tripoli and later Damascus. He had been working on the Indian connection for some time and believed that his fellow dynast Indira Gandhi would be naturally sympathetic to him. Initially, his thinking seemed to be validated – when he had asked for a meeting in December 1979 she granted him one, after which Murtaza expressed his group's 'great respect for Indira Gandhi'.[76] The personal relationship between the two did not develop, however, and when he tried to secure another meeting six months later she palmed him off on her son Sanjay. Murtaza's outreach to India was a move his father would surely have disapproved of, but Murtaza believed Delhi offered him opportunities. According to former Al Zulfikar members, the Indian authorities trained them in a facility north of Delhi and then helped them slip back into Sindh to launch attacks. But by the time Al Zulfikar started getting significant Indian support, the nature of the organisation had changed. Increasingly, it was becoming a Sindhi nationalist outfit. India, which later provided support for the Mohajir Quami Movement's (MQM) violent campaign in Karachi, was always willing to support organisations that undermined Pakistan's national unity. There is no evidence that Al Zulfikar changed its focus at the request of the Indians, but certainly India would have been more interested in backing an organisation that had a realistic chance of causing problems in Sindh than one that had little possibility of overthrowing the regime. Most of the volunteers at this stage were Sindhi youths who mounted actions in Karachi and interior Sindh.[77] Nusrat and Benazir were aware of the contact between Murtaza and the Indians, and certainly, Indira Gandhi took an interest in both of them. In May 1982, when Indira Gandhi visited London, she handed British Prime Minister Margaret Thatcher a memo from Bashir Riaz demanding that Benazir be allowed to go abroad. The appeal fell on deaf ears: one of Thatcher's officials recorded that 'the prime minister does not think that any action is required'.[78] But Gandhi kept at it. In October 1982 she wrote to Thatcher saying that Nusrat's ill health had moved her and that 'it seems cruel not to allow Mrs. Bhutto to go abroad for medical treatment'.[79]

Despite the Indian help, the number of attacks mounted by the organisation dwindled, in part because Zia's campaign against it – including a series of infiltrations into its ranks had been effective, and also because, with the anti-Soviet religious warriors, the *mujahideen,* a growing force in the Afghanistan–Pakistan border area, it was increasingly difficult for Al Zulfikar members to slip between the two countries. By 1985 the CIA was making withering assessments of Al Zulfikar and in April 1986 concluded that the group had 'virtually collapsed'.[80] While Al Zulfikar looked increasingly like a spent force, Nusrat and Benazir remained a problem for the government, which treated them ever more harshly. When Sanam visited Benazir at this time, she was shocked by what she saw. 'She looked so ill, so skinny. I saw to my horror that her hair had got thin. I could see her scalp.'[81] The imprisonment took an even heavier toll on Nusrat. When Benazir met Nusrat in her prison cell, she too was shocked: 'The pale, haggard woman with her nervous movements and gray hair parted in the middle and tied into a plait looked so different from the elegant and self-confident woman I knew as my mother.'[82]

The regime, though, had failed to break Benazir's spirit – she repeatedly spurned offers of release in return for giving up her political activity. In a sign that the military regime acknowledged that the best they could hope for was to keep her quiet, and after her friend Peter Galbraith organised sustained pressure from Washington, Benazir was moved to house arrest in Larkana in December 1981. She could not do any politics, but she could recover her strength. But there was no such recovery for Nusrat, who was always a diminished figure after her time in solitary confinement. With her health deteriorating, she was repeatedly refused permission to travel abroad for treatment, until in November 1982 she went to Germany with suspected lung cancer. While Nusrat was out of Pakistan, Benazir faced another fourteen months of house arrest. It was a time of real danger for the PPP, which now had no leader able to run the party effectively. And with Zia keeping up the pressure on anyone who showed loyalty to the PPP, there were signs of the senior members peeling away. But that period of PPP inactivity was about to end. By January 1984 Benazir too needed medical treatment, for an ear issue that had dogged her throughout her various imprisonments. And with more pressure from Peter Galbraith, Zia relented, and she was set free and headed for London.

Benazir initially planned a short stay in the UK, but then doctors said she could require at least nine months of medical attention, and, realising she wasn't going back home for a while, she rented a flat in London's Barbican. Zia hoped that by letting Benazir go abroad she would become a less potent source of opposition to him. But she threw herself into organising almost daily protests outside the Pakistan High Commission and handwriting piles of letters, most of them highlighting the plight of PPP workers being held as political prisoners and, in some cases, lashed and hanged.[83] While many young UK-based Pakistanis were attracted to Benazir, some senior party members in London had become used to running the exiled wing of the party themselves and found her arrival irritating. Leftists worried that she was insufficiently committed to the socialist ideas that Zulfikar had espoused when he founded the party. The rightists, meanwhile, were still advocating building bridges to the regime. A third group, led by Mumtaz Bhutto, argued for greater rights for Pakistan's different ethnic groups. Many chafed at the idea that such a young woman – the same age as their daughters – might eclipse them. As Benazir recorded in her autobiography, their sentiments were summed up by a remark one PPP leader made when she first arrived in London: 'It is not in my destiny to follow the father, then the mother and now the daughter'.[84]

Ever since Zulfikar's hanging there had been tension within the party about the family's role. Even though he was living in Kabul, Murtaza was aware of these disputes. In an autumn 1979 letter to Bashir Riaz, his successor as the editor of the PPP newspaper *Musawat*, Murtaza urged him to use the publication to back the family. 'If Punjab Working Committee recommended Begum

Sahiba as the Chairman for life and Miss Benazir Bhutto as the Acting Chairman, well then that is final. That is what the newspaper will carry and that is what our newspaper will propagate.'[85] Murtaza's focus on that issue reflected another concern: was Nusrat Bhutto really putting herself forward as a possible future prime minister? And was she medically fit to do that? In a letter to senior party organisers in Punjab on 30 May 1984, Benazir wrote, 'Begum Sahiba gets exhausted and therefore is not in a position to resume an active role by her presence although she continues to be well informed about all events.'[86] It was the start of her campaign to take over the PPP, but Benazir still needed to nod towards her mother's nominal authority. When, for example, she made some senior personnel changes in the PPP in March of that year, she took care to say that 'both Begum Sahiba and I' had made the decision.[87] But increasingly she was now writing with an air of easy command. In another March letter to party officials she began by stating that Begum Sahiba supported her but went on to issue instructions in her own name: 'I have decided to increase the number of the members of the Central Executive Committee . . . I may also be requiring the said committee to meet and consider matters that I feel are needed to be discussed and advise me thereof.'[88] And then in August she issued an instruction that no decisions about PPP organisational matters or any appointment to a party post could be made without her clearance.[89]

This assertion of authority provoked a backlash, and, for Benazir, matters came to a head in October 1985 when a meeting of the PPP Central Executive Committee in Quetta made a series of decisions about which she was informed a month later. She hit back hard, telling her loyalists that it was intolerable that she should read of party decisions in the newspapers before she heard them from the party itself. 'I do not want to be placed in the position where after every CEC meeting I am informed this is the unanimous position. Or consensus on this issue has been obtained. That presents me with a fait accompli.' She again insisted that the CEC should not take any decision without her approval: she was the leader of the party and the final decision should be left to her. She asked her loyalists to resist any unanimous decisions by always devising counterproposals, thereby ensuring there was always division and at least two contrasting points of view on which she could then declare a final verdict.[90] This Machiavellian tactic is clear evidence that power did not just come to Benazir – she fought for it.

Some of the older generation – 'the uncles', as she called them – realised that, with Benazir in her thirties, she could be there for decades. Zulfikar's former chief minister of Punjab, Mustafa Khar, tried to outflank her by setting up a series of party 'action committees', ostensibly to organise anti-Zia agitation but in fact, Benazir suspected, to establish a structure within the party loyal to him and on the basis of which he could make an accommodation with the Zia regime. In a letter to one of her loyalists in Punjab, Jehangir Badar, she explained that she was under such pressure in London that she might have to give ground on the action committees but insisted that she, Badar and other loyalists would need to choose the committee leaders, 'so control will remain'.[91] Another loyalist, General Tikka Khan, urged her not to give in to the demand for action committees: 'there should be no parallel organisation in the party – specially in Punjab and no pressure groups should be formed', he wrote to her.[92] In managing these machinations, Benazir was to a significant degree guided by her deep resentments against those who she believed had failed to do enough to save her father from the gallows: while she had been in prison defending her father, many had remained silent or even left the country. Her friend and lifelong supporter Naheed Khan had many discussions with Benazir about her sense of grievance that her father's senior colleagues had failed him: 'The ones who came out and were lashed,' Naheed recalled, 'were the party workers, not the leaders.'[93]

If Mustafa Khar was a problematic 'uncle', so was Benazir's real one, Mumtaz Bhutto. He and Zulfikar had shared a remarkably similar education: a degree at Christ Church, Oxford, before being called to the bar. Zulfikar went on to appoint Mumtaz as governor of Sindh and later its chief minister. But there was some family history. Zulfikar once showed his adviser Rafi Raza a letter in which Sir Shahnawaz blamed his 1937 defeat on members of Mumtaz Bhutto's branch of the family, who, he believed, had conspired against him. 'Throughout, ZAB and he had a difficult relationship,' Rafi Raza recalled. 'As Special Assistant I sometimes managed to smooth this out, but after I left government in July 1973, tension increased, and Mumtaz followed a few months later.' According to Rafi Raza, Mumtaz was removed as chief minister at the end of 1973 because Zulfikar resented both his independence and his popularity.[94] After Zulfikar's death, Mumtaz became increasingly insistent on Sindhi rights within a looser federal structure. This was not so unusual: the regionalists, as they were known, were a significant faction within the PPP. But in 1985 he took his campaign on the issue to a new level by becoming a founding member of the Sindh Baloch Pakhtoon Front, arguing for greater decentralisation. Nervous that expelling Mumtaz, who was a member of the PPP Central Executive Committee, would be interpreted by some as pandering to Punjabi chauvinism, Benazir asked PPP Secretary General Tikka Khan for advice. 'How can an individual belong to two different political organisations with separate political aims and objectives?'[95] In September she told Mumtaz he could not have his cake and eat it and expelled him from the party. Mumtaz did not go quietly, insisting that as a founder of the PPP, no one who had subsequently joined had the right to expel him. Benazir dismissed that out of hand. Mumtaz, she said, had not only failed to save Zulfikar's life but was so compliant at the time of the hanging that Zia had not even bothered to arrest him as part of his effort to forestall any agitation. Mumtaz could point out that he did take part in protests against the hanging and that the authorities limited his freedom of movement but Benazir insisted that many PPP leaders had done more. And she believed that by advocating Sindhi rights, he was causing a split between Punjabis and Sindhis within the PPP.[96] Mumtaz could not prevent his expulsion, and, more shocking still for the old feudal, it was all done by a young female relative.

As these power struggles played out, the question for leftists was: where actually did Benazir stand? Initially Tariq Ali was encouraged: 'She had moved to a tiny flat in London, where we would endlessly discuss the future of the country. She would agree that land reforms, mass education programmes, a health service and an independent foreign policy were positive, constructive aims and crucial if the country was to be saved from the vultures in and out of uniform. Her constituency was the poor, and she was proud of the fact.'[97] Benazir was at the time a genuine radical who took strength from the commitment of diehard leftist PPP activists – the so-called *jiyala* – who were prepared to face imprisonment or worse for the party. But as time passed she moved away from the left, and by 1987 she knew which direction she wanted to take the party in. She spoke with the British Labour leader Neil Kinnock about how he had moved his party from the left to the centre. She was worried, she told him, that if she moved too far the PPP would become less distinct from Zia and she would lose her leftist activists.[98] It was all a question of timing:

during her period in exile she needed the leftists, who were not only more willing to oppose Zia but also less prone than the right wing to try to oust her. Once she got into power and had complete control of the party, it was the turn of the leftists to feel they were being sidelined. By the 1990s, after the collapse of communism, the socialist vocabulary was dropped in favour of trickle-down economics.[99] She even became an admirer of the right-wing Margaret Thatcher and expressed some views that most Pakistanis might have found difficult: 'I grew up at a time when colonialism had just ended. The whole inspiration behind colonialism had been to discover the world and achieve more . . . Now things are much leaner and meaner.'[100]

While Benazir was asserting her authority over the PPP, Murtaza settled in Damascus and Shahnawaz was based in the French resort of Cannes. Many thought Shahnawaz had never really been cut out for life as a militant: even when he was Al Zulfikar's head of operations he had been unable to resist nights out in fashionable Paris nightclubs.[101] When he looked forward to the day Zia fell, he didn't fantasise about wielding great power; rather, he would say he wanted to become the minister of tourism. The brothers had their Afghan wives – the sisters Fauzia and Rehana Fasihudin – with them. Al Zulfikar had not been formally disbanded but was increasingly inactive. Nusrat, having received treatment for suspected lung cancer in Germany, had initially moved to Geneva and asked Benazir to join her there. Benazir declined, arguing that London was a far better place from which to run the PPP campaign. Nusrat then joined Shahnawaz in Cannes and again asked Benazir to move from London, telling her daughter that she had already spent too much of her youth in prison and should now settle down and seek happiness. When Benazir remained adamantly opposed to the idea, Nusrat cut off her monthly allowance, obliging Benazir to fall back on the generosity of friends. After three months Nusrat relented and restored the funds.[102]

Although she refused to live in France, Benazir did agree to her mother's idea of an annual family holiday in Cannes each July. In 1985, the second year they had all gathered, Nusrat, Shahnawaz and Rehana, and Murtaza with his wife and young daughter Fatima joined up with Sanam, Benazir and some other cousins. The family reunion turned into a tragedy when, on 18 July, the twenty-seven-year-old Shahnawaz was found dead in his apartment. As ever with high-profile deaths in Pakistan, even basic facts soon became contested.

According to Pakistan's ambassador to France at the time, Jamsheed Marker, the evening started going wrong when Murtaza and Shahnawaz argued about some money given to them by Colonel Gaddafi and an Emirati prince. Murtaza wanted to use it for Al Zulfikar but Shahnawaz preferred the idea of setting up a business. 'Benazir tried to calm them down,' Marker later reported, 'but she didn't succeed.' Murtaza went home with Shahnawaz, where the argument was said to have continued. The next morning Shahnawaz was found dead in his flat. British officials in Paris told the Foreign Office about reports that pathology tests indicated that Shahnawaz was poisoned by a substance not available in France but said to be standard issue in the Syrian secret service. There were rumours the two brothers carried small phials of poison in case they were captured,[103] and Benazir later confirmed that that was the case and that Murtaza found Shahnawaz's broken phial in a bin in the apartment.[104] The British Embassy in Paris also reported that further evidence from the autopsy suggested that the poison did not kill Shahnawaz immediately and that he had suffered a slow and painful death.[105] In her initial interrogation Rehana reportedly told investigators that she had heard her husband moaning but paid no attention because she was angry with him.[106] The French report into the murder is not publicly available but according to one witness who saw a copy some years ago it contained a suggestion that Rehana had cooked an omelette while Shahnawaz was dead or dying close by.[107] Marker, citing a senior French intelligence official, said that when French police arrived on the scene they arrested Rehana and Murtaza, who immediately produced a Syrian diplomatic passport, was released and left the country.[108] Rehana was charged for failing to assist a victim in distress.[109]

Marker's account cannot be taken at face value: he was, after all, one of Zia's ambassadors, with a track record of hostility towards the Bhutto family. Indeed, Benazir gave a very different account of the evening, not mentioning any argument between Murtaza and Shahnawaz and with different details of everyone's movements.[110] In her interviews with Linda Francke, who helped her write her autobiography *Daughter of the East*, Benazir also claimed that Shahnawaz had told her he wanted a divorce – something she tried to dissuade him from doing – and Benazir described how she shouted accusations at his wife.[111] There have been a bewildering number of explanations of Shahnawaz's death. Pakistani officials told the press that he had died of a drug overdose.[112] Rehana

Bhutto said her husband had killed himself. At the time, her lawyer, Maître Richard Banon, said that his client and her husband had not been on good terms for some time and that Shahnawaz was depressed.[113] Fatima Bhutto, who looked into the case closely, quoted a French lawyer who had been involved in the original hearings and who suggested that Benazir had blocked an investigation into the death because she wanted to avoid antagonising American intelligence, who had wanted to neutralise Al Zulfikar by killing the brothers.[114] In a 1989 interview in Damascus, the Indian journalist Shyam Bhatia discussed Shahnawaz's fate with Murtaza, who described how he and his wife had gone for a drink to Shahnawaz's apartment. Murtaza told Bhatia that as he and his wife returned to their own place, he thought his wife was trembling and sweating and could not understand why. The next day, when Shahnawaz was found dead, he challenged his wife, who denied any knowledge of what had happened.[115] He later divorced her but, according to Fatima, Murtaza went on to have doubts about his initial assessment of the role of the sisters in the death.[116] Both women went on to live in the US and have consistently denied any wrongdoing. Years later various interpretations were still being made: in 2018, Bilawal Bhutto tweeted that Shahnawaz had been assassinated 'on the orders of General Zia-ul-Haq'. And the passage of time also seemed to erode Benazir's anger. She not only undertook to pay for the education of Shahnawaz and Rehana's daughter Sassi, but also met Rehana in the US.

It is tempting to see Benazir's rise to power as having been preordained. Her American publishers tapped into this aspect of her story when they gave her autobiography the title *Daughter of Destiny*. She was the third generation of high-level political operators, born to power and seemingly assuming it effortlessly. Her study of politics at the world's greatest universities prepared her for office. Her timing was fortuitous. The fact that she had completed her education just as Zulfikar was arrested meant she was well placed to organise the campaign attempting to save him. And when it came to running things, she had aristocratic command. A letter she wrote to senior party official Jahangir Badar revealed what supporters might call a natural sense of authority, and what less sympathetic observers see as hubris. When Badar, after a row with her, resigned as president of the PPP in Punjab, she apologised for having taken him for granted. But she also urged Badar, who was ten years older than her, to accept her right to criticise him. 'As a sister and a leader, it is my duty to guide and correct you . . . in future you will not be so sensitive.'[117] Zulfikar is often credited with having raised the aspirations of Pakistanis used to centuries of feudal oppression. But both he and Benazir drew deep on the well of feudal authority as they asserted their right – or, as they would have put it, their duty – to rule.

And yet Benazir still had to struggle for power. When Zia allowed her to leave Pakistan in 1984, many in the military regime and others too thought she was finished. In their political reporting from Islamabad in January 1984, British officials believed that the PPP would split and that Benazir would become increasingly irrelevant.[118] From her Barbican flat, Benazir had to assert herself. Failure to do so would mean that, like the ailing Nusrat, she would be more of an adornment to the party than its leader. After all, other Bhuttos also had ambitions. Having run a militant outfit, Murtaza enjoyed the support of the PPP radical elements. And had Mumtaz Bhutto had the requisite drive, vision and willingness to suffer, he might have made a bid for the PPP leadership after Zulfikar's arrest. That last quality – of making personal sacrifices – was key. Many politicians of the developing world have had periods of exile in Europe. Some, such as Ayatollah Khomeini of Iran and Tunisia's Rachid Ghannouchi, have gone back home to assume power after the fall of the ancien regime. Benazir was different. She returned to Pakistan in 1986 while the dictatorship was still in place and Zia's power base was secure. She knew she was likely to face arrest, impressment and solitary confinement, and could not rule out being put on trial. As she later said, even her husband doubted it could work: 'when he married me, he thought that I was under delusions that I could beat a military dictator, and he thought that, "When she wakes up and finds out that it's all wrong and she can't then I'll be there to console her." '[119] But as Zardari and others soon discovered, Benazir's willingness to emulate her father and endure hardship resonated with the Pakistani people and created a strong bond.

Her opportunity to lay down a challenge to Zia arose because of his attempt to legitimise his regime by lifting martial law in December 1985. Within weeks of that being announced, Benazir was planning her return. This was not to be a low-profile move to 70 Clifton, but rather a rolling national tour in which she would directly confront the general. And it would begin in Punjab, the province that she had to win if she were ever to have power. The PPP calculated that either Zia would have to arrest her, underscoring her image as a political martyr, or he would have to let her agitate, rendering him ever weaker. Defying a series of anonymous death threats, she landed in Lahore on 10 April 1986. PPP officeholders had been told that, if they wanted a future in the party, they had to deliver a large crowd to welcome her. As they organised the food and transport that would enable party supporters to reach Lahore, the PPP had a number of factors in its favour. The press coverage surrounding her return, and months of speculation about the date, imbued a sense of drama. So too did the overarching narrative: a young woman returning to face down a harsh, all-powerful man who had had her father killed. It was the stuff of legend, and it struck a chord. But when it happened, the scale of the event exceeded all expectations. The pictures of the crowds in Lahore are astonishing. There were people as far as the eye could see. It is impossible to count crowds that big, but everyone could agree it was hundreds of thousands strong and even sober commentators wondered if it reached over a million. And when she addressed the crowds Benazir made an emotional pitch: 'I have willingly taken the path of thorns,' she told the crowd in a speech which Tariq Ali helped her write, 'and stepped into the valley of death.'[120] There was no sense of her moderating her message regarding General Zia. 'Will you workers and labourers help to destroy this man?' she asked the crowd. 'Yes! Yes!' it roared back.[121] It was street power on such a massive scale that no one could now doubt her command of the PPP and her role as leader-in-waiting, and she quickly moved to formalise her status. At a May 1986 Central Executive Committee meeting in Lahore, Nusrat was taken by surprise when Sheikh Rafiq proposed that Benazir be made chairman of the party before a compromise was reached, making both co-chairmen.[122]

Benazir took her stump speech to all four provinces in a series of mass demonstrations. Matters came to a head in August 1986. Both the government and the opposition had been planning rallies to mark 14 August, Independence Day. Citing concerns about violence, but perhaps fearing the opposition would attract bigger crowds, Prime Minister Muhammed Khan Junejo cancelled the Muslim League's official, government-backed rally. In her autobiography, Benazir claimed that the PPP's decision not to follow suit was foisted on her by other opposition parties in the Movement for the Restoration of Democracy, of which the PPP was a part. The choice she was presented with, she wrote, was between participation in the rally and breaking up the opposition alliance.[123] But when the opposition rally went ahead, the government cracked down, arresting Benazir and using force to maintain peace and stability. She now discovered that the mass rallies had given her a somewhat false impression. While huge numbers were willing to come to hear her speak, not so many were willing to court arrest or worse by going out onto the streets to demand her release. Thrown off balance, she stopped calling for elections. The balance of power between the PPP and the government was becoming clearer. The PPP was a formidable force, but the state's ability to use violence and detain people gave it the upper hand.

With the two sides in something of a stalemate, Benazir attended to an important domestic matter. As a single woman, she was subject to politically damaging rumours. Male chauvinism ran deep in Pakistan, and if she were ever to have a one-on-one meeting with a man, many would assume that there had been impropriety. The question of whom she might marry excited much idle chatter among Pakistan's elite, with various names discussed as possibilities. Even after her death, the question of who might have married Benazir comes up with surprising frequency. But finding a husband was not so easy. She was in her mid-thirties, knew her own mind and came with the prospect of troubles ahead. Anyone who married her had to be willing to take on the risk of having their business ruined by the regime. They would also have to play a supportive role to the main act – Benazir herself. That was not something many Pakistani men were willing to do. Despite all that, some did show interest. In 2011 the cricketer-turned-politician Imran Khan claimed that he nearly pulled off a bit of matchmaking. 'One of my cousins was interested in her and she also took an interest when I introduced them to each other. At one point, marriage was virtually on the cards.'[124] There were a number of flirtations, but Benazir could not start dating a man for fear that it would lead to scandal. As a way out of the problem, Benazir accepted the idea of an arranged marriage. She believed that her family could be relied upon to find someone suitable and that she would then be able to carry out her politics without the constant risk of gossips chipping away at her reputation. And there was a candidate: a young man by the name of Asif Zardari, whose family was pushing him forward. With Nusrat keen to marry off her daughter, the Bhuttos' research on Asif Zardari was distinctly lacklustre. The Zardaris, for example, said that Asif had studied at the London Centre of Economic and Political Science[125] and later the London School of Economics and Business. In fact, as British officials later confirmed, no such institutions existed: it was a rather feeble attempt to suggest he could keep up with Benazir because he had been to the world-famous LSE. But Asif Zardari was no intellectual.

Originally from Iranian Balochistan, the Zardari tribe settled in the Nawabshah district of Sindh several centuries ago. In feudal terms they were far from the first rank: as a WikiLeaked State Department cable rather crushingly put it: 'Post contacts suggest the Zardari tribe has little social standing with the Sindhi elite; there is a story that as children, Sindhis were told "a Zardari stole it" if something went missing.'[126] Asif Zardari's father, Hakim Ali Zardari, like many in his generation, tried branching out into urban life, buying a large house in Karachi and running the Bambino cinema there. His son attended not the top-flight Karachi Grammar School but the Cadet College Petaro and grew into a young man said to have touted his own father's cinema tickets and to have run a disco in his basement that would often go on until four in the morning. And he was ambitious, always wanting to make a splash. One story told by a contemporary makes the point. As a schoolboy, Zardari told his friends he wanted to borrow 5,000 rupees – the equivalent of thousands of dollars in today's money. He wanted to give it to a charity called the Lion's Club, because with that sum, he figured, he would be made the chief guest and garlanded on the stage in front of some of the great and the good of Karachi. He craved status. 'He was never your friend,' the school contemporary recalled. 'He was your boss. You had to say boss. Literally.'[127] Zardari came into adolescence at a time of change in Karachi. The swinging sixties brought nightclubs and bars to the city, attracting young men and women eager to escape the constraints of traditional, conservative family life. Alcohol and widely available weapons made for a high-octane mix, and Asif Zardari was among those fuelled by it. Often seen on his 125cc motorbike, he is said to have hitched up his trousers so that everyone could see the dagger tied to his ankle and to have bristled at any insults to his honour.[128] Shortly before Zardari met Benazir he had gone into business in the construction industry.[129]

On the face of it, he was a most unsuitable candidate for Benazir's hand, a cartoon character, like the archetypical blackguard who enslaves the passions of his lover through a combination of cruelty and charm. But the Bhuttos' innate sense of social superiority had been shaken by the family's political diffi-culties. Nusrat was fighting battles on many fronts, and finding a suitable husband for her wilful daughter was just one of a multitude of challenges she faced. The initial discussions between the two families were derailed by the premature death of Shahnawaz and by Benazir's triumphant return to Lahore the following year. But the Zardaris were persistent, and in 1987 Nusrat urged her daughter to consider Asif seriously. Benazir asked some of her friends and relatives to advise her. Her brother Murtaza, cut off in exile in Damascus, watched these developments with dismay. 'What the hell is she doing?' he asked. 'Stop her! How can she marry Hakim Zardari's son?'[130]

Tariq Islam took on the role of the father and interviewed Asif on the basis of a list of questions Benazir had given him. There were three main points: could he afford to keep her? Would he agree not to interfere in her politics? Would he be capable of not being jealous of her meeting male politicians? Charming to a fault, Asif gave all the right answers.[131] But that did not convince some of Benazir's girlfriends, who looked at his beautifully coiffed handlebar moustache with disdain and saw a provincial hick and social climber. Some advised against the match, but others thought she didn't have much choice, which is exactly how Benazir saw it. 'For me,' Benazir told the *Los Angeles Times*, 'the choice was not between a love marriage or an arranged marriage but between agreeing to this or not getting married at all.'[132]

The engagement took place in London in July 1987, and Benazir cele-brated by issuing a press release. 'Conscious of my religious obligations and duty to my family, I am pleased to proceed with the marriage proposal accepted by my mother, Nusrat Bhutto. The impending marriage will not in any way affect my political commitment to my country, my people or the trail blazed by Shaheed Zulfikar Ali Bhutto for a free, federal democratic and egalitarian Pakistan.' Even as she looked ahead to married life, she was thinking of her father. It didn't sound like love and many saw it as a union born of pragma-tism. In her autobiography, Benazir praised Sir Shahnawaz, her grandfather, for having allowed his daughters to choose their husbands. Zulfikar backed that up by raising Benazir as a highly independent woman. And yet here she was, allowing her mother and other close relatives to select a partner, even if she still had the final say. And many close to her believe that it worked. In the early years of the marriage the couple seemed to fall in love.

As ever when a wedding is being planned, there were tensions. Asif's mother was quoted in the Pakistani press saying that she would invite General Zia to the wedding – something totally unacceptable to the Bhuttos. It was a potential dealbreaker, and the Zardaris backed down. In *Daughter of the East* Benazir tactfully described the incident as a case of a 'false interview' carried by the press.[133] Next came the question of what name Benazir would use. For Zardari, this was a big issue: he was thinking in terms of furthering the glory of the house of Zardari. When Benazir refused to change her name, Zardari reluctantly accepted it, but it was a point he would return to in subsequent years. Typically, upper-class Pakistanis were married in lavish parties thrown in one of the five-star hotels. But Benazir – ever the politician – wanted something on a grander scale. In her home in Clifton she celebrated with friends from all over the world. Then she went to Karachi's slum district of Lyari – a PPP stronghold – for a second event, where an estimated 75,000 of the party's supporters and hangers-on joined in the fun with music, fireworks and free food.[134] 'It was amazing,' one party supporter later wrote. 'It was like one huge festive rally. Zia was alive but you could do anything, we drank, we smoked dope, we danced. Nobody could stop us.'[135] There was a world between Benazir's foreign guests and her adoring impoverished supporters, but both groups could agree they had never seen anything like it.

While Benazir had resolved the marriage issue, her politics were static. The enthusiasm that followed her return in 1986 was dissipating, and she despaired of ever seeing an end to Zia's regime. He remained firmly entrenched and showed no sign whatsoever of giving up power. She knew full well that if the PPP looked like they would win elections, he would simply prevent any vote taking place. Neither Benazir nor Zia hid their feelings about each other. In November 1987 Benazir's old friend Mark Siegel was in Pakistan heading a delegation monitoring some local elections. The group had a meeting with Zia, who asked Siegel to stay behind as the others left. 'I know who you are,' Zia said. And then: 'The greatest mistake of my life was letting your friend live.' In the event, Zia was the first to die. On 17 August 1988, General Zia's eleven and a half years in power were brought to an end by his assassination. That someone killed him was beyond doubt. To this day, the identity of his assassin remains a mystery, although no serious claim has ever been made that the PPP or Al Zulfikar was involved. Asked whether his men were responsible, Murtaza rather lamely replied, 'not to my knowledge'. Zia died in Bahawalpur after watching a display of M1 Abrams tanks, which the US was hoping to sell to Pakistan. Together with thirty others, including the US ambassador to Pakistan, he was flying back to Rawalpindi when his Lockheed C-130 Hercules blew up in mid-air. Villagers reported having seen the plane lurching up and down in the sky, before descending nose first to the ground. A series of US and Pakistani investigations failed to establish what happened – or at least failed to publish any substantive findings. But one suggestion has stuck in the public imagination – that a bomb was smuggled on board hidden in a crate of mangoes. It was a sudden, shocking end to the military regime. While many Pakistanis mourned – Zia's funeral was a major public event – many were relieved. A period of military rule was over and the hope of a democratic dispensation restored. Benazir realised immediately that she had to take care not to be seen to celebrate the death. When some PPP supporters started passing around sweets, Benazir told them to contain themselves and to show respect for the dead. But a statement issued by the PPP caught the feelings of many in the party. 'Internationally Zia may be remembered as the man who stood up to the Soviets after they entered Afghanistan but in Pakistan he will be remembered as the man who illegally seized power and after 11 and a half years of repressive rule left nothing behind but debt and mortgages, hunger and unemployment, exploitation and discrimination, drugs and corruption.' Benazir's struggle for power had entered a new phase.

6

BENAZIR TRIUMPHS

A state of emergency was proclaimed shortly after Zia died, and, with a significant proportion of the army command dead, there was an urgent need to fill the power vacuum. The main beneficiary was Zia's vice-chief, General Mirza Aslam Beg. For some reason the highly ambitious Beg, despite having been with Zia on the day of his death, had not been with him at the precise moment he was assassinated. Rumours spread that Beg had turned down a last-minute invitation from Zia to join him on board, but in the panicked hours that followed the assassination such questions were buried: the army's need to demonstrate continuity of command meant that there was no challenge to Beg taking over. He would work alongside the director general of the ISI, General Hamid Gul. Both Beg and Gul were Islamists who saw the world through a prism of Muslim victimhood. Gul would later become a highly articulate champion of the Taliban and almost certainly had a role in the concealment of Osama bin Laden in Pakistan for so many years after 9/11.[1] General Beg, among many other eccentric positions he adopted in retirement, went on to express strong support for Somali pirates and North Korea's murderous regime – and both for the same reason: they were being confronted by the Americans.[2]

The constitution provided for the acting chairman of the senate, the seventy-three-year-old Ghulam Ishaq Khan, to take over as interim president. Whether or not that would happen depended on the army deciding if it wanted another period of martial law. If he were to govern, Ghulam Ishaq would need a period of civilian rule, and with that in mind, he made a point of going to GHQ to pay obeisance to the army command. Ghulam Ishaq had started out as a mid-ranking civil servant in the NWFP administration, rising to the federal-level bureaucracy in the 1950s. By 1966 he had become the top civil servant in the Ministry of Finance and after that, under Zulfikar, he ran the State Bank.

He was subsequently made secretary general at the Ministry of Defence, which brought him into frequent contact with Zia. He held various posts under the martial law regime and was seen as Zia's key economic policymaker before being elected to the senate. Ghulam Ishaq had resented Zia putting him in the senate, as he considered it a largely ceremonial job.[3] But in fact it was his springboard to real power, and he went on to become a key figure in Pakistan's political development, and in particular its nuclear programme.

The new triumvirate, Ghulam Ishaq, Beg and Gul, were typical Zia acolytes who combined Islamism, nationalism, contempt for the West and disdain for politicians. But on that last point they had to compromise. On 2 October 1988 the Supreme Court ruled that, contrary to what Zia had been planning before his death, political parties could participate in the forthcoming elections. Benazir, fearing that the army might extend martial law, was pleased to participate. In an interview some months later, her brother Murtaza, who was in London, said: 'The PPP had been out in the cold for 10 years and Benazir was afraid that if the army launched another coup, we would be out for 10 more'.[4] But Beg's promise of fair elections was false: during the campaign, thousands of air-dropped leaflets showed doctored photographs of Benazir dancing in a Paris nightclub and her mother, in a sequined Western evening gown, waltzing at the White House with President Gerald Ford. 'Anti-Islamic' was scrawled across the leaflets in thick lettering.[5]

As the election campaign got underway, Beg and his colleagues bolstered the opposition. The new ISI chief, Hamid Gul, assembled an opposition alliance – the Islami Jamhoori Ittehad (IJI) – made up of small religious parties together with the Muslim League and Jamaat-e-Islami. The election contest narrowed to a two-horse race, with the establishment openly helping the IJI. There were many examples of interference in the process, but perhaps the most egregious was a requirement that voters present ID cards at polling stations. As everyone knew, many potential PPP voters in rural areas didn't have ID cards. Benazir not unreasonably complained: while Zia had tried to disqualify candidates, his successors were disqualifying voters. Despite many such provocations, Benazir reached out to the military. She tried to reassure them that she would look after their interests. She had long realised the importance of not alienating the army; while she had often accused Zia of being a tyrannical usurper and murderer, she had always taken care not to extend such rhetoric to the entire military. Before the vote Benazir praised the army's decision to allow elections and insisted it was only the 'dregs of the Zia regime' who would try to disrupt the return to democracy.[6] In private, though, it was a different story. In July 1989 she told her British counterpart Margaret Thatcher that many in the army would take back control of the government 'at the drop of a hat'.[7] Indeed, some PPP insiders worried about how far she was prepared to go to appease the army. One of her close advisers, Iqbal Akhund, had recorded his surprise when in 1988, before Zia was killed, Benazir even implied she might work with the dictator. The issue had come up when he raised the question of what she would do after the elections that Zia was planning. At the time few had asked this question. Zia had said political parties would not be allowed to participate in the elections, and although the PPP had started legal proceedings to challenge that, little thought had been given to the implications of the ban being reversed. Akhund asked what would happen if parties could take part, she won and Zia was forced to ask her to become prime minister. Would she take the oath of office from the man she considered her father's murderer? Benazir's less-than-direct reply was that Zia would not be allowed to stay on as army chief. It was far more equivocal than Akhund had expected, as it left open the possibility that she would indeed consider being prime minister under or at least alongside President Zia.[8] According to one of Murtaza's activists, Benazir had decided as early as 1986 that she would be prepared to work under Zia – something she told her brother as he accompanied her to Heathrow airport on the day she flew out to her massive reception in Lahore. The siblings had an argument about the issue, which was left unresolved.[9]

Her pragmatism went far further than many of her supporters would have expected or, in some cases, accepted. And while Benazir was contemplating what she might need to do to win power, many army officers were wondering whether she would emulate her father's compulsion to settle scores. Was her statement 'democracy is the greatest revenge' just a slogan or did she really believe it? Everyone was trying to work out how she would handle power. The US ambassador at the time of Benazir's first government, Robert Oakley, worked with her closely and believed she had inherited some of her father's authoritarian traits, born, he believed, of her sense of insecurity. 'She was also very vengeful,' he said. 'She always referred to actual or perceived damage that had been done to her, her family, her father, her followers. She used that as a rationale for taking action against her enemies.'[10] But, as her willingness to contemplate compromises with Zia demonstrated, what the ambassador missed was that even if she complained about her family's suffering, that didn't mean she was necessarily going to act on it – especially if doing so could jeopardise her getting into power. Although she sought political advantage by citing slights against her and the PPP, she was never as vengeful as her father.

When the election results came in, the PPP emerged as the party with the most votes but without an overall majority: 38.5 per cent of the national vote gave it 93 of the 207 directly contested seats in the National Assembly. The IJI won 30.1 per cent of the votes, and just fifty-five seats. The third largest party was the MQM, which represented the families that had moved to Pakistan from India at the time of partition. It won thirteen seats. The PPP victory rested on its solid base in Sindh, and in Punjab it was level pegging with the IJI: both won 40 per cent of the vote there. The provincial elections held on 19 November produced PPP-led administrations in Sindh, Balochistan and NWFP. But in Punjab, the IJI prevailed and Nawaz Sharif, once again, became chief minister. As she contemplated the results, Benazir, imbued with the sense of martyrdom and grievance that pervades PPP politics, readied herself to address the press and complain about rigging. Her old Harvard friend Peter Galbraith, who was with her at the time, suggested a subtler strategy: she should not complain about the result but rather proclaim it as a victory. She did so, and as a result all over the world she was declared the winner of the election, increasing the pressure on the regime to accept her as prime minister. Even so, it was a result the establishment could work with, and Ghulam Ishaq set about trying to weaken her. First, he championed the idea of a broad PPP–IJI alliance. Calculating that she did not have to give that much ground, Benazir turned the idea down, all the while complaining that PPP National Assembly members and independents were being advised by senior military figures to desert her.[11] Some in the PPP thought Benazir should go into opposition and await developments. But she never saw it like that. She argued that after eleven years of martial law PPP supporters desperately needed relief in the form of a friendly government that would reward their loyalty – otherwise the PPP could decline into irrelevance.

Eventually she broke the deadlock by visiting the MQM leader, Altaf Hussain, in his residence in Karachi. And in a sign that she was not governing alone, she took her new husband, Asif Zardari, with her. The meeting with the MQM was also notable as a moment which revealed the fluidity of Pakistani politics. The party had arisen out of Mohajir grievances about Zulfikar's policies on Sindh national issues and had been created in large part to oppose the PPP. But the two parties now shared an interest: together they could win power, and they quickly did a deal consisting of fifty-nine specific points, including detailed pledges such as commitments to provide the Mohajir-dominated city of Hyderabad with more PIA flights and to keep the cost of postage stamps to India down.[12]

With the MQM's thirteen votes, and those of some independents, Benazir could command a National Assembly majority, and the president had no choice but to invite her to form a government. At a dinner meeting with Beg – with Asif Zardari again present – the army chief expressed concern that she might change Afghan and Kashmir policy. He also raised the question of her brother's involvement in Al Zulfikar. In response Benazir offered assurances that key areas of foreign policy decision-making would remain with the army and that there would be no cuts in the military budget.[13] Ghulam Ishaq secured other concessions, such as the appointment of Yaqub Khan, an establishment, non-PPP politician, as foreign minister and securing for himself Benazir's agreement that he would be the permanent rather than interim president. Since the president would be elected by the members of the new national and provincial assemblies, it was a decision over which she would have considerable influence. In a sign of her nervousness that power would be denied her, but also because the PPP lacked the strength to force through its own candidate, she reluctantly agreed. It was no small matter: Zia's Eighth Amendment to the 1973 constitution enabled the president to dismiss the prime minister and make senior appointments in all branches of the state, including the provincial administrations and judiciary. Later in her political career Benazir would probably not have given so much ground and would have waited him out: Ghulam Ishaq would have had no choice but to let her become prime minister on her terms. But she was in a hurry. And she worried that some of the 'electables' to whom she had given PPP tickets – including some who had served under Zia – could switch sides once again. 'I was called very reluctantly,' Benazir later wrote. 'They tried to make a deal with everyone under the sun. None of them had the number. We had the magic number and they were unable to make a deal. And when they were unable to make a deal, I was invited.'[14] On 1 December 1988, less than a decade after her father's hanging, Benazir won back the post he had held.

At the age of just thirty-five she had become the first female prime minister of a Muslim-majority country. And that fact irked some of her opponents. When she had returned to Pakistan in 1986, the Jamaat-e-Islami leader, Qazi Hussain Ahmed, said that the West would love to see a Westernised girl such as Benazir come to power. He complained that she wore Western clothes and was a standard-bearer of Western civilisation.[15] Now she was in power, the attacks intensified. Within days of her becoming prime minister, a Saudi cleric declared that no Muslim country should have a female leader and that if it did, it was doomed to fail. 'They issued *fatwas* that I must be stopped,' Benazir later recalled, 'and they circulated pamphlets saying that the Holy Prophet was weeping tears of blood.' Moves were made to take the issue to the Organisation of the Islamic Conference with a view to securing a declaration that Pakistan was in breach of religious tenets and should be expelled.[16] She later said: 'pamphlets were distributed claiming it was the religious duty of the country to assassinate me as I was a woman who had usurped a man's place in an Islamic society'.[17] In one piece of Bhutto-related literature, the Indian politician, lawyer and writer Rafiq Zakaria tested the arguments by writing an imaginary courtroom drama pitting Benazir against some of the great Islamic scholars from through the ages.[18] The arguments used by Zakaria's learned clerical critics included the idea that a woman's role was to look after the family and that, since a woman should be subordinate to a man, one could not be prime minister. Zakaria's clerics also railed against Benazir's lifestyle: having initially been led astray by a Christian nanny, she cut her hair short, used cosmetics, mixed freely with men, had not performed hajj, wore Western clothes and had behaved in an unspeakably immoral way at Harvard and Oxford. In the military and bureaucracy, too, there were deeply ingrained sexist attitudes. The issue of pregnancy was repeatedly used to argue that she could not hold high office. In fact, Benazir believed that the date of the 1988 election had been chosen to coincide with the expected birth date of her first child. In the event, Bilawal was premature and, after a short rest, Benazir was free to get back on to the campaign trail. The issue arose again with her second pregnancy, which came during her first term in office. Giving birth to her second child while being prime minister was very likely to lead to significant difficulties with senior officials, who would argue that she could not perform her duties at such a time. Her solution was to have a caesarean section earlier than anyone was expecting. After some cloak-and-dagger manoeuvres to get her into the hospital unnoticed, she delivered Bakhtawar before the opposition even knew what was happening. By the time they did she was back at her desk.[19]

Benazir credited her father, not her mother, with her views on gender equality. While her mother might have been 'the first woman in Karachi to own a car and to drive', Nusrat had also complained that Zulfikar was ruining his daughter's chances in life by encouraging her to be so independent: 'When I look back on it,' Benazir later recalled, 'it was my mother who taught that a woman grew up to be married and to have children and she would tell my father in front of me, "Why do you want to educate her? No man will want to marry her."' In reply her father said, 'Boys and girls are equal. I want my daughter to have the same opportunities.'[20] There were limits to Benazir's feminism: rather than insisting on strict gender equality, she held that female leaders were more generous, flexible and forgiving than men. But she also believed that she had to show she was as good as a man. 'I adopted a very aggressive stance. I thought I had to prove that I was as tough as a man because I was in a man's world.'[21] And she believed Pakistani men opposed not only her but also her husband. 'As men in traditional homes dictate the way their women folk should behave, I believe there is male rage against my husband directed at him not keeping me at home'.[22] Seeking to overcome these prejudices, she took practical steps to counter criticisms as they arose. She arranged an early trip to the holy sites in Saudi Arabia and managed to persuade the king to drop his normal practice of not meeting senior politicians visiting Saudi Arabia on pilgrimage. He received her in her official capacity of head of the Pakistani government. Benazir also formulated a range of arguments she could use to answer her male critics. Generally, these were couched not in terms of Western liberal thought but rather with reference to religious arguments. 'Sovereignty belongs to God,' she said, 'men and women are his trustees. The trustees vote for a government. Therefore, as the trustees have voted for a government, that government has come into being by the will of Allah as the expression of his sovereignty. So, it is Islamic to have a government led by a woman.'[23] And on another occasion, she argued: 'The Holy Book of all the

Muslims refers to the rule of a woman, the Queen of Sabah . . . The Holy Book alludes to her wisdom, and to her country being a land of plenty.'[24] For many Pakistanis used to a decade of conservative Islamism under General Zia, these were shocking statements suggesting that Pakistan could be on a new path, a development many opposed.

When it came to policy, Benazir wanted to act on issues of direct relevance to women. Her manifesto contained pledges to sign the UN Convention on the Elimination of All Forms of Discrimination against Women (CEDAW), to repeal all discriminatory laws against women and to introduce special measures to promote the literacy of women. In March 1988 as she campaigned for power, she issued a statement on International Women's Day that gave a bleak assessment of the situation of women in Pakistan. Pakistan, she wrote, was a patriarchal society to the point of caricature, and women, often treated like cattle, were in a state of dependence, unable to take decisions for themselves. The fact that the PPP was led by women, she argued, demonstrated that it was setting a good example.[25] Against that, however, the PPP's 1988 slate of candidates for the National Assembly included just three women: Benazir, her mother Nusrat and one other.[26] And once Benazir got into office, there were more mixed signals. Even when the cabinet was expanded in March 1989 to include a new women's minister, there were just five female ministers out of a total of forty-three. The key issue, though, was whether Benazir would keep her promise to repeal the various Zia-era laws that put women in an inferior position in the legal system. Initially Benazir enjoyed the support of Western women's groups, who saw her electoral victory as a sign that their cause was prevailing. But within a few months, the same groups were criticising her lack of action. In May 1989 the Women's Action Forum, a group that had earned great credibility for opposing the Zia regime's attitude to women, complained that she had not taken steps to repeal the Hudood Ordinances, which, among other things, stated that the testimony of a woman was worth less than that of a man, and which failed to draw a distinction between adultery and rape.[27] Benazir's critics argued that she should have given the issue higher priority, although most accepted that repealing the measures needed a two-thirds majority in parliament and that she could not muster the necessary numbers.[28]

During her second government, Benazir led a delegation to the United Nations Development Programme (UNDP)'s Population and Development

Conference in Cairo, thereby alienating a significant number of clerics who had long held that the UN's support of birth control was part of an international plot to reduce the number of Muslims. With those objections in mind, Benazir pitched her speech in Islamic terms, saying that her faith led her to oppose abortion on the grounds that Allah would provide for however many children a woman gave birth to.[29] While she did sometimes make tactical retreats of this kind, there were also occasions on which she spoke her mind about clerical conservatism on gender issues. In August 1995 at a meeting in Islamabad of female Muslim parliamentarians from thirty-five countries, she said: 'Many of us face challenges from obscurantist groups, which declare that women should not leave their home. Such views are a direct contradiction to the message of liberation contained in Islam'.[30] The Islamabad Declaration that was issued at the end of the meeting demanded an end to discriminatory legislation and insisted that those who used Islam to justify discrimination against women were misusing their faith. It was a line of argument Benazir used many times subsequently. A month later she spoke in Beijing, explaining her commitment to the issue: 'As the first woman ever elected to head an Islamic nation, I feel a special responsibility towards women's issues and towards all women.'[31]

But as she settled into office these were battles to come, and, looking at the broad sweep of policy, there were many other issues to worry about. Her government's first announcements suggested real change was coming: thousands of political prisoners were released, Zia's system of parallel military-run special courts was dismantled, trade unions were legally acknowledged and the media were no longer censored. All of the Zia-era laws and regulations would be reviewed to see that they were compatible with the constitution and democratic practices. But while Benazir could make these announcements, actually governing was a different matter. A civil servant working in the prime minister's office, Shafqat Mahmood, who later went on to have a long ministerial career, recalls that Benazir was working in a siege atmosphere, surrounded by Zia remnants who feared a stable PPP government would act against them. 'In one of my first meetings with Benazir as joint secretary there were just two of us. She turned on the radio and then she pointed to the ceiling. She was saying the room was bugged.'[32] That was the least of it. 'For three days not a single file arrived at my desk,' she later wrote. 'It was because he [the president] had ordered all the files to go to him.' Ghulam Ishaq only let her see material when she threatened to go public about his being so obstructive.[33] Similarly, the foreign ministry failed to pass on invitations for foreign visits. 'Countries such as Germany and Turkey were sending messages trying to get her to visit. But the foreign ministry never passed on the message. They were cutting her out all the time. I remember two of the ambassadors went to Dr. Niyazi [her dentist] to say they didn't think their messages were getting through.'[34] Faced with bureaucrats trying to thwart her, Benazir might have taken her case direct to the people, but again she opted for conciliation, not confrontation. 'We are moving very cautiously', she told the *Washington Post*, 'so as to not ruffle feathers, to permit people to get to know us.'[35]

Nevertheless, Benazir wanted to appoint more sympathetic individuals to the top posts. She thought that, having given him a clear commitment about his remaining in office, Beg was, for the moment anyway, untouchable. But she had made no promises to Gul, and she had every reason to see him as a threat. Not only was his religious and political outlook antithetical to her own, he had also played a key role in assembling the IJI coalition. During the campaign he had also convened meetings of senior military leaders to discuss how to frustrate the PPP. His efforts were thwarted in part because many of his colleagues refused to believe his intelligence that the PPP was doing well: many officers, blinded by their own view of the world, could not believe that the IJI would not win.[36] As long as General Hamid Gul remained in charge of the ISI, Benazir could not feel safe. Aware that removing Gul would be seen as an affront to the military as a whole, she moved slowly, establishing a commission headed by a sympathiser, retired Air Marshal Zulfiqar Ali Khan, to review the role and relationship between the government and the intelligence agencies. It was obviously all about General Gul, but, in a somewhat futile attempt to deflect potential objections, she instructed the review to consider the civilian-run Intelligence Bureau and other agencies too. The commission duly reported that the ISI, while competent in many respects, was too prone to meddle in domestic politics, and it recommended top-level changes. By May Benazir was ready to strike, and, overriding Beg's objections, she used the failure of an ISI-backed mujahideen effort to take the Afghan city of Jalalabad as a pretext for firing Gul. Even then, rather than humiliate him, she gave him a soft landing in the form of the corps command in Multan. In an attempt to weaken the hold of Zia loyalists, she also used the committee's findings to secure the retirement of forty senior officers – most of them brigadiers – who had passed retirement age anyway, and she ordered the ISI to stop conducting political surveillance and instead concentrate on counter-intelligence and military-related security affairs.[37] For many in the army, these decisions were an unwelcome indication that the new prime minister was not prepared to keep her promise to let them run their own affairs. A more experienced politician would have replaced Gul with a senior, well-regarded officer, thereby undermining the unity of the army leadership's opposition to the sacking. Instead, disregarding the three names suggested by Beg, she appointed a retired officer, Lieutenant General Shamsur Rehman Kallu, who, because he had already left the army, did not have a support base among serving officers. Since most ISI officers were from the army, they looked to please General Beg: Kallu soon found himself ostracised as the army leadership simply ignored him and worked through his deputy, who was their own appointee.

The relationship between the army chief and prime minister had got off to a difficult start, and it would deteriorate still further. She didn't help her cause by being so ignorant of Pakistani power structures. General Asad Durrani has recorded how she mistook the name of the organisation he ran, Military Intelligence. Despite its being one of the most powerful agencies in the country, he had to correct her when she referred to it as 'M-one' rather than by its commonly used acronym, the letters 'MI'.[38] She could also be petty. Her decision, for example, to cut Ghulam Ishaq's hospitality allowance was never going to achieve anything other than irritate him. Other rows were more substantial but equally futile. For example, she tried to assert a right to appoint the chairman of the joint chiefs of staff committee. The incumbent was Admiral Iftikhar Ahmed Sirohi. Benazir wanted to retire him and to 'promote' Beg to the largely ceremonial slot. President Ghulam Ishaq pointed out that the Zia amendments to the 1973 constitution meant he had the right to make such appointments, and he insisted that Sirohi would stay in for another two years. It was an argument that she was bound to lose and that once again revealed her inexperience: she wasn't picking her battles well. Next, Benazir tried to extend the term of the Lahore corps commander, Lieutenant General Allam Jan Mehsud. But the system again pushed back, disregarding her wishes. Benazir made little secret about what she was up against. Asked whether she could exercise her power to cut defence expenditure, she replied: 'Surely . . . if you want to invite martial law.'[39]

Benazir also faced opposition in Punjab. Nawaz Sharif had only gone into politics because his father had wanted to protect his business interests by placing a family member in a position with political influence, thereby accidently launching one of the most successful political careers in Pakistan's history. His three terms in power would eventually teach Nawaz Sharif, as Benazir and Zulfikar had learnt before him, that it is virtually impossible for a civilian politician to overcome the military's desire for control. But at this stage of his career, he was everything the military wanted: conservative, biddable and hostile to the Bhuttos. Hitherto in Pakistan, the conflict between the central and the provincial power hubs had taken the form of the weaker provinces resisting Punjabi domination. But during Benazir's government it was different: Punjab had lost control of the central government and took on the role of victim. The struggle between Lahore and Islamabad was to be prolonged, bitter and at times petty. The PPP complained that Nawaz Sharif was fanning the flames of Punjabi nationalism, and, as chief minister, he did indeed launch a Punjabi TV and radio station and found a Punjabi bank. He also rejected appointments in Punjab made by the federal government. For her part, Benazir devoted much of her political capital to trying to dominate Punjab, with the result that officials in the province found themselves having to pick sides – they could be loyal to the Punjabi authorities or to the federal government but not both. Some of her efforts were vindictive and unproductive. Pakistan Railways, for example, said it was unable to shift scrap iron from the port in Karachi to the factories of the Sharif family's Ittefaq group in Lahore.[40] And for all her complaints that the IJI tried to bribe her supporters into switching sides, she tried exactly the same with IJI provincial assembly members. But if it came down to a graft contest, the inexperienced Benazir was no match for Punjab's grizzled political operatives.

The wrangling with the army and Punjab sometimes involved disputes over policy, not least when it came to the relationship with India. Rajiv Gandhi, the grandson of Nehru and son of Indira Gandhi, made his first trip to Islamabad – to attend a South Asian Association for Regional Cooperation (SAARC) summit – shortly after Benazir formed her government. The two leaders were both young – Rajiv forty-four and Benazir thirty-five – and Western-educated, and they carried with them the hope that they could leave the past behind and instead look ahead. In both countries people wondered: could these two political aristocrats see the bigger picture and forge a new future? The summit made the Pakistani establishment, and its counterpart in India, nervous. In her keynote address Benazir said that military expenditure was out of control and that the focus instead should be on poverty alleviation: 'our people face the same common problems of poverty, disease, slums and ignorance and it is for the vanquishing of these enemies that we should direct all our efforts',[41] she said. It was tentative and vague, but it was an attempt to push back. The sense of new possibilities was enhanced when the two leaders agreed to meet again in Islamabad a few months later, in July. Speaking at a banquet at that second meeting, Rajiv Gandhi said India and Pakistan should seek peaceful coexistence. Benazir responded in kind: both countries had the same aspirations and should agree to arms control. When Gandhi met the president the atmosphere was, inevitably, less positive, with Ghulam Ishaq saying that if India wanted to dispel the impression that it wanted to impose its hegemony over the region it would need to put confidence-building measures in place.

While the young politicians wanted to move things forward, the security establishments on both sides could see that their fears of real change had been exaggerated. The politicians were weaker than they seemed. Benazir and Rajiv could talk for as long as they pleased about arms control, but it was never going to happen without army agreement. Meanwhile, unbeknown to either leader, the ISI had launched a Kashmir insurgency that would last a decade, without, Benazir later insisted, having consulted her first.[42] Taking a broad view, the hawks in both countries concluded that they could relax: the two young leaders had not been able to break out of the constraints the securocrats imposed on them. Nevertheless, the army was concerned about Benazir's policy towards Afghanistan. In line with the US, she favoured trying to find a political settlement through negotiations between the various Afghan armed factions. In particular, she sympathised with Washington's view that the murderous Islamist, Gulbuddin Hekmatyar, should be frustrated in his desire to conquer Kabul and form a government there. The difficulty was that, throughout the anti-Soviet struggle, Hekmatyar had been an ISI-funded Pakistani proxy. Why on earth, the generals wondered, would Benazir want to alienate a Pakistani asset just at the moment he was about to deliver the influence in Afghanistan that

Islamabad had always craved? And there was more. Their suspicions that Benazir was too close to the US were bolstered when she failed to stop US officials holding direct meetings with mujahideen leaders. Despite strong US objections, Zia had always managed to prevent this, insisting that if Pakistan were to be used as a channel for US military supplies it would have complete control of communications with Islamist commanders. Under Benazir, that degree of control had been lost.

The differences between the government and the military spilled over into the National Assembly, where the opposition planned a no-confidence vote for October 1989. The military's first step was to persuade the MQM to switch sides, which it did just a few weeks before the vote. The PML leader Chaudri Nisar was reported as saying that it was army chief Aslam Beg who delivered these MQM votes to Nawaz Sharif.[43] But the MQM leader Altaf Hussain was no longer as important as he used to be. Since the PPP had used its powers of patronage to win over more independent National Assembly members, even with the MQM, the IJI still needed some PPP defectors. In October the Intelligence Bureau, which owed its loyalty to the government, not the military, became aware that senior serving military officers were meeting with the IJI leadership. In a sting that became known as Operation MIDNIGHT JACKAL, it revealed a conspiracy in which one serving and one retired ISI officer attempted to bribe some PPP National Assembly members to switch sides. The Intelligence Bureau managed to record audio and video footage of the secret meetings. According to Benazir, the ISI officer was taped saying 'The army does not want her, the President does not want her and the Americans don't want her.' Believing the officer should be tried for treason, she gave the tape to Beg who decided instead to dismiss him.[44] Although at the time it was never fully established who had ordered the officers to manipulate the National Assembly in this way, Benazir claimed Osama bin Laden financed the attempt to unseat her. She believed that Nawaz Sharif and a corps commander met with bin Laden, who at the time was known as a wealthy supporter of the anti-Soviet struggle in Afghanistan, and persuaded him to contribute $10 million to finance the no-confidence move against her.[45] Nawaz Sharif has always denied wrongdoing but Benazir was sufficiently convinced of bin Laden's relationship with him that she called King Fahd of Saudi Arabia and asked him to recall 'his man'. Failure to do so, she threatened, would lead to speculation in the Pakistani press about Saudi Arabia using bin Laden to interfere in Pakistan's internal affairs.[46] King Fahd responded saying that the Saudi government was not involved and that it was the act of a private citizen.[47] In 2006 the leader of Jamaat-e-Islami, Qazi Hussain Ahmed, appeared to confirm the story, claiming that he had been aware of bin Laden's willingness to use his money to install Nawaz Sharif as prime minister in Bhutto's place.[48] And then, in 2009, one of the conspirators was reported as confirming what had been rumoured: they had acted on the orders of the army chief.[49] Aslam Beg has always denied any involvement. While Operation MIDNIGHT JACKAL made for some salacious stories in the press, it also had a much more significant long-lasting impact. Having seen politics close up when her father was in power, Benazir had long been aware that money played a part in Pakistani politics. But now it could not have been clearer: if one of her National Assembly members was being offered a bribe to switch to the opposition, she needed to be able to match it.

Accounts of Benazir's first government have tended to explain her deteriorating relationship with the army and the establishment as having been the result of such issues as historic distrust going back to her father's time, the struggles over appointments, Punjabi nationalism, concern about her foreign policy, and army-led efforts to manipulate the National Assembly. Two other sources of tension have received relatively little attention, in part because they were so shrouded in secrecy. But on both the nuclear issue and Pakistan's burgeoning heroin trade, Benazir ran into significant problems with the military. Ever since 1947, drug production in both Pakistan and Afghanistan had been increasing. The decisions of Iran and Turkey to ban production meant Afghan farmers could supply increasing numbers of users. Then, during the anti-Soviet struggle, the Pakistan-backed mujahideen used the trade to finance their operations. 'We must grow and sell opium to fight our holy war against the Russian non-believers,' one farmer told the New York Times in 1986.[50] US officials could see the advantage of this, and, in retirement, the US ambassador Robert Oakley was open about the CIA's role. 'I could not get it to report on the narcotics traffic in Afghanistan . . . I suspect that the Pakistani intelligence services may have been involved and that the CIA was not going to rock their relationships over this issue.'[51]

By reverse engineering the US arms supply lines into Afghanistan, the drugs syndicates could move significant quantities of heroin to the West.[52]

Containers that went into Afghanistan filled with arms came back full of drugs. Tests undertaken in the US and the UK indicated that 90 per cent of the heroin entering Europe and 60 per cent going to the US originated from Afghanistan and Pakistan.[53] The profits were enormous. In the mid-1980s the Pakistani press started carrying stories about the Pakistan Army's National Logistics Cell (NLC) moving drugs out of Afghanistan. 'The drug is carried in NLC trucks,' one Pakistani news magazine reported in 1985. 'This has been going on now for about three and a half years.' Customs officials in Karachi who demanded they should be allowed to search NLC trucks were told to back off or face being transferred.[54] From the Islamists' perspective there was no downside: the mujahideen got funds for arms, the middlemen made huge profits and the infidel Americans got higher rates of addiction. But the scale of the drug industry made some worry that Pakistan was headed in the same direction as Colombia and could become a full-blown narco-state. But then the geopolitics changed. Having defeated the Soviet Union in Afghanistan, and with violent jihadism not yet a threat to the West, limiting the drug trade became the highest priority in Washington's South Asia policy and there were hopes in the US that Benazir would act on the issue. Unaware of just how powerful the syndicates were, she saw no reason not to offer Washington full cooperation. After all, domestic drug use was a major issue and the drugs trade was, along with the much-discussed 'Kalashnikov culture', holding back the development of a progressive Pakistan. As she saw it, her country's interests and those of the US were aligned on the issue.

Benazir took action as soon as she got into power, teaming up with the US Drugs Enforcement Agency to organise a four-day seminar in Islamabad. In January 1989 she ensured that the joint communique issued after the Islamabad SAARC summit included a commitment to work on stronger anti-trafficking laws and better sharing of intelligence information.[55] Next, she announced the establishment of a separate narcotics ministry complete with a 500-strong elite force under the Pakistan Narcotics Control Board. When she visited Washington in June 1989, she said she would discuss 'economic and military aid and the question of narcotics control, which is an urgent issue on our list of priorities'.[56]

What she seems not to have appreciated was the level of military involvement in the drug trade dating back to Zia's time in power. After arresting a Pakistani trafficker at Oslo airport in December 1983, Norway had followed up by formally requesting three named men. The difficulty was that when one of them, Hamid Hasnain, was arrested, it turned out he had General Zia's personal banking records in his briefcase. When Zia called in senior police officers to explain themselves, they insisted that a formal Norwegian request for arrests could not be ignored.[57] Rumours circulated that Hasnain was 'like a son to General Zia', a claim rejected by Zia's real son Ejaz ul-Haq. Evidence at the trial of a trafficker in the US revealed that 'certain Pakistani military units' could help move drugs through customs and out of the country.[58] Other cases also involved the military. In 1986 a major who was driving from Peshawar to Karachi was found with 220 kilos of heroin. Two months later an air force lieutenant was caught with the same quantity. These were massive amounts worth billions of rupees, and yet both men 'escaped' from custody.[59] Money on that scale was inevitably going to feed into the political system, and, speaking after the fall of her daughter's government, Nusrat Bhutto said the timing of Benazir's dismissal had been motivated by fear of an imminent series of arrests of prominent persons for drug running.[60] Benazir's failure to dismantle the drug cartels meant that her successor, Nawaz Sharif, was to face many of the same problems. In an extraordinary *Washington Post* interview after he too had been removed from power, Nawaz Sharif claimed that three months after his becoming prime minister, General Beg and General Durrani, who had moved on from MI to the ISI, both suggested raising money for covert operations through drug sales. 'General Durrani told me, "We have a blueprint ready for your approval",' said Sharif, who turned down the idea. Both Beg and Durrani denied the allegation, and Sharif tried to retract it.[61]

The drug traffickers and their deep-state backers were a formidable opponent. But the greatest of all Benazir's enemies were those involved in building Pakistan's nuclear bomb. As we have seen, Zulfikar had taken the decision that Pakistan should acquire nuclear capability, and without his determined attitude on the issue, the Pakistani programme would almost certainly have never got started. To give Pakistan a greater chance of success, Zulfikar had created two parallel programmes, one run by the Pakistan Atomic Energy Commission (PAEC), which relied on plutonium technology, and the other, using uranium enrichment, run by A.Q. Khan. By the time Zulfikar was hanged, work was well underway, and it fell to General Zia to maintain the momentum by providing the required resources.

For Pakistan's nationalists there were many arguments in favour of going nuclear. First, there was a straightforward deterrence argument. By conducting a successful test in 1974, India had shown that it was a nuclear power. Pakistani strategists in Rawalpindi could use precisely the same argument as the Western powers did in relation to the Soviets: the best way to prevent nuclear conflict was to deter it. But there was more to it than that. After the humiliation of losing East Pakistan and the failure to force any movement on the Kashmir dispute, Pakistan's sense of weakness vis-à-vis India was acute. Building a nuclear bomb worked at every level: it showed India that Pakistan remained a serious rival while also compensating Pakistan for its inevitably having a smaller army than India: the threat of an Indian invasion was diminished if Delhi faced the prospect of any conventional aggression being met by a nuclear response. It also gave Pakistan a claim to be the leader of the Muslim world, not just in ideological terms but in the technological sphere too. And there was also a measure of postcolonial reckoning: what better riposte to Western arrogance than to master its most advanced and powerful technology?

In general terms, Benazir always wanted to build on her father's achievements, and the bomb was a crucial element of his legacy. But many within the Pakistani establishment, and some in US intelligence circles too, wondered whether, in the course of her education in the US and the UK, the liberal values she picked up included some sympathy for the anti-nuclear movement. The nuclear issue had come up during the election campaign, with the IJI arguing that Benazir would give in to US pressure and stop the nuclear programme.[62] General Gul and his ISI officers briefed sympathetic journalists that the ISI had gathered intelligence that Benazir had promised the Americans that she would roll back the nuclear programme.[63] And there is good reason to think the ISI was right. Her old friend Peter Galbraith had tested the waters when he was with her in Larkana as news of her 1988 election victory came in. 'We thought she was persuadable on nuclear issues,' he later recalled, 'she was amenable'. He was leaving for Delhi a few days after the election, and, offering to take a letter to her counterpart Rajiv Gandhi, he started drafting a handwritten letter to him. Sitting next to her as he wrote, he began with some lines about improving relations, strengthening democracy and her need and desire to control the military, which would be made easier if she had good relations with India. He then included a paragraph on the nuclear programme, saying she did not want either country to have nuclear weapons and that Pakistan would not go ahead with nuclear weapons. When Benazir copied out the draft in her own hand she used all of it except the paragraph relating to the nuclear issue. 'Should I convey that orally?' Galbraith asked. She agreed.[64] A record of a 1989 meeting with Margaret Thatcher gives a hint of a back-room deal: Thatcher stressed 'the importance of limiting Pakistan's nuclear programme to peaceful uses' and said that 'she knew that Miss Bhutto had given certain assurances to the Americans [and that] it was very important that these should be honoured or US aid would be cut off'.[65] In her first news conference after being sworn in as prime minister, Benazir said that she was committed to the peaceful use of nuclear technology and that Pakistan would be nuclear weapon-free. It was nothing more than the standard line that General Zia had used before her. When Zia said it, everyone knew it to be a lie. But when it came from Benazir Bhutto, generals in the Pakistan Army and diplomats in Washington all wondered if she might just mean it. That Benazir in 1988 almost certainly wished to roll back or at least pause the nuclear programme will shock many Pakistanis who today almost universally take pride in the country's nuclear status. But at the time it made sense to Benazir. As she looked to her premiership, she wanted to spend government funds on social programmes rather than defence. And there was another factor. She knew she owed her freedom in part to Peter Galbraith and the US senators he had been working for. Many of this group were also very keen on nuclear non-proliferation issues: her support for a non-nuclear-armed Pakistan was related to an important US political constituency for her.

Within weeks of Benazir becoming prime minister, General Beg emphasised that the nuclear programme was a no-go area for her. She later recalled, 'I asked the army chief and he said, "It's got nothing to do with me. It's the president"'.[66] Although Beg was being disingenuous – it obviously had something to do with him – it was true that Ghulam Ishaq had long taken a close interest in the nuclear programme. In a 2015 article praising Ishaq, A.Q. Khan wrote that the former president had been in charge of the nuclear programme for seventeen years. Counting back from the time he resigned as president, that would have meant he had started overseeing the programme as early as 1976.[67] On another occasion Khan wrote that, as president, Ghulam Ishaq visited the Kahuta uranium enrichment facility every month.[68] So, for Benazir to discuss the issue with the president made some sense. But he rebuffed her too: 'There is no need for you to know,' he said.[69] Some clerics shared the deep state's suspicion of Benazir's intentions. One of the leading religious hardliners, Sami ul-Haq, who went on later to champion both the Taliban and al-Qaeda and in 2007 hosted Benazir's assassins as they plotted to kill her, said: 'Pakistan's nuclear weapons capability simply cannot be safe under the leadership of a westernized woman,' adding that, 'she cares more about American approval than ensuring the ummah's first nuclear bomb'.[70] As for the man spearheading the nuclear weapons programme, A.Q. Khan, he was also hostile, or at least soon became so. Never one to suffer from self-doubt, he had long believed that the nuclear programme would advance more rapidly if he had complete control of it. Within days of her becoming prime minister, he reportedly approached Benazir to see if she would allow the PAEC to be brought under his command. When she turned him down, he seemed to decide he had no use for her and allied himself instead to the army chief and the president.[71]

Part of the reason the army chief, the president and A.Q. Khan were so dismissive of Benazir was because of their concerns about Pakistan's relationship with Iran. Benazir first became aware of Iranian interest in nuclear technology when she attended a conference in Tehran in the autumn of 1989. During a break in the conference, President Rafsanjani asked her to go to a quiet corner to talk about a sensitive matter. He said the two countries had reached an agreement on special defence matters and he wanted to reaffirm it. Unaware of any such arrangement, Benazir asked him: 'What exactly are you talking about, Mr. President?' President Rafsanjani replied: 'Nuclear technology, Madam Prime Minister, nuclear technology'.[72] When she returned home and asked the president and army chief what Rafsanjani had been talking about, they reportedly pretended not to know anything about it.[73] Benazir had stumbled into the opening stage of what would be the long-running saga of Pakistani nuclear proliferation.

The US had seen Benazir's election as an opportunity to advance its non-proliferation agenda. In a sign of just how much the US trusted Benazir, in June 1989 the CIA took the opportunity presented by her being on an official visit to Washington to brief her on her own nuclear programme. The session was handled by the CIA director, William H. Webster, who showed Benazir a football-shaped mock-up of a Pakistani bomb. Pakistani scientists, he said, were now able to turn uranium gas into metalised bomb-grade material, and if they did so the US would consider that Pakistan had a bomb, at which point US aid would be replaced by economic sanctions. Each year the White House had to certify that Pakistan did not have a bomb in order to avoid being obliged by law to impose sanctions. During the years of the anti-Soviet struggle the US had overlooked the issue, but now that the Russians had withdrawn from Afghanistan, there was more attention focused on exactly what point Pakistan had reached. Having established exactly where the US considered the line to be – turning the gas into metal – Benazir assured Webster it would not happen.[74] Benazir subsequently told her American lobbyist Mark Siegel that the extent of the Americans' knowledge took her by surprise. The briefing was far more detailed than any information that she, as prime minister, had been provided by her own officers: 'It also showed what the military was doing behind her back,' Siegel said.[75] And it had the desired effect. 'The message I took away,' she later said, 'was the need to wrestle back control of the programme from Khan.'[76] Jamsheed Marker, the Pakistani ambassador who had been in Paris at the time of Shahnawaz's murder and who had since moved on to the US, has implied that he was also at the briefing and complained that the Americans revealed to Benazir just as much or as little as they thought she should know. 'Webster revealed the CIA had detailed knowledge of our nuclear programme and gave a serious warning about the consequences of its continuation.'[77] No doubt the American briefings were self-serving, but Marker rather missed the point that it should have been Pakistani, not American, officials telling Benazir about Pakistan's nuclear progress. A classic elitist bureaucrat, he celebrated her being kept in the dark about the nuclear programme. 'It became clear to me (with a barely concealed sense of relief) that the Prime Minister was not fully aware of the nuances of the situation. That old Pathan tiger Ghulam Ishaq Khan, had kept it under close lock and key and was guarding the contents like the fierce watchdog he always was.'[78]

Benazir believed that, if she told the army to stop short of turning the gas into metal, she could say Pakistan had not built a bomb. The day after the Webster briefing she told the US Congress: 'I can declare that we do not possess nor do we intend to make a nuclear device. That is our policy'. It may have been her policy but the reality was in the hands of Beg and Ghulam Ishaq, and in early 1990, with Kashmir tensions rising, the army chief and the president decided to press ahead with weaponisation, a development that soon became known to US intelligence.[79] Benazir staved off US sanctions for another year. But it became increasingly clear that she would not be able to perform a similar feat again. To the army's perception that she was unreliable on the nuclear issue was added the thought that the one thing she could deliver – pre-empting nuclear-related US sanctions – was a diminishing asset.

Given that the nuclear programme was so secret, it is difficult to assess how big a factor it was in Benazir's dismissal. But speaking after the fall of her government, in a speech at the National University of Sciences and Technology, A.Q. Khan boasted that he had repeatedly asked Beg to get rid of Benazir Bhutto because she was hindering the nuclear programme.[80] It was a boast, no doubt, but probably not an entirely idle one. Benazir's situation was further complicated by the fact that the drug trade and nuclear programme did not operate completely independently. The link between the two was the notoriously corrupt Bank of Credit and Commerce International (BCCI). The driving force behind the bank was founder Aga Hassan Abedi, and early backers included the Bank of America and the president of the UAE, Sheikh Zayed.[81] Ghulam Ishaq, who at the time was heading Pakistan's State Bank, supported Abedi's proposal for the bank, thereby laying the foundations for what would become an important relationship. Abedi was aligned with the establishment and against Zulfikar. Indeed, Benazir once said that she believed Abedi conspired against her father, helping persuade Zia to go ahead with the hanging.[82] Abedi was a master of cultivating people in power, and in 1981 he offered Ghulam Ishaq chairmanship of the BCC Foundation, the bank's charitable arm. In return Ishaq gave BCCI tax-free status in Pakistan. In the course of its work the BCC Foundation funded one institution particularly generously: the Ghulam Ishaq Khan Institute of Engineering Sciences and Technology. In 1987 alone, BCC gave the institute $10 million.[83] The institute's director was none other than A.Q. Khan, who went on to use the bank to process his purchases of nuclear supplies.[84] That BCCI was viewed by the establishment as a nationally prized asset became clear to Benazir after a January 1989 meeting with Ambassador Oakley, who told her that BCCI was under investigation in the US. He asked her to rescind its operating licence.[85] Benazir agreed but soon ran into obstacles. The Americans seemed to have believed that powerful interests – including generals, a government minister and civil servants – were in the pay of BCCI and were blocking her attempts to move against the bank.[86]

Tensions between the politicians on one side and the president and military officers on the other had been there from the outset and they were getting worse. There was increasing talk that Benazir would not be allowed to remain in office. The tipping point came in February 1990, when MQM-led strikes in Karachi turned violent and Beg told Benazir that the corps commanders wanted to intervene. Highly aware of what had happened when her father had given the army free rein in Balochistan, Benazir was reluctant. But she also knew she was powerless to resist the army. 'Go ahead and do what you please,' she told Beg, 'I can't stop you.' After the exchange she discussed it with her adviser Iqbal Akhund: 'What else could I say to him?' Worse still, she said, a mere brigadier had said to her: 'Another strike like the recent one in Karachi and the army would have to move in.'[87] If a brigadier felt free to be so insolent to the elected prime minister, it couldn't be long before the army would act.

Matters came to a head in May 1990 when there were multiple deaths in Pucca Qila, a Mohajir district of Hyderabad named after an old fort there. The violence began when Sindhi police tried to recover illegal weapons held by Mohajirs. As the police approached, the MQM sent out a procession of women and children holding copies of the Koran above their heads. When the police opened fire on the column, the army, without waiting for orders from any civilian authority, intervened. Benazir's adviser Shafqat Mahmood, who was following developments closely, had no doubt – and Benazir agreed with him – that the army had intervened to protect the MQM weapons cache from being exposed.[88] Jubilant MQM celebrations followed as they rejoiced at having been saved by the army. The perception that the military was using the issue to assert itself was hardly assuaged by Beg, who, having been on a trip to Bangladesh, rushed to Hyderabad as soon as he landed, not stopping to see the prime minister. He said he needed to be with his troops. Benazir said he was acting as if he were facing a foreign invasion.[89] The sense of an irreversible decline in civil–military relations wasn't helped by the slogans Beg saw when he reached Hyderabad: 'Impose Martial Law!' they read, and 'Remove Benazir Bhutto!'

It was a mess. The Hyderabad violence soon spread to Karachi. Faced with open, running street fights in the country's commercial capital, Benazir told the police to capture those responsible for the violence. Predictably, the MQM turned to the army and, not for the first time, nor the last, the military establishment was reluctant to leave the field clear to the police, who, when they tried to make arrests, faced stiff MQM resistance.[90] Senior military officers complained that if they were called in to restore law and order they would effectively be shoring up the PPP against its political opponents: if the military was going to intervene, it would do so on its own terms. And the extent of the government's reliance on the army was striking. In 1989 the army had been called on to restore peace on 284 days out of 365.[91] Beg said he wanted to declare martial law throughout Sindh. The prime minister insisted on a limited action to restore law and order. For the army, it was the final grievance, and Benazir later said that her relations with Beg finally broke down over Pucca Qila.[92] At the corps commanders' meeting on 21 July 1990, the generals decided they could no longer accept the supremacy of the government, and the army chief conveyed their decision to the president.[93] Lacking allies in important places, Benazir, like her father before her, didn't realise what was happening.

That's not to say no one told her. An official from the Intelligence Bureau picked up on what was going on and, on the morning of her dismissal, informed her about what was to happen to her government later that day. Having heard him out, Benazir called the president and asked if he was going to dismiss her government. He denied it. Later in the day, the Intelligence Bureau official reconfirmed the facts, returned to Benazir and told her the president was lying to her. Benazir called him again and repeated her question. He denied it again, but just a few hours later Ghulam Ishaq made an address to the nation, which included his reading out twenty-three pages of allegations. The Bhutto government, he declared, had been dismissed on charges of, among many other things, corruption, inefficiency, nepotism and misconduct of power.[94] The president also dissolved the four provincial parliaments and governments. As Roedad Khan, the senior civil servant liaising between the army and the president, later recorded, Ghulam Ishaq and his team had been anxious that their plans would be disrupted: 'we were apprehending a pre-emptive move by the prime minister but with every passing day and with D-Day approaching and nothing happening, an eerie feeling gripped us all. Why was the prime minister not making any move? Was she going to spring a surprise? What if she went on air, addressed the nation and disclosed that a plan was afoot to dissolve the National Assembly and dismiss the elected government?'[95] But despite the tip-off she got from the Intelligence Bureau, Benazir did nothing.

Benazir's election had been a time of great hope. Notwithstanding the fears of army officers who worried about what the daughter of the man Zia had killed might do, many Pakistanis viewed her as young, principled, highly educated, democratic and full of promise. Twenty months later her government ended with a sense that she had failed to make the most of a great opportunity. Many believed that she was too domineering and that she failed to understand the need to encourage her supporters. As early as August 1989 an old friend of the Bhutto family, the chairman of the Foreign Relations Committee, Senator Claiborne Pell, together with US Ambassador Robert Oakley visited Benazir and her mother. The senator told them that while he hoped Benazir would enjoy many years in power, he thought she would not last as prime minister through to the end of 1989. 'He told her that compromise and consensus building were the key essences of a democratic process – not authoritarianism. Bhutto was completely stunned, knowing that the comments were coming from a friend. But she did not change her behavior.'[96] She could also be erratic. She wondered, for example, if it would be possible to reach a modus vivendi with the Punjabi chief minister Nawaz Sharif, and asked Oakley to take a message to him, saying she wanted to end the wrangling and was prepared to meet him more than halfway. A week after he delivered that message, she told Oakley that she had changed her mind and had decided that Sharif had to go and that she was determined to oust him as chief minister. 'I was flabbergasted,' Oakley later recalled. 'How could anyone send a message of reconciliation to a person one week and the next week try to eliminate him? But that was Bhutto! Unfortunately, that unpredictability was part of her modus operandi. This event was not an exception.'[97]

When Zulfikar had taken over in the wake of the 1971 defeat, the military had been caught off balance. For the first part of his government the military didn't have the self-confidence to block his attempts to set up a parallel power structure answerable to him, and he had a far better opportunity than Benazir to assert civilian control. By the mid-1970s the army had regained its balance and once again believed that it alone was capable of working for the 'national interest' and delivering the governance Pakistan needed. By the time Benazir was prime minister, the army was not just self-confident but increasingly arrogant too. Benazir realised she would have to give the army some space. If they asked, for example, for higher defence spending, she was not going to oppose them. But she could never do enough. The army's doubts about her commitment to the nuclear programme, the attempts of some officers to protect drug racketeering and the sense that only the military could maintain law and order all contributed to her removal. Some of her mistakes were perhaps inevitable for someone who had never held political office before, especially as she was operating in a system with no institutions worth speaking of. But even if Benazir could cite mitigating circumstances for her disappointing performance, that could not hide her failure to deliver the change people hoped for. And it wasn't just that she had been sinned against. As we will see, when President Ghulam Ishaq Khan complained about the corruption of Benazir's government, he had a point.

7

BENAZIR: POWER AND EXILE

Zulfikar described himself as having had two very different influences: his feudal background in Sindh and his Western education. Benazir was in a similar situation. As the Pakistani leftist Tariq Ali put it, the author of *Daughter of the East* was really a 'daughter of the West'. The historian Ian Buruma wrote that Benazir had a double life: the Larkana Bhutto and the Radcliffe Bhutto. The Larkana Bhutto used to sit in the family home in Sindh listening to her father telling stories about the family history. The Radcliffe Bhutto had got to know about apple cider and Joan Baez, gone on peace marches in Boston and owned a sports car in Oxford.[1] Buruma's analysis irked Benazir's loyalists, who saw it as overly simplistic and not without a hint of orientalism. Her national security adviser, Iqbal Akhund, wrote: 'In one respect Benazir defied orientalist stereotypes: she was no willowy, veiled seductress skilled in the ways of fascinating men. Rather she was a powerful woman who dominated those around her . . . she was imperious: when she spoke, she expected people to listen whether they be voters in a village, colleagues at the cabinet table or the rulers of foreign states.'[2] Buruma argued that *Daughter of the East* had been written to 'enchant Western readers'. In it she described her life in a way which played to Western perceptions of the East and resonated with Western mythic traditions: hers was the story of a vulnerable young woman overcoming archaic tradition and deep prejudice, surviving years of hardship and exile to avenge her father's death at the hands of a wicked, all-powerful man. But while Westerners saw a heroine, many Pakistanis, wearily familiar with their feudal masters, saw something else. By her own admission, Benazir was 'moody, impetuous, given to irritation'. In 1999 she said she had tried for twenty years to control her emotions but 'I still fly off the handle'.[3] When Westerners admired a highly educated modern champion of democracy, many Pakistani voters responded to an aristocrat tapping into ancient, ingrained patterns of authority.

If there is a common theme running through Benazir's speeches, it is her adoration of her father. 'All my life and even spiritually to this day, it was my father who guided me, who mentored me, who encouraged me, who gave me the strength and confidence to express my views. His soul and his values are alive within me, wherever I go.'[4] She could not accept he had a single fault. That was true at Harvard, when she took on professors in class, defending his record in East Pakistan with such vehemence that she would shake, and it was true in 1986 when a *New York Times* journalist wrote that 'a shadow crosses her face when she is asked about her father's record of repression, the stories of jailings and torture documented by Amnesty International and other human-rights groups. Friends say that Miss Bhutto cannot accept any criticism of her father. "You can never bring it up with her," said a senior party leader. "She won't accept it. Her demand for loyalty is total."'[5] Some have suggested that the subsequent falling out with Nusrat was an indication that she had the Electra complex, whereby a daughter competes with her mother for her father's attention, or, in the Bhuttos' case, his legacy. Piloo Mody saw the father–daughter relationship close up. Having shared formative years at school with Zulfikar, he was one of the few people who could tease him, and when he did so, he was struck by Benazir's reaction: 'she completely worships her father and thinks the world of him, and she was rather surprised to hear me talk to him in the manner in which I did, because she had never heard anyone tackle Zulfi in that fashion. But having got over the initial shock she thereafter relaxed and seemed to enjoy seeing her father's leg being mildly pulled.'[6]

Perhaps, as some of those closest to her have suggested, Benazir transferred some of her strong feelings for her father onto her husband: Asif Zardari did, after all, take on some of her father's roles, such looking after the family finances. For Benazir, having large amounts of cash to hand was both a natural state of affairs and a political necessity. If she could not buy the loyalty of her parliamentary supporters, then her opponents would. As another of her political advisers later recalled, 'Asif's role became more prominent when she beat back the motion of no confidence. There was some wheeler dealing in that. Some buying of votes. The moment money transactions came into play, Asif was in his element.'[7] Asif Zardari has consistently denied any financial malpractice.

During her second government, Benazir told an aide that you needed to have $200–300 million to go into an election so that you could fund your candidates and secure their loyalty.[8] While many of her advisers gave her plenty of interesting suggestions about what to do, Zardari actually did things, proving himself to be a man she could rely on. His ability to understand what she needed and to do it without fuss or even discussion was the foundation of their relationship. Throughout the marriage, whatever complaints she had about him – and there were many – he delivered for her, perhaps explaining why she described him as 'my lion'. The TV journalist Daphne Barak, who knew the couple, believed Benazir was 'completely and utterly in love with her husband' and always wanted to please. In turn, he was charming and chivalrous. Barak recalled telling Benazir in front of Zardari that the French politician Ségolène Royal resembled her: 'Asif responded forcefully and immediately. "Nobody is as beautiful as my wife," he said. Benazir blushed deeply. She loved him saying that.'[9] It was a relationship most outsiders could not fathom. Benazir made little secret of how her husband at times hurt her feelings. She revealed some of what she felt in a heart-to-heart with Hillary Clinton in the White House at the height of the Lewinsky scandal. 'We both know from our own lives that men can behave like alley cats and it is accepted,' she told Hillary.[10] Divorce was never a possibility, first because it would have been an admission of failure, but secondly because Benazir was too conservative to give up on the marriage. After all the years of his imprisonment they both became used to living separate lives, but for all that there was a genuine bond to the end.

As the prime minister's consort, Zardari found himself in a difficult situation. Pakistani men of his era expected to be in charge, and, more often than not, he found himself trailing in the wake of a woman who attracted adulation wherever she went. The fact that most of her posh friends looked down on him as socially inferior made it worse. During a visit to the UK in 1989 Benazir and Zardari attended a dinner party in London. As they left, she signed the hosts' visitors book: 'Benazir Bhutto, Prime Minister of the Islamic Republic of Pakistan, Government House, Islamabad'. He wrote: 'Asif Zardari, a nobody'.[11] He knew his place. When Benazir became prime minister, the newly married couple moved into a government building near the parliament called Sindh House and she worked in the prime minister's secretariat. Zardari also started working from an office in the secretariat. When officials asked Benazir what to do about the large numbers of people thronging into his office, she told them that their job was to keep him happy.[12] In the early years of her time in power she thought she had enough to cope with and wanted to avoid picking fights with her assertive husband too. But senior PPP colleagues did not see it like that and insisted he should conduct his business elsewhere. Frustrated and refusing to back down, Zardari moved to Karachi, obliging Benazir to fly down with baby Bilawal every weekend to see him. Rumours about Zardari's financial dealings started circulating just months into the administration. Perhaps mindful of the Bhuttos' estates, Zardari always believed that the ownership of property conferred social weight and power, and as early as mid-1989 the newspapers were asking questions about his growing property interests. Prime Minister's House, one opposition leader complained, had become a stock exchange run by Zardari.[13] There were also complaints about nepotism, with his father becoming chair of the parliamentary Public Accounts Committee and his brother-in-law head of the Karachi Development Authority, although Asif Zardari has consistently denied any wrongdoing in public office. But while Benazir was content to let him do his business uninterrupted, Zardari did not get a free pass on everything. The couple's marital disputes trickled down to their advisers, who used to joke that there was an 'A' team backing Asif and a 'B' team with Benazir. In 1991 there were rumours that Benazir briefly considered leaving him and some on the 'B' team encouraged her to do so.[14] But those on the 'A' team reckoned that, either for personal reasons or to avoid a scandal, she would never walk out of her marriage. They were right – as Benazir's closest friends have said, she was at heart a conservative woman who believed that marriage, however difficult, was for life. Or as Zardari rather unromantically put it when asked about the rumours: 'She behaves as an Eastern wife should behave. Why should she dump me?'[15]

After the fall of Benazir's first government, the search for evidence of financial malpractice began. One of President Ishaq's most trusted advisers, the civil servant Roedad Khan, was made a federal minister in the caretaker government and given the task of securing some corruption convictions. Khan set up a special cell with dedicated tribunals to process cases against Benazir, her husband and some of her ministers. Zardari was the prime target, and the status of the various cases against him were to become a running theme of Pakistani politics for the next two decades. After some initial investigations Roedad Khan selected six cases, one of which alleged that Benazir had allotted 545 residential plots in Islamabad to PPP leaders at throwaway prices. Khan told the president that the court proceedings should not take more than two months. Yet, for all his much remarked upon capability as a bureaucrat, Roedad Khan had not appreciated the slothful practices of the Pakistani courts. Two years later, none of the six cases had made any significant progress. 'We soon realised', he later wrote, 'that under our existing judicial system it takes longer to get an answer from a respondent in a reference case than it takes to send a man to the moon and bring him back'.[16] As for Zardari, on 11 October 1990, during the election campaign, he was arrested in connection with the alleged kidnapping of someone who owed him money. The allegation was that he strapped a bomb to the man and said that if he did not go to a bank to withdraw $800,000 there and then, the bomb would be exploded by remote detonation. Zardari denied the charge, but the case led to his first period of imprisonment. There would be many more. But the whole process was hopelessly politicised: when the PPP was in power, the cases against him went away. When it was in the opposition, they came back.

If she believed an interlocutor was discreet Benazir would, on occasion, discuss the issue of corruption as a generalised practice. In a surprisingly unguarded interview with the American Academy of Achievement in 2000 she said, while denying personal involvement, that she wished she had done more to tackle corruption: 'We all knew kickbacks must be taken . . . these things happen.'[17] Politicians everywhere, she argued, made money. The difference was that while Western politicians did so after they left office, their counterparts in the developing world did not have that option. The US journalist Ron Suskind once put it to her that his high-level sources in the US government had told him that she was making 'real money'. There was no denial. Rather she said, 'Let me explain how it works. In your part of the world Dick Cheney is vice president and then he goes to Haliburton to make his money. In this part of the world you make your money whilst you are in office. It is not that different.'[18] There were many other rationalisations. She had to provide for the next generation. Didn't her children deserve some compensation for being brought up in the glare of publicity? Should politics lead to her premature death, wasn't it reasonable that her offspring should have enough to look after themselves? If she had given industrial permits to relatives and friends, what was wrong with that? Wasn't it fair to make up for what General Zia had taken off them?[19] While Benazir was sometimes willing to have private conversations about these matters, there were lines she would not cross. US Ambassador Robert Oakley, who got to know her well during her first government, later said she would justify making money with the argument: 'my enemies practised it; why shouldn't I?' But the moment Oakley raised Zardari's alleged activities, she would clam up, with strong denials of any wrongdoing. 'She was fiercely defensive about her husband. She was terribly in love with him; she could never deny him anything. And he took and takes advantage of that.'[20] The only time that Benazir gave any ground on Zardari came when it was politically expedient for her to do so. In 2001, when she was at the start of her long campaign to return for a third stint as prime minister, she faced a barrage of criticism about Zardari's conduct during the first and second governments. For PPP loyalists, nervous of criticising Benazir, it was convenient to say that all the corruption had been his fault and he had led her astray, and that if she wanted to make a comeback, she should do so alone. She responded to this criticism with unusual frankness: 'OK. He is not an angel. Maybe he did things that were wrong. He is man enough to say, "I did it" in a fair and impartial enquiry. But what about all those others . . .'[21]

A 1998 exchange of letters with the highly regarded PPP senator, lawyer and human rights activist Iqbal Haider revealed another aspect of her personality that even some of her most ardent supporters found difficult to defend: the feudal mindset she never escaped. Unlike virtually any other senior member of the PPP, Iqbal Haider had had the courage to tell Benazir what he thought of her husband, writing to her that he believed Zardari had been one of the main reasons for the dismissal of the PPP government and that if his role was not diminished the party would continue to suffer. Benazir's response brimmed with her sense that, while she had the right to lead, others with more modest backgrounds did not. She accused Iqbal Haider of failing to show enough gratitude for having been made a senator and of forgetting where he came from. Her feudal attitudes were never far from the surface.

The corruption cases were just one of many methods used to besmirch the PPP's reputation during the 1990 election campaign. Another involved a crudely forged letter from Benazir to her American friend Peter Galbraith. In the letter Benazir supposedly urged Galbraith to stop all US aid to Pakistan and to 'use your influence on V.P. Singh the Indian Prime Minister, to engage the Pakistan Army on the borders, so that they do not impede my way'. In return Benazir would keep a check on Pakistan's nuclear programme. The fakery was obvious: the forger misspelt Galbraith's name and addressed the letter to the National Democratic Institute, whereas in fact he worked for the Senate Foreign Relations Committee. Forgeries aside, the most unusual aspect of the campaign to influence the 1990 vote was that one of those who organised it, former Director General of the ISI Lieutenant General (Retd) Azad Durrani, later admitted to his manipulations. In 2012 Durrani recorded in a Supreme Court affidavit that he had been instructed by the chief of army staff, General Beg, to provide 'logistic support' for the disbursement of funds to Benazir's electoral opponents. According to Durrani, the ISI opened bank accounts in Karachi, Rawalpindi and Quetta and transferred money to other accounts, on the instruction of the chief of army staff and the election cell in the presidency. The recipients included Nawaz Sharif ($58,000), Jamaat-e-Islami ($83,000) and a whole series of anti-PPP politicians based in Sindh, although both Nawaz Sharif and Jamaat-e-Islami have denied ever having received the money. When this activity came to light, General Beg brazenly told the Supreme Court: 'It would be in the fitness of things that further proceedings on this matter are dropped.' As to the substance of the allegations, he did not deny that the ISI had been involved in disbursing the funds. Rather, he argued that such activity was quite normal, proper and even lawful. 'A full account was maintained of all the payments made by the DG ISI and no amount was misappropriated or misused.'[22]

With the establishment determined to prevent her from doing well, no one was very surprised when the October 1990 election results gave the IJI 115 seats and the PPP just 45: Nawaz Sharif was installed as prime minister. While Benazir denounced her overthrow in the strongest possible terms, she couldn't deny that the actual dismissal of her government had been done legally. And with no effective means of challenging the flawed election process, she was now, de facto, the leader of the opposition and had to decide the extent to which she would confront or cooperate with Nawaz Sharif's new government. Not for the first time, one of the considerations was fear of creating a crisis that would provoke a coup. Keen to avoid that, the Central Executive Committee of the PPP decided it would perform as an opposition party under protest.[23] For his part, Sharif, who had risen to power under General Zia, picked up where the caretaker government left off and tried to secure convictions against the PPP leaders, hoping to take Benazir out of politics for good.

Despite Sharif being, at this point in his career, the establishment's man, it only took thirty months for President Ghulam Ishaq to find him as intolerable as he had found Benazir. The relationship broke down for a number of reasons. Just as Benazir had discovered, Sharif found that Karachi was a big problem. Altaf Hussain's MQM had grown in strength and a few elements had become increasingly violent. When, during Sharif's term, the army launched a crackdown, it found caches of weapons and torture cells. As the pressure on the MQM mounted, a breakaway faction, MQM Haqiqi, emerged and, with establishment backing, started to use violence against the mainstream party. It was at this time that Altaf Hussain moved to London, where for the next two decades he would harangue Karachiites with his impassioned speeches. But when the army tried to get control of Karachi, Sharif began to resent its display of power in the city, fearing what it might presage. There were other tensions. General Beg – always more anti-American than anything else – was unhappy with Sharif's failure to support the religious parties in their objections to the US war against Saddam Hussein in Iraq. There was also the question of President Ghulam Ishaq's political future. The president wanted another five-year term, and to achieve it he would need a majority of the members of the provincial assemblies and National Assembly to vote for him. With Sharif openly reluctant to back that second term, the president wanted him out. But perhaps the most important issue of all was the familiar one of who had the power over senior military appointments. When General Beg retired, Sharif wanted an army chief whom he could trust not to launch a coup. On two occasions during his short tenure, the army came up with generals – Asif Nawaz Janjua and Abdul Waheed – with whom Sharif was not comfortable. His attempts to gain control of the right to appoint army chiefs was one of the factors that persuaded President Ghulam Ishaq that Sharif, like Benazir before him, should be removed from office. Seeing where the danger was coming from, Sharif wanted to repeal the Eighth Amendment so as to strip the president of his power to remove the government. That would require a two-thirds majority in parliament, which could only be achieved if the PPP voted for it. Suddenly Benazir found that both the president and the prime minister needed her parliamentary votes.

Sharif asked her to chair the Parliamentary Committee on Foreign Affairs. For his part, the president, using his mastery of the hidden corners of Pakistan's corridors of power, ensured that all the legal cases against Zardari started to fall away. It was a manifestation of a perennial problem in Pakistan. Despite all the rhetoric, Pakistan is yet to find a leader who views corruption cases as a moral or good governance issue rather than a tool with which to manipulate rivals. Just four years before, Benazir had said the Eighth Amendment was a travesty of justice and law and that 'our government will not rest until this amendment goes'.[24] Faced with a choice between helping Sharif repeal it or going for power, Benazir chose power.

The elections of October 1993 – like those of 1970 – are generally reckoned to have been well conducted. And the result was close. The PPP won 86 out of 202 seats, while the Nawaz Sharif faction of the Pakistan Muslim League, PML(N), won 72. With such a narrow margin it wasn't clear Benazir could get back into power, but this time she knew what to do. As soon as the results were in, a somewhat disappointed Benazir hit the phones, gathering up support so that with the backing of minor parties and independents, she once had enough members of the National Assembly to declare victory. Just as in her first government, the MQM's support, together with that of some minor parties and independents, gave her enough to declare victory. As she took office for the second time, Benazir was determined not to repeat the key mistake of her first administration: this time she would do everything she could to remain in the army's good books. She would not interfere in the army's senior appointments. If she had a strong view on a particular issue, she would attempt to nudge the system rather than order it around. In addition, she tried to please the military by using some of her political capital on the world stage to secure arms supplies. Despite pressures from the IMF and the World Bank, she refused to cut military expenditure.[25]

Benazir also took a new line on the nuclear issue that had caused such problems in her first administration, leaving the generals, scientists and the president to manage the programme and vowing there would be no rollback. 'We will protect Pakistan's nuclear program and will not allow our national interest to be sacrificed,' she said shortly after taking power.[26] There is some evidence she went further than that, actively seeking not only the preservation of the Pakistani bomb but also its proliferation. The *Observer* journalist Shyam Bhatia has claimed that Benazir told him in 2004 that, while she was prime minister in 1993, she personally carried discs with data on uranium enrichment into Pyongyang and carried out discs containing information about missile technology. That the two technologies were traded is now well established, but Bhatia is the only person to suggest that Benazir played such a direct role in it.[27] She told him she even purchased an overcoat with especially deep pockets to conceal the discs as she travelled. Bhutto and Bhatia had known each other at Oxford. The reason they met in 2004 was that she wanted to ask him about a 1989 meeting he had had with her brother Murtaza in Damascus. After Bhatia told a distressed Benazir that Murtaza had repeatedly called her a bitch – something he had not published at the time – she gave him an interview on the nuclear issue, a specialist subject of his. While much of it was recorded, Bhatia says, she asked for the tape machine to be switched off when she told him about taking the data to Pyongyang. She said he should not use those comments until after her death. Bhatia respected that wish, but when he did publish, loyal friends of Benazir's strongly rejected the story and insisted that Bhatia hardly knew Benazir.[28] That appears not to be the case. The parts of the interview that were recorded clearly indicate the two knew each other well. While there is no way to resolve the issue with certainty, it seems somewhat unreasonable for Benazir's friends to dismiss Bhatia's account out of hand. To accuse a veteran foreign correspondent of fabrication was a serious charge. Two of the leading experts on Pakistan's nuclear programme, Douglas Frantz and Catherine Collins, have written that after her 1993 election win Benazir was determined to keep the nuclear establishment on side and agreed to personally carry missile designs from North Korea to Pakistan. They make no comment on her having taken discs in, but then again it should be no great surprise that more people are aware of – and more willing to talk about – her having helped Pakistan's cause by bringing missile technology into the country than her having furthered proliferation by taking nuclear technology out.[29]

Even if Benazir assuaged the deep state's concerns about her attitude to the bomb, there were other issues on which she remained vulnerable, not least religion. Many Pakistanis, including the violent jihadists who went on to kill her, believed Benazir was Shia despite her stating on a number of occasions that that was not the case. The confusion went back generations. While descendants and Larkana family friends insist that Sir Shahnawaz was Sunni, others state he was Shia. The Pakistani political scientist Hassan Abbas, for example, who has studied the issue closely, gathering evidence over many years, has described Sir Shahnawaz as a Shia politician.[30] Similarly with Zulfikar there are competing claims. A childhood friend who knew him as a boy in Bombay wrote that Suraiya Currimbhoy's family rejected Zulfikar's youthful proposal because he was Shia.[31] Over the years many Shia voters have cast their ballots for the PPP thinking the family was from their community. This was in part because Zulfikar's second wife, Nusrat, was Shia, and she taught her daughters about Shia rituals. Less well known, his first wife Shirin, the daughter of a Sunni father and Shia mother, also considered herself Shia. The PPP also made use of coded messages intended for Shia voters: its election symbol in the 1970 election was a sword, an image that Bhutto and other party leaders referred to as 'Al-Zulfikar' during the election campaign. 'Al-Zulfikar' was the title associated with Ali's sword – a powerful emotional symbol for Shia.[32] Against that, however, close relatives such as Sanam Bhutto, Tariq Islam and Muslim Bhutto insist Zulfikar was Sunni.

It is possible that these competing accounts reflect Zulfikar having switched allegiance for political reasons, but there is insufficient evidence to settle the matter. As for his children, one of them, Sanam, followed her mother: since she wasn't going into politics, Sanam could adopt Shiism. The other three children stuck with their father's Sunni practices.[33] When Benazir and Zardari were married, as an eyewitness correspondent reported in a Karachi newspaper, the ceremony was handled by the Bhutto family's Sunni maulvi from Garhi Khuda Bakhsh.[34] But like her father, Benazir had married a Shia: early in her marriage Benazir told friends that she was Sunni and her husband was Shia. But even here there are some complexities. Zardari at times showed that he was a Shia by, for example, putting a Shia symbol on the roof of Bilawal House. But he has also said both his parents were Sunni,[35] although some close to the family have suggested that his mother's antecedents might have been Shia. His Shiism, it seems, was at least in part a matter of choice: many young people in Karachi in the 1960s and 1970s adopted Shiism because they were drawn to the dramatic Muharrem ceremonies, in which some Shias lashed their backs with sharp blades to commemorate the tragedy at Karbala, where the grandson of the Prophet was massacred. After he became president in September 2008, in public Zardari would pray in the Sunni manner, but when with other Shias he adopted Shia practice. He also gave money to Shia charities.[36]

But even if religious conservatives accepted that the Bhuttos, with the exception of Nusrat and Sanam, were Sunni, they had another objection. It was always clear that the family followed Sufi Islam in its Sindhi manifestation rather than the more literalist Deobandi or Salafi sects favoured by most conservatives. The Bhuttos had a long history in the Sufi tradition. Back in the nineteenth century, when he was acquitted in his legal cases brought by Colonel Mayhew, Sir Shahnawaz's father, Mir Ghulam Murtaza, gave thanks at a Sufi shrine near Larkana dedicated to the memory of the twelfth-century mystic Lal Shahbaz Qalandar.[37] Shahnawaz's wife Begum Khurshid was also a regular at the shrine.[38] 'My grandmother had gone to pray at his [Qalandar's] shrine when my father became very ill as a baby and nearly died,' Benazir later wrote.[39] Perhaps told that the prayers offered there had saved his life, Zulfikar also visited the shrine often and urged Benazir to do so too. After the police attack on Nusrat Bhutto at Lahore Gaddafi stadium, some PPP supporters managed to get hold of some of the blood that came from her scalp, took it to the shrine and wiped it on the cloth covering the saint's tomb. As a sign of his devotion, Zulfikar used his authority as president to order his newly created Ministry of Religious Affairs to donate two golden doors to the shrine.[40] Back in the precolonial days in Sindh, tribal leaders such as the Talpurs had shown off their wealth by donating gold doors to important shrines. Zulfikar was copying them.

Benazir made no secret of her religious attitudes, saying that Sufis had set examples of love and fraternity through their deeds and that their eternal message of love for humanity could create national unity.[41] 'I come from a land of mystic saints who preached the message of love,' she said.[42] Her beliefs sometimes strayed into superstition. After a nightmare she would tell her staff to sacrifice a goat, and she believed it was not mere chance that those involved in her father's death had subsequently had bad luck: some of the judges who sentenced him had died relatively young and one had a swarm of bees attack his funeral.[43] Zulfikar's hangman, Tara Masih, had died of cancer, and Zia had died in the plane crash, something she described as an act of God. When she bought a multi-million-dollar Manhattan apartment in 2007, she told the vendor that she would be moving the front door because the 'feng shui' wasn't right.[44] Benazir's interest in spiritualism even led her to visit the celebrity British mystic Doris Stokes, who claimed in a séance to be able to commune with her father. According to a media report on the séance, Zulfikar's spirit said: 'There were 12 of them they came for me in the night and they strangled me.' And then: 'Get the people behind you. It's the people who count. You can't fool the people.'[45] In participating in such practices, Benazir was following her father, whose minister of religious affairs recorded how, on a visit to Colombo, Zulfikar told his Sri Lankan counterpart Sirimavo Bandaranaike that he would like to see her official astrologers. When he met them, he asked for their view on the date he had fixed for the next election – 7 March 1977.[46] On another occasion Zulfikar sent a print of his palm to a renowned Pakistani palmist, who later claimed that, since he foresaw Zulfikar's death, he did not give the prime minister a full reading.

For all her interest in spiritual matters, Benazir – like her father – was constantly on the back foot in the face of the religious lobby. In August 1992 the question of Benazir's religious beliefs came into sharp focus when the minister of religious affairs said on the floor of the National Assembly that Benazir was a *kafir*, or non-believer – a statement that implied she was worthy of death. The reason the minister made such an extraordinary claim, which, as one newspaper report put it, produced pandemonium just short of physical violence, was that Benazir had opposed Sharif's attempt to introduce the death penalty for blasphemy cases.[47] While it was easy for advocates of the measure to paint themselves as especially devout, critics of the death penalty pointed out that false blasphemy allegations were often made to settle scores on unrelated matters such as property disputes. The introduction of the death penalty in such cases would run a severe risk of miscarriages of justice. Responding to Niazi, Benazir told the National Assembly that 'As a Muslim I accept the supremacy of the Koran and Sunnah', adding that it was time to be rid of the 'monopoly of the Mullahs'.[48] She did not believe in the Islam of mullahs but in an enlightened Islam.[49] 'I do not know from where the clergy has sprouted up to tell us what is a good Muslim and what is not a good Muslim . . . it is only God who can decide on the day of judgement.'[50] Benazir was well aware that the leader of Jamaat-e-Islami routinely claimed that she would drive the country towards 'secularism' in an attempt to win the favour of the Indo-Israel lobby backed by the US.[51] She responded to this by making a conscious effort to avoid the criticism her father faced about his lifestyle. While campaigning in the late 1960s, he made little secret of his drinking and womanising. Benazir, by contrast, at least when she was in Pakistan, lived the life of a conservative Muslim woman, refusing to shake men by the hand and always covering her hair, or at least some of it.

There was an irony to the violent jihadists' hostility to her: during her second government, Benazir – along with Americans – helped establish the Taliban by providing the movement with arms and logistical support. At the time, Afghanistan was suffering from the rolling civil conflict that followed the withdrawal of the Soviet forces. With no one group strong enough to control the whole country, a number of competing forces reduced much of Kabul to rubble as they struggled for supremacy. When there was talk of a new emerging force in Afghan politics – a movement of religious students who wanted to unify the country and put an end to the fighting – the US and Pakistan governments were interested. Washington was thinking that a strong central Afghan government could help it build an oil pipeline from central Asia through Afghanistan, even going so far as to invite a Taliban delegation to Texas to discuss the matter. With their habitually patronising attitude towards violent jihadists, Pakistan's strategic planners thought that a Pashtun religious government would form exactly the kind of biddable, pro-Pakistan administration they were hoping for. After the fall of her second government Benazir was understandably reluctant to talk about her role in creating the Taliban. Generally, she brushed the subject aside. But on a few occasions, she did admit her part in it. 'Many of us, including our friends from the US, initially thought they would bring peace to that war-torn country,' she said in 2007. 'And that was a crucial, fatal mistake we made. If I had to do things again, that's certainly not a decision I would have taken.'[52]

Although many of the Taliban had been educated in Pakistani madrasahs, their initial political and military campaign was focused on Afghanistan. Other hardline groups were active in Pakistan itself. Since the late 1980s a cleric in the picturesque Swat Valley, just a few hours' drive from Islamabad, had established the Tehrik-e-Nafaz-e-Shariat-e-Mohammadi to agitate for sharia law. By November 1994 Sufi Mohammed had launched a full-blown insurgency in the valley. Over a decade later his movement would prevail, and for some months the valley suffered a brutal period during which violent jihadists took control, beheading opponents and leaving their dismembered bodies in the streets. The disaster in Swat was generally blamed on the army, which hesitated to confront the problem and win back control of the valley. Eventually they did so and, with heavy loss of life on both sides, managed to reassert the writ of the central government. While the army does deserve much of the blame, the prevarications in fact started with Benazir, who signalled her willingness to make major concessions, including an acceptance that the valley and nearby areas would, as the militants demanded, live under sharia law. Benazir's support for the Taliban and toleration of the hardliners in Swat revealed something she had in common with her father. Both father and daughter took policy decisions relating to Islam on purely pragmatic grounds, seeing Islam as a political lever which could be used to achieve other policy objectives. Zulfikar knew his declaration on the Ahmadis as non-Muslims was morally wrong: he was not a hardline sectarian keen to excommunicate those who held different beliefs any more than Benazir was a violent jihadist seeking clerical rule. For both, religious policy was a means to an end rather an end in itself.

For some Pakistanis, such attitudes to Islam were unacceptable. In September 1995 police disrupted a plot to overthrow Benazir's government by stopping the car of a serving brigadier – Mustansir Billah – as he drove from Pakistan's tribal areas.[53] Inside his vehicle they found a cache of Kalashnikovs and rocket launchers that had been purchased by Qari Saifullah Akhtar, a member of a militant outfit, Harakat ul-Ansar. Thinking he could pull rank, the brigadier called GHQ hoping to get someone to force the police to release his car. When they didn't help, he realised he had just walked into a trap. The leader of the plot was a major general, Zahir ul-Islam Abbasi, who had first hit the headlines in 1988 when he was serving as Pakistan's military attaché in Delhi. When Indian intelligence agents beat him up and threw him out of the country, he returned to Pakistan a national hero. Seven years later, the ambitious major general, seeing Benazir as an obstacle to Islamic reform, took matters into his own hands. When Abbasi and his co-conspirators were later put on trial, it emerged that he had intended to storm the GHQ, kill the corps commanders and impose sharia law. He planned to have a staff car lead a busload of thirty Harakat ul-Ansar militants dressed in commando uniforms into the military headquarters. Once inside the perimeter they would storm the building and establish control. Abbasi planned to proclaim himself not only the chief of army staff but also the leader of the faithful, or Amir ul-Momineen. The major general's intended address to the nation left no doubt as to the kind of administration he had in mind: 'We are thankful to almighty Allah and, with complete confidence, after declaring Pakistan a Sunni state, we announce the enforcement of the complete Islamic system.' The draft speech also announced bans on films, music, interest payments, contraception and photographs of women. Benazir could take heart from the fact that Abbasi's coup attempt was not only against her but also against the army leadership and that he looked for reliable foot soldiers from the ranks of Harakat ul-Ansar rather than the military. Nonetheless, over thirty serving officers were involved: she had good reason to feel anxious.

The Islamists were just one of many problems threatening Benazir's second term. There was also a challenge from within her family. The question of which of his children Zulfikar favoured has been hotly disputed. In previous generations the issue would not have arisen. For centuries, the Bhuttos had treated women as little more than mechanisms to secure land and produce heirs. That had begun to change with Sir Shahnawaz Bhutto, who, unlike most of his landed peers, allowed his son to make a love match and his daughters to marry outside the family. Zulfikar took Sir Shahnawaz's liberal instincts to a new level, allowing his daughter to go abroad alone to university. No doubt there were many factors behind Zulfikar's decision, but one of them may well have been Benazir's precociousness. A short piece of mid-1960s film showing Zulfikar and his four children seated on a veranda in Karachi gives a hint of the sibling rivalry that was to become much more intense. When Zulfikar asks where Nusrat is, a bright-eyed Benazir explains that she had taken herself off to the city to organise something she was running. 'Now we have two leaders in the family,' Benazir jokes. She is rewarded by her father's indulgent smile. One of the boys, trying to keep up, mutters somewhat awkwardly 'Or six', meaning the family has six leaders. For the Bhutto children, the rivalries began early. While much has been made of the idea that Benazir was always destined for great things, there is no evidence that Zulfikar ever reached a settled view on which of his children he considered his political heir. Benazir, seeking dynastic legitimacy, claimed otherwise: 'he always believed that his daughter would one day be prime minister, when such a thing was unheard of in the Muslim world'.[54] And it is true that in his writing in his death cell Zulfikar compared her favourably with Indira Gandhi: 'I have no hesitation in saying that my daughter is more than a match for the daughter of Jawaharlal Nehru.'[55] But while Zulfikar did prepare his daughter for public life, he did just the same for Murtaza. He too went to Oxford and before that to Harvard, where he studied politics, sociology, history and environmental science. And while much has been made of how Benazir accompanied her father to the Simla summit, Zulfikar also involved Murtaza in his diplomatic travels; in 1972 on trips to China and Moscow, for example, Zulfikar took Murtaza with him.[56] At a White House dinner in 1973 at which Murtaza was present, President Nixon remarked that some considered the nineteen-year-old as a future prime minister of Pakistan. 'The only young politician I can think of who might have been launched earlier was Winston Churchill,' the American president said.[57] In 1993 Nusrat insisted that Zulfikar had never favoured Benazir over Murtaza. 'He didn't choose Benazir – *I* did,' she told the *New Yorker*. '*I* was to have been my husband's political heir. But, because I was ill, *I* told the Party that I would like Benazir to stand in my stead. They couldn't make her chairman, because I already was, so they coined the phrase "co-chairman", which we *both* still are.'[58] Zulfikar's close adviser Rafi Raza, who saw the family close up when the children were in their adolescence, commented that Murtaza was underestimated by his father.[59] 'Murtaza was always conscious that he valued [Benazir's] opinion and judgement and the political sense and her academic capability over and above his. Sanam was his little princess but in terms of intellectual affinity it was Benazir.'[60] At the same time, Murtaza often said he was the chosen one. An Al Zulfikar publication of 1982 quoted Murtaza as saying he was the successor of Ali Bhutto,[61] and in 1989 in Damascus he said the fact his father had made him his political agent for Larkana in 1977 showed that 'I should be the PM not her.'[62]

Murtaza's widow, Ghinwa Bhutto, dates the differences between the two siblings to the time Benazir was in the Barbican, that is to say, 1984 to 1986. 'She came back a different person from England. She wasn't working for Pakistan. She came back with deals with American lobbyists. She wasn't any more Pakistani. She changed. She was not any more standing on the manifesto of PPP.'[63] Increasingly, Murtaza positioned himself as the heir to the PPP's radical traditions. By February 1989, shortly after Benazir became prime minister, the breach was complete. Murtaza gave an interview in Damascus in which he criticised his sister's decision to compromise with General Beg and Ghulam Ishaq Khan when she formed her first government. Murtaza said: 'If it had been me, I would have taken the PPP majority and gone into opposition and watched if they could find another government.'[64] Off the record he was far ruder, describing Benazir in highly disparaging terms and again saying that as Zulfikar's son he, not she, should be prime minister.[65]

Nonetheless, Murtaza saw one benefit in his sister's coming to power in 1988: it was an opportunity for him to return to Pakistan, and he asked her for a safe National Assembly seat. Benazir and Zardari, however, saw very little upside to Murtaza's becoming politically active in Pakistan. He could base a claim to her job on solid dynastic credentials and would attract the support of disaffected elements in the PPP: it was inevitable that he would become the focus of a rival power centre, and she turned him down, saying he should not come back to Pakistan directly from Syria but should first clean up his image by having a stay in London, which would help him combat the charges he faced in Pakistan of abetting murder, terrorism and air piracy.[66] In a 1993 statement from Damascus, Murtaza declared not only that he would return to the country but also that he would contest the elections, standing for his own party PPP Shaheed Bhutto (PPP SB), opposing the PPP, which he said 'has been taken hostage by agents of the Pakistan intelligence agencies'. Nusrat was so keen to have Murtaza in Pakistan that, going behind Benazir's back, she sent emissaries to the army and the president to negotiate his return. 'He must be given an amnesty,' she said, 'and his return must be announced two weeks in advance. I don't want him to come back in secret, through the back door. He must be received properly by the people of Pakistan. He is, after all, Zulfi Bhutto's son.' When asked how she could undermine her daughter in this way, Nusrat described Benazir as a viper who she could never forgive. 'There are many families in Pakistan where four or five members are politicians. Benazir will be here, and Murtaza will be here. Murtaza is really interested only in his own province of Sindh, not in being the prime minister of Pakistan.'[67] The two women managed to maintain the veneer of a familial relationship, seeing each other and exchanging pleasantries, but the political divide in the house of Bhutto was plain to see: Zardari's Karachi home, Bilawal House, became the campaign headquarters of the PPP, while 70 Clifton housed Murtaza's PPP SB.

Murtaza wanted to run over twenty candidates in Sindh for the national and provincial assemblies. Benazir complained that having what would amount to two PPP candidates in so many constituencies would confuse voters, and she suggested she could withdraw the PPP's candidates from one national and one provincial seat, thereby allowing Murtaza to get into the National Assembly. Murtaza, however, refused on the grounds that his supporters wanted the chance to stand and contest. And in a significant blow to Benazir, Nusrat declared she would be running her son's campaign.[68] Benazir made no secret about her hurt, complaining that her mother said 'awful, awful, awful things against me' and that she got angry reading them. 'All my mother wants to do is hurt me. Each allegation of hers is like a bullet in the heart,' Benazir said. 'She tells a lot of lies, this daughter of mine,' Nusrat answered back.[69]

When in November 1993 Murtaza took the plunge and flew back to Karachi, the authorities refused permission for his plane to land, diverting him to the Gulf. Next Murtaza tried an Ethiopia Airlines flight from Dubai, and on the second attempt, after seventeen years abroad, he made it back to Pakistani soil and was immediately taken into custody. Nusrat had been on hand to greet him at the airport and had to watch him being led away. 'Nusrat wanted to help him and she helped him,' Ghinwa later recalled. 'She went to the airport to meet him and she slapped the officer.'[70] Benazir's revenge was swift. At a meeting of the PPP Central Executive Committee she secured her mother's removal as co-chairman of the party. 'My daughter stabbed me in the back,' declared Nusrat,[71] adding that Benazir no longer deserved the name Bhutto and should now call herself Benazir Zardari. 'She will be nowhere. She is because of her father, because of being Bhutto. She should test her popularity anew. Stop calling herself as Benazir Bhutto and see what happens to her.'[72] But Benazir was having none of it. 'For me it is a case of pure male prejudice,' Benazir said. 'My mother has come on record as saying the male is the one who should inherit the traditional crown.'[73]

There were moments when the family row span out of control. In January 1994 Nusrat said members of Benazir's government could not visit her husband's grave on the anniversary of his birth. When Benazir insisted the day would be marked as normal, there were clashes as the two Bhutto women led separate groups of followers to the family tomb: three people died and twenty were wounded. 'I want to ask her how she could be so ruthless,' Nusrat said at the time, charging that her daughter's government was worse than that of Zia. Murtaza issued a statement from jail accusing his sister's administration of being 'responsible for the bloodbath'.[74] The violence perhaps served as a reminder of how much the two factions in the family had to lose. And for Benazir there were tactical considerations. Having Murtaza in prison was one thing. Actually convicting him could result in an irrevocable family split, and after seven months behind bars he was let out, albeit on bail.[75]

Murtaza was now free to organise politically, although, as he did so, he found it hard to adjust to the new realities of Pakistan. When he used some of his father's language about socialism and revolution, many Pakistanis thought it sounded dated and irrelevant, and the PPP SB never enjoyed great electoral success: Murtaza became its sole representative in the Sindh Provincial Assembly. Nonetheless, he campaigned hard, railing against his sister's incompetence and arrogance: 'she fancies herself as a master strategist. Here she is, a latter day Machiavelli, grossly exaggerating her own concept of her manipulative abilities.'[76] Increasingly, though, his complaints focused on Zardari, who he openly described as 'Asif baba and the 40 thieves'.[77] He now called his sister 'Benazir Zardari', adding that he had been appalled by her choice of husband when she was engaged.[78] Zardari, he said, should have an apolitical or at least a minimised political role,[79] and to make clear the level of his disdain he apparently put a photograph of Zardari on the toilet in a bathroom at 70 Clifton so that when male visitors were urinating they would see his image.[80] For all the angry words, though, both sides in the dispute could see the benefit of reaching some sort of accommodation, and in July 1996 Murtaza attended a meeting at Prime Minister's House attended by, among others, Benazir and Nusrat. 'All three of them, tears were rolling down their cheeks,' a friend later recalled.[81] When she described the meeting, Benazir would always say that she and her brother had settled their differences. Even a decade later she told a close colleague that she had achieved a reconciliation in July 1996. But that wasn't true, at least according to one source close to Murtaza. As the meeting progressed, Zardari walked in – which Murtaza had not expected. Zardari asked Murtaza if he would like a drink and poured him a regular measure. 'Murtaza was a heavy drinker, took the bottle and saying "I'll show you how to drink," made it half a glass,' one of those present recalled. When Murtaza asked, 'Why are you persecuting my people?' Benazir replied that there had been some incidents – acts of terrorism – that had to be dealt with. Zardari then raised Murtaza's hostility towards him. 'Murtaza, you have your difference with your sister. But what have I done?' Murtaza banged his whisky tumbler on a glass-topped table. 'What haven't you done?' he yelled. 'You have a bloody cheek asking me what my problem is. Your corruption has screwed up my father's political party.'[82] The encounter at Prime Minister's House was the last time the three would meet.

The antagonisms were so raw that it was ever clearer that the PPP was heading for a split, with Murtaza leading a radical, breakaway faction. He even called for the army to help create a caretaker national government for five years to replace Benazir.[83] It was obvious that Benazir needed to deal with her brother but there seemed to be no way of doing so. On 16 September 1996, just two months after the disastrous meeting at Prime Minister's House, Zardari and Murtaza found themselves on the same flight to Karachi. They exchanged pleasantries, but when Zardari was later seen in Karachi without his moustache, rumours spread that the two men's armed supporters had faced off in the city's airport, where Murtaza's people had grabbed Zardari and humiliated him by shaving off half of his famous moustache, thereby obliging him to remove the whole thing. There is no evidence that this ever happened, and had it done so there would almost certainly have been an exchange of fire – but nonetheless, the story took hold. The next day an official at Prime Minister's House sent a document to Murtaza headed 'Subsequent to meeting of Benazir Bhutto and Murtaza Bhutto in Islamabad the following was decided'. The document consisted of an incoherent account of the July meeting, saying that in return for 'huge compensation', Murtaza had agreed to form a new terrorist wing of Al Zulfikar that would kill Sharif and other leaders of the Muslim League and generally help the PPP in conducting acts of terrorism. Benazir referred to the incident in 2001. She said the director general (DG) of the ISI had given her the report. 'I had a copy sent to Murtaza and I told the DG ISI that the report is incorrect. He replied that the DG MI received the report and gave it to the [army] chief who asked that it be brought to the prime minister's attention.'[84] Whatever the truth of the letter's provenance and content, it only heightened the feeling that trust levels were reaching an all-time low.

Then, late on 17 September, the Karachi police detained Ali Sonora, a veteran PPP activist who, after a row with Benazir during her first government, had switched allegiance to her brother. Murtaza immediately went to several Karachi police stations where he thought Sonora might be held. According to Fatima Bhutto, her father became hot-tempered with the police.[85] Others, including senior police officers in the city at the time, say that that was the least of it and that Murtaza roughed up some police officers and made armed threats. The next day, Murtaza's forty-second birthday, there was a series of explosions in Karachi, which the authorities said were the work of Murtaza's activists pressing for Sonora's release. Tensions were rising, and Fatima Bhutto has said that by 20 September there were four armoured vehicles parked near their home, 70 Clifton,[86] and Murtaza was telling friends he expected to be arrested. That afternoon Murtaza held a press conference demanding the release of Ali Sonora and saying his own life was at risk. 'There is a plot against me formulated by the most criminal elements in the police,' he said. He then moved on to a Karachi suburb to address a rally of his supporters.

Murtaza was killed as he returned from that rally. Much of what happened is contested, but it is generally accepted that he was heading back to his house in a convoy of four cars when he came across a police checkpoint right outside 70 Clifton. When he got out of his car, there was shooting; he was hit and left bleeding to death on the street for at least twenty minutes. He was belatedly given some highly unsatisfactory medical treatment before he succumbed. But the fact that he was left on the tarmac for so long is the clearest single piece of evidence that his death was not an accident. This was, after all, the prime minister's brother, and that no one was interested in getting him timely medical attention was utterly extraordinary. Benazir did make some efforts to investigate the death, or, at least, appear to do so. She hired a team of retired Scotland Yard police officials and a British Home Office-approved pathologist who went to Karachi for four days in October 1996, just before her second government was dismissed. The brief was simply to find out what had happened.[87] The British investigators complained that there appeared to have been a clean-up of the crime scene: over 100 bullets had been fired, and all had been removed. The pathologist, Peter Acland, later recorded what he had discovered: Murtaza had been attending a rally and was returning to Clifton in a convoy accompanied by armed bodyguards and associates; the convoy was stopped at a police checkpoint just outside his residence; an exchange of fire took place, injuring two police; and of Murtaza's party, eight were killed, four injured, six arrested without injury and some others got away. The post mortem showed that Murtaza had suffered gunshot wounds. While some of the police manning the checkpoint had been clearly visible, others had been in more hidden locations at the side of the road – making it look more like an ambush.[88]

Much of the press coverage in the days after the killing centred on the two injured police officers. A panel of doctors declared that the two men had self-inflicted their injuries so as to give the appearance that there had been a firefight when, in reality, only the police had fired. The situation became even more charged when one of the police officers accused of shooting himself was found dead and a police surgeon claimed he had been murdered. In his report, Peter Acland rejected that conclusion. Having examined the physical evidence and the scene of the shooting, he concluded that the officer had not self-inflicted any injury during the clash outside 70 Clifton. His foot was hit by a bullet when he was hiding behind the door of a car. As for his death, Acland also found that the nature of the soot marks in his head wound, and the location of the gun that killed him, were strongly suggestive of suicide, not murder. Acland speculated that the police officer might have killed himself after being faced with the false accusation of self-inflicted injury.

The fate of the police officers was, however, a distraction from the question: why had Murtaza been killed? Shortly after his death Nusrat Bhutto said, 'If I am guaranteed justice I will register a case against Asif Ali Zardari and Benazir Bhutto for killing my son.' She later retracted the remark.[89] Fatima Bhutto continued to believe that Zardari was at least in part responsible for her father's death, as she wrote in her book published in 2010.[90] At a judicial inquiry into the killing, it has been reported that one witness claimed that Zardari, during his stay in Karachi in the days before Murtaza's death, met with Wajid Durrani,[91] the police officer who was in charge of the operation outside 70 Clifton. The judicial inquiry into Murtaza's death raised this point, asking Benazir if she was aware that the day before Murtaza's death Zardari had been in the Chief Minister's House meeting officials.[92] She reportedly replied that she was not aware. Durrani's boss, the man in charge of police in Karachi, Deputy Inspector General Shoaib Suddle, has claimed in a recent interview that not only did Durrani meet Zardari in the Chief Minister's House but that Durrani had brought his own gunmen to reinforce the police officers outside 70 Clifton.[93] Durrani denies all the allegations against him. Zardari too has always insisted on his innocence, and when he was charged with involvement he was not convicted, despite a lengthy legal process. A year into Zardari's presidency, the Sindh High Court acquitted him, and the next year all the policemen who had participated in the shootout, Durrani included, were also acquitted.[94]

In her autobiography Benazir relied on all-purpose stock villains, suggesting the killing was carried out by members of the establishment trying to destabilise her government. Misleadingly, and again referring to the 7 July meeting, she said that the death came at a time when she had just reconciled with Murtaza.[95] In Ghinwa Bhutto's view, only Benazir could have given the go-ahead for the operation. 'She was very much in knowledge of it – no one else could have allowed it. Asif could not have told them to arrest Mir . . . she is the one who enabled them.'[96] For their part, the police have always insisted it was a case of an arrest gone wrong. Shoaib Suddle says to this day that he gave an order to disarm and arrest Murtaza on his own initiative and not because the government told him to.[97] After a conversation with Benazir on 17 September, however, he amended the order so as to leave Murtaza at liberty but to arrest and disarm the guards. As for the operational detail, he said his juniors decided to set up the checkpoint outside 70 Clifton without his knowledge. Suddle lived in the house opposite 70 Clifton, and as Murtaza's convoy approached he was sitting on his lawn unaware, he claims, that just the other side of his garden wall the police had put men armed with submachine guns in place to make the arrests. He says the first he knew about it was when a shot rang out, followed by many others, which went over his head and into the walls of his house.

The judicial inquiry that followed Murtaza's death was intended by Benazir to be a whitewash. One hundred and four witnesses were examined, but Zardari was not called to give evidence. According to one of the judges on the three-member panel, the decision that Zardari should not appear was taken by the Sindh government, but clearly it was a matter that would have involved Benazir, who did appear. To no one's surprise, the commission could not find who was responsible. It even failed to find who had given the order to arrest Murtaza's men, concluding that it came from an unnamed 'very high authority', a phrase with just enough ambiguity to leave the matter totally unclear.[98] To this day the judges argue that they were only able to reach conclusions on the basis of the evidence that came before them. But many Pakistanis still have strongly held opinions about Murtaza's killing. Those who think Murtaza was murdered to order hold on to their view. Those who think it was an arrest gone wrong stick to theirs.

When Benazir began her second stint as prime minister, there was every reason to believe she would still be in power at the end of her five-year term. The arch-manipulator of Pakistani politics President Ghulam Ishaq had gone, and she was able to replace him with Farooq Leghari, an ultra-loyalist and fellow feudal who had also been to Oxford. Ideally, she would have liked to have over-turned the Eighth Amendment too, but she lacked the required two-thirds majority and with Leghari in place it was no longer an urgent priority. At least that's how it seemed in November 1993. But just thirty-six months later Benazir was out of power and the man who wielded the axe was none other than her handpicked president, who had succumbed to establishment pressure to over-throw her. He gave a number of reasons for doing so. The administration was widely seen as incompetent or worse. The non-stop corruption allegations were draining her support. When she sent in the security forces to deal with MQM violence in Karachi there was widespread, brutal suppression of the Mohajir movement, causing, at times, scores of deaths every night. She also implemented a tough economic policy. Leaving her youthful leftism behind, she said she now favoured right-wing market reforms. 'I was in England when Margaret Thatcher introduced the economics of privatization. I was also in America to see the economics of deregulation. And I took these lessons from the West to the East.'[99] While that approach pleased the international funding agencies, it left little money for welfare spending. 'We would argue,' Tariq Ali said, 'and in response to my numerous complaints – all she would say was that the world had changed. She couldn't be on the "wrong side" of history.'[100] For leftists there seemed little to choose between the PPP and the centre-right Muslim League. Zulfikar Ali Bhutto's old ally Sheikh Rashid vented his frustrations, complaining that since the first heady days of the PPP the party had been taken over by millionaires, feudals, capitalists and opportunists who, seeing the success of the party, had wormed their way in, encouraged by Benazir, who in her anxiety to win power had not just backed out of her father's political legacy but even reversed it. As well as these internal PPP divisions, the government had also alienated the judi-ciary by appointing over twenty loyal but unqualified judges, who were so inex-perienced that some could not find their way into the court buildings. When the Supreme Court ordered that the judges appointed by Benazir should be sacked, the government refused to implement the order. The criticism of Benazir was intense. As one journalist put it: 'she was an arrogant, reckless, capricious and corrupt ruler who surrounded herself with sycophants, lackeys and flunkies and squandered away a second opportunity to serve the people of Pakistan'.[101] But even if the invective was powerful, did such complaints amount to a constitutional case for the dismissal of the elected government?

Even those close to Leghari had difficulty fully understanding his decision. Twenty years later the veteran politician Shafqat Mahmood, who worked closely with Leghari through the crisis, said: 'If you ask me to put my finger on it, I can't.' Leghari told Mahmood that the country was being run into the ground, that the economy was collapsing and that Benazir and Zardari were corrupt: 'but was that enough reason for dismissal? I don't think so.' Other factors that might have played into the decision included Leghari's personal animosity towards Zardari, Leghari's inability to influence day-to-day government decisions and, possibly, hidden resentments of Benazir, who in the past had been high-handed in her treatment of him.[102] The president's dismissal order listed other items: there had been extra-judicial killings, and Benazir had resisted implementing a Supreme Court decision overturning her judicial appointments. And to cap it all, Leghari said, there had been illegal phone-tapping, corruption and nepotism. The problem was that none of this seemed very different to what had occurred under Nawaz Sharif, or, for that matter, Ayub Khan. That Leghari made his move in cooperation with the army was obvious. Benazir's government was dismissed after midnight and all airports and broadcasting stations were shut down and placed under army guard. Robert Oakley, the US ambassador who had been so close to Benazir during her first term, later said that Leghari's reasons were similar to those of his predecessor President Ishaq Khan:

I was told of a cable from Ambassador Simons [US ambassador to Pakistan from 1995 to 1998] reporting on a conversation he had with the present President, Sardar Leghari, in which the latter remarked that he had to get rid of Prime Minister Bhutto. I had to laugh because it sounded very much like the conversation I had with President Ghulam Ishaq Khan in 1990; he had made exactly the same comments about Bhutto as his successor had – authoritarian, wilful, corrupt, unbending, unwilling to listen to advice, stubborn. Bhutto seems to get worse and worse; she is not growing. That is unfortunate.[103]

That was one way of looking at it, but, understandably enough, Benazir had a different perspective: the army simply could not tolerate civilian politicians and Leghari had been unforgivably weak.

Within hours of the fall of her government Zardari was taken to prison. Although never convicted, he stayed there until 2004 on charges pertaining to money laundering, corruption and murder, all of which he denied. And when elections were held, the PPP found itself at a low ebb, winning just 19 seats against 125 for Sharif's Muslim League. With a two-thirds majority, Sharif seemed unassailable, but he remained deeply anxious that he would be removed from power. His concern led him to focus his efforts not on policy but rather on staying in power. When the Supreme Court threatened to find him in contempt over a case it was hearing, a mob, which included one of his ministers, ransacked the court buildings. The chief justice accused Sharif of bussing demonstrators from around the country to Islamabad and ensuring the police did not intercede – all of which the government denied.[104] Sharif also increased his efforts to remove his main opponent by securing some convictions against Benazir, establishing an accountability bureau under a close adviser, Saifur Rehman, who spent significant sums of money trying to investigate allegations against her.

After the collapse of her second government, Benazir even considered pulling out of politics. She told friends that when she was younger she had not been sure if she wanted to go into politics, especially when she saw her friends start families, and now those doubts had returned. Following Murtaza's death, she said, she felt totally isolated. Previously she had thought that if anything happened to her then Murtaza would take over, but with that possibility gone she was unsure how to view the future of the dynasty. In April 1997 she told PPP Secretary General Chaudhry Ahmed Mukhtar that she wanted to take a lower profile in politics. She said that after the killing of her brother she was concerned as to what could happen to the PPP in the event of an attack on her. Consequently she wished to transfer power to a more collective and democratic leadership to ensure that the party would not fragment without the children of Zulfikar Ali Bhutto to lead it.

If senior party officials who heard these views thought they was uncharacteristic, they were right: by 1999 Benazir had got over her doubts and declared herself PPP chairperson for life.[105] And when, in that year, a PPP member put forward a resolution to make Zardari co-chairman of the party, he was immediately expelled and only readmitted after writing a letter of apology. Benazir now demanded total loyalty. Legislation introduced in 2002 by General Musharraf, who had become president in June 2001, meant that Benazir could not lead the PPP in elections because she had been declared an absconder. Rather than hand the PPP to someone else, she decided that for the purposes of elections she would form the PPPP – Pakistan People's Party Parliamentarians. While Benazir would continue to lead the PPP, the PPPP was run by a loyal senior party member, Amin Fahim. In the crucial party meeting that finalised these arrangements, Benazir was so moved by the potential loss of control that she wept. And she immediately moved to tighten her grip.[106] Prospective PPPP senators had to sign an oath declaring their 'dedication and devotion to Benazir who is the guiding inspiration of Pakistan People's Party Parliamentarians even though she is not leading it'. The second paragraph continued in much the same vein: 'Given the respect I have for Mohtarma Benazir Bhutto's leadership I swear to abide by all her directions, advice and suggestions (including resignation) as I may receive'. She also required senators to write undated, irrevocable letters of resignation.

But for all her efforts to bolster her political position Benazir was still vulnerable legally, and on 15 April 1999 Sharif's longstanding efforts to investigate her corruption finally paid off: a two-judge panel of the Lahore High Court headed by Justice Qayyum convicted Benazir Bhutto and her husband Asif Ali Zardari in a corruption case concerning kickbacks from two Swiss companies which had been awarded contracts in her second government, Geneva-based Société Générale de Surveillance and Cotecna Inspection. Since he was already in prison the outcome of the case didn't make so much difference to Zardari, but for Benazir it was a significant development, and it forced her into exile. She was to remain abroad for the next nine years. Although she often described this period as one of enforced exile, she was in fact free to return to Pakistan at any time – but had she done so she would have run headlong into the various corruption cases she faced. As for the SGS/Cotecna case, she was saved by the incompetence of Sharif's anti-corruption investigator, Saifur Rehman. At the start of the trial which ended with her conviction, the government ordered the monitoring of the office, home and mobile telephones of the judge in the case, Justice Malik Abdul Qayyum, in order to keep him under constant observation[107] – in previous cases against the family, officials had become aware of judges being threatened. But when the recordings were leaked by a PPP sympathiser in the Intelligence Bureau in 2001, it turned out the government had scored an own goal. They revealed that the judge had come under sustained pressure from government officials to convict Benazir and Zardari or face losing his job. In one call, Saifur Rehman discussed when the verdict would come, saying: 'Give me 100% confirmation that it will be done tomorrow'. The judge then asked him what punishment he should give. 'Not less than 7 years,' Saif said. When the judge pointed out that that was the maximum sentence, which was hardly ever awarded, Saifur Rehman said he would seek guidance from the prime minister. In a subsequent conversation Saifur Rehman told the judge that he had asked Sharif about the punishment, to which the prime minister had said, 'Give them full dose'.[108] In what can only be described as a very limited display of judicial independence, he sentenced them both to five years.

In April 2001, on the basis of the leaked recordings, the Supreme Court overturned the conviction and ordered a retrial. But that was not the last of the SGS/Cotecna case. In 2003 a Swiss magistrate, Daniel Devaud, found Benazir guilty of money laundering. His finding centred on a sapphire and diamond necklace that Benazir had bought in 1997 in New Bond Street, London, for $175,000. Devaud seized the jewellery from a safety deposit box in Geneva and found that she had paid for most of the necklace with kickbacks: 'Benazir Bhutto knew she was acting in a criminally reprehensible manner by abusing her role in order to obtain for herself or her husband considerable sums in the sole private interest of her family at the cost of the Islamic Republic of Pakistan.' He sentenced her and Asif Zardari to 180 days in prison and ordered them to pay $11.9 million back to Pakistan. 'I certainly don't have any doubts about the judgments I handed down,' Devaud said in 2007. 'Nor have I had any reason to start having any doubts . . . These judgments came after an investigation lasting several years and involving thousands of documents from several sources including banks, lawyers and the two companies concerned, SGS and Cotecna.'[109]

Benazir and Zardari both denied any wrongdoing, but when she tried to defend herself against Devaud, Benazir ended up adopting absurd positions, such as describing the Swiss authorities as 'the Swiss regime' and accusing them of making a mistake by taking sides in a political battle.[110] But like generations of Bhuttos before her, she always understood the importance of paying for the best legal advice, which in this case was to refuse to appear before Devaud or answer any of his questions – he eventually convicted her in absentia. Under Swiss law, this meant that she had the right to demand a retrial – which she did. The Devaud judgment was not overturned but it was set aside pending the outcome of the new trial. The Swiss authorities then increased the stakes by including a more serious charge of aggravated money laundering.

The Swiss case showed that by the time of the second government, the nature of Benazir and Zardari's financial dealings had changed. Business was no longer something she let her husband do – it had become more of a joint enterprise. There were many other accusations of malpractice, including the so-called 'Karachi affair', which concerned an attempt by Benazir's government to purchase three Agosta-class submarines from France in 1994, a deal that led to allegations of massive kickbacks taken by both military officers and civilians. The Pakistani authorities subsequently successfully secured the extradition from the US of the head of the Pakistan Navy at the time of the deal, but, as ever, the military protected their man, saying an open trial would undermine trust in the armed forces. Despite the rumours that civilian politicians also benefited, none were ever charged, let alone convicted. In the normal course of events the case would have faded away, but in 2002 eleven French naval engineers working in Karachi were killed by violent jihadists. There were suspicions in France that the bombing was an act of revenge after President Jacques Chirac ordered an end to paying bribes relating to the arms deal. Pakistan dismissed that suggestion, saying the attackers mistook the French engineers for Americans. The case came back into the headlines again in 2019, when the former French prime minister Edouard Balladur went on trial accused of financing his 1995 bid for the presidency by accepting 'retro-commissions' related to the arms deal. Balladur denied any wrongdoing.

There were many other cases. A leading French military contractor was accused of planning to pay $200 million in bribes for a $4 billion jet fighter deal that fell apart only when Benazir's second government was dismissed. A Dubai-based gold bullion-dealing company was accused of depositing $10 million into an account controlled by Zardari, after the company was given a monopoly on gold imports to Pakistan. The company denied the allegation, saying the bank documents that showed its money transfers to Zardari were faked by someone in the bank.[111] Zardari also denied the charge, and he was never convicted. Other allegations concerned luxury properties owned in France and the US and the purchase of Polish tractors for Pakistan's farmers. Next, Western governments started investigating allegations that Benazir and her husband had been involved in drug-related cases. Realising just how damaging such claims would be, Benazir moved fast to persuade the authorities in Switzerland and the UK that such suggestions were politically motivated slander by her opponents. The PPP convincingly argued that the Pakistani government had come to realise that, as soon as it raised drug cases, Western governments such as the Swiss and the British would provide the authorities in Islamabad with much more information about Benazir's and Zardari's bank accounts. The Pakistani authorities consequently found some people to make false allegations about drug-related crimes.[112]

But even if those allegations were beaten back, others found traction. In the UK, Lord Justice Collins made a preliminary finding about allegations that Benazir or Zardari had used ill-gotten gains to buy and refurbish a country estate near London called Rockwood, or, as the Pakistan press dubbed it, Surrey Palace. The purchase might have remained a secret had it not been for the shipping of crates of antiques and other furnishings to the UK in diplomatic bags. In what became known as 'the container case', it was later revealed that they had eighty-three pieces of furniture in crates sent from Lahore and Bilawal House. In 2006 the British judge concluded: 'There is a reasonable prospect of Pakistan establishing that the funds used to refurbish the Rockwood estate were the proceeds of payments by SGS and Cotecna, that those funds were the fruits of corruption, that the funds used to purchase the Rockwood estate were also the fruits of corruption.' It was a complicated case because Rockwood was owned by a series of Isle of Man companies and blind trusts in various jurisdictions. Investigators insisted that Benazir and her husband were the ultimate owners – something they denied, until, that is, liquidators eventually sold the property for £4 million and, given that no one said they owned it, wondered what they should do with the proceeds. The Pakistan government argued that since the money had originated in kickbacks on government contracts, it should have the money. At that point, Asif Zardari told an Isle of Man court that he was indeed the beneficial owner and wanted his money back.

It is possible that Benazir was unaware of the Rockwood purchase. A British lawyer trying to help the Pakistan government push the case through the London courts conceded that there was no document linking Benazir to the purchase nor any evidence that she had even seen the property.[113] It all left Benazir increasingly frustrated that her name was being tarnished and her reputation damaged within PPP circles. One PPP activist reflected widespread opinion in the party when he said: 'The wedding was the worst thing that ever happened to the PPP.'[114] But it was by no means fair to blame everything on Zardari. At the time this internal PPP discontent was growing, Benazir's business activities entered a new phase: she branched out on her own. In 1996 the UN set up the Oil-for-Food Programme with the intention of allowing the Iraqi government to sell its oil as long as the funds generated were used for humanitarian supplies. Saddam Hussein's officials managed to subvert the scheme in a number of ways, one of which was to sell the oil to selected traders – many of whom were politically influential – at low prices. And a UN inquiry, the Volcker Commission, subsequently found that the kickbacks paid to the Iraqi oil minister totalled $228 million, of which $2 million came from a UAE company named Petroline FZC. Documents unearthed by Pakistan's National Accountability Bureau showed that Benazir was the chairperson of Petroline FZC. Because of a property in Marbella, the allegations became the subject of legal hearings in Spain.[115] The fact that Zardari was not involved in the Oil-for-Food deal was a sign of how they had grown apart, which, given how long he had spent in prison, was perhaps inevitable.

The legal cases were mounting up and Benazir needed a way out. On her fiftieth birthday she wrote an epic 400-line poem to express her feelings about living in exile in Dubai.

Waiting for news in dreams and day
Waiting for messengers in dreams and day
When will the message come
Taking me from here to there
I want the answer to my heart
I want to pass God's test
O God, I wait the messenger
Taking me to where I belong.[116]

When the messenger eventually came, he had been sent by General Musharraf. Benazir and Musharraf had met before. In 1995 he had come to her when she was prime minister with a plan to occupy the Kargil heights – something he actually did three years later. But Benazir turned him down, pointing out that, even if Pakistan took the heights, the UN would insist on a withdrawal – which is exactly what eventually happened. Benazir believed Musharraf had been embarrassed by her criticism of his plan, not least because it was done in front of his colleagues.[117] But that was all in the past. By 2005 they both had plenty to discuss. Musharraf needed more political support and Benazir needed to get out of her legal cases. In 2005 and 2006 there were at least five meetings between Benazir and Musharraf's officials, including Tariq Aziz, the ISI chief Parvez Kayani and, at a later stage, Musharraf's chief of staff, General Hamid Javed. Meetings between the two sides were originally facilitated by the British Foreign Office, but when it looked as though an agreement might actually be possible, London let the US take over. The military said they wanted to deal with Benazir alone, excluding Zardari – a suggestion which Benazir successfully resisted. After a process that she described as a rollercoaster, which involved not only building trust with the army but also facing down internal PPP opposition, a direct meeting between Musharraf and Benazir took place on 24 January 2007.

For Musharraf, the deal was not too complicated. Faced with declining popularity and a growing crisis of legitimacy, he needed the PPP's support to keep on ruling after parliamentary elections due in 2008. Benazir had three demands: first and foremost, Musharraf would have to resign from the army. Secondly, the ban on third terms for prime ministers should be lifted, thereby enabling her – and Nawaz Sharif, with whom she signed a so-called Charter of Democracy – to participate in Pakistani politics. Finally, all the legal cases against her and her husband should be subject to an amnesty. American and British diplomats believed that an administration run by Musharraf and Benazir would combine the kind of strong government needed to confront the Taliban with the political support necessary to remain in power and the democratic façade to give the whole set-up more international legitimacy. Benazir persuaded them that if Musharraf could give her greater control of the army and the ISI, she could at last make progress on confronting violent jihadism and improving relations with India. But it was an arrangement that was never going to work.

The depth of mistrust between the two was so great that there was no chance of them establishing a stable power relationship. Benazir routinely described Musharraf as a dictator. And he had genuine contempt for most civilian politicians, who he believed had enriched themselves in office. When he had taken over power, his primary stated goal had been to clean up the system and bring on a new generation of clean, competent politicians. 'Bhutto', he wrote in his 2006 autobiography *In the Line of Fire*, had 'twice been tried, been tested and failed', and should be denied a third chance. He compared her becoming the PPP's chairperson for life to the tradition of old African dictators. But that was then. Now, he needed her.

In public Benazir insisted it was doable. Asked if she could work with General Musharraf, she hedged her bets. 'It would depend on how the event unfolded . . . we are risking our popularity by even having this dialogue, but we understand Pakistan is a critical country. We understand that instability in Pakistan could threaten our own security as well as that of the region, so we've taken the risk.'[118] The final deal was a compromise: he did agree to step down as army chief and she did get let off all her cases. The ban on third-term prime ministers remained in place, but Benazir figured that if she did well in the elections, she could deal with that later. And so the deal was done. With the basic outlines agreed, teams from the two leaders thrashed out a National Reconciliation Ordinance for politicians who faced allegations between 1996 and 5 October 2007, dates which neatly excluded Nawaz Sharif from the deal. Musharraf signed the NRO on 6 October. In September 2007 Benazir announced a date for her return. Her years of exile were about to end, but, as everyone knew, great dangers lay ahead.

8
ASSASSINATION

While American and British diplomats were organising Benazir's political come-back, al-Qaeda and the Pakistan Taliban were planning her murder. Osama bin Laden had first identified Benazir as a target in 1989 when he funded the plot to remove her from power uncovered by Operation MIDNIGHT JACKAL.[1] Four years later al-Qaeda went further. It tried to kill her. There were two attempts, involving men who would go on to the front ranks of violent jihadism: Ramzi Yousef, the man who was later convicted of the first, failed, 1993 World Trade Center bombing, and his uncle Khalid Sheikh Mohammed, the al-Qaeda planner who succeeded in destroying the twin towers in 9/11. In August 1993 Yousef and an accomplice attempted to place a bomb in a sewage drain outside Benazir's home, Bilawal House, in Karachi. The idea was to detonate the bomb when her car drove over it, but the plan failed when suspicious police officers asked what the men were doing. Next Yousef tried to organise Benazir's assassi-nation at an election rally in Nishtar Park, Karachi. A nearby rooftop was selected for an ex-army sniper provided by the Punjabi sectarian militant group Sipah-e-Sahaba. According to Benazir, Yousef later told the Pakistani authorities: 'We had her right in our sights but the weapons did not arrive in time.'[2] The details of both plots came out in 1995, when one of Ramzi Yousef's teenage friends, Adbul Shakoor, was arrested in Pakistan. Shakoor was reported as saying that Yousef wanted to kill Benazir because 'she is a female and according to Islamic religion, she could not become a prime minister'.[3] Benazir subsequently claimed that when he was in US custody, Yousef admitted that both he and Khalid Sheikh Mohammed had tried to kill her. 'So, they succeeded with the World Trade Towers but they didn't succeed with me,' she said.[4]

From bin Laden's point of view, targeting Benazir again in 2007 made sense for a number of reasons. First, she had declared her opposition to both al-Qaeda and the Pakistan Taliban in much clearer terms than any other Pakistani politician. Even General Musharraf was reluctant to name the Taliban as his enemy: he preferred to talk in terms of 'terrorists' without specifying which group they belonged to. Benazir brooked no such equivocation and, as bin Laden saw it, had declared herself to be an enemy, for whom a deadly response would be entirely appropriate. Killing her would not only eliminate a potentially powerful pro-American politician in Pakistan but also send a warning to others that open criticism of jihadis carried a high price. And there was something else. The American drone campaign in north-west Pakistan and Afghanistan had severely damaged al-Qaeda's capacity. Far from being able to follow up on 9/11 with another spectacular attack, it had proved difficult for bin Laden to mount even relatively small actions. But while al-Qaeda was on the back foot, the Pakistan Taliban was ascendant, mounting significant operations almost every day. Bin Laden wondered whether he might be able to leverage the Taliban's strength and at least associate al-Qaeda with a major attack. He asked one of his most senior operatives in Pakistan, Abu Obaidah al-Masri, to discuss the issue with the Pakistan Taliban leader Baitullah Mehsud. Some reports suggest that a second senior al-Qaeda operative, Ilyas Kashmiri, was also present at the meeting.[5] The Pakistan Taliban was not in the habit of taking orders from al-Qaeda, but on the question of Benazir the two organisations shared an interest: both believed that the US had tasked her with crushing violent jihadist forces and that she was therefore a threat. Once the decision had been taken, Baitullah Mehsud made no secret of his intention to assassinate Benazir. A week before her return, the Pakistani media reported that he had, according to a Pakistani senator who had met him, 'sent his people to welcome her'.[6] Haji Omar, a Taliban commander in Waziristan, confirmed the Taliban thinking: 'She has an agreement with America. We will carry out attacks on Benazir as we did on General Pervez Musharraf.'[7] Benazir responded with characteristic robustness. Anyone who attacked her, she said, would 'burn in hell'.[8]

Baitullah Mehsud had no shortage of recruits willing to mount a suicide attack. Allegedly, one of them was fifteen-year-old Aitzaz Shah.[9] The mullahs running suicide bomb factories preferred young students: it took less time to train an impressionable teenager to kill himself than someone in their late teens or twenties, who often had sufficient strength of personality to resist indoctrination. Aitzaz Shah was born in Karachi, where his father worked for twenty years in a cotton mill, rising to the rank of machine master. Like many Pakistani parents, the father relied on madrasahs or Islamic seminaries to educate his son. Not only were they free, but they also opened up the possibility for his son to become a respected member of the community with a reliable, if modest, income as a cleric. In the course of his religious education, Shah learnt the Koran by heart – an exercise that took some years. He could not understand the Arabic that he was reciting, but he could articulate the sounds of the entire text. Then, after watching some films about jihad, he decided he wanted to fight the Americans in Afghanistan. He asked his mother's permission and, when she refused, decided to volunteer anyway. On 2 May 2007 he began a twenty-seven-hour journey from the bus station in Karachi to the tribal area of Waziristan near the Afghan border. Contacting the Taliban could not have been easier. A fellow madrasah student, who went to see him off in Karachi, told the bus driver that Aitzaz was going on jihad. When they reached Waziristan, the driver asked someone with a pickup if he could run the boy down to the Taliban office in Makeen, a small town nearby. The pickup owner was so impressed by Aitzaz Shah's piety that he agreed to do it free of charge. The young Karachiite now found himself with a group of forty to fifty boys and men being given basic physical and firearms training. Anxious about his mother, he called home to find out how she had taken his disappearance, but because he used a landline, the family was able to trace the number's location. An uncle was dispatched to Waziristan to recover him, but Aitzaz Shah did not want to go back home, and when he heard the uncle had come to find him, he hid: the uncle left empty-handed.

Once his training was complete, Aitzaz Shah was granted his wish to fight in Afghanistan. After a three-day trek in which he crossed the border, he took part in a forty-day-long attack on a US army camp. Eight of his fellow Taliban fighters were killed, but Aitzaz survived and claimed he was among those who walked through the camp after the Americans deserted it. On his return to Pakistan he spent some days listening to clerics talking about suicide attacks, which, they said, were the greatest of sacrifices for Islam and, as a result, generously rewarded. While a martyr defending Islam could take seventy people to paradise, a suicide bomber could take an unlimited number. Not only that, he would also be guaranteed seventy-two virgins. Convinced, Aitzaz Shah volunteered for a suicide mission and in July 2007, less than three months after he had left Karachi, he found himself in a specialist suicide bomber training facility with a group of ten to twelve others who had made the same commitment. Now it was time for some driving lessons in case he was selected to undertake a mission in which he would need to drive to his target alone. In October 2007 his training was complete, and Aitzaz Shah was informed he had been selected for an important mission. He would kill Benazir. His confession does not record whether he had ever heard of her but in all likelihood he had not. He was told she was too pro-American, would probably launch an attack on the Taliban if elected and, to cap it all, was a woman, who should not run for office. Faced with this request, the court heard, Aitzaz Shah agreed to do it.

Since the Taliban did not let recruits watch TV, Aitzaz Shah was unable to see the breaking news being played out on screens around the world on 18 October 2007. Having bid farewell to her husband and two daughters (Bilawal had stayed in Oxford studying), Benazir battled her way through the Dubai terminal, followed by a retinue of party activists and journalists. 'This is the beginning of a long journey for Pakistan back to democracy,' she declared, 'we must believe that miracles do happen.'[10] After take-off, the plane lurched in the air as over-enthusiastic party workers crowded around her, becoming so rowdy she had to call for calm on the plane's public address system. As soon as the plane landed in Karachi, she showed her political experience. Instructing the journalists to disembark first, she waited until the cameras were rolling before walking down the steps. Wearing a green and white shalwar kameez to represent Pakistan's national colours, she raised her hands, palms upwards, in prayer as someone held a copy of the Koran above her head. Her campaign had begun and she had the initiative. A procession was planned from Karachi airport to Mohammad Ali Jinnah's mausoleum, where she would give a speech. The huge crowds who had come to welcome her made for powerful TV images, but at the same time Benazir knew she was vulnerable. As she had written just days before her departure from the US: 'Once I leave the airport, I pray for the best and prepare for the worst'.[11] Distrusting the army, she wanted her own people to handle her security arrangements but realised they did not have the skills. She had made considerable efforts to persuade the Americans to provide her with security, figuring that it would not only make her safer but also send Musharraf an important message about how much the US valued her. The

Americans declined to help because, she believed, of opposition from Vice President Dick Cheney, who wanted to show continued American support for Musharraf.

The single contribution of the Pakistan Army was to provide her convoy with vehicles fitted with devices that would jam any signal sent to detonate a remote roadside bomb. It wasn't much, and even that measure proved ineffective: subsequent investigations showed that because the procession took so long to progress, the batteries drained, rendering the jammers useless. For its part, the PPP had adapted a truck, cladding it with armour. It had also recruited thousands of volunteers – the so-called 'Benazir martyrs' force' – who linked arms to form a human chain around the vehicle. The bus was fitted with a three-sided bulletproof cubicle, but Benazir refused to use it, saying she did not want to disappoint people who had travelled a long way to see her. Standing on the double-decker vehicle's open-air top floor, she was an easy target. People on bridges along the route found themselves within a couple of metres of her when the truck passed underneath them.

The suicide bombers struck just after midnight, triggering their devices manually, meaning that the lack of working jammers made no difference. The first blew himself up as he approached the Benazir martyrs' force, clearing a path for the second bomber, who walked over the dead and dying guards. Bright white flashes filled the air and the explosion rocked the vehicle, killing three people on board. But on the road it was much worse: 146 people were dead or dying, with body parts spread over a large area. Benazir survived, but it was a very lucky escape: tired after hours of waving and with her ankles swelling, she had retreated into the body of the bus just ten minutes before the attack. Within seconds of the bombs going off, she was rushed to her Karachi home where, the next morning, she held a press conference. 'It was no secret that the terrorists would attempt to assassinate me,' she thundered. 'So, all those who walked with us knew that it carried a risk. And still they did so, because they want a Pakistan that is democratic. They want a Pakistan that can provide hope and a better future for those who are hungry. For those who are poor. For those who are downtrodden.' She also revealed she had sent Musharraf a letter with the names of three people who she believed were behind the attack. It later emerged that the three were the former head of the ISI, General (Retd) Hamid Gul; the serving head of the Intelligence Bureau and former ISI official Brigadier (Retd) Ejaz Shah; and a Musharraf loyalist serving as chief minister of Punjab, Chaudhry Pervez Elahi – all of whom strongly denied the allegation. Initially, because she did not want a complete breach with the military, Benazir did not release those names. While she could claim to the military that she had behaved with restraint, resisting the temptation to name the trio in public, the existence of a secret list whetted the appetite of the media, who immediately started guessing which deep-state figures might be on it. Having set those hares running, Benazir put the PPP's martyrdom machine to work: her first trips out of her house in Karachi were to hospitals to visit some of those who had sustained injuries trying to protect her.

The police investigating the double suicide bombing knew they would have to tread carefully. As a general rule, senior Pakistani officers assume that the perpetrators of a politically important attack probably have protection from elements within the ISI. Their task, therefore, is to give the impression of investigative activity without actually uncovering too much. The 128-page document produced by the Joint Investigation Team investigating the Karachi attack appears to be a work of deliberate obfuscation.[12] While there is page after page of useless information naming, for example, hundreds of police officers who were posted to various locations in the city, there is not even a single reference to Benazir's letter or the three men she named in it. Nor are there any phone records of who called whom in the vicinity of the attack. Normally such records are available, but the police subsequently said that they had been unable to get any information from the phone companies. 'It's quite difficult to get,' the head of the Karachi investigation Saud Mirza later said. 'At times, even if you have clues, you are totally stumped because all the mobile detectors are totally under their control.' Asked to elaborate on the phrase 'their control' and specifically whether he meant the intelligence agencies, he said: 'Yeah. It's not only the military ones. It's the civilian ones as well. The Intelligence Bureau . . .' he said, trailing off to avoid further specificity. 'It's really frustrating. It is really very wrenching for us. The counterterrorism department of Sindh police has a very glorious history. But this is one case which really challenges us and so far we haven't been able to crack it.'[13] He might have added – but didn't – that the man running the Intelligence Bureau at the time was none other than Ejaz Shah – one of the three men Benazir had named in her letter.

Another major gap in the police report concerned the physical appearance of the suspects. As a result of dealing with so many suicide attacks, the Pakistani police had noticed that the force of a suicide bomb blast often peeled the bomber's face clean off the skull and propelled it far from the epicentre. Police could gather these so-called 'facemasks' and get a very good idea what the bomber looked like. The police in Karachi found a facemask 78 feet from the blast point, as well as a head. For some reason they decided not to publish images of them, but it seems they did show them to the Americans: a confidential US cable ten days after the attack reported, 'The heads of the bombers were recovered and it appears they are from the northern areas.' Amid all the omissions and deliberate distractions, the police report included just two pieces of useful information. The first concerned the suicide bombers' equipment. An army explosives expert scoured the crime scene and found a detonator. Similar devices, he said, with the same lot numbers and factory code, had been used in eleven other Taliban attacks in different parts of the country earlier that year.[14] The second interesting aspect of the report concerned a militant named Qari Saifullah Akhtar. A well-known jihadi, Akhtar became a suspect in the Karachi case because Benazir named him in her posthumously published book, *Reconciliation*.

> I was informed of a meeting that had taken place in Lahore where the bomb blasts were planned . . . a bomb maker was needed for the bombs. Enter Qari Saifullah Akhtar, a wanted terrorist who had tried to overthrow my second government. He had been extradited by the United Arab Emirates and was languishing in the Karachi central jail . . . The officials in Lahore had turned to Akhtar for help. His liaison with elements in the government was a radical who was asked to make the bombs and he himself asked for a fatwa making it legitimate to oblige. He got one.[15]

Saifullah Akhtar and Benazir had history. In 1995 he had procured the weapons for Major General Zahir ul-Islam Abbasi's coup attempt (see Chapter 7). Later, in what turned out to be a very successful militant career, he became head of Harkat-ul-Jihad al-Islami (HUJI), an organisation with operations in Uzbekistan, Tajikistan, Burma, China and Chechnya as well as Pakistan and Afghanistan. He also formed a close relationship with the Afghan Taliban leader

Mullah Omar: the two men are said to have shared the same motorbike as they fled Kandahar after 9/11. Even though the ISI had good relations with Saifullah Akhtar, the publication of his name in *Reconciliation* left the Pakistani authorities little choice but to question him. Towards the end of October, the ISI detained him, together with three of his sons.[16] He was interviewed, but nothing came of it. As for his possible role in Benazir's killing, the published version of the interrogation in the Joint Investigation Team report did not even refer to the Karachi attack. Conveniently enough, there was a gap in the transcript between August 2007 and January 2008. Saifullah Akhtar was released once again. He was killed in 2017 fighting the Americans in Afghanistan.

With the police doing their best to avoid finding out what had happened, Benazir returned to the campaign trail. Her first foray outside Karachi was to her hometown of Larkana. Despite attempts to keep the visit secret, by the time she arrived buildings were bedecked with PPP green, red and black flags and the streets filled with people chanting her name. Security men wielding AK-47s clung on to her vehicle, swatting away supporters with the butts of their weapons. She now took care not to have direct contact with the crowds, preferring to put her head and shoulders through the emergency hatch fitted into the roof of her armoured vehicle. Her first stop was at the family mausoleum at Garhi Khuda Bakhsh. Draped in a shawl inscribed with Islamic verses, Benazir sprinkled rose petals on her father's grave. And as she looked at the cameras, she said: 'I am not afraid of anyone but Allah.'[17] Her campaign was back on track.

On her return to Karachi, Benazir turned to the task of honing her message. She called together the senior party leadership and explained her thinking. The imminence of the elections – they were due on 8 January – would help her maintain party unity, but, even so, she knew she was treading a fine line. She avoided outright criticism of General Musharraf, holding back from saying he was behind the Karachi attack, for example. 'I am not accusing the government, but I am accusing certain individuals who abuse their positions, abuse their powers,' she said.[18] While some in her party feared what direct confrontation with the military would bring, others had always opposed her decision to strike a deal with Musharraf, seeing it as a betrayal of the PPP's oft-stated policy of shunning military rulers. To take just one example of this strand of thinking in the party, Raheel Iqbal, a former province-level information secretary, said that Benazir had betrayed her father's cause. 'Zulfikar Ali Bhutto's manifesto was anti-imperialist, anti-general and anti-dictatorship. We spent years in jail to stand up for this manifesto, and now Benazir arrives with American support, and has been making meetings with General Musharraf. Democracy does not require a deal with a dictator.'[19] But party activists who thought this way hadn't been paying attention. Zulfikar had done deals with two dictators, Ayub Khan and Yahya Khan, whose declaration of martial law he had accepted without complaint. Benazir had reacted in much the same way when Musharraf ousted Nawaz Sharif: 'normally coups take place against democratic leaders,' she told a TV reporter in London. 'Here a coup has taken place against an unpopular despot ... I would like to urge the Western community, stay away from Nawaz Sharif. He is not liked by the people of Pakistan. You support democracy, so talk to the army'.[20]

Five days after the attack Benazir met with US Ambassador Anne Patterson at Bilawal House. She requested that the Americans 'undertake an evaluation of existing executive security procedures and recommendation of additional resources necessary for maximum safety'. The ambassador told Benazir that, while there were situations in which the US government provided security to foreign leaders – former President of Haiti Jean-Bertrand Aristide and President Karzai, for example – it did not do so for opposition leaders running political campaigns. Afterwards, in a telegram to Washington, Patterson advised not to offer help. 'We also believe it highly unlikely that the PPP would follow professional recommendations not to hold rallies in large crowds,' she said with some perspicacity. Any US government evaluation would inevitably conclude that Benazir's security arrangements did not meet American standards. The question would then arise as to whose job it was to fix the problem. 'Responsibility for security belongs with the Government of Pakistan,' the ambassador argued. 'We will keep stressing to both sides that government and Benazir's party must work directly together to resolve any questions or issues regarding Benazir's personal security.'[21] But the Patterson meeting was not just about security. 'You want me to cooperate,' Benazir complained, 'with someone who is trying to kill me.' Although she did not spell it out in so many words, the message was clear: after the Karachi attack, the deal she had struck with Musharraf was open for renegotiation.[22]

As Benazir contemplated the remaining weeks of the campaign, the Taliban were also refining their plans. They decided to work with a young man from

Rawalpindi who had volunteered to fight with them. Husnain Gul[23] had been an active jihadist from the age of sixteen, when, in 2005, a friend took him for weapons training in North Waziristan. A couple of years later his commitment to the cause intensified when the friend who had introduced him to jihad was killed in the 2007 siege of the Red Mosque. Husnain Gul vowed revenge. In September 2007, without telling his family, he went to the Haqqania madrasah on the road between Islamabad and Peshawar to see if he could get involved in militant activities. He had gone to the right place. Soon he was talking with an expert bomb-maker, Nadir Khan, whom Gul had first met two years earlier on the jihadist weapons training course and who was now living at the madrasah. Nadir Khan used to be with the Haqqani Network but, frustrated that it was active only in Afghanistan, joined the Pakistan Taliban (TTP) instead, developing a close relationship with TTP leader Baitullah, whom he visited frequently. He suggested that Gul might want to join a group he had established to attack government targets.

Husnain Gul not only agreed but also secured the help of another young jihadi, his twenty-four-year-old cousin, a Rawalpindi-based taxi driver called Rafaqat Hussain. They were soon put to work. The first suicide bomber they handled was a boy called Usman, who, on 4 September 2007, drove his motorbike into a military car near the city's main market. Usman blew himself up, killing a colonel. Some weeks later, on 30 October, they helped another suicide bomber attack a police checkpoint in the city. There were some failed operations too, but still, with successful attacks under their belts, the two young men from Rawalpindi were gaining a reputation for competence, and when Husnain Gul was back at the Haqqania madrasah in November he was given a far more important task. When Nadir Khan gathered his group in room 96 on the fourth floor of the madrasah's hostel, he told them the Pakistan Taliban leader had given them their next target: Benazir Bhutto.

While Benazir campaigned and the Taliban plotted, General Musharraf fretted. Having failed to keep Benazir out of the country before the elections, he now faced Pakistan's most charismatic politician, emboldened by the outpouring of sympathy after the Karachi attack, charging around the country drumming up support. Regretting his weakness in ever having given in to Western pressure to come to an accommodation with her, Musharraf decided he had to act. On 3 November he declared a state of emergency, closed down newspapers, put TV stations off air, arrested thousands of his opponents and sent troops into the Supreme Court building. Benazir was in Dubai taking a few days off the campaign when the state of emergency was declared. Musharraf had hoped she would decide that the risks were too great and stay there, but in fact she flew straight back to Pakistan. Again, though, her statements were more nuanced than they first appeared. 'The people of Pakistan will not accept martial law,' she said.[24] But rather than calling for Musharraf to resign, she instead asked the international community to persuade the military ruler to restore the constitution. Despite her restraint, though, it was becoming increasingly clear that the two principal figures in Pakistani politics were headed for a direct confrontation, in which only one could emerge still standing. The Western-brokered deal in which she would provide a democratic veneer for his military campaign against the militants – always an utterly unrealistic plan – was unravelling. But she still had some wiggle room. 'It's very difficult,' she said, 'to work with a military dictator.'[25] Difficult, but not, perhaps, impossible. Benazir had not yet called on her party activists to take to the streets, but she did decide to increase the pressure on Musharraf by announcing a rally in Rawalpindi on Friday, 9 November.

Benazir and Musharraf then performed the sort of political theatre at which Pakistan excels. Using emergency powers to declare that the Rawalpindi rally would never happen, police surrounded Benazir's home in Islamabad with personnel, vehicles and barbed wire but insisted she was not under house arrest. And it was true that, because Musharraf did not want to irritate Washington, she faced fewer restrictions under the state of emergency than other party leaders. Yet when Benazir on a number of occasions tried to leave her house, she was physically prevented from doing so because, the police said, they were concerned about her security. From Benazir's point of view the resulting TV pictures were perfect, showing an embattled democratic leader facing military oppression. Musharraf was again on the back foot: he wanted to limit her actions but could not afford to upset Washington by formally arresting her. All the while, the Americans were mediating behind the scenes, and eventually a deal was done. Benazir called off the Rawalpindi rally and, in return, when she made a twenty-minute statement to reporters outside her house, it was relayed on state television. But just in case, Musharraf deployed 6,000 police to Rawalpindi, blocking all routes to the place where the rally would have been held.

Musharraf and the PPP had patched together a deal for the day, but it resolved none of the underlying issues. When Benazir moved on to Lahore, she vowed to increase the pressure. 'To get Pakistan from the clutches of dictatorship we are organising a long march,'[26] she said, as she asked her candidates in constituencies on the road from Lahore to Islamabad to organise rallies she could address as she progressed towards the capital. 'Pakistan under dictatorship is a pressure cooker. Without a place to vent, the passion of our people for liberty threatens to explode.'[27] Again the government blocked her, this time declaring the house she was staying in a sub jail, meaning the restrictions on her movements were not only physical but, this time, legal too. Musharraf had upped the ante. Benazir responded in kind, openly raising the possibility of boycotting the vote and adding that, if the election did go ahead, she would not work with Musharraf. 'He has made his decision,' she said in a TV interview. 'He has refused to adopt the democratic course. So he should resign'.[28] Later she added: 'I will not serve as prime minister as long as Musharraf is president.'[29] It sounded definitive, but Benazir was always willing to listen to the Americans. A visit from the US consul general in Lahore and a phone call from Deputy Secretary of State John Negroponte were enough to persuade her to back down. Working with Musharraf, she now said, would be 'difficult'. Once again, the rifts had been papered over, but Musharraf was increasingly frustrated, describing her as 'the darling of the West'.[30]

Benazir made an effort to visit as many parts of Pakistan as she could: this was a national campaign and she did not want to be accused of spending too much time in her own province of Sindh or the electorally important one of Punjab. With six weeks of campaigning to go, she headed for Balochistan and the north-west. 'I ask our Pashtun brothers to come forward for peace. They have supported the Pakistan People's Party in the past', she said, 'and once again they must support the Pakistan People's Party.' This was heartland Taliban country, but she lashed out at the militants, insisting that many Pashtuns, whatever their reputation for conservatism, in fact shared her liberal values. 'We should not sit as silent spectators while terrorists are killing innocent people,' she told the crowd there.[31]

As she moved around the north-west, Benazir also turned her attention to the unfinished business of the rally she had been forced to cancel in Rawalpindi, setting another date: 27 December. But the Taliban were one step ahead of her. In late November Rafaqat Hussain, Husnain Gul and another Haqqani student, Nasrullah Khan, had carried out a recce of Rawalpindi's Liaquat Park, the location in the city which generally hosted political rallies. Having satisfied themselves that an attack could be staged there, it was a question of waiting for Benazir to come to them. And they had made a significant tactical break-through. A young would-be suicide bomber, Bilal, had been sent to observe Benazir's rallies in the north-west. When he saw her in Pubbi, near Naushera, on 12 December, he noticed that her security was less intense as she left the rally. He approached her departing vehicle and, having managed to touch it, told his handlers that he had worked out how to mount an attack. When the 27 December date was announced, the final planning began. Nadir was in overall charge. Husnain Gul and Rafaqat Hussain would be responsible for the accommodation, and Nasrullah Khan, working with another Haqqania student, Rasheed Ahmed, would bring the suicide bomber to Rawalpindi and be in charge on the day. Others were asked to make and deliver the suicide vests. Nadir Khan and Nasrullah Khan left the Haqqania madrasah and headed for South Waziristan to see Baitullah Mehsud. When they returned, they had $1,000 of spending money, and Bilal, together with another fifteen-year-old, was about to make global headlines.

The precise circumstances of the attack in Liaquat Park and the announce-ment of Benazir's death at the hospital in Rawalpindi have been described in the introduction. Most Pakistanis were deeply shocked: even her opponents were appalled by what had happened. But one teenager was rejoicing. Having watched Bilal hit his target, Ikramullah, the backup bomber, realised both that his mission had been accomplished and that his services were no longer required. He made his way back to Nasrullah so that he could be transported back to Waziristan. For many years, the Pakistan state insisted that Ikramullah was dead. In July 2017, for example, the chief prosecutor Mohammad Azhar Chaudhry said that, on the basis of information he had been given by the Federal Investigating Agency, civil servants in the tribal area and relatives, Ikramullah had died in a drone strike in Waziristan. 'Ikramullah is dead,' he said. In fact, he was alive, and in time rose to become head of the Taliban in the Kurram tribal agency.[32] For some reason, in August 2017 the Pakistani state stopped saying he was dead and included him on a list of most-wanted terrorists.[33] While the state took years to give accurate information about

Ikramullah, it acted within hours to supply information about a phone call it had secretly recorded hours after the assassination. After getting clearance from Musharraf, the Ministry of Interior published what it claimed was a phone conversation between a militant mullah and the Taliban leader Baitullah Mehsud. This is the transcript of the tape:

Mullah: Asalaam Aleikum [Peace be with you].

Baitullah Mehsud: Waaleikum Asalaam [And also with you].

M: Chief, how are you?

BM: I am fine.

M: Congratulations, I just got back during the night.

BM: Congratulations to you, were they our men?

M: Yes, they were ours.

BM: Who were they?

M: There was Saeed, there was Bilal from Badar and Ikramullah.

BM: The three of them did it?

M: Ikramullah and Bilal did it.

BM: Then congratulations.

M: Where are you? I want to meet you.

BM: I am at Makeen [a town in the South Waziristan tribal area], come over, I am at Anwar Shah's house.

M: OK, I'll come.

BM: Don't inform their house for the time being.

M: OK.

BM: It was a tremendous effort. They were really brave boys who killed her.

M: Mashallah. When I come I will give you all the details.

BM: I will wait for you. Congratulations, once again congratulations.

M: Congratulations to you.

BM: Anything I can do for you?

M: Thank you very much.

BM: Asalaam Aleikum.

M: Waaleikum Asalaam.

A BBC correspondent who had met and spoken with Baitullah Mehsud confirmed that the voice on the tape was his. When the boys at the suicide bomber training facility heard the news of the assassination on BBC radio, they cheered. But one of their number, Aitzaz Shah, could not help feeling disappointed. He had been told he had missed out on the Karachi attack because of a logistical problem caused by the arrests of the two Taliban organisers who were supposed to get him there on time. Now it had happened again. Aitzaz Shah complained to the head of the suicide bomber training facility, Wali Mohammed: 'I was told I would kill Benazir,' he said. Wali Mohammed did his best to reassure him. 'It's a question of luck,' he said, 'your chance will come.' Perhaps as a result of that conversation, Aitzaz Shah was within a few days sent to carry out a suicide attack in Karachi. But he was to be frustrated once again. On 17 January 2008 police picked him up as he made his way south. He was arrested together with another jihadi, Sher Zaman. Aitzaz Shah's confession would give the police their first insights into the plot and lead to a series of arrests of low-level conspirators.

As TV channels reported Benazir's death, governments around the world condemned the assassination and hailed both her bravery and her commitment to democratic values. In Pakistan there was chaos. All over the country rioters expressed their rage by attacking banks, police checkpoints, fuel stations, factories and restaurants. It was particularly bad in Sindh, where roads were blocked with burnt-out vehicles and smouldering tyres. As young men ran amok brandishing handguns, shopkeepers pulled down their shutters hoping to avoid the mob. But many banks were looted and businesses burnt to the ground. By the time the violence subsided, more than thirty would be dead. Part of the problem was that the police, anticipating widespread violence, stayed at home. The army, seeing the crisis deepening, had to deploy soldiers to maintain law and order, and the paramilitary Rangers were told they could shoot troublemakers on sight. All domestic flights were cancelled and, as the rioters started attacking trains, the railway network was closed down too. There were disturbances even in Lahore, well away from Benazir's power base.

Isolated in north-west Pakistan, caught up in the world of religious institutions, Baitullah Mehsud had no idea just how popular Benazir had been. He soon found himself being criticised by Mehsud tribesmen who, over the years, had built up major stakes in the transport business in Karachi. Assuming that the Taliban had done it, Benazir supporters were setting fire to Mehsud vehicles moving out of the city. Baitullah Mehsud calculated that he had to dissociate the Taliban from the assassination. A Taliban spokesman, Maulvi Umar, called round the news agencies denying any involvement. He said that it was against tribal tradition and custom to attack a woman. And, because the Taliban generally claimed their attacks, the denial carried some weight: even though it was a total lie, many were inclined to believe it. While the Taliban were dissociating themselves from the attack, al-Qaeda saw it rather differently: the assassination was an opportunity to establish its continued relevance. In a telephone statement to a Pakistani journalist, the al-Qaeda spokesman Mustafa Ahmed Muhammad Uthman Abu al-Yazid said 'we terminated the most precious American asset which vowed to defeat [the] Mujahideen'.[34] Al-Qaeda's involvement was later confirmed after the raid on bin Laden's Abbottabad home in 2010. While the Americans took a significant amount of printed and digital material from the house, they also left some behind. Those documents, later analysed by Pakistan's intelligence agencies, included a message to bin Laden from Abu Obaidah al-Masri, the man who had first discussed with the Taliban the possibility of assassinating Benazir. Written two days after Benazir's assassination, he said al-Qaeda could take credit for the 'operation in Pindi'.[35]

It would be November 2017 before the Taliban came clean by publishing a book, *From British Raj to American Imperialism*, recounting the organisation's history. The author, Abu Mansoor Asim Mufti Noor Wali, confirmed that Baitullah Mehsud had approved the attack. 'Bilal alias Saeed and Ikramullah were assigned to carry out the attack on Benazir on December 27,' he wrote. 'Bomber Bilal first fired at Benazir from his pistol and the bullet hit her neck. Then he detonated his explosive vest and blew up people in the procession.' The book also gave the first solid information ever published about the Karachi attack, naming the bombers as Mohsin Mehsud and Rehmatullah Mehsud. They had missed their target, the book said, because, fearing discovery, they abandoned the location near the stage that had been planned for the attack. Needing to improvise, they ended up trying to do it in a hurry.

As the militants calibrated their responses, the Bhutto family gathered for the funeral. Benazir's sister, Sanam, made the journey from London, and Asif Zardari flew in from Dubai with his three children. Because the University of Oxford was on Christmas vacation, Bilawal was at home at the time of the Rawalpindi attack. Soon after they reached the Chaklala military airbase in Rawalpindi, Zardari was offered the option of a post mortem. In a decision that was later to prove controversial, he turned it down. Whether this was for religious, cultural or other reasons has never been clear. He may have just thought there would be no purpose served: the nature of her death had been clear for all to see. And then, as his three children went into the room where the coffin had been placed, he stood guard at the door, giving them time to start the process of grieving. It wasn't long before they were airborne again, as Benazir's body followed the route that had been taken by her father's twenty-nine years earlier: a flight to Sukkur followed by an overland drive to Larkana. But whereas Zulfikar Ali Bhutto's burial had been hidden from public view, his daughter's was an international event. Supporters, many holding photographs of her, came from all over Pakistan by bus, car, overloaded motorbikes and even on foot. As the vehicle carrying her coffin, draped in the PPP flag, drove by, many wept and beat their chests in despair. Men hugged each other as young boys ran through dust trying to keep up with the cortege. And then it was on to the family mausoleum in Garhi Khuda Bakhsh. The mourners organised them-selves into hundreds of rows under the cavernous onion-shaped domes. Their despair was mixed with anger. 'Shame on the killer Musharraf!' they chanted. 'Long live Bhutto!' As the final prayers were offered, a period of silence came over the crowd, and Asif Zardari and his son, flanked by the PPP leadership, stood by the coffin as it was lowered into a hole dug in the ground close to the grave of Zulfikar. And as she was finally laid to rest, no one could doubt that she had fulfilled one of the main driving forces of her life: meeting, even exceeding, every hope her father had reposed in her.

The cover-up began within an hour and forty minutes of Bilal detonating his suicide vest. Shortly after the dead and dying had been removed from the road, Superintendent of Police Khurram Shahzad instructed the fire brigade to hose down the crime scene. It was littered with pools of blood, clothes, shards of glass and, of course, thousands of pieces of evidence. But it was all washed away: at the time of the order the police had gathered just twenty-three items. It was such a bizarre thing to do that the district emergency officer, Dr Abdul Rehman, told the fire brigade to stop while he double-checked. He found Shahzad and asked for confirmation. After talking with someone on his phone, Shahzad repeated his instruction. So, to whom had he spoken? Although he would never answer that question in court, the press reported the obvious answer: his boss, the chief police officer for Rawalpindi, Saud Aziz. Which raised in turn the question: who told Saud Aziz to hose the scene down? In December 2010 the state prosecutor of the case, Chaudhry Zulfikar, claimed that Aziz had admitted that four senior ISI and MI officials were in contact during and after the assassination. Multiple Pakistani press reports claimed that one of the men who wanted the hosing done was the director general of MI, Major General Nadeem Ijaz Ahmad. Saud Aziz and Khurram Shahzad refused to provide the court with the cell phones they had used on the day of Benazir's assassination. Both suspects initially claimed that they had lost them, and also reportedly provided the police with phones they hadn't used that day.[36] The issue of who had called whom was never resolved. Colleagues explained that the two men really had no choice but to block these questions. If the two police officers named senior members of the military establishment as having ordered the clean-up, there was a real risk that they would become such awkward witnesses that they would be killed. They both calculated that it was better to offer themselves up as fall guys. Khurram Shahzad and Saud Aziz were sentenced to seventeen years in prison, but they didn't serve their sentences. Their convictions were suspended in 2017 and both men were reinstated: Khurram Shahzad became a senior superintendent of police and Saud Aziz was made the director general of the National Crisis Management Cell. The deep state had rewarded their silence.

The hosing down was just the first of numerous steps to thwart investigators. Immediately after the murder, a Joint Investigation Team, or JIT, was established. Its first task was to view the crime scene. But achieving even that simple task was not easy. On 28 January Saud Aziz held the JIT up with a long lunch that lasted until dusk. By that time Benazir's vehicle had been taken away. When the JIT found it in a police car park on 29 January, it was in the process of being cleaned so that there was not a speck of blood or any other evidence to be seen. The JIT was shown photographs of the Mauser pistol that the police had found at the crime scene. But the team could not see the pistol itself because the ISI had taken custody of it.[37]

Initially General Musharraf wanted to keep the investigation within Pakistan. But he was soon persuaded that no one would trust Pakistani officials to act independently: if he wanted to give the impression of genuinely seeking the truth, he would need to bring in some outsiders. The UK obliged, offering the services of a Scotland Yard team that arrived in Pakistan on 11 January

2008. As officials close to the Scotland Yard investigation freely concede,[38] their position was not unlike that of the police in Karachi: their main goal was to avoid getting drawn into Pakistani politics. The British government accepted – in fact welcomed – very restricted terms of reference: Scotland Yard was only allowed to look into how Benazir died, rather than who killed her, why and at whose behest. The resulting sixty-nine-page document was as anodyne as both governments hoped. For example, rather than ask why the crime scene had been hosed down so quickly, Scotland Yard unquestioningly accepted the obviously inadequate police story, saying in its report: 'it is believed the Senior Officer feared a total breakdown of law and order, which led directly to the request for the local fire service to hose down the scene'. There was just one point of interest in the report. Some of Bilal's body parts were sent to Cambridge for examination. Scientists there, using the little-known work *Radiographic Atlas of Skeletal Development of the Hand and Wrist* by W.W. Greulich and S.I. Pyle, calculated that he was just fifteen years and six months old when he blew himself up. Much of the press had reported him as clean-shaven. In fact, he may never have shaved at all. The Pakistani police barely bothered investigating Bilal, not even locating and talking to his parents. 'Why bother?' they argued – he was just a tool in someone's hands. All that emerged about his short life was that he had been born near the Afghan border in June 1992, when the fighters who would become the Taliban were gaining strength. By the time he was four, they controlled most of Afghanistan. He was nine when the US went to war in Afghanistan after 9/11. Benazir's killer was the product not only of his handlers but also of his time and his geography.

The PPP rejected the Scotland Yard report out of hand, and Asif Zardari pushed for something better. A few days after the murder, Benazir's friend Peter Galbraith called Zardari: 'You need to have an international investigation of this,' he told him. 'Demand a UN investigation just like the one that took place in Lebanon after the Hariri assassination.' Galbraith was referring to the Lebanese prime minister Rafiq Hariri, who had been murdered in Beirut in 2005. The Special Tribunal for Lebanon set up to investigate Hariri's death had wide-ranging powers, including the capacity to prosecute and try those it believed were responsible. Galbraith had no doubt as to why such a body was needed in the Benazir case. 'The reason for having the commission,' he later recalled, 'was precisely because of the evidence that existed of the involvement of both the Pakistani military and intelligence services . . . If it had been a pure terrorist operation there would have been no need for a UN commission.'[39] Zardari made the demand for a UN commission part of his election manifesto and, once in power, stuck with the idea, achieving a Security Council vote authorising a three-member commission of inquiry. It was a significant step forward, although it fell short of what had been decided in relation to Hariri: the Benazir Inquiry would not have judicial powers. Nonetheless, in a sign that Zardari had nothing to fear from an investigation, he pressed UN Secretary General Ban Ki-moon to invite Peter Galbraith to be one of the commissioners. As Benazir's lifelong friend, Galbraith could be expected to put his loyalties to her above Asif Zardari's interests. In the event, though, Galbraith's appointment didn't happen. A few days after Ban Ki-moon agreed to Zardari's proposal, Galbraith was given the job of UN deputy envoy to Afghanistan.[40]

The UN Commission of Inquiry into the Facts and Circumstances of the Assassination of Former Pakistani Prime Minister Mohtarma Benazir Bhutto was formally established in July 2009. It interviewed over 250 people, including the two police officers who had ordered the hosing down of the crime scene. For the head of the UN commission, Heraldo Muñoz, this was one of the most 'astonishing' aspects of the whole affair. In its report, the UN commission named General Nadeem Ijaz Ahmad, saying one of its sources, speaking anonymously, had told them that he had ordered the hosing down. For the UN to blame a serving general by name indicates they had a very high degree of confidence in the veracity of the information. Muñoz later wrote: 'I am convinced that Police Chief Saud Aziz did not act independently in deciding to hose down the crime scene.' By the standards of UN reports, the commission's conclusions were hard-hitting. It complained about 'the efforts of certain high-ranking Pakistani government authorities to obstruct access to military and intelligence sources'. One high-ranking authority they were presumably referring to was Rehman Malik, who told the press quite bluntly that the UN 'would not be allowed access to military officials'. Heraldo Muñoz gave more detail in a book he wrote about the commission's work. The level of physical protection the commission members and staff were initially granted diminished over time. The government, for example, had at first provided a secure location, Sindh House, from which they could do their work. Later, the government tried to withdraw that facility. Distrust reached the point where

UN officials suspected that PIA flights were cancelled in order to make it more difficult for them to reach Pakistan to do their work.[41]

Even though the police, some elements of the government and the military had done an effective job of limiting and undermining the investigations of the JIT, Scotland Yard and the UN, there were still some loose ends that needed tidying up. A remarkable number of people connected with Benazir's assassination subsequently met violent deaths themselves. Two of them worked for the state. Nawaz Ranjha was the initial investigation officer of the Karachi case. In that capacity he had interrogated at least ten suspects belonging to the banned groups Lashkar-e-Jhangvi, Jaish-e-Mohammed, the TTP and the Afghan Taliban.[42] In August 2010, when he was on a routine patrol in Karachi, men on motorcycles surrounded his car and sprayed it with bullets, killing him and his driver. Bilawal Bhutto has said Ranjha was killed because of his work on the Benazir case, but the Karachi police are unsure. In September 2010 they arrested a former police officer – Ishtiaq, alias 'Police Wala' – who, they said, had killed a number of other police as well as Nawaz Ranjha.[43] They could not confirm a link with the Benazir case.

While little is known about Ranjha's death, there is more information concerning the murder of a lawyer who for four and a half years was the chief prosecutor in the Benazir murder case. Chaudhry Zulfikar told friends he was making real progress with his inquiries shortly before gunmen killed him on 13 May 2013. He was on his way to a hearing in the case when he was ambushed. His guard, despite being shot in the back, returned fire, hitting two of the assassins, injuring one and killing the other, who, it later transpired, was called Haris. A third assassin, trailing in a car behind, collected the injured gunman and Haris's body. The police gathered samples from a trail of blood left on the road by the injured man and, realising that someone with such severe injuries would need medical attention, searched every hospital within a 50-mile radius. They found him, paralysed from the waist down, in a hospital in Rawalpindi. His father, who was at his bedside, said his son had been attacked by bandits. But the blood samples from the crime scene matched the patient's blood.[44]

It turned out that the injured man was a well-known jihadi by the name of Abdullah Umar Abbasi. His father, a former colonel of the Pakistan Army, had himself been imprisoned and court-martialled ten years earlier for helping to hide the mastermind of 9/11, Khalid Sheikh Mohammed. The most suspicious aspect of the whole affair was that after Abdullah Umar Abbasi was charged with the chief prosecutor's murder, he was released on bail and vanished. Later, the Islamabad police – responding to a petition filed by Abdullah's wife for the recovery of her husband – told the Islamabad High Court that he might be with the ISI. Once more the deep state had protected, but also silenced, one of its own.

As well as working on Benazir's case, Chaudhry Zulfikar had also been trying to prosecute those involved in the 2008 Lashkar-e-Taiba attack on Mumbai. Might that have been the reason someone wanted him dead? While there is no certainty, many of his colleagues and his son, who worked closely with him and was familiar with the many threats his father had been receiving, believe the Benazir case and not the Mumbai attack motivated his killers. There is some circumstantial evidence to support that view. From his hospital bed, Abdullah Umar Abbasi admitted his role in the attack on Chaudhry Zulfikar and gave information about a safe house on the outskirts of Islamabad owned by two brothers, Adnan and Hammad Adil. In the safe house's backyard, police recovered Haris's body from a shallow grave. Adnan and Hammad, it turned out, were major-league jihadis who had been involved in a number of significant attacks, including an attempt to kill General Musharraf. But one of their actions seemed especially significant. They said they had been part of an attack on the Pakistan Air Force aeronautical engineering complex in Kamra. Leaked documents from the Benazir trial showed that one of the men being prosecuted by Chaudhry Zulfikar in the Benazir murder case, Rasheed Ahmed Turabi, was also involved in the Kamra attack.[45] The links between the assassins of Chaudhry Zulfikar and the Benazir case were clear.

It wasn't just state officials who were killed after the assassination: jihadis were also murdered. As we have seen, Nadir Khan and Nasrullah Khan were senior members of the conspiracy who, according to confessional evidence, collected Bilal and Ikramullah from the Taliban leader and delivered them to the Haqqania madrasah. Official records describe how, on 15 January 2008, nineteen days after Benazir died, a jeep carrying Nadir Khan, Nasrullah Khan and a boy approached an official checkpoint manned by the Mohmand Rifles on a remote mountain road in Malakand, near the Afghan border.[46] It is not clear exactly what happened, but within a few minutes Nadir Khan was shot dead, while Nasrullah Khan was injured and taken to hospital, where he died a week later. The incident had the appearance of a so-called 'police encounter', a term used in Pakistan to refer to extrajudicial killings. Police believed that Nadir Khan and Nasrullah had been detained by the intelligence agencies straight after the assassination and held secretly before being dispatched to their deaths.[47] But if that were the case it raises the questions why wasn't Nasrullah Khan killed there and then at the checkpoint, and why would he have been taken to the hospital? A minister with a reputation for having ordered some police encounters offered a possible explanation: 'Yeah well,' he said, 'some of these security guys on the checkpoints – they're not well trained.'[48]

Others to die included three people associated with the Haqqania madrasah, where the assassins had stayed on their way to Rawalpindi. Mullah Naseeb was a senior figure at the madrasah, with connections to both the Haqqani Network and al-Qaeda. After the assassination Naseeb went with a driver to attend a religious function at a madrasah in north-west Pakistan. He was picked up by two men on bikes on a road near the function and his body was found twenty-four hours later.[49] A secret PowerPoint presentation given by the Pakistan government to the Assembly in Benazir's home province of Sindh named another conspirator: Abdullah, alias Saddam, who like so many others in the plot was an alumnus of the Haqqania madrasah. According to the briefing, he was involved in the manufacture and transport of the suicide vests ahead of the assassination. He was killed in Mohmand agency in northern Pakistan in an explosion on 31 May 2008, reportedly because one of his own bombs went off by mistake. Then there was Abadur Rehman. A former Haqqania student and bomb-maker, he also helped with the provision of the suicide jackets. He was killed in a Pakistan Air Force strike on 13 May 2010. According to Rehman Malik, who was the minister of the interior at the time, there was quite a backstory to Abadur Rehman's death. Malik says his men were on the point of arresting him in the Khyber tribal agency when they got a message from a mobile phone company saying Abadur Rehman's phone signal showed he had moved location. Malik diverted his men to the new location only to find that the information was false. Abadur Rehman was killed in a drone strike in the Khyber agency the next day. Inquiries established that the mobile phone company executive who had given the false information had been pressured to do so by members of the intelligence services.[50] There was another indication that the death was unusual. The Pakistan Army's public relations outfit was normally keen to boast about killing militants, but on this occasion it was uncharacteristically coy, issuing a statement saying they generally didn't confirm or deny the killing of particular militant leaders.[51] And there is one more death to consider – that of Khalid Shahenshah, an aide of Asif Zardari's who doubled up as a security expert. As Benazir was giving her last speech in Rawalpindi, he was standing on the stage a couple of metres from her. Online videos show him making a series of strange movements. He kept his head completely still as he raised his eyes towards Benazir while simultaneously running his fingers across his throat. It is possible he was trying to indicate that Benazir was wearing a bullet-proof vest up to her neckline. The pictures went viral and have been the subject of endless speculation. On 22 July 2008, seven months after Benazir was killed, gunmen on motorcycles rode up to Shahenshah outside his Karachi home and killed him.

While the extent of the cover-up remains unclear, the blocking of the UN commission alone is enough to establish that there was one. So what exactly were the government and the army trying to hide? The most benign explanation is that they were trying to avoid any embarrassment that would follow revelations about rogue intelligence or army officers being involved in the plot. In 2017 General Musharraf gave weight to this explanation when he was asked whether some elements in the army could have been in touch with the Taliban regarding the murder. Musharraf replied: 'Possibility. Yes indeed . . .' Especially after 9/11, he said, Pakistan society was polarised. 'A lady who is known to be inclined towards the West is seen suspiciously by those elements.'[52] For many years senior Pakistani officers interacting with Western officials and journalists have used the idea of rogue elements within the ISI to explain away various militant attacks that seemed to have state backing. It was difficult for Westerners to assess these explanations. Little was known about the internal workings of the ISI: the degree to which it was supporting militants remained controversial. In the years after 9/11, however, the scale of the American engagement in Afghanistan and the US military's close working relationship with the ISI meant that Washington slowly acquired a better understanding of how Pakistan's spies operated. The killing of Osama bin Laden led to even greater scrutiny, as the world sought an answer to the question, 'Did Pakistan know he was there?'

In 2017 a groundbreaking book, *The Exile* by Cathy Scott-Clark and Adrian Levy,[53] gave a very detailed account of bin Laden's story from the time of 9/11 until his death in Abbottabad. According to Scott-Clark and Levy, the ISI's 'S' Wing did have knowledge of his whereabouts. The 'S' Wing had been created at the time of the anti-Soviet struggle by the then ISI chief General Hamid Gul – one of those referred to by Benazir in her press conference after the Karachi attack. One of Pakistan's most articulate public figures until his death in 2015, Gul combined nationalism, Islamism and a deep contempt for the West. He and likeminded officers continued to hold sway over 'S' Wing after they retired. This afforded successive subsequent ISI chiefs plausible deniability should the West get worked up about a particular jihadi group or attack. But the arrangement also gave the 'S' Wing's employees, many of whom shared the religious and political outlook of their contacts, considerable discretion in deciding how much support should be given to which violent jihadists. Scott-Clark and Levy argued that 'S' Wing could sometimes frustrate army policy. In 2004, for example, when Musharraf ordered one of the first offensives against militants in South Waziristan, 'S' Wing tipped off local al-Qaeda and Taliban members, who made good their escape before the Pakistani soldiers arrived. 'S' Wing also stretched the authority given to it. The 2008 Mumbai attack started as an officially approved proposal for which some initial planning was made. It was meant to stay that way, but someone inside the system gave the green light without the senior ISI leadership ever asking for that to happen. So might 'S' Wing have been involved in facilitating Benazir's murder? Did semi-official and official elements of the state help the Taliban and al-Qaeda achieve their objective? Benazir certainly thought so. Immediately after the Karachi attack, she named an officer who she believed was actively seeking to undermine her security. The same ISI officer had been heard bragging before her arrival about how, if she did return to Pakistan, she would be stopped.[54] A former Pakistani intelligence official named the same officer as having played an active role in facilitating the Taliban bombers on the day in Karachi.[55]

There is one piece of evidence that strongly suggests that even if 'S' Wing played a role, the ISI's top leadership was not involved: General Taj's visit to Benazir, during which he warned her that people were in Rawalpindi planning to kill her. It turned out to be very good advice. But his action does raise the question, why was Benazir not given a similar warning by the ISI before the

Karachi attack? It seems unlikely that the ISI source inside the Pakistan Taliban was aware of one plot but not the other. A more plausible explanation is that Nadeem Taj was unaware of the planning for the Karachi attack. After all, he had been made director general of the ISI on 22 September, just twenty-seven days before Benazir returned to Karachi. He barely had time to read himself in. A third possibility is that once Taj took over and established his new leadership he changed ISI policy.

But why would the deep state have wanted Benazir killed? There is no firm evidence as to what motivated her murder, but here are some strong possibilities. First, she was a woman who was perceived, with justification, as being pro-American. Second, she had been very critical of people in a position to harm her. While she tended to tread carefully when discussing Musharraf, she had been less cautious when it came to others, such as the head of the Intelligence Bureau, Ejaz Shah. In an interview in August 2007 she said: 'I would very be uncomfortable . . . [if] the intelligence bureau which has over 100,000 people . . . [was] being run by a man who worked so closely with militants and extremists.'[56] There was a third reason to believe she was at particular risk. In September 2007, during the run-up to her departure from Washington, Benazir addressed an audience in Congress under the auspices of the Middle East Institute. In the course of the question and answer session she was asked about Pakistan's leading nuclear scientist, A.Q. Khan, who in 2004 had accepted personal responsibility for the export of nuclear technology to Iran, North Korea and Libya. His live TV confession was always considered suspect by the International Atomic Energy Agency (IAEA) and the US, both of which believed that no single individual could have exported planeloads of nuclear material without the army's knowledge. As she gave her answer, Benazir spoke hesitantly, as if aware that she was getting into very dangerous territory. But she was still clear – perhaps too clear: 'Many Pakistanis are cynical about whether A.Q. Khan could have done this without any official sanction,' she said. 'While we do not agree at this stage to have any Western access to A.Q. Khan, we do believe the IAEA . . . would have the right to put questions to A.Q. Khan.'[57] Her stance sent shockwaves through the Pakistani establishment. Benazir's political rival Nawaz Sharif soon made it clear that he would never allow any access whatsoever to A.Q. Khan. And in remarks that revealed deep-state thinking, Hamid Gul made his views quite plain. Following the US agenda, he wrote in the Pakistani press, Benazir wanted to roll back the nuclear programme. The deep state's distrust of her on the nuclear issue had contributed to the downfall of her first government and may well have had a role in her death.

General Musharraf has said that his initial reaction to being informed of Benazir's death was to say: 'Bloody hell . . . this will further complicate the situation'.[58] It certainly complicated his. Prior to her death Benazir had come to view her letter to Musharraf in which she named three people as being behind the Karachi attack as something of a mistake. By not naming Musharraf in that letter she felt she had let him off the hook. On 26 October she decided to send an email to Mark Siegel, which, she said, he should forward to Wolf Blitzer of CNN in the event of her death. It read: 'Nothing will, God willing, happen. Just wanted you to know if it does in addition to the names in my letter to General Musharraf of 16 Oct I would hold Musharraf responsible. I have been made to feel insecure by his minions and there is no way what is happening in terms of stopping me from taking private cars or using tinted windows or giving jammers or four police mobile outriders to cover all sides would happen without him.'[59] As a result of that email, within hours of her assassination, CNN was running her posthumous claim that General Musharraf was responsible.

Musharraf was later charged with murder, criminal conspiracy for murder and facilitation for murder. The legal case against him relied not on the Wolf Blitzer email but on a phone call he was alleged to have made to Benazir on 25 September 2007, some three weeks before she returned to Pakistan, when she was doing the rounds on Capitol Hill, trying to drum up political support to put pressure on the White House to tell Musharraf that he needed to protect her. She was in the office of Californian Congressman Tom Lantos, head of the Foreign Relations Committee, when her mobile phone rang. 'She looked down at the phone,' Mark Siegel later recalled, 'as if she was reading a phone number and looked back up at me and mouthed the word, Musharraf.' Siegel led Benazir to a small room off the congressman's office so she could talk to the general in private. She closed the door behind her. After the call Siegel recalled she was pale and perspiring. 'She looked physically and emotionally upset. She told me that she felt personally threatened by him. She said, "He threatened me. He told me not to come back. He warned me not to come back. He said he will not be responsible for what's going to happen to me if I come back." '60 Siegel's account was supported by a journalist, Ron Suskind, who was also on Capitol Hill that day, covering Benazir's lobbying effort. Suskind later described what she had told him about the call. 'Musharraf had told her "Your security, your safety is based on the nature of our relationship." '61 General Musharraf denies these claims outright, describing the account of the phone call as a total lie. 'Honestly I laugh at it,' he said. 'Why would I kill her? Why would I get her killed?'62 The legal case against Musharraf relied entirely on circumstantial evidence, but it would eventually force him into exile in Dubai, where he continued to insist on his innocence. And in making his denials he lashed out. 'What a lot of Pakistanis can't understand is this: after Benazir was killed, her husband won power.' Musharraf was relying on the age-old, arid reasoning of conspiracy theorists that whoever benefited from an event must have caused it to happen. There is, in fact, no evidence whatsoever to implicate Asif Zardari in his wife's murder.

Bilawal Bhutto and his father have different views about Musharraf's possible role in the assassination. Bilawal has rejected Musharraf's denials out of hand. 'Musharraf exploited this entire situation to assassinate my mother,' he said. 'He purposely sabotaged her security so that she would be assassinated and taken off the scene'. For reasons that will be discussed in the next chapter, Zardari has said he does not think Musharraf was involved. But even if President Zardari seemed to show no interest in the case, the police were still holding the low-level Taliban conspirators who after their arrests had confessed to their parts in carrying out the plot. But no one was in a hurry. It took four years to charge the men. Even then the trial consisted of occasional desultory hearings. Everyone, it seemed, had moved on. That the state did not want proceedings to advance was clear: the legal authorities changed the trial judge no fewer than seven times. Each new judge to be appointed took months to read himself in. Asked why his office hadn't been able to accelerate matters, the chief prosecutor Mohammad Azhar Chaudhry said, 'We are helpless',63 and laughed. But in 2017 something changed. For some reason the eighth judge to handle the trial, Muhammad Asghar Khan, wanted to reach a conclusion and declared that from 21 August there would be daily hearings. After nearly ten years of delays, the whole trial was wrapped up in ten days. And when the verdict came on 31 August 2017, there was widespread astonishment. Rafaqat

Hussain, Husnain Gul and three others were found innocent. PPP lawyers immediately appealed, meaning the case could drag on for many more years.

In reaching his verdict, the judge Muhammad Asghar Khan debunked evidence including the retracted confessions, phone records and physical evidence. The shawl, cap and trainers found in Husnain's house, for example, had been sent to an FBI laboratory, which had confirmed that Bilal's DNA was on them – it was a direct link between Husnain and the bomber. The judge also needed to address the intercepted phone call in which a Maulvi told Baitullah Mehsud that Bilal and Ikramullah had done it – a claim that was corroborated by the confessions. Muhammad Asghar Khan's judgment amounted to a long list of technical errors which he argued had been made by the police and prosecutors. Baitullah's phone call was declared inadmissible because the prosecution had not produced in court the ISI operative who had recorded it. The operative had apparently told the police that since both Benazir and Baitullah Mehsud were dead, he did not see why he should take the risk of provoking the Taliban by giving evidence. Aitzaz Shah was cleared on the grounds that he had been arrested when he was a child, and yet his age in the official records was given as nineteen years old. Rafaqat Hussain and Husnain Gul, meanwhile, had been arrested six days before their confessional statements were recorded. The judge said the delay made their confessions inadmissible. And he found that even a delay of one day in the case of Rasheed Ahmed was enough for him to dismiss his confession as unreliable too. Next there was Sher Zaman, the man whom Aitzaz Shah had been with when he was arrested. The judge reasoned that if he had dismissed the confession of Aitzaz Shah on the grounds of the age discrepancy then there was no basis for holding Sher Zaman. That still left the phone records. The judge dismissed them out of hand: who was to say the phones belonged to the accused? The landline was more difficult. After all, it was in the house used by Husnain Gul and the court had heard evidence from Husnain Gul's landlord. The judge did not challenge that evidence but said that, since no rental agreement had been produced before the court, he could not be sure Husnain Gul did use the room. As for the very awkward point that Bilal's clothes had been found in Husnain Gul's room, the judge remained silent and simply asserted that the prosecution had 'miserably failed' to make its case.

9
THE DYNASTY'S FUTURE

Benazir's death left her many friends and acquaintances in Pakistan and around the world wondering how to assess her life. Those who most vehemently opposed her, the violent jihadists and hardline Islamists and nationalists, fell silent. Their ilk had already given their verdict when they had her killed. A decade later the veteran bureaucrat Roedad Khan, who had been so active in conspiring against Benazir's first government, gave voice to the establishment's perspective: 'The contours of historical judgment are already emerging, she will be remembered for destroying financial institutions, rampant corruption, lot and plunder, widespread lawlessness, political vindictiveness and senseless confrontation with the senior judiciary and the president.'[1] To that, the military might add that she would be judged as having been too pro-American and insufficiently committed to the nuclear programme. The fact that she was more fluent in English than in Urdu, and that she was so comfortable in the West and had so many admirers there, always rankled. Another highly critical verdict came from Stanley Wolpert, whom she had commissioned to write her father's biography. He complained that rather than focusing on how to help the poor, Benazir had instead 'worried about how best to immortalize her father, planning costly monuments and hoping to persuade the World Court to exonerate him'.[2]

While her detractors found plenty to criticise, there was also much to praise. Throughout her life Benazir had articulated liberal positions, supported democratic development, spoken up for Pakistan's minorities and provided not just a role model to women but also practical support: the Benazir Income Support Programme, launched after her death, recognised this by providing low-income families with cash transferred twice monthly into the bank account of a female member of the household. And there was her courage. In the years before her murder she was virtually alone in Pakistan in making clear, unambiguous and direct denunciations of the Taliban and their allies. Neither the army nor the right-wing politicians dared do so. Her bravery had been apparent too in 1986, when she gave up the comforts of London to take on General Zia. The optics of a young, single woman confronting a formidable and harsh military machine struck a chord in Pakistan and around the world. But for all that, even her keenest advocates conceded that her governments did not deliver as much as they had hoped. Weakened by her military, political, bureaucratic and clerical opponents, she never managed to assert her authority over the Pakistani state as a whole. And her democratic instincts did not extend to the PPP, which declared her, North Korea-style, chairman for life. She never managed to transform the organisation into a modern political party with internal democratic procedures. While many in the West saw her as a leader of moral clarity, advancing moderate Islam and democracy, many Pakistanis were more aware of how, like her father before her, she had always been willing to make compromises with the men in uniform if it eased her path to power. And then there was the corruption. While she may have seen making money as a necessary political tactic to help her compete against those who tried to outbid her, the well-filled foreign bank accounts gave opponents a stick with which to beat her, and her use of some of the money to buy very expensive jewellery made her a kleptocrat as well as a democrat.

But what Roedad Khan missed in his ungenerous assessment was that, as people look back on Benazir's life, the way it ended might well assume greater significance than her faults. Those who criticise her fail to appreciate that her death was, at least to some extent, an act of redemption which should be weighed in the balance. After the Karachi attack on the day she returned to Pakistan in 2007, she knew she was unlikely to survive the election campaign. But she accepted what might happen without complaint. The first line of *Daughter of the East* stated, 'I didn't choose the life; it chose me.' There was some truth in that, but more striking was the way she chose her death. Her acceptance of her fate, as she saw it, remains one of the most impressive acts of defiance against violent jihadists in Pakistan's history and will remain an enduring inspiration for Pakistan's secular-minded democrats. For as long as Pakistan society produces people as defiant as Benazir, liberal values will remain part of Pakistan's national debate.

Her death also gave new life to the Bhutto dynasty at a time when, in Pakistan and elsewhere, populist nationalism was gaining ground against entrenched elites. The dynastic tradition remains a force to be reckoned with, not only in the Pakistan polity as a whole, but also within the Bhutto family. Although they have been settled farmers for centuries, the Bhuttos still describe themselves as a tribe,[3] and as such they have a tribal leader, or *sardar*. Arrangements for choosing a sardar in Afghanistan and Pakistan vary from tribe to tribe and are often somewhat opaque. In the Bhuttos' case, a sardar was chosen in the late nineteenth century, and the turban denoting that officerholder's authority has been passed down from father to son ever since. Each transition required a gathering of Bhutto elders to confirm the new sardar, whose most important function is still to resolve intra-Bhutto disputes. The advent of democratic politics has somewhat overshadowed these arrangements: the political success of Zulfikar and Benazir led to the unusual situation that they were better known and more powerful than their sardar, whose authority, according to tribal tradition, they should respect. When Benazir was busy doing her politics in Islamabad, for example, back in Sindh the Bhutto sardar – Wahid Bakhsh Bhutto, also known as Bobby – was a figure little known to the public. In fact, many first heard of him when he was brutally murdered in 2000. As the Pakistani press did not hesitate to point out, his death came at a time when the position of sardar was being contested. Three years earlier, Mumtaz Bhutto had gathered thousands of people at the municipal stadium in Larkana to advance his view that he should be sardar. A few days after the murder, there was a ceremony at Mumtaz's residence in which a hundred or so elders gathered to place confidence in him.[4] That failed to settle the matter, and it appears that as far as the political branch of the family is concerned, the current sardar is Wahid Bukhsh Bhutto's brother Aamir.[5] The Bhutto habit of bitter family disputes lives on.

Despite the advent of electoral legitimacy as an important factor in the life of nations, Pakistan is by no means the only South Asian country with a living tradition of dynastic politics. In India, power won by Jawaharlal Nehru was bequeathed to Indira and then Rajiv Gandhi. In 2019, the fourth generation, in the form of Rahul and his sister Priyanka, campaigned for power – albeit unsuccessfully – in that year's elections. The Bandaranaikes of Ceylon and Sri Lanka wielded power for three generations. When the Oxford graduate Prime Minister S.W.R.D. Bandaranaike was killed, his wife Sirimavo Bandaranaike filled his shoes, and in turn their daughter, Chandrika Bandaranaike Kumaratunga, became president. In Bangladesh, politics has long been a grudge match between the wife and daughter of the two towering figures at the time of the country's birth, Mujibur Rahman and General Ziaur Rahman, and, to the east, Aung San Suu Kyi stepped into her father's shoes in Burma. As for Pakistan, the Bhuttos are by no means unique. As well as their main rivals the Sharifs, there are other dynasties: Fatima Jinnah tried to lay claim to some of her brother's power and, at the regional level, the Pashtun nationalist Awami National Party and many of the Baloch parties have also been run on dynastic principles.

Dynasties confer both privilege and danger. Some of the risks flow from wealthy lifestyles: Sanjay Gandhi died piloting his private plane, and, further afield, John F. Kennedy Jr met the same fate. But the main cause of dynasts' premature deaths is politics. Zulfikar and Benazir were by no means alone in this respect. S.W.R.D. Bandaranaike was shot by a Buddhist monk, Indira Gandhi was killed by her Sikh bodyguard and her son Rajiv was murdered by a Tamil woman who was one of the world's first suicide bombers. It is striking how many of South Asia's dynastic rulers have been women. Indira Gandhi, Khaleda Zia, Sheikh Hasina, Chandrika Bandaranaike Kumaratunga and Benazir all defied deep prejudice in their societies. That said, there are precedents for female rulers in South Asia. As the eleventh-century Sanskrit pillar near Jaisalmer reveals, the Bhuttos produced powerful women nearly a millennium ago. In the princely state of Bhopal a continuous line of four generations of women ruled from 1819 until 1926. And better known is the case of Raziya, the ruler of the Delhi Sultanate in the thirteenth century, whose life has frequently been celebrated in popular culture. She not only wore men's clothing but also refused to accept the title Sultana, the feminine form of Sultan. Eight centuries later, as Benazir toured her feudal estates, she remarked that she too had transcended gender.[6]

Whether they be in South Asia or the US, dynasts have wealth, connections, name recognition and, crucially, a self-fulfilling sense of entitlement. As Nusrat had pointed out, were it not for politics, after her wedding Benazir would have been known as Benazir Zardari. In the early years of his marriage, Asif Zardari, determined to show he was unimpressed by the Bhuttos' social superiority, taunted Benazir with the thought that his son would take his name, not hers. But by the time Benazir was killed, he better understood the source of the power and wealth he had enjoyed and accepted a compromise: Bilawal, it was announced at Benazir's funeral, would henceforth be known as Bilawal Bhutto Zardari.

Dynastic politicians in the West tend to play down their heritage for fear that it will upset voters' ideas about a level playing field. Benazir, by contrast, was unembarrassed by her undemocratic origins. In 1998 she organised a seminar on her grandfather, Sir Shahnawaz Bhutto. The next year she marked the twentieth anniversary of her father's death by inviting Anura Bandaranaike to give a lecture on 'The Impact of Political Dynasties in South Asia'. Himself a member of parliament, Anura Bandaranaike was the son of two prime ministers and the brother of President Chandrika Bandaranaike Kumaratunga. 'The policies of South Asia,' Benazir said in introducing him, 'have been dominated to a large extent by the political struggles of the Nehrus, the Bhuttos and the Bandaranaikes who embodied the hopes and aspirations of the teeming masses of the Sub-Continent.' The fabric of South Asian politics, she said, had a crimson stain: 'Bandaranaike, Indira, Bhutto were murdered because they could not be defeated.'[7]

Over the course of her life Benazir became more attached to the dynastic principle, not less. In 1987 when she was recording interviews to provide material for *Daughter of the East*, she clearly had not given any thought to where she might be buried.[8] And when he visited the family tombs in 1988, Peter Galbraith saw some simple graves with bits of cloth on them.[9] But by the time of her death in 2007, Benazir had completed a decade-long project to construct a monumental mausoleum proclaiming the family's pre-eminence. The domed, marbled building dominated the surrounding sparsely populated and somewhat desolate landscape. Anyone constructing such a building can only have hoped that centuries later people would still be marvelling at it. When vast crowds gathered at the mausoleum for Benazir's burial, their mourning had a religious quality, in line with Sindh's Sufi traditions. Like her father, she was beginning to take on the quality of a saint, or pir. It is quite possible to imagine that, a century from now, the political aspects of Zulfikar's and Benazir's lives will be relatively unimportant to devoted followers who ascribe to the family special spiritual powers passed down through the generations. In fact, that process has begun: already the impoverished of Larkana visit the graves in the hope of making the sick well, the infertile pregnant and the jobless employed. Benazir's biographer Brooke Allen has quite reasonably raised the question of whether Benazir herself thought she possessed such powers. 'I find that whenever I am in power, or my father was in power,' Allen quotes her as saying, 'somehow good things happen. The economy picks up, we have good rains, water comes, people have crops.'[10]

That may be the family's future, but in the immediate aftermath of her death the issue was Benazir's political rather than spiritual legacy. After the burial, forty of the party's most senior figures gathered in the Bhuttos' dining room, with Benazir's portrait in the chair at the head of the table. Zardari then produced a sheet of paper that, he said, was his wife's political will. Given its importance to his subsequent career, it is perhaps not surprising that he later had it framed and hung on the wall of his home in Dubai. Zardari was too savvy to read it out himself: he gave that task to Bilawal.[11] The crucial passage stated: 'I would like my husband Asif Ali Zardari to lead you in this interim period until you and he decide what is best. I say this because he is a man of courage and honour. He spent 11½ years in prison without bending despite torture. He has the political stature to keep our party united.' Dated 16 October 2007, the letter had been written just before she left Dubai for Karachi. Zardari did not encourage any discussion of the document; he just said he would do his best to justify the trust placed in him and, in a gesture to his internal PPP critics, announced that Bilawal would be his co-chair. 'The torch of leadership in the PPP has been passed to a new generation, to our son Bilawal Bhutto Zardari,' he said disingenuously. He also tried to downplay his ambitions, insisting he was not interested in any position: 'I see myself as a Sonia Gandhi advisory figure, but without the seat in parliament'.[12]

For many in the PPP it was a shocking, almost unimaginable outcome. The man many blamed for the PPP's failures was taking over. Immediately there were rumours of a forgery. But the PPP stalwarts at the dining table had to concede that the handwriting looked like Benazir's – a finding subsequently confirmed by handwriting experts. Later there would be further confirmation that the letter was genuine. On her last evening in New York, before heading for Dubai and Karachi, Benazir and Zardari had a dinner with her key aide in the US, Husain Haqqani, and his wife Farahnaz Ispahani. In the course of that meal she said that she did not believe that Bilawal – still a student – was ready to run the party: Asif would have to lead until her son was in a better position to take over.[13] By handing power to her husband, Benazir had technically broken with the idea that the PPP's ideology was passed down a bloodline. But she kept power within the family and, in effect, had appointed Asif as regent, holding the reins until Bilawal was ready. It was an act that showed once again that she had failed to escape her feudal background. The thought that her successor should be chosen by internal party elections probably never occurred to her. The decision caused ructions within the family. As far as some Bhuttos are concerned, there are only two people in the current generation who can legitimately use the family name: Murtaza's children Fatima and Zulfikar Jr. Neither, however, is interested in electoral politics; Fatima has dedicated herself to writing and Zulfikar Jr makes a living as a poet, visual artist and sometimes cross-dressing performer in San Francisco, whose artwork includes textile portrayals of imagined queer Muslim revolutionaries.[14] In that sense, the field was clear for Zardari and Bilawal.

With Benazir alive, it was generally expected that the party would have done well in the 2008 elections, but so too would the PML(N). Her death meant there was a greater chance of a clear PPP victory. Tired of years of military rule, and with Musharraf an ever less credible figure, voters were looking for change, and, with memories of Benazir's sacrifice fresh in the minds of many voters, the PPP rode a wave of sympathy and ended up with 119 seats. The PML(N) won eighty-nine and Musharraf's party, the PML(Q), just fifty. As he contemplated turning that result into power, Zardari had to overcome significant disadvantages. Some Benazir loyalists, despite having no evidence whatsoever, wondered if he had played a role in his wife's murder. Aware of these perceptions, Zardari's first visit as president was to the Bhutto mausoleum, no doubt to remember his wife but also to make the point that he considered himself her political heir. He also followed the practice of Zulfikar, Nusrat and Benazir of attending the shrine of Lal Shahbaz Qalandar and in his early speeches spoke of 'the Bhutto doctrine'. But none of that convinced his in-laws. Fatima Bhutto made no secret of her dislike of Zardari, despite his acquittal of involvement in her father's murder, saying her 'blood froze' on the day Zardari became the country's president.[15] Mumtaz Bhutto, Zulfikar's cousin and old ally, was also appalled: 'It is most unfair that the name of an old and noble family which has provided leadership to the country and had made many sacrifices in the political field should be held responsible for the misdeeds of the Zardaris,' he said.[16]

There were also anxieties about Zardari's physical and mental health: in addition to rumours about his suffering from heart issues and bouts of depression, there was the awkward fact that, when he was facing his legal cases in the UK and Switzerland, a doctor had diagnosed him with dementia.[17] While there was no evidence that he had that ailment, foreign interlocutors were dismissive of his abilities. WikiLeaks later revealed that the UK's most senior Foreign Office official considered Zardari to be 'clearly a numbskull'.[18] A NATO official would later describe him as 'unable to engage PermReps [i.e. national governments' Permanent Representatives or ambassadors to NATO] in a strategic level discussion of the situation in South Asia'.[19] Across the Atlantic, one of the US's most senior diplomats on South Asia, Zalmay Khalilzad, described as 'madness' Zardari's view, apparently expressed in all earnestness, that the US was arranging the Taliban's suicide-bombing campaign in Pakistan.[20] And Zardari's meetings with Barack Obama did not help either. To the irritation of the US president, Zardari would speak for up to forty minutes at a stretch, repeatedly refer to US aid to Pakistan as 'my money', and say that while Obama may be surrounded by highly educated people, he, Zardari, had the advantage of a PhD in life. It wasn't long before Obama was apparently trying to avoid one-on-one meetings with him.[21] Pakistan's close ally Saudi Arabia also had its doubts, with King Abdullah describing Zardari as a 'rotten head' and 'the greatest obstacle to Pakistan's progress',[22] although in that case the insult may have had as much to do with Zardari's Shia background as his capacity or conduct. And even China had its reservations, seeing him, like his wife, as too pro-American. Beijing also resented Zardari's failure to ensure that China was his first foreign visit. His excuse – that trips to London and Dubai were made in a private capacity – and his commitment to honouring Zulfikar's legacy in respect of the Pakistan–China relationship did not assuage them. Nor did the substance of his first encounter with the Chinese leadership, when it became clear that his overriding concern was to avoid the strictures of an IMF reform programme by relying on huge amounts of Chinese money. His requests for funds were turned down.[23]

Zardari, however, never lacked confidence, and in the wake of the election he simply pressed on with winning power. With no overall majority he needed allies, and reached out first to his wife's old adversary, Nawaz Sharif. Zardari's experience of political horse-trading back in the 1980s now came in useful, and somehow he found a way, highly unusual in Pakistan politics, of securing the support of, or at least a lack of opposition from, virtually every political party in the country. In part, this was a question of timing – his initial alliance with the PML(N) was only possible because both parties had a shared interest in removing President Musharraf. But there was more to it than that: Zardari's evident lack of interest in ideology meant he could convince everyone that he was at least to some extent on their side. As he once said, politics is all about giving people what they want – something he was happy to do, however unpalatable he found it.[24]

With the PML(N) onside, Zardari had enough backing to force Musharraf's resignation. Once that was achieved, he simply disregarded commitments he had given to back a neutral presidential candidate and in August 2008 won enough support in the national and provincial assemblies to become president himself. To ease the process – and to the disgust of many PPP old-timers – he offered Musharraf what he wanted: an amnesty.[25] These Machiavellian moves meant the PPP and PML(N) were moving apart, and the divide deepened over the question of whether some Supreme Court judges dismissed by Musharraf, including Chief Justice Iftikhar Chaudhry, should be restored to office. The restoration of the judges became the biggest issue in Pakistani politics. Nawaz Sharif was supportive of the protesting lawyers and wanted the judges restored. But Asif Zardari, fearing they might annul the National Reconciliation Ordinance, leading to all his legal cases being revived, was not prepared to do it. By March 2009 the lawyers' demands for the restoration of the judges had intensified, with thousands of protestors on the streets. As long as the demonstrations were restricted to PML(N) supporters, Zardari held firm, arresting hundreds of them, leading Nawaz Sharif to pull the PML(N) out of the ruling coalition. But the army also had an interest. As the politics played out in Islamabad, it was coping with the Taliban insurgency in the north-west of the country. It was a time when Pakistan needed national unity in the face of the violent jihadist threat, and eventually General Kayani told Zardari he would have to back down. Zardari complied. In similar circumstances, Zulfikar Ali Bhutto would have lashed out and Benazir would have deeply resented the encroachment on her authority. But Zardari simply issued a statement saying that restoration had been his intention all along. It was much the same story when he reacted to the violent jihadist attacks in Mumbai in November 2008 by agreeing to a British suggestion to send the ISI chief to India. When the army said that was unacceptable, he just dropped the idea. The humiliations were so glaring that *Foreign Policy* magazine put him in its top five list of political losers. 'He is on the ropes, his opposition is gaining strength and meanwhile dangerous, complex Pakistan is hardy being governed at all.'[26] Maybe. But because of his willingness to climb down when he needed to, he was still the president.

While he mastered some political arts, others eluded him. Despite having spent so long at Benazir's side, he seemed unaware of what was expected of a head of state. In 2011, for example, he failed to see the importance of attending the funeral of one of his most senior colleagues, Governor of Punjab Salmaan Taseer, who had taken up the case of a Christian woman, Asia Bibi, accused of blasphemy. Despite a lack of credible evidence against her, Bibi had ended up in prison facing a death sentence, and Taseer denounced the law that put her there. As soon as he described the blasphemy legislation as a 'black law', Taseer found himself being strongly criticised by clerics and TV journalists, who began accusing him of being a blasphemer. Despite warnings that he was putting himself in danger, Taseer refused to back down and on 4 January 2011 was murdered by one of his own bodyguards. Given that Taseer was an old friend of Zardari's and a senior state official, it was widely expected that the president would attend the funeral. Some hoped he might also publicly defend the Christian minority. Zardari did neither, leaving it to Bilawal to make a statement from London: 'Shaheed Salmaan Taseer fought back. He spoke without fear . . . The assassination of Salmaan Taseer is not about liberals versus conservatives or moderate Islam versus radical Islam. It's about right and wrong.'[27] Rumours circulated in the PPP that the president – who, in clear contrast to his wife, made no secret of his fears of being killed – had not attended the funeral for fear that it might be attacked.

As well as failing to stand up for friends, colleagues and principles, he made so many foreign visits as president – at the state's expense – that it started to hurt him politically. The most infamous trip was in August 2010, when one-fifth of Pakistan's total landmass was under floodwater and over 3 million people displaced. Despite this being covered day in and day out by the domestic and even international media, President Zardari travelled to the UK and France, culminating in him being photographed alighting from a helicopter at a sixteenth-century French château in Normandy, the Manoir de la Reine

Blanche. He wasn't just ignoring the suffering of the Pakistani people; he seemed to be revelling in his family's wealth.[28] These blunders all raise the question: how did such a man become, in terms of not being removed from power, the most successful civilian politician in Pakistan's history? In the 1990s two much more popular politicians – Benazir and Nawaz Sharif – had twice failed to complete their terms in office. And while Zulfikar had been in power for five and a half years, he ended up being dismissed and hanged. Zardari outdid them all, surviving a full term and handing over power to a democratically elected successor, Nawaz Sharif. How did he do it?

Like every other civilian politician in Pakistan, Zardari realised his key relationship was with the army. Within a few days of Benazir's funeral, Rehman Malik, the man who had fled the scene of Benazir's assassination, advised Zardari that if he wanted to be president he would have to talk to the generals. Initially Zardari was reluctant, saying it was too soon: if people found out, they would accuse him of being in league with his wife's killers. But Malik's view prevailed, and just four days after Benazir's death he set up a meeting with the army leadership at the Pano Aqil military base near Sukkur. Zardari was flown in by helicopter. In the immediate aftermath of his wife's assassination there was anxiety in the senior military leadership that the violence in Sindh was so widespread, and the anger so deep, that Pakistan's unity was threatened. So there was considerable relief when Zardari reacted to her death not by stoking up Sindhi grievances but with a public statement that 'Pakistan will survive'. It was just what the army wanted to hear, and it responded positively. According to sources familiar with the Pano Aqil meeting, senior military officers told Zardari that if he could get the votes, the army would not stand in the way of his becoming president after Musharraf.[29] The obvious question that arises is whether Zardari offered a quid pro quo in the form of an undertaking not to investigate his wife's murder. When he put forward the name of Peter Galbraith as commissioner of the UN inquiry into his wife's murder in January 2008 Zardari seemed intent on installing someone who could be relied upon to conduct a proper investigation. But by October 2008, his attitude seemed to have changed, and he appeared to be actively blocking progress in the case. At that time, the authorities in Sindh were making the legal preparations to question Chaudhry Pervez Elahi, one of the men named by Benazir in her letter to General Musharraf. Zardari apparently ordered his officials in Sindh to drop the matter.[30] Zardari has denied that the issue of how vigorously he would investigate his wife's murder came up in Pano Aqil. But even if nothing was explicitly stated, it may be that the army officers at the closest meeting reached the view that Zardari could be relied upon not to rock the boat. And there is no doubt that, over the course of his term in office, Zardari did very little to investigate his wife's murder. In terms of personal loyalty to his wife's memory, it was very disappointing for those who had been close to her. In terms of power politics, it made perfect sense.

The army had long considered Zardari to be a potential partner. According to Benazir, some individual officers had considered the idea of working with him as early as 1989, when a corps commander, complaining that he could not salute a woman, said to Zardari, 'let her make you prime minister as we have no problems with the PPP'.[31] Fifteen years later, when the army was back in power and Benazir was in exile, Musharraf had contacted senior PPP leaders to see if he could tempt them into accepting an alternative leader of the party. Zardari was one of the possibilities. Musharraf probably realised that he could never persuade the party as a whole to abandon Benazir, but he hoped he might be able to organise a sufficiently large breakaway faction to split the party and to secure the backing of at least part of it. As part of Musharraf's outreach, an intermediary passed on a message from him to Benazir's cousin, Tariq Islam, saying that if Benazir stepped back from politics they would release Zardari from prison.[32] Tariq Islam declined to pass on what he considered an insulting offer, but when the suggestion reached Benazir through another channel, she rejected it outright, leading to arguments between her and her husband.[33] After Benazir's death, Musharraf's advisers told US officials that the Pakistan military 'prefer working more with Zardari than they did with Benazir because he is a straightforward, practical dealmaker'.[34] The cooperation became quite real: after Zardari was released from prison in 2004, he persuaded Benazir that he should have a chance to do something political on his own account and even held some public rallies. Zardari had never complained about his years of imprisonment, and whenever he had been let out for a day to attend parliament he was always seen on TV smiling, apparently unconcerned by his incarceration. The dignity he displayed won him admirers, and there were some in the PPP who flirted with the idea of his playing a bigger political role. While Benazir did not welcome Zardari's attempt to project himself at this time, as one of her closest advisers put it, she 'went along with it'.[35] But it was not to last. If some PPP activists had positive feelings towards him, a greater number were opposed. In 2005 Benazir decided she had had enough and told her husband to desist for fear he would split the party. He did so and took himself off to New York, and the couple lived increasingly separate lives. According to their friend Daphne Barak, by the last three years of her life Benazir would only spend around twenty-five days a year with Zardari. They did, however, remain affectionate to the end and were often seen holding hands. There was never any serious suggestion of ending the marriage.[36]

There was a story that, during his long years of imprisonment, Zardari made a point of refusing to stoop when passing through the small door within a door that constitutes the entrance to Sindh prison. Guards had to open the main door itself so that he could enter with his head held high. Such defiance delighted his fellow inmates. But Zardari's sense of dignity only went so far. For all his ingrained Sindhi pride, Zardari, throughout his presidency, allowed the military and the bureaucracy to do what they wanted without interference. That is not to say there were not tensions over some issues – there were – but as a general principle, Zardari was willing to give ground whenever he thought he needed to, even if doing so was embarrassing. For example, in July 2008 his government announced that the ISI would henceforth be under the direct control of the Ministry of Interior. The idea was to assert greater civilian, and possibly US, oversight by giving control of the ISI to a favourite of the Americans – Interior Minister Rehman Malik. In the face of an angry army pushback, Zardari immediately reversed the decision and issued another notification which said that the earlier one had been 'misunderstood' and the ISI would 'continue to function under the prime minister'.[37]

There were other difficult issues. As with so many other civilian leaders, relations with India were a major bone of contention. A month after the election, Zardari was talking about increasing trade with India, suggesting, for example, that Karachi could take in goods destined for India, moving them across the international boundary in high-speed trains.[38] Early in his administration, in a videoconference with a gathering in India, Zardari said that he not only wanted more India–Pakistan trade but also was ready to drop Pakistan's traditional nuclear policy of refusing to commit to no first use of nuclear weapons. 'I am glad I can say it with full confidence that I can get my parliament to agree upon that,' he said.[39] The army was shocked: it could scarcely believe that the long-established nuclear doctrine, according to which the possibility of Pakistan's first use deterred an overpowering Indian conventional attack, had been overturned without any consultation whatsoever. Senior officers not unreasonably took the view that Zardari had simply not understood the implications of what he had said. But the crucial point was that while Zulfikar and Benazir tended to double down in such situations, Zardari retreated: he announced that henceforth the prime minister rather than himself would be the most senior government figure to sit on the Nuclear Command Authority.[40] In practice, this made little difference – the whole nuclear programme was firmly in military hands anyway – but it took a potentially difficult policy area out of contention. There were to be other remarks that caused great anxiety in GHQ. Zardari told the *Wall Street Journal*, for example, that the militants fighting in Kashmir were terrorists, directly contradicting the longstanding Pakistani policy that they were freedom fighters. He also meddled once again in nuclear policy, failing to support the Pakistan military's concerns that the US was moving to give India's nuclear status de facto international recognition while not doing the same for Pakistan. 'Why would we begrudge the largest democracy in the world getting friendly with one of the oldest democracies in the world,' he said, apparently failing to see the point. But worst of all, from the army's perspective, was the idea that 'India was never a threat to Pakistan'. The religious parties and the military were outraged, forcing the presidency to claim that Zardari had been misquoted.[41]

There was also the question of who would manage the relationship with Washington. Throughout the Zardari presidency, the US wanted Pakistan to take strong action against the Taliban, which was inflicting significant blows against US forces in Afghanistan. Shortly before Obama's inauguration, Vice President-elect Joe Biden visited Islamabad to ask Zardari for his support in return for an enlarged aid package. But Zardari was hesitant. While he was happy to take the aid money and would articulate his opposition to the Taliban in private, he was not prepared to do so in public: he did not want to be hated, he said, for being an American stooge.[42] Zardari's reluctance suited the army well, as it allowed the chief of army staff, General Kayani, to exploit his direct line of communication with his US opposite number, General Mullen. Nonetheless, a potential clash between Zardari and the army arose over the so-called Kerry–Lugar aid package. In line with the advice of the US military, the senators John Kerry and Richard Lugar believed that the single most helpful thing Islamabad could do to further US interests in Afghanistan was to stop allowing militant groups to use Pakistan as a location where they could train violent jihadis, handle logistics and find sanctuary. Consequently, the senators proposed offering Pakistan a $7.5 billion aid package if the country would agree to greater civilian oversight of military policy. Zardari enthusiastically supported the package, largely because he wanted the money. But the army saw it differently and leaked that it had secretly recorded Asif Zardari and his US ambassador Husain Haqqani discussing how to use the Kerry–Lugar bill to reduce the power of the military.[43] When General Kayani rejected the Kerry–Lugar offer as an unacceptable interference in Pakistani sovereignty, Zardari accepted the decision without public protest. It was much the same when it came to military personnel issues: both Zulfikar and Benazir had tried to assert some authority over senior military appointments. Zardari simply gave the high command what it wanted: in March 2010 Lieutenant General Shuja Pasha, the director general of the ISI, was given an extension beyond his retirement date, and in July that year Kayani received a full three-year extension of his term.

There was one issue on which Zardari at least gave the appearance of holding firm: the passage of the Eighteenth Amendment, which contained many changes to Pakistan's constitution and in general terms distributed power away from the president and the centre towards the prime minister, National Assembly and the provinces. The key provision was the removal of the presidential power to dismiss the prime minister, but there were many other significant reforms: for example, the amount of time the president may consider bills passed by parliament before approving them was limited, and the prime minister only had to inform rather than consult the president on policy matters. In one of the most eye-catching changes, laws governing marriage, contracts, firearms, education, the environment and many other areas were devolved to the provinces, with each provincial assembly given responsibility for drafting legislation on these matters. Zardari's success in getting the amendment unanimously passed by the parliament is rightly seen as one of the landmark moments of his presidency. As ever, he was motivated not so much by any reforming zeal but rather by the need, as he saw it, to respond to pressure exerted on him by people inside and outside his party who wanted change. Nonetheless, these were reforms that many other governments had talked about but which he succeeded in enacting. His achievement rested in part on the fact that the army did not seem to have a clear view on the Eighteenth Amendment; while it was nervous of some measures in the package, such as the removal of the president's power to dismiss the prime minister, it liked others, such as greater autonomy over military appointments. But that in itself was testament to Zardari having managed to assemble a collection of reforms that contained something for everyone: it was deal-making of a high order.

While the army was a big problem for Zardari, he also had to cope with the resurgent and hostile judiciary. As the restored Iftikhar Chaudhry settled back into his job as chief justice, the pressure on Zardari started to build. Chaudhry became very hostile to the PPP and in December 2009 rescinded the National Reconciliation Ordinance: at a stroke, Asif Zardari's hard-won amnesties were void. It was the start of the second phase of his presidency. Before the restoration of the chief justice, Zardari believed he was secure. After the National Reconciliation Ordinance was rescinded, he felt more vulnerable and was almost constantly on the back foot. He could still rely on presidential immunity for all the domestic cases, but that left the foreign ones, of which the most advanced was that in Switzerland. The proceedings surrounding SGS/Cotecna had been stopped almost as soon as Zardari got into power, when the Pakistan government wrote to the Swiss authorities saying that they were no longer seeking to recover any missing funds. The cancellation of the National Reconciliation Ordinance, however, meant the case could be revived. Wajid Shamsul Hasan, Pakistan's high commissioner to London and a trusted Zardari loyalist, went to the Pakistan government's lawyers in Geneva to recover twelve boxes of documents relating to the SGS/Cotecna case. When the high commissioner was filmed shifting the boxes into a car before moving them to London, he offered the explanation that they were being kept for archival purposes, as leaving them in storage in Geneva would have been costly.[44]

The chief justice realised that reviving the Swiss case would in fact not be easy. He told Prime Minister Yousaf Raza Gilani that he must write to the Swiss authorities asking them to get proceedings underway again. After a long tussle Gilani refused on the grounds that the president had immunity: an act of defiance that led to his being convicted of contempt of court and disqualified from office, forcing him to resign as prime minister. Further, bitter arguments ensued, until Zardari appointed a prime minister, Raja Pervez Ashraf, who in November 2013 did write the letter to the Swiss authorities asking for the case to be restarted. But by the time he did so, the Swiss were no longer willing to be used as a political football in Pakistan's domestic affairs; they said that the case had become time-barred under Swiss law, and not only called off the proceedings but also said that they had released $60 million of frozen assets, although Zardari claimed that figure was an exaggeration and even offered $30 million to anyone who could prove it was true.[45] Asif Zardari argued that the Swiss decision to drop the case showed that he had been innocent all along and that all the charges against him had been politically motivated. And to some extent he was right. Had it not been for Nawaz Sharif's determination to undermine a rival, the evidence would never have been amassed in the first place. The final twist came when Zardari, never able to let matters rest, raised the issue of the famous necklace that Benazir had been accused of buying in London's New Bond Street for $175,000 and which the Swiss had found in a safety deposit box. Zardari's lawyers argued that the offshore companies used to buy the item should be allowed to recover their property. The Swiss Federal Court rejected that claim and decided the jewellery would stay in Switzerland.[46]

The gruelling political struggle over the Swiss case illustrated the weakness of Zardari's way of doing politics. Early in his career the difficult times came only when the PPP was in opposition. By the end, he was having to fend off cases even when he was in power. But the biggest political crisis faced by the Zardari presidency had its origins not in corruption allegations but in the killing of Osama bin Laden in his hideout in Abbottabad in north-west Pakistan on 2 May 2011. It was an event with ramifications for many elements of the Pakistani state – including the army, which once again had been humiliated. Despite hogging the lion's share of the country's resources, the armed forces had been unable to detect that US helicopters had penetrated deep within Pakistan territory, killed bin Laden, searched his compound and left. Even if it wasn't as bad as the aftermath of the wars in 1965 and 1971, it was still a major blow to the military's prestige. When a commission of inquiry established that bin Laden had been living in Pakistan for nine years, moving between various locations, the army and its intelligence services were faced with accusations of either complicity or incompetence. It now seems that, while the senior military leadership including the ISI and army chiefs were unaware of bin Laden's whereabouts, some retired and serving officers were in the know and helped protect him. The bin Laden killing left many Pakistanis confused: most had no love for bin Laden's violent tactics, but that was often overpowered by their deep anti-Americanism and the sense that the US action had demeaned the whole country. Zardari, however, saw things rather more clearly: for him, the killing of bin Laden was an opportunity. With the army on the defensive, he had the chance to assert civilian control. As he contemplated how he could turn the situation to his advantage, he acted with calculated restraint. In not dissimilar circumstances, after the 1971 defeat Zulfikar had put a documentary on TV showing the army surrendering in Dhaka. Zardari reacted differently, trying to shield the army from too much media criticism. Consequently, in the immediate aftermath of bin Laden's killing, it seemed as if Zardari and the army had managed to smooth things over: the damage to the army's reputation was kept to a minimum and Zardari remained in office. But a memo to the US high command then emerged that revealed that behind the scenes Zardari had all the time been asserting himself.

The 'memogate' scandal centred on the alleged actions of the Pakistani ambassador to Washington, Husain Haqqani. The army believed that in May 2011 he arranged for a Pakistani businessman, Mansoor Ijaz, to send a written message to Admiral Michael Mullen.[47] The memo told the Americans that there was an unprecedented tussle as the army tried to pin the blame for its failure over bin Laden on the civilian government. There was 'a unique opportunity for the civilians to gain the upper hand over the army and intelligence directorates'. The document urged the US to side with the civilians, in return for which the government would give the US six significant concessions. Pakistan would order an independent inquiry into the allegations that it had harboured and helped bin Laden. The memo said it was certain that the commission 'will result in immediate termination of active service officers in the appropriate government offices and agencies found responsible for complicity in assisting' bin Laden. The US would also get a 'green light' to conduct the necessary operations to capture or kill al-Qaeda operatives on Pakistani soil: 'This commitment has the backing of the top echelon on the civilian side of our house'. There was also an offer to bring Pakistan's nuclear assets under a 'more verifiable, transparent regime', to better control the ISI support of violent jihadists and to bring to justice the perpetrators of the 2008 Pakistan militant attack on Mumbai.

When news of the memo leaked into the public domain, the Pakistani press went into a frenzy about who authored it and whether Zardari had approved it. Mansoor Ijaz, whose credibility was damaged by the emergence of some old video footage showing him umpiring some naked female wrestling bouts, accused Husain Haqqani of writing the memo. However, citing security concerns, Ijaz declined to return to Pakistan to testify, giving evidence by video link instead. Haqqani consistently denied the claim. For his part, Zardari's handling of memogate once again showed his political acumen: he left it to his prime minister to say that the military's efforts to identity the author of the memo were unconstitutional and illegal. The military hit back in kind: 'There can be no allegation more serious than what the honourable prime minister has levelled against COAS [the chief of army staff] and ISI DG and has unfortunately charged the officers for violation of the constitution of the country. This has very serious ramifications with potentially grievous consequences for the country,' a military statement said.[48] As both sides dug in, the underlying power dynamics came to the fore, which inevitably meant the civilians would have to back down: Zardari was forced to accept Haqqani's resignation.

For some, the scandal was a missed opportunity to change the political settlement in Pakistan and to assert greater civilian control of the armed forces. When the ISI chief was summoned to the National Assembly to explain himself, it seemed the balance of power was shifting. But that was not the case. After all, the 1971 defeat had offered an even better opportunity for the politicians, yet the military had proved to be too strong for the civilians to prevail. And in the case of memogate there was another factor. It was far from clear that, despite all its rhetoric, the US establishment wanted democratic change in Pakistan: many US generals preferred working with their military counterparts. If the civilians were ever to wield real power in Pakistan, they would have to grasp it themselves. Memogate took a heavy personal toll on Zardari, who experienced some kind of depressive episode of such severity that he was in urgent need of medical treatment. Friends reported that at this time the president would ring them up and ramble incoherently for significant periods of time. The army's offer that he could use their medical facilities only served to reveal the depth of the distrust between the politicians and the generals: Zardari steadfastly refused to go to any military medical facility, for the simple reason that he did not trust military doctors not to harm or even kill him.

Eventually a mobile medical unit came from the UAE and he was taken for treatment there.

Zardari's presidency was never short of incident. He had to cope with an assertive military, street protests, judicial activism and a Taliban insurgency. A politician who only won power because his wife had been murdered, he managed to do something no Pakistani leader before him had accomplished – handing over power to another civilian after a full term. That said, the election result at the end of his term was a rout: the PPP was all but wiped out in Punjab and pinned back to its heartland in rural Sindh. In 2008 the PPP had won 119 seats. In 2013 it won just thirty-three, leading some to wonder if the party would henceforth be little more than a regional outfit representing the Sindhi rural interest.

Zardari's presidency had significant consequences for the PPP. In terms of its vote share, the party he left for his son, Bilawal, was considerably weaker than the one he inherited. He had also opened up internal fissures. As far back as Benazir's first term in the late 1980s, senior PPP figures had worried that they needed to make a choice: were they with Asif or Benazir? In keeping with his Sindhi background, Zardari was not one to let bygones be bygones, and those who had aligned with Benazir found themselves pushed out when he became president. The most striking case was that of Naheed Khan and her husband Safdar Abbasi. Having met Benazir way back in her Barbican days in the mid-1980s, they had proved to be among her most loyal and hard-working associates, with Naheed Khan bearing the load of internal PPP management. Both had been with her in the car in Rawalpindi on the day she died. But Zardari never called on their services and replaced them with his own relatives and friends. As he tightened his grip on the party, PPP propaganda posters slowly but surely reflected the changing power dynamics: as images of Zardari's face got ever bigger, those of Benazir's shrank.[49] WikiLeaked documents from 2008 and 2009 revealed how Zardari tried to shift control of the PPP to his own relatives. Benazir had opened the door for this by, for example, giving a National Assembly seat to Zardari's father, Hakim Ali. But she had drawn lines. When Zardari asked for National Assembly seats for relatives, she sometimes turned him down.[50] But now, with Benazir no longer restraining him, Zardari focused his efforts on his politically inexperienced sister Faryal Talpur, who was given Benazir's old National Assembly seat in Larkana and made guardian to the three children. In February 2009 Zardari told US officials that in the event of his death he had instructed Bilawal to name Faryal Talpur as president.[51] It is unclear exactly what he meant by this – according to the constitution the presidency would pass automatically to the chairman of the senate. He may have been talking about who would take over the running of the PPP. If so, it is unlikely that the party would have accepted her, but, in any event, it was clear that Zardari was thinking in terms of his own dynasty rather than a Bhutto one. There was one other hint that Bilawal's status as successor was not an entirely settled matter. Hakim Ali had been the head of the Zardari tribe, and after his death in 2010 the question of who would succeed him in that role arose. In the normal course of events that title should have gone to his eldest son, Asif. But in May 2014, in a break with tradition, it was announced that Bilawal would get the job, presumably to tie him in to the Zardari side of the family.[52] For some reason, however, that never happened, and in December 2014 Asif Zardari himself took the title, with a newspaper report saying somewhat enigmatically that 'elders of his tribe advised him to refrain from handing over the position to Bilawal'.[53]

These attempts to promote Zardari family interests were possible in part because, following Benazir's death, there was no Bhutto in place to defend the family's interests. While Bilawal was studying in Oxford, Nusrat Bhutto was suffering from Alzheimer's and remained housebound in Dubai until her death in 2011. And while Mumtaz did churn out vitriolic newspaper articles denouncing Zardari, he was widely regarded as a spent force. Despite being aware that many in the PPP continued to distrust his father, Bilawal remained loyal to him. In 2013 he wrote an assessment of his father's term in office, in which he said that Zardari's legacy would be written in golden letters and that he would go down as one the most successful leaders Pakistan had ever seen: he had lasted a full term, held an election and handed over power to another civilian politician, despite having had to deal with sustained jihadist violence, a hostile Supreme Court, a power-hungry army and a parliament in which he did not have an overall majority. More than that, he surrendered key presidential powers and imposed a moratorium on the death penalty.[54] Bilawal did not mention that the president's reputation remained tarnished, governance continued to be poor, tax was still uncollected, the rule of law was still a distant aspiration and, by the time Zardari left the presidency, the country had so many power cuts that the opposition's promise of ending them was a significant factor in the PPP's election defeat. Once he was out of power, Zardari was again unable to protect himself from legal cases brought by his opponents, and would once again find himself behind bars.

Whatever ambitions Zardari may have harboured for his family, as his presidency receded into history it became clear that the PPP remained a Bhutto possession. That was in part because Bilawal left no doubt that he was committed to seeking power. That had not always been clear. Asked about his plans in 2004, he said: 'I don't know. I would like to help the people of Pakistan, so I will decide when I finish my studies. I can either enter politics or can enter another career that would benefit the people.'[55] The death of his mother put an end to any such options: as soon as he was named co-chairman of the party by his father after the burial of his mother, Bilawal realised that the PPP and its vast number of dependants, from ministers to lowly activists, needed him to keep the party in business. The pressure for him to go into politics proved irresistible. By 2018 Zardari's health was visibly deteriorating and Bilawal was holding rallies up and down the country, proclaiming liberal values and attracting significant crowds, giving the PPP hope that it did have a future.

As Bilawal looks ahead, he knows his first task is to secure control of the PPP itself. That has proved harder than many in the party hoped: Zardari is such a domineering character that it has been difficult for Bilawal to avoid being overshadowed. Bilawal does have the support of his sisters, Bakhtawar and Aseefa, both of whom have undertaken limited amounts of social work, particularly, in Aseefa's case, concerning polio eradication. In 2019 she told the BBC: 'My brother speaks for the entire Pakistan, and we will therefore continue to speak up and stand by our chairman, Bilawal Bhutto Zardari.'[56] If he tightens his grip on the party, he next faces the task of winning over the voters. The problem he faces is not just that Zardari left the party electorally weak; there are broader trends at play. South Asia's dynastic parties look increasingly outmoded. The paternalism and elitism implicit in dynastic politics do not chime in an era in which emerging middle-class voters with conservative, nationalist values are driving change. The failure of the Gandhis' Congress Party in the face of Narendra Modi, the tea boy turned prime minister, would seem to hold bleak lessons for the Bhuttos' PPP.

For all that, if the past is a guide then the most important factors in determining Bilawal's future will be his relationships with the West and with the army. The prospect of continued instability in Afghanistan, the Pakistan military's insatiable appetite for US aid, the worldwide concerns about nuclear security and the risk that the next violent jihadist attack on US soil could originate in Pakistan all suggest that Washington will remain deeply involved in Pakistani affairs. As Bilawal knows from his family history, finding an accommodation with the global power, as his great-grandfather Sir Shahnawaz and later his mother Benazir did, provides an easier path to power than opposing it. Even Zulfikar gave up on his anti-imperialist rhetoric of the 1960s, and, when he won power, came to appreciate that reassuring the US was more advantageous that criticising it. And Bilawal is well placed in this regard: his liberal outlook means he may well be able to persuade the next generation of American powerbrokers that he could be someone they could do business with.

But even if he can make friends in high places in Washington, that still leaves the Pakistan Army. Whatever his private view of the matter, Zardari never accused General Musharraf of being responsible for his wife's murder. Bilawal, however, has unambiguously blamed him, and he consequently finds himself in the same situation as his mother – simultaneously criticising a former army chief and reassuring the institution as a whole that he is not so hostile that they can never work together. It is certainly possible to imagine a scenario in which the army would need to install a civilian government with at least a modicum of legitimacy, meaning that it might turn to Bilawal as one of the few civilian politicians with genuine national visibility. The history of the Bhutto family suggests that, if that moment comes, Bilawal will probably make the necessary adjustments. He may give speeches demanding democracy, but his mother and grandfather did that too and yet found a way to work with GHQ. Indeed, ever since Doda Khan Bhutto worked out how to manipulate the British colonialists so as to secure the financial viability of his estates, the Bhuttos have always believed that, when the ultimate prize of power is at stake, a deal can be done.

A NOTE ON SOURCES

This is not an authorised history of the Bhutto dynasty. As a journalist covering Pakistan I have had some limited dealings with leading members of the family, but these were occasional encounters that barely got beyond the blandness associated with broadcast journalists' interviews of politicians. Having said that, Chapter 8, which deals with the plot to assassinate Benazir Bhutto, did benefit from interviews granted by her widower Asif Zardari and her son Bilawal Bhutto. These were used in *The Assassination*, a series of ten podcasts put online in 2018. Having completed the podcasts, I informed Asif Zardari both directly and through PPP officials that I was next going to attempt a book. Initially I had in mind a biography of Benazir Bhutto but later expanded it to cover the dynasty as a whole. None of my various messages ever received a reply. I also approached Bilawal and, despite an agreement that we should meet to discuss it, our repeated attempts to fix a date proved fruitless. While I would doubtless have benefited from the cooperation of these two highly political members of the family, this is primarily a study of the Bhutto dynasty and, although the Zardari presidency is of relevance, it is by no means central to the story. As for Bilawal, he is just at the start of his career and it is too soon to know what he will achieve.

As for other members of the family, Ghinwa Bhutto kindly agreed to a discussion at the Bhuttos' famous Karachi residence, 70 Clifton, but she did not reply to my request to see the material in the library there. I am, however, very grateful to Sanam Bhutto and Tariq Islam, both of whom generously gave me time whenever I asked for it. Many family friends and PPP members also contributed, and they are mentioned, subject to the degree of anonymity they asked for, in my acknowledgements and the endnotes.

I was able to access some useful primary sources. The National Documentation Centre in Islamabad has a number of declassified records from both the cabinet secretariat and other parts of the Pakistani government. These all relate to Zulfikar Ali Bhutto's time in power – nothing from the two Benazir Bhutto governments has yet been declassified. The India Office Records in the British Library contain material on the relationship between the Bhuttos and British officials in the late nineteenth and early twentieth centuries. The National Archives of the UK at Kew has now declassified many files relating to Zulfikar Ali Bhutto, the Al Zulfikar militant group and Benazir Bhutto. Also relating to Al Zulfikar, I benefited from the account of the hijacking of flight PK326 written by one of hostages, Jeffrey Balkind. A former World Bank employee, he has deposited his memoir in the World Bank archive.[1] Increasingly, material that would have been inaccessible to any author without a very significant travel budget is becoming available online. Navigating the US digital archives is by no means easy, but between the presidential libraries and the sites of the State Department, the CIA, the military in various forms and the Office of the Historian, there is a huge amount of US material available to scholars online.

Many PPP officials have kept various documents relating to the family, thinking that they should be preserved for posterity. Most notably, Jahangir Badar, one of Benazir's most trusted advisers, kept and published some of her correspondence with senior party leaders.[2] Having reported on Pakistan for over twenty years, I have also gathered my own collection of primary source material, including some correspondence and documents concerning the plot to kill her. These include the confessions of some of the conspirators who say they helped the assassin, as well as official reports produced by investigators. I also had access to what might be called the 'Linda Francke tapes'. Linda Francke worked with Benazir Bhutto on her autobiography *Daughter of the East* (published in the US under the title *Daughter of Destiny*).[3] In the course of producing that book she recorded over sixty hours of interviews with Benazir Bhutto and close allies, and she was kind enough to make those tapes available to me. I also recorded over thirty of my own interviews with members of the family and those close to them and had many more off-the-record conversations.

The Bhuttos have produced a number of books. Many of those published in Zulfikar Ali Bhutto's name are collections of his speeches, affidavits, articles, statements and interviews. Examples include: *Awakening the People, Commitment to History, My Pakistan, Let the People Judge, A South Asian View, Marching Towards Democracy, Pakistan and the Muslim World* and *Thoughts on Some Aspects of Islam*.[4] Published in 1963, *Bilateralism: New Directions* and *Pakistan and Alliances* advanced a particular policy position and could perhaps better be described as a pamphlet. The two works that are generally considered to be full-blown books are *The Myth of Independence*, published in 1969,[5] and *The Great Tragedy*, published in 1971.[6] The former was an extended denunciation of the international order at the time; the latter an attempt by Zulfikar to explain, or perhaps explain away, his role in the loss of East Pakistan. After his death various books came out either describing his trial or consisting of material he had produced in prison prior to his execution. Two are noteworthy: *My Dearest Daughter: A Letter from the Death Cell*[7] begins with the sentence 'How does a condemned prisoner write a letter of birthday greetings to a beautiful and brilliant daughter fighting for the life of her father, being in bondage herself, knowing that her mother is suffering the same suffering as herself?' Much of the letter is a review of global politics with reference to history, military power and ideology. As such, it has aged better than the longer *If I Am Assassinated*, which consists mainly of a rebuttal of the many allegations made against him by the military regime during his trial.[8]

Benazir Bhutto also authored a volume better described as a pamphlet. *Foreign Policy in Perspective* was written when she was in detention between December 1977 and January 1978. As for her speeches, some of her early ones were recorded in *The Way Out*,[9] which was followed by a 600-page volume, *Benazir Bhutto: Selected Speeches 1989–2007*.[10] But Benazir's main literary contribution was to write (with Linda Francke's help) *Daughter of the East* and then (with the help of her US lobbyist and friend Mark Siegel) *Reconciliation*. Both were autobiographical in nature. *Daughter of the East* dealt with her life up to the end of her second government. *Reconciliation* was written after 9/11 and tried to address one of the key policy issues in Washington at the time: how might Islam and the West live together. It was finished shortly before her death and published posthumously.

I have not relied on a third book, published in India in 1984 under her name, with the title *The Gathering Storm*. Benazir adamantly denied having ever written the book and said she first became aware of it when she saw a newspaper article saying that she had. The book ascribed to Benazir a number of radical positions, such as encouraging supporters to subvert Friday prayers at the mosques, to attack magistrates or judicial officers responsible for punishing agitators, and to spread subversive jokes about the generals. The book also discussed the possibility of violent action: 'Let Zia choose with which means he wants to be defeated: non-violent or violent.'[11] The book had been put out by an Indian publisher, Narendra Kumar, who believed that it had been written by Benazir when she was under house arrest and that the text was subsequently smuggled to India because publication in Pakistan would have been impossible. He said the manuscript had been passed on to him by an 'unimpeachable' person. However, Benazir's strong denials and the threat of legal action meant that Kumar's major scoop became worthless. He was especially frustrated because, he said, he had not found anything in the book which was not in keeping with what she had been saying. It was an interesting point: they were the sort of things she might have said in the heat of the moment, but possibly taken out of context and lumped together to make her look more radical than she really was. Benazir's loyal supporter, the dentist Dr Niazi, suggested that the material in *The Gathering Storm* could have been a compilation of the 'Foundation Document' of the PPP drafted by J.A. Rahim in 1968; the fourteen-hour speech delivered by Benazir in court when she was called upon as witness in 1983 in the trial of Jam Saqi, a Sindhi communist leader; and a speech she gave to the Karachi Bar Association in 1981.[12] However, a reading of the Jam Saqi trial transcript does not support that view. To take one example, *The Gathering Storm* repeatedly attacks the armed forces: 'Let us be quite clear,' the book states, 'who the enemy is. It is not one man, Zia, who is the nominal ruler. It is the entire military officer class who today stands solidly behind Gen. Zia, sustaining his rule, and may tomorrow put up another General. Let us guard against that danger.' In her evidence to the Jam Saqi trial, by contrast, she explicitly limits her criticism to General Zia while exonerating the armed forces as a whole. Benazir herself said she was unsure if *The Gathering Storm* was written by a friend or a foe. Given that the author had full mastery of the arguments put forward by PPP leftists, it is unlikely that it was a military propagandist trying to undermine her: it seems too well written to be misinformation produced by an apparatchik. That's not to say that Pakistan's deep state does not attempt forgeries – it does, but other examples, such as the letter supposedly written by Peter Galbraith, are ham-fisted and contain obvious errors. *The*

Gathering Storm is too well done to be a deep state forgery. It seems more likely that it was the work of a radical member of the PPP trying to associate Benazir with his or her political views.

While the Bhuttos have written a lot, far more has been written about them. The first Bhutto to become a prominent public figure, Zulfikar's father, Sir Shahnawaz Bhutto, was discussed at a seminar in Karachi organised by Benazir in 1998. A record of that meeting was published privately, and I am grateful to Sanam Bhutto for lending me her copy.[13] Friends and admirers of Zulfikar have written memoirs and analyses almost entirely devoted to their relationship with him. The Indian politician Piloo Mody, who knew him as a schoolboy in Bombay and a student in California, described Zulfikar's education.[14] Some fellow Sindhis, such as the educationalist Sayid Ghulam Mustafa Shah and Zulfikar's lifelong associate Chakar Ali Junejo, picked up the narrative thread in Oxford and later Karachi, describing how their hero rose through the political system.[15] Both produced hagiographic accounts of his life which include some revealing anecdotes. Other memoirs, such as those of trusted adviser Rafi Raza,[16] Finance Minister Dr Mubashir Hasan[17] and Information Minister Kausar Niazi,[18] all deal with his time in power, offering not only praise of Zulfikar but criticism too. The memoirs of military men such as General Gul Hassan[19] and General Arif[20] give the army's perspective.

The first attempt at a full biography was by Salmaan Taseer,[21] then a PPP activist from a well-known Lahore family. Taseer, who went on to become the governor of Punjab, was so much his own man that in 2007 he courageously defended a Christian woman accused of blasphemy, a stance that led to his assassination. So it is no surprise that, while generally sympathetic, his biography is by no means fawning. In his best passages, Taseer powerfully evokes Zulfikar's capacity to bewitch mass audiences, but he also describes some of his flaws. The year 1993 saw the publication of Professor Stanley Wolpert's more thorough biography.[22] Wolpert worked in the 70 Clifton library and revealed that it contains possibly the only copy of Sir Shahnawaz Bhutto's memoirs, as well as an archive of Zulfikar Ali Bhutto's papers, including highly sensitive documents such as his early instruction to the army chief General Tikka Khan about how he wanted the military to prepare for future conflict with India. The Bhutto family, however, did not enjoy Wolpert's book, accusing him of being impertinent, overly critical and taking far too close an interest in Zulfikar's sexual activity. Access to the library has been severely restricted ever since. Syeda Hameed, author of the recently published book *Born to be Hanged*, did get access but does not seem to have seen all the material that Stanley Wolpert saw.[23] Zulfikar continues to interest historians of Pakistan. In 2018 Shamim Ahmad's *Zulfikar Ali Bhutto: The Psychodynamics of His Rise and Fall* attempted to unravel and describe the psychological compulsions driving Zulfikar's conduct.[24]

Wolpert and Taseer both made the point that Zulfikar was the product of conflicting, contradictory influences: his Western education and his feudal background. It's an obvious observation but no less valid for that. However, in a PhD dissertation on the Bhuttos' PPP, Maleeha Lodhi, who went on to have a distinguished career as a newspaper editor and diplomat, rejected the idea that the way to understand Zulfikar was through the prism of the conflict between his Sindhi feudal influences on the one hand and his Western education on the other. The key, she argued, was his ambition and preoccupation with his personal destiny. 'His manipulation of different interests was not the product of a schizophrenic personality but revealed a balance of power strategy of a practitioner of realpolitik.'[25] In fact, both insights into his personality can be valid simultaneously – and both are.

Just as some of Zulfikar's ministers and advisers wrote books about him, so some of Benazir's colleagues described their perspectives on her. The most noteworthy were by Iqbal Akhund and Muhammed Ali Shaikh.[26] Particularly after her death, an enormous amount was written about Benazir Bhutto. But the only attempt at a biography is Brooke Allen's short book *Benazir Bhutto: Favored Daughter*.[27] Despite relying on many US-based friends and colleagues, it's a beautifully written and insightful introduction to her life. Another book written after her death, by an old Oxford friend, Shyam Bhatia, was more controversial.[28] *Goodbye Shahzadi* made some astonishing claims about how Benazir had told him that she had smuggled nuclear technology to North Korea, and its publication was followed by a chorus of disapproval from close friends of Benazir's, who said that Shyam Bhatia didn't know her very well and that, anyway, she would never have divulged nuclear secrets to an Indian national – arguments I have assessed in Chapter 7.

Supporters of the Bhutto family have set up two websites with useful material. The first, www.sanipanhwar.com, focuses on Zulfikar Ali Bhutto. There are PDFs of most of the significant books by him and about him, as well as interviews with people such as Zulfikar Ali Bhutto's first wife. The second website, the Bhutto Legacy Foundation, organised by Benazir's loyal press officer, Bashir Riaz, has material not easily available elsewhere, such as a collection of Bilawal's speeches. Inevitably, less has been written about some of the supporting characters in the Bhutto drama, including Zulfikar's wife Nusrat and their two sons Mir Murtaza and Shahnawaz. Raja Anwar's *The Terrorist Prince*[29] has come to take on an important role – too important, some argue – in defining the life and times of Mir Murtaza Bhutto.

Finally, there is the only one attempt, other than my own, to write about the dynasty as a whole – although it was published before Bilawal came to prominence. Fatima Bhutto's *Songs of Blood and Sword: A Daughter's Memoir*[30] was written on the basis of the author's very good access to family archives and interviewees, including relatives and family friends. It presents some new material on aspects of the dynastic story, with a detailed account, for example, of the circumstances surrounding the death by poisoning of Benazir and Murtaza's brother, Shahnawaz Bhutto. *Songs of Blood and Sword* is not only suffused with the author's longing for her father Mir Murtaza but is also full of disparagement for Fatima's aunt, Benazir.

No doubt much evidence remains to emerge. The Pakistani, American and British state archives all hold material still classified as too sensitive to be released. As time passes, those documents will come into the public domain. And it can only be hoped that the many Bhutto family associates who told me that they had material somewhere in the house but would have to go through all their papers to find it, do just that! But the single largest untapped archive lies with the Bhutto family itself. Aware of the centrality of their historical reputation to the dynasty's future, the Bhuttos have been assiduous in gathering, preserving and securing control of any papers or other material they have been able to locate. From what I have been able to gather, this material has not been read or assessed – rather it is seen as potentially troublesome, should it contain politically awkward revelations. We can only hope that if at some time in the future the family withdraws from politics, future generations of Bhuttos will see that the material they hold has historical as well as political value.

NOTES

INTRODUCTION

1. I should say that throughout the book I refer to the key family members by their first names – 'Zulfikar', 'Benazir', 'Bilawal' and so on. This is not an attempt to claim some sort of familiarity with them – it's simply to help the text flow: I found that constant repetition of the full names was somewhat cumbersome.
2. Author interview with Rehman Malik, December 2017, and author interview with senior Pakistani security officer, Karachi, July 2017.
3. Author interviews with Bilawal Bhutto and Asif Zardari, Dubai, December 2017.
4. Interview with Benazir Bhutto, interviewed and recorded by Linda Francke for *Daughter of the East*.
5. Author interviews with Naheed Khan and Safdar Abbasi, July 2017.
6. Author interviews with Rehman Malik and Farhatullah Babar, 8 December 2017.

1. THE BHUTTOS AND THE COLONIALISTS

1. Bhutto, Fatima, *Songs of Blood and Sword: A Daughter's Memoir*, Vintage, London, 2011, Preface.
2. O'Brien, Anthony, 'The Bhuttos and the Bhattis in the Twelfth Century A.D.', *South Asian Studies*, vol. 4: 1 (1988), p. 35.
3. Tod, James, *Annals and Antiquities of Rajasthan: Or the Central and Western Rajput States of India*, vol. 2, OUP, London, pp. 1194–6.
4. Din, Malik Muhammad, *Gazetteer of the Bahawalpur State 1904*, Sang-e-Meel, Lahore, 2001, p. 360.
5. O'Brien, 'The Bhuttos and the Bhattis in the Twelfth Century A.D.', pp. 29–31.
6. Author interview with Ashiq Bhutto, Karachi, May 2019.
7. Author interview with Zulfikar Ali Bhutto's nephew, Tariq Islam, London, April 2019.
8. Siddiqui, Habibullah, *Son of the Desert: A Biography of Quaid-a-Awam Shaheed Zulfikar Ali Bhutto*, SZABIST, Karachi, 2010, p. 11.
9. Postans, T., *Personal Observations on Sindh: The Manners and Customs of Its Inhabitants*, Longman, Brown, Green and Longmans, London, 1843.
10. McMurdo, James, 'An Account of the Country of Sindh', *The Journal of the Royal Asiatic Society of Great Britain and Ireland*, vol. 1: 2 (1834), p. 241.
11. Ansari, Sarah F.D., *Sufi Saints and State Power: The Pirs of Sind, 1843–1947*, CUP, Cambridge, 2002, pp. 9–56.
12. McMurdo, 'An Account of the Country of Sindh', p. 243.
13. Wolpert, Stanley, *Zulfi Bhutto of Pakistan: His Life and Times*, OUP, New York, 1993, p. 331.
14. Author interview with Ghinwa Bhutto, Karachi, August 2018.
15. Wolpert, *Zulfi Bhutto of Pakistan*, p. 5.

16. Advani, A.B., 'The Early British Traders in Sind', *Journal of the Sindh Historical Society*, vol. 1: 2 (1934), available at https://www.sahapedia.org/the-early-british-traders-sindh.

17. Advani, 'The Early British Traders in Sind'.

18. Bhutto, Fatima, *Songs of Blood and Sword*, p. 40.

19. Report of Sir George Clerk on the Administration of Scinde, House of Commons, 11 August 1854, p. 39, para. 197. Ordered, by the House of Commons, to be printed, 11 August 1854, House of Commons sessional papers, 483, London, 1854.

20. *Evening Mail*, London, 5 March 1847.

21. Report of Sir George Clerk on the Administration of Scinde, p. 121.

22. Burton, Richard, *Sind Revisited*, vol. 1, Richard Bentley & Son, London, 1877, p. 298.

23. Cheesman, David, 'Rural Power and Debt in Sind in the Late Nineteenth Century 1865–1901', PhD thesis, SOAS, University of London, 1980, p. 188.

24. Cheesman, 'Rural Power and Debt in Sind in the Late Nineteenth Century', p. 233.

25. Cheesman, 'Rural Power and Debt in Sind in the Late Nineteenth Century', p. 246.

26. Bhutto, Fatima, *Songs of Blood and Sword*, p. 41.

27. Bhutto, Zulfikar Ali, 'Is Aid Charity?: 27 October 1961', in Panhwar, Sani H. (ed.), *Z. A. Bhutto: Speeches and Interviews: 1948–1966*, p. 162, www.sanipanhwar.com, accessed 18 May 2020.

28. Bhutto, Zulfikar Ali, *The Myth of Independence*, OUP, Lahore, 1969.

29. Smith, Louis J. (ed.), *Foreign Relations of the United States, 1969–1976*, Volume E-7, Documents on South Asia 1969–1972, Government Printing Office, Washington D.C., 2005, Document 193.

30. Zulfikar Ali Bhutto's prison cell holograph in 70 Clifton, as reported in Wolpert, *Zulfi Bhutto of Pakistan*, p. 3.

31. Junejo, Chakar Ali, *Zulfikar Ali Bhutto: A Memoir*, National Commission on History and Culture, Islamabad, 1996, p. 11.

32. Cheesman, David, *Landlord Power and Rural Indebtedness in Colonial Sind, 1865–1901*, Curzon Press, Richmond, Surrey, 1997, p. 56.

33. Junejo, *Zulfikar Ali Bhutto*, p. 12.

34. Cheesman, 'Rural Power and Debt in Sind in the Late Nineteenth Century', p. 91.

35. Taseer, Salmaan, *Zulfikar Ali Bhutto: A Political Biography*, Vikas, New Delhi, 1980, p. 15.

36. Wolpert, *Zulfi Bhutto of Pakistan*, p.7. The quote comes from Sir Shahnawaz's unpublished memoir.

37. Bhutto, Benazir, *Daughter of the East: An Autobiography*, Pocket Books, London, 2008, p. 30.

38. Bhutto, Fatima, *Songs of Blood and Sword*, p. 42.

39. Cheesman, 'Rural Power and Debt in Sind in the Late Nineteenth Century', p. 101.

40. Bhutto, Ali, 'Murder Ink', *Newsline*, 23 June 2018.

41. Cheesman, *Landlord Power and Rural Indebtedness in Colonial Sind*, p. 94.

42. Cheesman, *Landlord Power and Rural Indebtedness in Colonial Sind*, p. 94.

43. 'Letter of Lt. Col. Mayhew regarding the (late) Commissioner of Sind Henry E.M. James', India Office Records at the British Library, L/PJ/6/565, File 614: April 1901.

44. Wolpert, *Zulfi Bhutto of Pakistan*, p. 10.

45. 'Hindu Woman's Death', *Sunday Times*, 13 January 1929.

46. 'The Khanzadi Murder Case in Larkana, Sind, withdrawal of the case against Mr. Wardero Wahid Bakhsh Bhutto', IOR/L/PJ/6/1989, File 4385: September 1929–May 1930.

47. House of Commons Hansard, available at: https://hansard.parliament.uk/Commons.

48. Bhutto, Ali, 'Murder Ink', *Newsline*, 23 June 2018.

49. Shah, Sayid Ghulam Mustafa, article in a booklet published in Karachi recording contributions to a 'national seminar' held Sunday, 8 March 1998, Hotel Avari Towers, Karachi.

50. Interview with Benazir Bhutto, interviewed and recorded by Linda Francke for *Daughter of the East*. Like the story about Ghulam Murtaza, this account may not be historically accurate but nonetheless gives insight into the issues that concern the family.

51. Khuhro, Hamida, *Mohammed Ayub Khuhro: A Life of Courage in Politics*, Ferozsons, Lahore, 1988, p. 33.

52. Syed, Ghulam Mustafa, article in booklet recording contributions to a 'national seminar' Hotel Avari Towers.
53. Taseer, *Zulfikar Ali Bhutto*, p. 20.
54. Pryde, Walter, British Library, MS. Eur R 149/4 side 1 recording.
55. Shah, Syed Mir Mohammad, article in booklet recording contributions to a 'national seminar', Hotel Avari Towers.
56. Khuhro, *Mohammed Ayub Khuhro*, p. 41.
57. Khuhro, M.A., *Dawn*, 19 November 1960.
58. Allama, Dr G.A., article in booklet recording contributions to a 'national seminar', Hotel Avari Towers.
59. Wolpert, *Zulfi Bhutto of Pakistan*, p. 17.
60. 'Sindh Muhammadan Association memorandum', *Report of the Indian Statutory Commission*, vol. 16, His Majesty's Stationery Office, London, 1930, p. 203.
61. 'Report of the Committee Appointed by the Bombay Legislative Council to co-operate with the Indian Statutory Commission', printed at the Govt. Central Press, Bombay, 1929, pp. 4 and 5.
62. 'Report of the Committee Appointed by the Bombay Legislative Council to co-operate with the Indian Statutory Commission', pp. 19–29.
63. Jones, Allen Keith, *Politics in Sindh 1907–1940: Muslim Identity and the Demand for Pakistan*, OUP, 2002, p. 20.
64. Wolpert, *Zulfi Bhutto of Pakistan*, p. 11.
65. Cheesman, 'Rural Power and Debt in Sind in the Late Nineteenth Century', p. 212.
66. 'Deputation from the All-Sind Hindu Association', *Report of the Indian Statutory Commission*, vol. 16, His Majesty's Stationery Office, London, 1930, p. 240.
67. *London Times* report on the Round Table Conference, 11 September 1930.
68. *Daily Mail*, 24 May 1930.
69. Bhutto, Shahnawaz, 'Letters to the Editor', *The Times*, 12 December 1930.
70. Jones, *Politics in Sindh 1907–1940*, p. 63.
71. Jones, *Politics in Sindh 1907–1940*, p. 75.
72. Shah, Sayid Ghulam Mustafa, article in booklet recording contributions to a 'national seminar', Hotel Avari Towers.
73. 'India Congress and Elections', *Observer*, 21 December 1937.
74. Khuhro, *Mohammed Ayub Khuhro*, p. 503.
75. ul-Islam, Munawar, 'A Sister Speaks', in *Zulfikar Ali Bhutto: Recollections and Remembrances*, Bhutto Memorial Society, Musawaat Publications, Lahore, 1993, p. 35.
76. Shah, Syed Mir Mohammad, *Dawn*, 19 November 1961.
77. Menon, V.P., *The Story of the Integration of the Indian States*, Longmans, Green & Co., London, 1956, pp. 124–50.
78. Bhutto, Nusrat, 'He Was a Loving Husband', in *Zulfikar Ali Bhutto: Recollections and Remembrances*, p. 20.
79. Bhutto, Fatima, *Songs of Blood and Sword*, p. 43.
80. Bhutto, Nusrat, 'He Was a Loving Husband', p. 19.
81. Sykes, E.L., 'Pakistan: Intrigue in High Places', 24 August 1965, The National Archives of the UK, DO 134/36.
82. Taseer, *Zulfikar Ali Bhutto*, p. 21.
83. Bhutto, Zulfikar Ali, *My Dearest Daughter: A Letter from the Death Cell*, Classic, Lahore, 1995.
84. Khuhro, *Mohammed Ayub Khuhro*, p. 50.
85. Author interview with a friend of Zulfikar Ali Bhutto's, Karachi, May 2019.
86. Interview with Benazir Bhutto, by Linda Francke.
87. Author interview with a relative who was an eyewitness to this remark, Karachi, May 2019.
88. Interview with Rafi Raza, interview by Ziad Zafar, copy in author's personal archive.
89. Interview with Mumtaz Bhutto, interview by Ziad Zafar, copy in author's personal archive.
90. Author interview with Tariq Islam, London, April 2019.
91. Interview with Benazir Bhutto, by Linda Francke.

2. ZULFIKAR'S ASCENT

1. ul-Islam, Munawar, 'A Sister Speaks', in *Zulfikar Ali Bhutto: Recollections and Remembrances*, Musawaat Publications, Lahore, 1993, p. 34.
2. Macaulay, Thomas Babington, *Speeches by Lord Macaulay*, OUP, London, 1935.
3. Fallaci, Oriana, *Interview with History*, available on www.sanipanhwar.com, p. 13.
4. Fallaci, *Interview with History*, p. 13.
5. Begum, Ameer, 'A Happy Man Always', in *Zulfikar Ali Bhutto: Recollections and Remembrances*, p. 30. The following quotes are all taken from the transcript of this interview, which she gave after Zulfikar Ali Bhutto's death.
6. Reminiscence of a Bombay friend, almost certainly Amina Rahimtoola. Document in author's private archive. Many thanks to Victoria Schofield for making this document available.
7. Mukerjee, Dilip, *Zulfikar Ali Bhutto: Quest for Power*, Vikas, New Delhi, 1972, p. 28.
8. Reminiscence of a Bombay friend, almost certainly Amina Rahimtoola. Document in author's private archive.
9. ul-Islam, 'A Sister Speaks', p. 36.
10. Bhutto, Zulfikar Ali, *The Myth of Independence*, OUP, Lahore, 1969, p. 171.
11. Bhutto, Zulfikar Ali, facsimile in *Zulfikar Ali Bhutto: Recollections and Remembrances*, pp. 13 and 14.
12. Junejo, Chakar Ali, *Zulfikar Ali Bhutto: A Memoir*, National Commission on History and Culture, Islamabad, 1996.
13. Wolpert, Stanley, *Zulfi Bhutto of Pakistan: His Life and Times*, OUP, New York, 1993, p. 27.
14. Bhutto, Zulfikar Ali, 'Reflections on New York: September 15, 1948', in Panhwar, Sani H. (ed.), *Z. A. Bhutto: Speeches and Interviews: 1948–1966*, p. 28, www.sanipanhwar.com, accessed 18 May 2020.
15. Bhutto, Zulfikar Ali, 'One World: University of Southern California, February 3, 1948', in Panhwar (ed.), *Z. A. Bhutto: Speeches and Interviews*, p. 12.
16. Wolpert, *Zulfi Bhutto of Pakistan*, p. 28.
17. Wolpert, *Zulfi Bhutto of Pakistan*, p. 39.
18. Interview with Benazir Bhutto, interviewed and recorded by Linda Francke for *Daughter of the East*.
19. Reminiscence of a Bombay friend, almost certainly Amina Rahimtoola.
20. Bhutto, Nusrat, 'He was a Loving Husband', in *Zulfikar Ali Bhutto: Recollections and Remembrances*, p. 21.
21. Begum, 'A Happy Man Always', p. 29.
22. Fallaci, *Interview with History*, p. 13.
23. Begum, 'A Happy Man Always', p. 32.
24. Sisman, Adam S., *Hugh Trevor-Roper: The Biography*, Weidenfeld & Nicolson, London, 2010, p. 420.
25. Wolpert, *Zulfi Bhutto of Pakistan*, p. 37.
26. Junejo, *Zulfikar Ali Bhutto*.
27. Author interview with a relative of Zulfikar's, Karachi, June 2019.
28. Interview with Mumtaz Bhutto, interview by Ziad Zafar, copy in author's personal archive.
29. Wolpert, *Zulfi Bhutto of Pakistan*, p. 35.
30. ul-Islam, 'A Sister Speaks', p. 37.
31. Bhutto, Zulfikar Ali, 'The Islamic Heritage: University of Southern California Los Angeles, April 1, 1948', in Panhwar (ed.), *Z. A. Bhutto: Speeches and Interviews*. For a fuller description of the speech see Chapter 3.
32. Abbasi, G.H., 'An Uncompromising Lawyer', in *Zulfikar Ali Bhutto: Recollections and Remembrances*, p. 63.
33. Abbasi, 'An Uncompromising Lawyer', p. 65.
34. Smith, Louis J. (ed.), *Foreign Relations of the United States, 1969–1976*, Volume XI, South Asia Crisis 1971, Government Printing Office, Washington, D.C., 2005, Document 327:

Memo of the President's files. Smith (ed.), *Foreign Relations of the United States, 1969–1976*, Volume E-7, Documents on South Asia, 1969–1972, Document 156: Transcript of conversation between Nixon, Kissinger and others.

35. Churchill, Rhona, 'Prince Bags 143 Ducks in 5 Hours', *Daily Mail*, 9 February 1959.

36. ul-Islam, 'A Sister Speaks', p. 38.

37. Bhutto, Zulfikar Ali, 'Role of Political Parties: Speech in the National Assembly, July 10, 1962', in Panhwar (ed.), *Z. A. Bhutto: Speeches and Interviews*.

38. Taseer, Salman, *Zulfikar Ali Bhutto: A Political Biography*, Vikas, New Delhi, 1980, p. 41.

39. A facsimile of the original note can be found in *White Paper on the Performance of the Bhutto Regime*, vol. 1, Mr. Z. A. Bhutto, His Family and Associates, Government of Pakistan, Islamabad, 1979, preface.

40. Video clip in author's personal archive.

41. 'Zulfikar Ali Bhutto Used to Call Ayub Khan "Daddy"': Omar Ayub, *Geo News*, 23 April 2019.

42. Wolpert, *Zulfi Bhutto of Pakistan*, p. 82. Overdose confirmed by close relative of Zulfikar Ali Bhutto who used to work closely with Nusrat in interview with author, Karachi, July 2010.

43. Nawaz, Shuja, *Crossed Swords: Pakistan, Its Army, and the Wars Within*, 2nd edition, OUP, Karachi, 2008, p. 190, n. 17.

44. Wolpert, *Zulfi Bhutto of Pakistan*, p. 56.

45. James, Morrice, *Pakistan Chronicle*, Hurst, London, 1993, p. 74, footnote.

46. Junejo, *Zulfikar Ali Bhutto*.

47. Marker, Jamsheed, *Cover Point: Impressions of Leadership in Pakistan*, OUP, Karachi, 2016, p. 98.

48. Mukerjee, *Zulfikar Ali Bhutto*, p. 37.

49. 'Man in the News', *New York Times*, 1 October 1963.

50. Junejo, *Zulfikar Ali Bhutto*.

51. Mukerjee, *Zulfikar Ali Bhutto*, p. 44.

52. Small, Andrew, *The China–Pakistan Axis: Asia's New Geopolitics*, Hurst, London, 2015, p. 24.

53. The phrase comes from his address to the All Pakistan Students Federation, Conway Hall, London, 13 August 1966, reproduced in Bhutto, Zulfikar Ali, *Awakening the People: A collection of articles, statements and speeches, 1966–1969*, Pakistan Publications, Rawalpindi, 1973, p. 13. Shaikh, Farzana, 'Zulfikar Ali Bhutto: In Pursuit of an Asian Pakistan', in Ramachandra Guha (ed.), *Makers of Modern Asia*, Belknap Press, Cambridge, MA, 2016, pp. 286–7.

54. Chaudhuri, Rudra, *Forged in Crisis: India and the United States Since 1947*, Hurst, London, 2014, pp. 136–46.

55. Mallon, Gabrielle S. and Smith, Louis J. (eds), *Foreign Relations of the United States, 1964–1968*, Volume XXV, South Asia, Government Printing Office, Washington, D.C., 2000, Document 12: Telegram from US Embassy in Pakistan to State Department.

56. Kux, Dennis, *The United States and Pakistan, 1947–2000: Disenchanted Allies*, OUP, Karachi, 2001, pp. 147–8.

57. Folder, 'South Asia, 1962–1966: Volume I, Tab B: 1–13 [1 of 2]', National Security Council Histories, NSF, Box 24, LBJ Presidential Library, accessed 7 September 2019, https://www.discoverlbj.org/item/nsf-nsch-b24-f02.

58. Mallon and Smith (eds), *Foreign Relations of the United States, 1964–1968*, Volume XXV, Document 12: Telegram from US Embassy in Pakistan to State Department.

59. Oral history transcript, McGeorge Bundy, interview 1 (I), 1/30/1969, by Paige E. Mulhollan, LBJ Library Oral Histories, LBJ Presidential Library, accessed 7 September 2019, https://www.discoverlbj.org/item/oh-bundym-19690130-1-07-17.

60. Bhutto, Zulfikar Ali, 'A Defensive Alliance: Speech at the Inaugural Session of CENTO Ministerial Meeting, Washington, D.C., April 28, 1964', in Bhutto, Zulfikar Ali, *A South Asian View*, Embassy of Pakistan, Washington, D.C., 1964, p. 5. Like many other Zulfikar-related books, this can be accessed at www.sanipanhwar.com.

61. Bhutto, Zulfikar Ali, 'Nehru: An Appraisal', in *Quest for Peace: Selections from speeches and writings 1963–1965*, Pakistan Institute of Foreign Affairs, Karachi, 1996. This can be accessed at www.sanipanhwar.com.
62. Musa, Muhammad, *My Version: India–Pakistan War 1965*, Peace Publications, Lahore, 2018, pp. 5 and 6.
63. Gauhar, Altaf, *Ayub Khan: Pakistan's First Military Ruler*, Sang-e-Meel, Lahore, 1998, p. 312.
64. *White Paper on Jammu and Kashmir Dispute*, Pakistan Ministry of Foreign Affairs, Jan. 1977, pp. 82 and 83, quoted in James, *Pakistan Chronicle*, p. 128.
65. Gauhar, *Ayub Khan*, p. 322.
66. Khan, Z.A., *The Way it Was*, Ahbab, Karachi, 1998, pp. 155 and 156.
67. Wolpert, *Zulfi Bhutto of Pakistan*, p. 90.
68. Address by Zulfikar Bhutto to the press conference held at Rawalpindi on 5 October 1965, www.sanipanhwar.com, accessed 13 May 2020.
69. Gauhar, *Ayub Khan*, p. 351.
70. Mallon and Smith (eds), *Foreign Relations of the United States, 1964–1968*, Volume XXV, Document 187: Telegram from US Embassy to State Department.
71. Taseer, *Zulfikar Ali Bhutto*, p. 61.
72. Barrington, N.J., 'Mr Bhutto and the Hawks', 3 March 1966, The National Archives of the UK, DO 134/36.
73. James, *Pakistan Chronicle*, pp. 152 and 153.
74. Mallon and Smith (eds), *Foreign Relations of the United States, 1964–1968*, Volume XXV, Document 271: Transcript of phone call between Johnson and Eisenhower, 4 November 1967.
75. Bhutto, Zulfikar Ali, Confidential British High Commission cable, March 1967, The National Archives of the UK, DO 134/36.
76. Wilson, Harold, Letter to Downing Street, 24 September 1965, The National Archives of the UK, DO 196/320.
77. This probably meant Straits dollars – around £125,000 at the time.
78. The National Archives, DO 196/320.
79. Gauhar, *Ayub Khan*, p. 385.
80. Sayeed, Khalid B., *The Political System of Pakistan*, Houghton Mifflin, Boston, 1967.
81. Wolpert, *Zulfi Bhutto of Pakistan*, p. 112.
82. Taseer, *Zulfikar Ali Bhutto*, p. 73.
83. Jones, Philip E., *The Pakistan People's Party: Rise to Power*, OUP, Karachi, 2003, p. 103.
84. Mirza, Afzal, 'The Truth about Bhutto's Indian Nationality "Scandal"', https://www.pakistanlink.org//Commentary/2006/Apr06/07/02.HTM, accessed 12 May 2020.
85. Mukerjee, *Zulfikar Ali Bhutto*, p. 29.
86. Author interview with Altaf Abassi, Rawalpindi, February 2020.
87. Brown, A.J., 'President Zulfikar Ali Bhutto', Letter to A.A. Hallily, The National Archives of the UK, DO 134/47.
88. Harrison, Ronald, 'Zulfikar Ali Khan Bhutto', Letter to A.A. Hallily, The National Archives of the UK, DO 134/36.
89. Author interview with Rafi Munir, Karachi, June 2019.
90. Paracha, Nadeem F., 'Bhutto's Ideologue: Friend, Mentor, Enemy', *Dawn*, 30 August 2015.
91. Sayeed, Khalid B., 'How Radical is the Pakistan People's Party?', *Pacific Affairs*, vol. 48: 1 (Spring 1975), pp. 42–59.
92. PPP 1970 Manifesto, www.sanipanhwar.com, accessed 13 May 2020.
93. Sayeed, 'How Radical is the Pakistan People's Party?', pp. 42–59.
94. 'Pakistan: Of Whisky, War and Islam', *The Economist*, 5 March 1977, p. 68.
95. PPP 1970 Manifesto, www.sanipanhwar.com, accessed 13 May 2020.
96. Jones, *The Pakistan People's Party*, p. 116.
97. Hasan, Khalid, *Rearview Mirror: Four Memoirs*, Alhamra, Islamabad, 2002, p. 110.
98. Reminiscence of a Bombay childhood friend, almost certainly Amina Rahimtoola.
99. Sayeed, 'How Radical is the Pakistan People's Party?', pp. 42–59.

100. Zaman, Arshad-uz, *Privileged Witness: Memoirs of a Diplomat*, OUP, Karachi, 2000, p. 96.
101. Ayoob, Mohammed, 'Profile of a Party: PPP in Pakistan', *Economic and Political Weekly*, vol. 7: 5/7 (Feb. 1972), pp. 215 and 217–19.
102. Sisson, Richard and Rose, Leo E., *War and Secession: Pakistan, India and the Creation of Bangladesh*, OUP, Karachi, 1990, p. 57.
103. Baxter, Craig (ed.), *Diaries of Field Marshal Ayub Khan, 1966–1972*, OUP, Karachi, 2007, p. 435.
104. Sisson and Rose, *War and Secession*, p. 67.
105. Choudhury, G.W., *Last Days of United Pakistan*, OUP, Karachi, 1998, p. 146.
106. Zaheer, Hasan, *The Separation of East Pakistan: The Rise and Realization of Bengali Muslim Nationalism*, OUP, Karachi, 1995, p. 149.
107. Salik, Siddiq, *Witness to Surrender*, OUP, Karachi, p. 36.
108. Raza, Rafi, *Zulfikar Ali Bhutto and Pakistan, 1967–1977*, OUP, Karachi, 1998, p. 47.
109. Hasan, *Rearview Mirror*, p. 93.
110. Author interview with an eyewitness, Lahore, May 2019.
111. Telegram 567 from Dhaka, The National Archives of the UK, RG 59, Central Files 1970–73, POL PAK.
112. Zaheer, *The Separation of East Pakistan*, p. 141.
113. Sisson and Rose, *War and Secession*, p. 85.
114. *Dawn*, 27 March 1971, p. 1.
115. Raza, *Zulfikar Ali Bhutto and Pakistan*, p. 70.
116. Smith (ed.), *Foreign Relations of the United States, 1969–1976*, Volume XI, Document 328.
117. Smith (ed.), *Foreign Relations of the United States, 1969–1976*, Volume E-7, Document 193.
118. *Dawn*, 29 March 1971.
119. Hasan, Khalid, 'Did Bhutto Break up Pakistan?', http://zabhutto.com/did_bhutt_%20 break_up_pakistan.htm, accessed 13 May 2020.
120. Khan, Roedad (ed.), *The American Papers: Secret and Confidential India–Pakistan–Bangladesh Documents, 1965–1973*, OUP, Karachi, 1999, p. 803.
121. Khan, M. Asghar, *We've Learnt Nothing from History: Pakistan Politics and Military Power*, OUP, Karachi, 2011, p. 54.
122. Smith (ed.), *Foreign Relations of the United States, 1969–1976*, Volume XI, Document 327: Memorandum for the President's Files, Washington, 18 December 1971.
123. Smith (ed.), *Foreign Relations of the United States, 1969–1976*, Volume E-7, Document 171: Conversation between Richard Nixon and his Assistant for National Security Affairs [Kissinger], Washington, 9 December 1971.
124. Smith (ed.), *Foreign Relations of the United States, 1969–1976*, Volume E-7, Document 267: Transcript of conversation between Kissinger, Chou En Lai and others.
125. Rushd, Abu (ed.), *Secret Affidavit of Yahya Khan on 1977*, Dhaka Bangladesh Defence Journal Publishing, Dhaka, 2009, passim.
126. Bhutto, Zulfikar Ali, *The Great Tragedy*, Vision Publications, Karachi, 1971.
127. Fallaci, *Interview with History*, p.6. Faruqui, Ahmad, 'The Enigmatic Z. A. Bhutto', https://www.pakistanlink.org//Opinion/2005/Jan05/14/01.htm, accessed 13 May 2020.

3. ZULFIKAR IN POWER

1. Faruqui, Ahmad, 'The Enigmatic Z. A. Bhutto', https://www.pakistanlink.org//Opinion/2005/Jan05/14/01.htm, accessed 13 May 2020.
2. 'How Leaders Look – and How They Ought to', *The News International*, 9 August 2009. Raza, Rafi, *Zulfikar Ali Bhutto and Pakistan, 1967–1977*, OUP, Karachi, 1998, p. 222.
3. Raza, *Zulfikar Ali Bhutto and Pakistan*, p. 119.
4. Bhutto, Zulfikar Ali, *If I Am Assassinated*, Vikas, New Delhi, 1979, pp. 122–3.

5. Interview with Benazir Bhutto, interviewed and recorded by Linda Francke for *Daughter of the East*.
6. Bhutto, Zulfikar Ali, *If I Am Assassinated*, pp. 122–3.
7. Bhutto, Benazir, *Daughter of the East: An Autobiography*, Pocket Books, London, 2008, p. 43.
8. Bhutto, Zulfikar Ali, 'Nehru: An Appraisal', in *Quest for Peace: Selections from speeches and writings 1963–1965*. Like many other Zulfikar-related books, this can be accessed at www.sanipanhwar.com.
9. For more on his attitude to Nehru see Shaikh, Farzana, 'Zulfikar Ali Bhutto: In Pursuit of an Asian Pakistan', in Ramachandra Guha (ed.), *Makers of Modern Asia*, Belknap Press, Cambridge, MA, 2016.
10. Burki, Shahid Javed, *Pakistan Under Bhutto, 1971–1977*, Macmillan, London, 1988, pp. 80–1.
11. Khan, Roedad (ed.), *The American Papers: Secret and Confidential India–Pakistan–Bangladesh Documents, 1965–1973*, OUP, Karachi, 1999, p. 432.
12. Azfar, Kamal, *Waters of Lahore*, Najam Printing Press, Karachi, 2010, p. 139.
13. Bhutto, Zulfikar Ali, 'Interview to the French Daily, "Le Monde", Released on December 26, 1972', in Nusrat Lashari (ed.), *Bhutto's Vision of Pakistan: Interviews of Quaid-e-Awam, Zulfikar Ali Bhutto*, Quaid-e-Awam Archives, Karachi, 2006.
14. Bhutto, Zulfikar Ali, 'My Debut in Journalism, The Pakistan Observer, Dhaka, 12 January, 1967', in Bhutto, *Awakening the People: A Collection of Articles, Statements and Speeches, 1966–1969*, Pakistan Publications, Rawalpindi, 1973.
15. Fallaci, Oriana, *Interview with History*, available on www.sanipanhwar.com, p. 16.
16. Shah, Sayid Ghulam Mustafa, *Bhutto: The Man and the Martyr*, Sindhica Academy, Karachi, 1993, p. 20.
17. Shah, *Bhutto: The Man and The Martyr*, p. 20.
18. Author interview with a family friend of Zulfikar Ali Bhutto's, Karachi, 19 June 2019.
19. Brown, A.J., 'President Zulfikar Ali Bhutto', Letter to A.A. Hallily, The National Archives of the UK, DO 134/47.
20. Mukerjee, Dilip, *Zulfikar Ali Bhutto: Quest for Power*, Vikas, New Delhi, 1972, p. 10.
21. Hasan, Khalid, *Rearview Mirror: Four Memoirs*, Alhamra, Islamabad, 2002, p. 48.
22. Hassan, Mubashir, *The Mirage of Power: An Inquiry into the Bhutto Years, 1971–1977*, Jumhoori, Lahore, 2016, p. 9.
23. Interview with Rafi Raza, interview by Ziad Zafar, copy in author's personal archive.
24. Bhutto, Zulfikar Ali, *Marching Towards Democracy: A Collection of Articles, Statements and Speeches 1970–1971*, Pakistan Publications, Lahore, 1971, p. 2.
25. Bhutto, *Awakening the People*, p. 176.
26. 'Bhutto's New York Visit', *Pakistan Forum*, vol. 2: 4 (Jan. 1972), p. 6.
27. Interview with Rafi Raza, by Ziad Zafar.
28. Smith, Louis J. (ed.), *Foreign Relations of the United States, 1969–1976*, Volume XI, South Asia Crisis 1971, Government Printing Office, Washington, D.C., 2005, Document 329, Telegram from the Embassy in Pakistan to the Department of State.
29. Bhutto, Zulfikar Ali, 'Interview with Australian Broadcasting Commission, May 22, 1972', in Lashari (ed.), *Bhutto's Vision of Pakistan*.
30. Niazi, Zamir, *The Press in Chains*, Karachi Press Club, Karachi, 1986, p. 150.
31. Raza, Rafi, *Zulfikar Ali Bhutto and Pakistan, 1966–1977*, OUP, Karachi, 1998, p. 118.
32. *White Paper on Misuse of Media, December 20, 1971–July 4, 1977*, Government of Pakistan, 1978. Annexes in the various White Papers produced by the Zia regime contained many documents lifted from the files of the Bhutto administration. Although he complained in *If I Am Assassinated* that the files reproduced in the White Papers had been selected to show him in a bad light and were not representative, Zulfikar Bhutto did not challenge their authenticity.
33. Bhutto, Zulfikar Ali, 'Interview to Der Spiegel, April 26, 1972', in Lashari (ed.), *Bhutto's Vision of Pakistan*.

34. Bhutto, Zulfikar Ali, 'Interview with Mr. Van Rosmalen, Chief Editor Elseviers Magazine, Amsterdam, October 1, 1972', in Lashari (ed.), *Bhutto's Vision of Pakistan.*

35. 'Global, Regional, and National Age-Sex-Specific Mortality and Life Expectancy, 1950–2017: A Systematic Analysis for the Global Burden of Disease Study 2017', *The Lancet*, vol. 392: 10159 (Nov. 2018), www.thelancet.com/journals/lancet/article/PIIS0140-6736(18)31891-9/fulltext#fig7. The PPP's 1970 manifesto gave an exaggerated figure of 33 years old.

36. Bhutto, Zulfikar Ali, 'Interview with Mr. Van Rosmalen, Chief Editor Elseviers Magazine'.

37. Ahmed, Feroz, 'Swing to the Right', *Pakistan Forum*, vol. 2: 9 (June–July 1972), p. 5.

38. Taped conversation between Zulfikar Ali Bhutto and his biographer Salman Taseer, as quoted in Lodhi, Maleeha, 'Bhutto, the Pakistan People's Party and Political Development in Pakistan: 1967–1977', PhD thesis, London School of Economics and Political Science, 1980, p. 124.

39. Bhutto, Zulfikar Ali, 'Let the People Judge', Address to the Hyderabad Convention, 21 September 1968.

40. Interview with Mumtaz Bhutto, interview by Ziad Zafar, copy in author's personal archive.

41. Mody, Piloo, *Zulfi My Friend*, Thompson Press, New Delhi, 1973, pp. 48 and 49.

42. Khan (ed.), *The American Papers*, p. 453.

43. Raza, *Zulfikar Ali Bhutto and Pakistan*, p. 15.

44. Bhutto, Zulfikar Ali, 'Interview to Mr. Fariborz Atapour, Correspondent of Tehran Journal, 10 September, 1976', in Lashari (ed.), *Bhutto's Vision of Pakistan.*

45. Bhutto, Zulfikar Ali, 'Interview with Walter Schwartz, Guardian, November 16, 1972', in Lashari (ed.), *Bhutto's Vision of Pakistan.*

46. Paracha, Nadeem F., 'Riding the Arrow: An Ideological History of the PPP', *Dawn*, 7 June 2012.

47. Ahmed, 'Swing to the Right', p. 4.

48. Sayeed, Khalid B., 'How Radical is the Pakistan People's Party?', *Pacific Affairs*, vol. 48: 1 (Spring 1975).

49. Interview with Rafi Raza, by Ziad Zafar.

50. Interview with Rafi Raza, by Ziad Zafar.

51. Fallaci, *Interview with History*, pp. 4 and 5.

52. Sham, Mahmood, *Larkana to Peking*, National Book Foundation, Islamabad, 2009, p. 74.

53. Chaudry, Aminullah, *Political Administrators: The Story of the Civil Service of Pakistan*, OUP, Karachi, 2011, p. 98.

54. 'Administrative Reforms, Before and After', *Pakistan Times*, 24 November 1976, quoted in Lodhi, 'Bhutto, the Pakistan People's Party and Political Development in Pakistan', p. 314.

55. Hassan, *The Mirage of Power*, p. 17.

56. Chaudry, *Political Administrators*, p. 92.

57. Burki, *Pakistan Under Bhutto*, p. 146.

58. Bhutto, Zulfikar Ali, 'Role of Political Parties: Speech in the National Assembly, July 10, 1962', in Panhwar, Sani H. (ed.), *Z. A. Bhutto: Speeches and Interviews: 1948–1966*, p. 182, http://sanipanhwar.com/Reshaping%20Foreign%20Policy%201946%20-%201966%20Z%20A%20Bhutto.pdf, accessed 18 May 2020.

59. PPP 1970 Manifesto.

60. Lodhi, 'Bhutto, the Pakistan People's Party and Political Development in Pakistan', p. 212 and footnote 237.

61. Lodhi, 'Bhutto, the Pakistan People's Party and Political Development in Pakistan', p. 661.

62. Lodhi, 'Bhutto, the Pakistan People's Party and Political Development in Pakistan', p. 712.

63. Wolpert, *Zulfi Bhutto of Pakistan*, p. 122.

64. Fallaci, *Interview with History*, p. 15.

65. Bhutto, Zulfikar Ali, 'Interview to Der Spiegel, April 26, 1972', in Lashari (ed.), *Bhutto's Vision of Pakistan.*

66. Fallaci, *Interview with History*, p. 15.

67. Bhutto, Ali Bhutto, 'Interview with American Broadcasting Corporation Telecast, May 14, 1972', in Lashari (ed.), *Bhutto's Vision of Pakistan*.
68. LaPorte, Robert, Jr, 'Pakistan in 1972: Picking up the Pieces', *Asian Survey*, vol. 13: 2 (Feb. 1973), pp. 187–98.
69. Gustafson, W. Eric, 'Economic Problems of Pakistan under Bhutto', *Asian Survey*, vol. 16: 4 (April 1976), p. 364.
70. Bhutto, Zulfikar Ali, 'Interview with Dr Walter Beg, German Television, April 2, 1972', in Lashari (ed.), *Bhutto's Vision of Pakistan*.
71. Hassan, *The Mirage of Power*, pp. 33 and 235.
72. Bhutto, Zulfikar Ali, 'Interview with Walter Schwartz'.
73. Sterba, James P., 'Bhutto Picks up the Pieces of Pakistan', *New York Times*, 25 June 1972.
74. Zaidi, S. Akbar, *Issues in Pakistan's Economy*, 2nd edition, OUP, Karachi, 2005, p. 265.
75. Faruqui, 'The Enigmatic Z. A. Bhutto'.
76. Kureshi, Omar, 'Early Years', in *Zulfikar Ali Bhutto: Recollections and Remembrances*, Musawaat Publications, Lahore, 1993, p. 61.
77. Bhutto, Zulfikar Ali, 'The Islamic Heritage: University of Southern California Los Angeles, April 1, 1948', in Panhwar (ed.), *Z. A. Bhutto: Speeches and Interviews*.
78. National Archives of Pakistan, 218/CF/72 Cabinet Division, 5 May 1972; 130/CF/72 Cabinet Division, 18 September 1972.
79. Hussain, Rizwan, *Pakistan and the Emergence of Islamic Militancy in Afghanistan*, Ashgate, Aldershot, 2005, p. 79.
80. Quoted in Kiessling, Hein G., *Faith, Unity, Discipline: The ISI of Pakistan*, Hurst, London, 2016, p. 34.
81. National Archives of Pakistan, 196/CF/72, 25 April 1972.
82. Hassan, *The Mirage of Power*, p. 214.
83. Interview with Hafiz Pirzada, interview by Ziad Zafar, copy in author's personal archive.
84. Bhutto, Zulfikar Ali, *Thoughts on Some Aspects of Islam*, Sh. Muhammad Ashraf, Lahore, 1976.
85. Babar, Nasrullah Khan, 'Mr. Bhutto as Prime Minister', in *Zulfikar Ali Bhutto: Recollections and Remembrances*, p. 107.
86. Bhutto, Zulfikar Ali, 'Bilateralism: New Directions', *Pakistan Horizon*, vol. 29: 4 (Fourth Quarter, 1976).
87. Raza, *Zulfikar Ali Bhutto and Pakistan*, p. 29.
88. Fraser, Gordon, *Cosmic Anger: Abdus Salam, The First Muslim Nobel Scientist*, OUP, Oxford, 2008, p. 250.
89. Niazi, Kausar, *Zulfikar Ali Bhutto of Pakistan: Last Days*, Vikas, New Delhi, 1992, p. 26.
90. Burki, *Pakistan Under Bhutto*, p. 174.
91. Wolpert, *Zulfi Bhutto of Pakistan*, p. 111.
92. Lawrence Ziring has a well-sourced but less convincing alternative account of what happened. Ziring, Lawrence, *Pakistan in the Twentieth Century: A Political History*, OUP, Karachi, 1997, p. 398.
93. Raza, *Zulfikar Ali Bhutto and Pakistan*, p. 218.
94. Richter, William, 'The Political Dynamics of Islamic Resurgence in Pakistan', *Asian Survey*, vol. 19: 6 (June 1979), p. 551.
95. Esposito, John L., 'Pakistan: Quest for Identity', in John L. Esposito (ed.), *Islam and Development*, Syracuse UP, Syracuse, 1980, p. 150.
96. Kennedy, Charles H., 'The Politics of Ethnicity in Sindh', *Asian Survey*, vol. 31: 10 (Oct. 1991), p. 942.
97. Bennett-Jones, Owen, *Pakistan: Eye of the Storm*, 3rd edition, Yale University Press, New Haven and London, 2009, p. 53.
98. See front-page stories in *Dawn* from 8 to 17 July 1972.
99. For Z.A. Bhutto's account of this affair see Khan (ed.), *The American Papers*, p. 888.
100. Smith (ed.), *Foreign Relations of the United States, 1969–1976*, Volume E-8, Documents on South Asia 1973–1976, Document 107: Intelligence Note.

101. Bhutto, Zulfikar Ali, *Speeches and Statements: January 1, 1973–March 31, 1973*, Government of Pakistan, Islamabad, 1972, p. 85.

102. Hassan, *The Mirage of Power*, p. 169.

103. Quoted in Lashari (ed.), *Bhutto's Vision of Pakistan*, p. 226.

104. Harrison, Selig, *In Afghanistan's Shadow: Baluch Nationalism and Soviet Temptations*, Carnegie Endowment for International Peace, Washington, D.C., 1981, p. 3. Ian Talbot also estimates the Pakistani force at 80,000 – Talbot, Ian, *Pakistan: A Modern History*, Vanguard, Lahore, 1999, p. 224.

4. ZULFIKAR'S DOWNFALL

1. An account of the Multan meeting can be found in Rehman, Shahidur, *Long Road to Chagai: Untold Story of Pakistan's Nuclear Quest*, Print Wises, Islamabad, 1999, pp. 16–19. Also see Malik, Zahid, *Dr A.Q. Khan and the Islamic Bomb*, Hurmats, Islamabad, 1992, p. 12.

2. Hassan, Mubashir, *The Mirage of Power: An Inquiry into the Bhutto Years, 1971–1977*, Jumhoori, Lahore, 2016, p. 27.

3. Burki, Shahid Javed, *Pakistan Under Bhutto, 1971–1977*, Macmillan, London, 1988. Burki traces this famous remark back to Bhutto's largely extempore speech made after he was sworn in as president, p. 249.

4. 'Bhutto's New York Visit', *Pakistan Forum*, vol. 2: 4 (Jan. 1972), p. 7.

5. Raza, Rafi, *Zulfikar Ali Bhutto and Pakistan, 1967–1977*, OUP, Karachi, 1988, p. 124.

6. Hamoodur Rehman Commission Report, supplementary report. General Niazi denied the accusations.

7. Hassan, Gul, *The Memoirs of Gul Hassan*, OUP, Oxford, 1993, pp. 354 and 361.

8. Hassan, *The Mirage of Power*, p. 82.

9. Arif, K.M., *Working with Zia: Pakistan's Power Politics, 1977–1988*, OUP, Karachi, 1995, p. 42.

10. Taseer, Salman, *Zulfikar Ali Bhutto: A Political Biography*, Vikas, New Delhi, 1980, p. 149.

11. Bhutto, Zulfikar Ali, 'Interview to Dilip Mukherjee of Times of India and B K Tiwari of Indian Express, March 14, 1972', in Lashari (ed.), *Bhutto's Vision of Pakistan: Interviews of Quaid-e-Awam, Zulfikar Ali Bhutto*, Quaid-e-Awam Archives, Karachi, 2006.

12. Bhutto, Zulfikar Ali, 'Interview to Kuldip Nayer of Indian Express, March 27, 1972', in Lashari (ed.), *Bhutto's Vision of Pakistan*.

13. Burki, *Pakistan Under Bhutto*, pp. 104–5.

14. Quoted in Kiessling, Hein G., *Faith, Unity, Discipline: The ISI of Pakistan*, Hurst, London, 2016, pp. 37, 44 and 45.

15. Rizvi, Hasan Askari, *The Military and Politics in Pakistan, 1847–86*, Progressive Publishers, Lahore, 1987, p. 202.

16. Cohen, Stephen, *The Pakistan Army* (1998 Edition), OUP, Karachi, 1998, p. 123.

17. Nawaz, Shuja, *Crossed Swords: Pakistan, Its Army, and the Wars Within*, 2nd edition, OUP, Karachi, 1998, pp. 336–7.

18. Rizvi, *The Military and Politics in Pakistan*, p. 150.

19. Nawaz, *Crossed Swords*, p. 344.

20. Arif, *Working with Zia*, p. 42.

21. Wolpert, Stanley, *Zulfi Bhutto of Pakistan: His Life and Times*, OUP, New York, 1993, p. 263.

22. Memorandum on Rao Rashid, Special Secretary, PM Secretariat, July 13, 1976, *White Paper on the Conduct of the General Elections of 1977*, Government of Pakistan, Rawalpindi, 1978, annexe 64, pp. A272 and 273.

23. Bhutto, Zulfikar Ali, *If I Am Assassinated*, Vikas, New Delhi, 1979, p. 124.

24. Niazi, Kausar, *Last Days of Premier Bhutto*, Vikas, New Delhi, 1992, p. 60.

25. *White Paper on the Conduct of the General Elections of 1977*.

26. *White Paper on the Conduct of the General Elections of 1977*, p. AI.

27. *White Paper on the Conduct of the General Elections of 1977*, p. A4.
28. *White Paper on the Conduct of the General Elections of 1977*, p. 289.
29. Interview with Hafiz Pirzada, interview by Ziad Zafar, copy in author's personal archive.
30. Raza, *Zulfikar Ali Bhutto and Pakistan*, p. 243.
31. Interview with Rafi Raza, by Ziad Zafar.
32. *White Paper on the Conduct of the General Elections of 1977*, p. 20.
33. *White Paper on the Conduct of the General Elections of 1977*, p. A 30.
34. *White Paper on the Conduct of the General Elections of 1977*, p. A22.
35. *White Paper on the Conduct of the General Elections of 1977*, p. A28.
36. *Amnesty International Report 1977*, Amnesty International UK, London, 1977, p. 203.
37. Weinbaum, M.G., 'The March 1977 Elections in Pakistan: Where Everyone Lost', *Asian Survey*, vol. 17: 7 (July 1977), p. 617.
38. Ali, Salamat, 'Heading for Hard Times', *Far Eastern Economic Review*, 15 April 1977.
39. Interview with Rafi Raza, by Ziad Zafar.
40. Niazi, *Last Days of Premier Bhutto*, p. 60.
41. Lt. Gen. Faiz Ali Chishti, interviewed by Ziad Zafar, copy in author's personal archive.
42. Arif, *Working with Zia*, p. 71.
43. Lt. Gen. Zaiz Ali Chishti, interviewed by Ziad Zafar.
44. Interview with Hafiz Pirzada, by Ziad Zafar.
45. Arif, *Working with Zia*, p. 93.
46. Hasan, Khalid, *Rearview Mirror: Four Memoirs*, Alhamra, Islamabad, 2002, p. 41.
47. Niazi, *Last Days of Premier Bhutto*, p. 242.
48. Chishti, Faiz Ali, *Betrayals of Another Kind*, Jang, Lahore, 1996, p. 56.
49. Aziz, Inam, *Stop Press: A Life in Journalism*, trans. Khalid Hasan, OUP, Karachi, 2008, p. 143.
50. Chishti, *Betrayals of Another Kind*, p. 60.
51. Schofield, Victoria, *Bhutto: Trial and Execution*, Cassell, London, 1979, p. 36.
52. Schofield, *Bhutto: Trial and Execution*, p. 37.
53. Schofield, *Bhutto: Trial and Execution*, p. 87.
54. Schofield, *Bhutto: Trial and Execution*, p. 31.
55. Schofield, *Bhutto: Trial and Execution*, p. 33.
56. Schofield, *Bhutto: Trial and Execution*, pp. 52–3.
57. Schofield, *Bhutto: Trial and Execution*, p. 176.
58. Schofield, *Bhutto: Trial and Execution*, p. 182.
59. 'Pakistan: The Case of Mr. Bhutto', The National Archives of the UK, FCO 37/2195.
60. 'Pakistan: The Case of Mr. Bhutto', The National Archives of the UK, FCO 37/2194.
61. Arif, *Working with Zia*, p. 202.
62. Bhutto, Benazir, *Daughter of the East: An Autobiography*, Pocket Books, London, 2008, p. 86.
63. Latif, Rahat, *--Plus Bhutto's Episode: An Autobiography*, Jang, Lahore, 1993, p. 230.
64. Weaver, Mary Anne, 'Bhutto's Fateful Moment', *New Yorker*, 27 September 1993.
65. Latif, *--Plus Bhutto's Episode*, pp. 232–3.
66. Bhutto, Benazir, interviewed by American Academy of Achievement, 27 October 2000, London, https://achievement.org/achiever/benazir-bhutto/#interview.
67. Weaver, 'Bhutto's Fateful Moment'.
68. Arif, *Working with Zia*, p. 208.
69. Z.A. Bhutto speaking to a young Benazir Bhutto, quoted from Bhutto, Benazir, *Daughter of the East*, p. 122.
70. Interview with Hafiz Pirzada, by Ziad Zafar.
71. Latif, *--Plus Bhutto's Episode*, p. 246.
72. Latif, *--Plus Bhutto's Episode*, p. 351.
73. Latif, *--Plus Bhutto's Episode*, p. 352.
74. Weaver, 'Bhutto's Fateful Moment'.
75. Chishti, *Betrayals of Another Kind*, p. 177.

76. Latif, *--Plus Bhutto's Episode*, p. 340.
77. Weisman, Steven R., 'The Return of Benazir Bhutto: Struggle in Pakistan', *New York Times*, 21 September 1986.
78. Hassan, *The Memoirs of Gul Hassan*.
79. James, Morrice, *Pakistan Chronicle*, Hurst, London, 1993, p. 75.
80. Bhutto, Zulfikar Ali, Confidential British Foreign Office 1965 memo, The National Archives of the UK, DO 134/36.
81. The National Archives of the UK, 1973, Pakistan Prem 15/1810.
82. Burki, *Pakistan Under Bhutto*, p. 238.
83. Wolpert, *Zulfi Bhutto of Pakistan*, p. 314.
84. Hassan, *The Mirage of Power*, pp. 280–2.
85. Smith, Louis J. (ed.), *Foreign Relations of the United States, 1969–1976*, Volume E–8, Documents on South Asia, 1973–1976, Government Printing Office, Washington, D.C., 2005, Document 84: Memorandum of Conversation, Washington, 2 April 1975.
86. 'Mujib Says That Bhutto Foiled an Execution Order by Yahya', *New York Times*, 17 January 1972.
87. Zulfikar Ali Bhutto, interviewed by the Australian Broadcasting Company, 22 May 1972.
88. Burki, Shahid Javed, *A Revisionist History of Pakistan*, Vanguard, New York, 1988, p. 66.
89. Hassan, *The Mirage of Power*, p. 150.
90. Taseer, *Zulfikar Ali Bhutto*, p. 152.
91. 'Benazir Defined Bhuttoism', *Dawn*, 20 October 1986.
92. Thapoor, Karan, 'If Pakistan Should Fall to Me: Interview', *Dawn*, 10 November 1987.
93. 'Benazir for "Bhuttoism", not for Democracy', *Dawn*, 7 May 1986, quoting Tempest, Rone, 'Pakistan: Democracy or Bhuttoism?: Exile's Return May Revive Cult', *Los Angeles Times*, 27 April 1976.

5. THE BHUTTOS RESIST

1. Radcliffe was a college for female students at which Harvard faculty repeated the courses they had given to the men. After a series of reforms bringing Radcliffe and Harvard closer together, the two were finally fully integrated in 1977. I shall follow Benazir's general practice of referring to her alma mater as Harvard rather than Radcliffe.
2. Author interview with Samiya Waheed, Karachi, September 2018.
3. Bhutto, Benazir, 'Address at World Leaders Summit – November 15, 2005', in Sani H. Panhwar (ed.), *Benazir Bhutto: Selected Speeches, 1989–2007*, M.H. Panhwar Trust, Hyderabad, 2009, p. 513.
4. Fadiman, Anne, 'Face to Face with the Woman who Wants to Rule Pakistan', *Life*, October 1986.
5. Author interview with Samiya Waheed, September 2018.
6. Author interview with Samiya Waheed, September 2018.
7. Interview with Benazir Bhutto, interviewed and recorded by Linda Francke for *Daughter of the East*.
8. Fadiman, 'Face to Face with the Woman who Wants to Rule Pakistan'.
9. Interview with Benazir Bhutto, by Linda Francke.
10. Bhutto, Benazir, 'Fight for Pakistani Democracy – August 7, 2001', in Panhwar (ed.), *Benazir Bhutto*.
11. Allen, Brooke, *Benazir Bhutto: Favored Daughter*, New Harvest, Boston, 2016, p. 24.
12. Allen, *Benazir Bhutto*, p. 33.
13. Bhutto, Benazir, 'Democratic Nations Must Unite – June 8, 1989', in Panhwar (ed.), *Benazir Bhutto*.
14. Bhutto, Benazir, *Daughter of the East: An Autobiography*, Pocket Books, London, 2008, p. 70.
15. Bhutto, Benazir, 'International Leadership Day – November 25, 1997', in Panhwar (ed.), *Benazir Bhutto*, p. 89.

16. Bhutto, Benazir, *Daughter of the East*, p. 77.
17. Bhutto, Benazir, 'Address at World Leaders Summit', p. 526.
18. Raza, Rafi, *Zulfikar Ali Bhutto and Pakistan, 1967–1977*, OUP, Karachi, 1998, p. 141.
19. Riaz, Bashir, 'Remembering Shahnawaz Bhutto', *Pakistan Today*, 17 July 2014.
20. Shaikh, Muhammed Ali, *Benazir Bhutto: A Political Biography*, Oriental Books, Karachi, 2000, p. 78.
21. Anwar, Raja, *The Terrorist Prince: The Life and Death of Murtaza Bhutto*, Verso, London, 1997, p. 27.
22. Mohammad, Dost, 'The Memoirs', in *Zulfikar Ali Bhutto: Recollections and Remembrances*, Musawaat Publications, 1993, p. 83.
23. Bhutto, Benazir, *Daughter of the East*, p. 150.
24. Bhutto, Benazir, interviewed by American Academy of Achievement, 27 October 2000, London, https://achievement.org/achiever/benazir-bhutto/#interview.
25. Ahmed, Sheikh Rafique, 'Four Important Meetings', memo. After the hanging, a party convention in Naudero unanimously elected her as party chairman.
26. Bhutto, Benazir, *Daughter of the East*, p. 116.
27. Husain, Irfan, 'A Death Foretold', in Sani H. Panhwar (ed.), *Articles Written to Pay Tribute to Mohtarma Benazir Bhutto*, http://www.sanipanhwar.com/bhutto.html, accessed 13 May 2020.
28. Bhutto, Benazir, *Daughter of the East*, p. 118.
29. Bhutto, Benazir, *Daughter of the East*, p. 165.
30. Bhutto, Zulfikar Ali, *If I Am Assassinated*, Vikas, New Delhi, 1979, p. 79.
31. Bhutto, Fatima, *Songs of Blood and Sword: A Daughter's Memoir*, Vintage, London, 2011, p. 169.
32. Islam, Tariq, 'Letter to the Editor', *Dawn*, 22 April 2010.
33. Bhutto, Sanam, 'Letter to the Editor', *Dawn*, 30 April 2010.
34. Durrani, Tehmina, *My Feudal Lord: A Devastating Indictment of Women's Role in Muslim Society*, Corgi, London, 1996, p. 141.
35. Paracha, Nadeem F., 'Revisiting the Al-Zulfiqar Saga: What Really Went Down', *Dawn*, 17 September 2015.
36. Raina, Asoka, 'Murtaza and Shahnawaz Bhutto Form Militant Group Al Zulfikar to Strike Back at Zia ul Haq', *India Today*, 31 July 1981.
37. Author interview with former AZO activist, UK, August 2019.
38. The Insight Team, 'Vengeance of "Baby" Bhutto', *Sunday Times*, 15 March 1981, p. 1.
39. Bhutto family member, interviewed by author, London, April 2019. That this call took place has been confirmed by Al Zulfikar activists who were in Karachi at the time and who say the phone was in the back room of a carpenter's shop.
40. Author interview with former AZO activist, UK, August 2019.
41. Weaver, Mary Anne, 'Bhutto's Fatal Moment', *New Yorker*, 27 September 1993.
42. Bhutto, Benazir, *Daughter of the East*, p. 182.
43. Bhutto, Benazir, interviewed by American Academy of Achievement.
44. Akhund, Iqbal, *Trial & Error: The Advent and Eclipse of Benazir Bhutto*, OUP, Karachi, 2000, p. 317.
45. Bhutto, Fatima, *Songs of Blood and Sword*, p. 223.
46. Ballantyne, Aileen, 'Bhutto Admits his Organisation Hijacked Plane', *Guardian*, 20 April 1981.
47. Bhutto, Murtaza, 'FSP 011/1 Pakistan Al Zulfikar Murtaza Bhutto Interview to BBC, 23 Oct 1983', The National Archives of the UK, FCO 37/3329.
48. Author interview with a senior Al Zulfikar leader, Karachi, July 2019.
49. Author interview with a friend of Murtaza Bhutto's, London, August 2018.
50. Bhutto, Fatima, *Songs of Blood and Sword*, pp. 224–5.
51. Hanif, Mohammed, 'Interview: Murtaza Bhutto', *Newsline*, August 1993, p. 35.
52. Ahmad, Malik Hammad, 'The Struggle for Democracy in Pakistan: Nonviolent Resistance to Military Rule, 1977–88', PhD thesis, University of Warwick, 2015, available online.

53. Balkind, Jeffrey, *Life and Death on a Tarmac – The Hijacking of PK326*, World Bank Group Archives, p. 107.
54. 'Pakistan – Al Zulfikar', 1982, The National Archives of the UK, FCO 37/2920.
55. National Foreign Assessment Center, 'Pakistan: Prospects for the Zia Government, An Intelligence Assessment', Central Intelligence Agency, February 1981, CIA-RDP06T00412R000200070001-1, NARA, p. 12.
56. National Foreign Assessment Center, 'The Pakistan People's Party: Search for Power, An Intelligence Assessment', Central Intelligence Agency, September 1981, CIA-RDP06T00412R000200490001-5, NARA, p. 19.
57. Anwar, *The Terrorist Prince*, p. 45.
58. Anwar, *The Terrorist Prince*, pp. 44 and 63.
59. Author interview with a senior Al Zulfikar leader, Karachi, July 2019.
60. Anwar, *The Terrorist Prince*, p. 44.
61. Ahmad, 'The Struggle for Democracy in Pakistan'.
62. Author interview with Mushtaq Lasharie, April 2019.
63. Bhutto, Benazir, *Daughter of the East*, p. 169.
64. Chandran, Ramesh, 'I Do Hope to Contribute to the Just Struggle of Our People: Benazir Bhutto', *India Today*, 15 February 1984.
65. Anwar, *The Terrorist Prince*, p. 140.
66. 'Benazir Denies Links with Al Zulfikar', *Dawn*, 20 April 1986.
67. Paracha, 'Revisiting the Al-Zulfiqar Saga'.
68. National Foreign Assessment Center, 'The Pakistan People's Party', p. 7.
69. Chandran, Ramesh, 'I Am Afraid and Fearing for Pakistan's Future: Nusrat Bhutto', *India Today*, 15 January 1983.
70. 'Al Zulfikar and the Bhutto Brothers', 1984, The National Archives of the UK, FCO 37/3807.
71. Bhutto, Murtaza, 'FSP 011/1 Pakistan Al Zulfikar Murtaza Bhutto Interview to BBC, 23 Oct 1983', The National Archives of the UK, FCO 37/3329.
72. Bhutto, Benazir, *Daughter of the East*, p. 218.
73. Emmer, Monica, 'Terror Plot a Signal Failure', *Sunday Times*, 15 July 1984.
74. 'Pakistan – Al Zulfikar', 1982, The National Archives of the UK, FCO 37/2920.
75. Bhutto, Murtaza, 'FSP 011/1 Pakistan Al Zulfikar Murtaza Bhutto interview to BBC, 23 Oct 1983', The National Archives of the UK, FCO 37/3329.
76. National Foreign Assessment Center, 'The Pakistan People's Party', p. 9.
77. Paracha, Nadeem F., 'Al-Zulfikar: The Unsaid History', *Dawn*, 9 April 2010.
78. 'India: No.10 Record of Conversation (MT, Indira Gandhi)', The Margaret Thatcher Foundation, PREM 19/801 f54.
79. 'Indira Gandhi Letter to MT', The Margaret Thatcher Foundation, PREM19/799 f20.
80. *Terrorism Review*, 22 March 1985, CIA Directorate of Intelligence, p. 18. *Terrorism Review*, April 1986, CIA Directorate of Intelligence, p. 38.
81. Bhutto, Benazir, *Daughter of the East*, p. 197.
82. Bhutto, Benazir, *Daughter of the East*, p. 203.
83. Author interview with Naheed Khan and Safdar Abbasi, Islamabad, February 2019.
84. Bhutto, Benazir, *Daughter of the East*, p. 267.
85. Author interview with Bashir Riaz, Lahore, February 2019.
86. Bhutto, Benazir, Letter to Farooq Leghari, Shaikh Rafiq, Shaukat Mahmood and Jehangir Badar, 30 May 1984, *Benazir Papers, The State and Government: Democracy, Historical Resistance and Resilience*, Series 1, Volume 1: Letters by Benazir Bhutto sent to Senator Dr Mohammed Jehangir Badar, Secretary General of the Pakistan People's Party, Aizaz-ud-Din TBM Publishers, Lahore, 2014, p. 6.
87. Bhutto, Benazir, Letter to General Tikka Khan, undated but early 1985, *Benazir Papers*, p. 68.
88. Bhutto, Benazir, Letter to General Tikka Khan, 24 March 1985, *Benazir Papers*, p. 68.
89. Bhutto, Benazir, Letter to Jehangir Badar, 28 August 1985, *Benazir Papers*, p. 97.
90. Bhutto, Benazir, Letter to Jehangir Badar, 21 October 1985, *Benazir Papers*, p. 127.

91. Bhutto, Benazir, Letter to Mohammed Jehangir Badar, 9 July 1984, *Benazir Papers*, p. 16.

92. Khan, Tikka, Letter to Benazir Bhutto, 20 November 1984, *Benazir Papers*, p. 16.

93. Author interview with Naheed Khan, Islamabad, February 2019.

94. Raza, *Zulfikar Ali Bhutto and Pakistan*, p. 1.

95. Bhutto, Benazir, Letter to Tikka Khan, 29 May 1985, *Benazir Papers*, pp. 16, 85 and 86.

96. Bhutto, Benazir, Letter to Jehangir Badar, 7 September 1985, *Benazir Papers*, pp. 16 and 99.

97. Ali, Tariq, 'A Tragedy Born of Military Despotism and Anarchy', *Guardian*, 28 December 2007.

98. Akhund, *Trail & Error*, p. 3.

99. Paracha, Nadeem F., 'Riding the arrow: An ideological history of the PPP', *Dawn*, 7 June 2012.

100. Bhutto, Benazir, interviewed by American Academy of Achievement.

101. Buruma, Ian, 'The Double Life of Benazir Bhutto', *New York Review of Books*, 2 March 1989.

102. Shaikh, *Benazir Bhutto*, p. 110.

103. 'Benazir Bhutto and the PPP', The National Archives of the UK, FCO 37/4195.

104. Interview with Benazir Bhutto, interviewed and recorded by Linda Francke for *Daughter of the East*.

105. 'Benazir Bhutto and the PPP', The National Archives of the UK, FCO 37/419637/4195.

106. 'Rehana Bhutto Sentenced to Two Years' Jail', *Associated Press*, 5 December 1988.

107. Author interview with Amna Paracha, June 2019. Amna Paracha had a full copy of the report and translated it into English, but it was stolen from her home. I have been unable to get hold of a copy, but Amna Paracha recalls the detail about the breakfast.

108. 'Rehana Bhutto Sentenced to Two Years' Jail', *Associated Press*, 5 December 1988.

109. 'Rehana Bhutto Sentenced to Two Years' Jail', *Associated Press*, 5 December 1988.

110. Bhutto, Benazir, *Daughter of the East*, p. 290.

111. Interview with Benazir Bhutto, interviewed and recorded by Linda Francke for *Daughter of the East*.

112. Paracha, Nadeem F., 'The Tragic Life and Death of Shahnawaz Bhutto', *Daily Times*, 23 July 2017.

113. Macdonald, Susan, 'New Light thrown on Bhutto's Death by Widow's Arrest', *The Times*, 25 October 1985.

114. Bhutto, Fatima, *Songs of Blood and Sword*, p. 272.

115. Author interview with Shyam Bhatia, London, 7 April 2019.

116. Bhutto, Fatima, *Songs of Blood and Sword*, p. 255.

117. Bhutto, Benazir, Letter to Jehangir Badar, 30 May 1984, *Benazir Papers*, pp. 144–6.

118. 'Mrs. Bhutto, Benazir Bhutto and the PPP', The National Archives of the UK, FCO 37/3765.

119. Bhutto, Benazir, interviewed by American Academy of Achievement.

120. Bhutto, Benazir, *Daughter of the East*, p. 325.

121. Weisman, Steven R., 'The Return of Benazir Bhutto: Struggle in Pakistan', *New York Times*, 21 September 1986.

122. Hassan, Ali, 'Benazir is now Co-Chairman', *The Star*, 14 May 1986.

123. Bhutto, Benazir, *Daughter of the East*, p. 334.

124. Khan, Afzal, 'My Cousin was Interested in Benazir, Says Imran', *Khaleej Times*, 10 July 2011.

125. Bhutto, Benazir, *Daughter of the East*, p. 351.

126. 'Profile: PPP Co Chair Asif Zardari', 31 March 2008, WikiLeaks, ISLAMABAD 00001368 003 OF 003.

127. Author interview with a school contemporary of Asif Zardari's, Karachi, July 2019.

128. Author interview with a resident of Zardari's home town of Nawabshah, 20 August 2018.

129. Author interview with a journalist who knew Zardari as a young man, Karachi, August 2018.

130. Author interview with Sanam Bhutto, London, April 2018.
131. Author interview with Tariq Islam, Karachi, August 2018.
132. Marshall, Tyler, 'Political Maverick Bows to Muslim Custom', *Los Angeles Times*, 7 August 1987.
133. Bhutto, Benazir, *Daughter of the East*, p. 358.
134. Omar, Kaleem, 'Huge Crowd at Benazir Wedding', *The Star*, 19 December 1987.
135. Author interview with Nadeem F. Paracha, Dubai, July 2019.

6. BENAZIR TRIUMPHS

1. Scott-Clark, Cathy and Levy, Adrian, *The Exile: The Flight of Osama bin Laden*, Bloomsbury, London, 2017, passim.
2. Beg expressed such views in tweets since deleted from his Twitter feed.
3. Marker, Jamsheed, *Cover Point: Impressions of Leadership in Pakistan*, OUP, Karachi, 2016, p. 152.
4. Bhatia, Shyam, 'Bhutto Dynasty's Outcast', *Observer*, 5 February 1989, p. 27.
5. Weaver, Mary Anne, 'Bhutto's Fatal Moment', *New Yorker*, 27 September 1993.
6. 'Benazir Praises Armed Forces Role, Interview with Maleeha Lodhi', *The Muslim*, 29 August 1988.
7. 'Prime Minister's Meeting with the Prime Minister of Pakistan', The National Archives of the UK, Kew, Prem 19/3872.
8. Akhund, Iqbal, *Trial & Error: The Advent and Eclipse of Benazir Bhutto*, OUP, Karachi, 2000, p. 21.
9. Panhwar, Sani H., 'Khakwani Deposes Before Mir Case Tribunal', *Murtaza Bhutto*, p. 439, www.sanipanhwar.com, accessed 13 May 2020.
10. Oakley, Robert B., interviewed by Charles Stuart Kennedy and Thomas Stern, 7 July 1992, 'Foreign Affairs Oral History Project: Ambassador Robert B. Oakley', *The Association for Diplomatic Studies and Training*, Arlington, VA, 1999, p. 149.
11. Shaikh, Muhammed Ali, *Benazir Bhutto: A Political Biography*, Oriental Books, Karachi, 2000, p. 119.
12. Declaration made by PPP and MQM, 2 December 1988, copy in author's personal archive.
13. Nawaz, Shuja, *Crossed Swords: Pakistan, Its Army, and the Wars Within*, 2nd edition, OUP, Karachi, 1998.
14. Shaikh, *Benazir Bhutto*, p. 120.
15. 'Jamaat Leader Dubs Benazir as "Westernised"', *Dawn*, 9 April 1986.
16. Akhund, *Trial & Error*, p. 58.
17. Bhutto, Benazir, 'International Leadership Day — November 25, 1997', in Sani H. Panhwar (ed.), *Benazir Bhutto: Selected Speeches, 1989–2007*, M.H. Panhwar Trust, Hyderabad, 2009.
18. Zakaria, Rafiq, *The Trial of Benazir Bhutto: An Insight into the Status of Women in Islam*, Sangam Books, London, 1989, passim.
19. Bhutto, Benazir, *Whither Pakistan: Dictatorship or Democracy?*, al-Hamd Publications, Lahore, 2007, p. 301.
20. Bhutto, Benazir, interviewed by American Academy of Achievement, 27 October 2000, London, https://www.achievement.org/achiever/benazir-bhutto/#interview.
21. Bhutto, Benazir, interviewed by American Academy of Achievement.
22. Bhutto, Benazir, 'Profiles in Courage – March 5, 1999', in Panhwar (ed.), *Benazir Bhutto*, p. 225.
23. Shaikh, *Benazir Bhutto*, p. 148.
24. Bhutto, Benazir, 'Islam Forbids Injustice against People, Nations and Women – September 4, 1995', in Panhwar (ed.), *Benazir Bhutto*, p. 22.
25. Bhutto, Benazir, *The Way Out: Interviews, Impressions, Statements, and Messages*, Mahmood Publications, Karachi, 1988, pp. 256–64.

26. Weiss, Anita M., 'Benazir Bhutto and the Future of Women in Pakistan', *Asian Survey*, vol. 30: 5 (May 1990), p. 434.
27. 'Pakistan: Feminists criticize Bhutto', *Off Our Backs*, vol. 19: 5 (May 1989), p. 5.
28. Crossette, Barbara, 'In Pakistan Women Seek Basic Rights', *New York Times*, 26 March 1989.
29. Weiss, Anita M., 'Islamic Influences on Sociolegal Conditions of Pakistani Women', *Oriente Moderno*, Nuova serie, Anno 23, vol. 84: 1, Islam in South Asia (2004), p. 316.
30. Weiss, 'Islamic Influences on Sociolegal Conditions of Pakistani Women', p. 316.
31. Bhutto, Benazir, 'Islam Forbids Injustice against People, Nations and Women', p. 21.
32. Author interview with Shafqat Mahmood, February 2019.
33. Shaikh, *Benazir Bhutto*, p. 125.
34. Author interview with Samiya Waheed, Karachi, September 2018.
35. Weintraub, Richard, 'Pakistan's Bhutto Sees Success in Conciliation', *Washington Post*, 7 December 1988.
36. Shaikh, *Benazir Bhutto*, p. 115.
37. '40 Top Pak Army Officers Retired', *Dawn*, 27 February 1989.
38. Durrani, Asad, *Pakistan Adrift: Navigating Troubled Waters*, Westland, Chennai, 2018, p. 132.
39. Kukreja, Veena, *Contemporary Pakistan*, Sage, New Delhi, 2002, p. 231.
40. 'PR Not to Yield to Ittefaq's Blackmail', *Dawn*, 22 July 1989.
41. 'Pakistan, India Renounce Attack on Each Nation's Nuclear Installations', *Pakistan Affairs*, Vol. 42, Washington DC, 16 January 1989, p. 4.
42. Haqqani, Husain, *Pakistan: Between Mosque and Military*, Carnegie Endowment for International Peace, Washington, D.C., 2007, p. 213.
43. Akhund, *Tia & Error*, p. 120.
44. Bhutto, Benazir, 'The Security Apparatus Has Run Amok', *The Nation*, 11 January 2001, available in Bashir Riaz (ed.), *Faith in People*, Bhutto Legacy Foundation, Lahore, 2010, p. 76.
45. Bhutto, Benazir, *Daughter of the East: An Autobiography*, Pocket Books, London, 2008, p. 405.
46. Bergen, Peter L., *The Osama bin Laden I Know: An Oral History of al Qaeda's Leader*, Free Press, New York, 2006.
47. Bhutto, Benazir, 'The Security Apparatus Has Run Amok', p. 77.
48. 'Osama Offered to Buy Votes for Nawaz: Qazi', *Dawn*, 19 March 2006; Asad, Malik, 'Claims that Nawaz Took Money from Bin Laden Resurface', *Dawn*, 29 February 2016.
49. Ahmed, Imtiaz, ' "Midnight Jackal" was Launched to Overthrow Benazir: Imtiaz', *Daily Times Monitor*, 28 August 2009.
50. Bonner, Arthur, 'Afghan Rebel's Victory Garden: Opium', *New York Times*, 18 June 1986.
51. Oakley, interviewed by Kennedy and Stern, 'Foreign Affairs Oral History Project', p. 152.
52. Haq, Ikramul, 'Pak–Afghan Drug Trade in Historical Perspective', *South Asian Survey*, vol. 36: 10 (Oct. 1996), p. 945.
53. Freemantle, Brian, *The Fix: Inside the World Drug Trade*, Tor, New York, 1985, p. 174.
54. 'Narcopower: Pakistan's Parallel Government?', *Newsline*, December 1989, p. 16.
55. 'Documents', *Pakistan Horizon*, vol. 42: 1 (January 1989), pp. 134–60.
56. 'Bhutto to Discuss drugs Afghanistan During Visit', *Deseret News*, 5 June 1989.
57. Lifschultz, Lawrence, 'Inside the Kingdom of Heroin', *The Nation* (New York), 14 November 1988, pp. 492 and 493.
58. United States District Court, Eastern District of New York, USA against Haji Mirza Mohammed Iqbal Baig, Haji Ayub Afridi, Mohammed Anwar Khan Khattak and Tariq Butt, 91CR 960 (S), Affidavit in support of request for extradition para. 33, evidence of Stewart Newton para. 19, evidence of John Rende, para. 2.
59. Rashid, Ahmed, *Taliban: The Power of Militant Islam in Afghanistan and Beyond*, I.B. Tauris, London, 2010, p. 120.

60. Langridge, Barry, 'Begum Bhutto speaks', *BBC*, 14 August 1990.
61. Anderson, John Ward and Khan, Kamran, 'Heroin Plan by Top Pakistanis Alleged', *Washington Post*, 12 September 1994.
62. Jalal, Ayesha, *The Struggle for Pakistan: A Muslim Homeland and Global Politics*, Harvard UP, Cambridge, MA, 2014, p. 262.
63. Haqqani, *Pakistan*, p. 202.
64. Author interview with Peter Galbraith, London, May 2019.
65. 'Prime Minister's Meeting with the Prime Minister of Pakistan', The National Archives of the UK, Prem 19/3872.
66. Abbas, Hassan, *Pakistan's Nuclear Bomb: A Story of Defiance, Deterrence and Deviance*, Hurst, London, 2018, pp. 106 and 107.
67. Khan, A.Q., 'An Indomitable Man', *The News*, 26 January 2015.
68. Abbas, *Pakistan's Nuclear Bomb*, p. 110.
69. Frantz, Douglas and Collins, Catherine, *The Nuclear Jihadist: The True Story of the Man Who Sold the World's Most Dangerous Secrets . . . and How We Could Have Stopped Him*, Twelve, New York, 2007, p. 164.
70. Haqqani, *Pakistan*, p. 217.
71. Chaudhri, M.A., 'Pakistan's Nuclear History: Separating Myth from Reality', *Defence Journal*, vol. 9: 10 (2006), http://www.defencejournal.com/2006-5/index.asp.
72. Abbas, *Pakistan's Nuclear Bomb*, p. 108.
73. Abbas, *Pakistan's Nuclear Bomb*, p. 108.
74. Burrows, William E. and Windrem, Robert, *Critical Mass*, Simon & Schuster, London, 1994, p. 80. Author interview with Mark Siegel, New York, February 2020.
75. Hersh, Seymour, 'On the Nuclear Edge', *New Yorker*, 29 March 1993.
76. Levy, Adrian and Scott-Clark, Catherine, *Deception: Pakistan, the United States and the Global Nuclear Weapons Conspiracy*, Penguin, London, 2007, p. 200.
77. Marker, Jamsheed, *Quiet Diplomacy: Memoirs of an Ambassador of Pakistan*, OUP, Oxford, 2010, p. 361.
78. Marker, *Cover Point*, p. 167.
79. Oakley, interviewed by Kennedy and Stern, 'Foreign Affairs Oral History Project', p. 144.
80. Abbas, *Pakistan's Nuclear Bomb*.
81. Smith, Louis J. (ed.), *Foreign Relations of the United States, 1969–1976*, Volume XXIV, Middle East Region and Arabian Peninsula, 1969–1972, Government Printing Office, Washington, D.C., 2005, Document 34: Jordan, September 1970, Airgram from the Embassy in the United Arab Emirates to the Department of State.
82. Beaty, Jonathan and Gwynne, S.C., *The Outlaw Bank*, Random House, New York, 1993, p. 283.
83. Philip, David, 'Ghulam the Grim Requiem for a Despot', *Economic and Political Weekly*, 21 December 1996, p. 3295.
84. Beaty and Gwynne, *The Outlaw Bank*, p. 291.
85. Philip, 'Ghulam the Grim Requiem for a Despot', p. 3295.
86. Beaty and Gwynne, *The Outlaw Bank*, p. 49.
87. Akhund, *Tia & Error*, p. 134.
88. Mahmood, Shafqat, 'My BB, My Boss', *The News*, 2 January 2008.
89. Akhund, *Tia & Error*, p. 142.
90. Shafqat, Saeed, 'Pakistan under Benazir Bhutto', *Asian Survey*, vol. 36: 7 (July 1996), p. 662.
91. 'Why Benazir Fell', *The News*, 6 August 1991.
92. 'Why Benazir Fell', *The News*, 6 August 1991.
93. Shafqat, 'Pakistan under Benazir Bhutto', p. 663.
94. *Dawn*, 7 August 1990.
95. Khan, Roedad, *Pakistan – A Dream Gone Sour*, OUP, Karachi, 1999, p. 109.
96. Oakley, interviewed by Kennedy and Stern, 'Foreign Affairs Oral History Project', p. 155.
97. Oakley, interviewed by Kennedy and Stern, 'Foreign Affairs Oral History Project'.

7. BENAZIR: POWER AND EXILE

1. Buruma, Ian, 'The Double Life of Benazir Bhutto', *New York Review of Books*, 2 March 1989.
2. Akhund, Iqbal, *Tia & Error: The Advent and Eclipse of Benazir Bhutto*, OUP, Karachi, 2000, p. 73.
3. Bhutto, Benazir, 'Leadership Lesson: How to Succeed, Benazir Bhutto', *The Nation*, 29 January 1999, available in Bashir Riaz (ed.), *Faith in People*, Bhutto Legacy Foundation, Lahore, 2010, p. 10.
4. Bhutto, Benazir, 'Leadership and Courage – March 14, 2000', in Sani H. Panhwar (ed.), *Benazir Bhutto: Selected Speeches, 1989–2007*, M.H. Panhwar Trust, Hyderabad, 2009, p. 311.
5. Weisman, Steven R., 'The Return of Benazir Bhutto: Struggle in Pakistan', *New York Times*, 21 September 1986.
6. Mody, Piloo, *Zulfi My Friend*, Thompson Press, New Delhi, 1973, p. 85.
7. Author interview with a former colleague of Benazir and Zardari's, who worked with them closely at this time, Lahore, February 2019.
8. Author interview with a senior civil servant and adviser to Benazir Bhutto, Karachi, August 2018.
9. Barak, Daphne, 'How Benazir Let Her Hair Down', *Daily Mail*, 30 December 2007.
10. Author interview with Mark Siegel, New York, February 2020. Siegel made contemporaneous notes of the one-and-a-half-hour meeting.
11. Palling, Studley Bruce, 'Asif Zardari – A Controversial Figure, *Dawn*, 27 July 1989.
12. 'Benazir Asked Me to Keep Zardari Happy Former Aide Alleges', *Daily Times*, 27 November 1998.
13. 'Zardari Defends Son', *Dawn*, 1 July 1989.
14. Author interview with a senior civil servant and adviser to Benazir Bhutto, Karachi, August 2018.
15. 'Asif Says Loving Wife Will Not Leave Him', *Dawn*, 6 October 1993.
16. Khan, Roedad, *Reflections at 94: Collected Works*, Vol. 1, PanGraphics, Islamabad, 2018.
17. Bhutto, Benazir, interviewed by American Academy of Achievement, 27 October 2000, London, https://www.achievement.org/achiever/benazir-bhutto/#interview.
18. Author interview with Ron Suskind, Boston, 2018.
19. Akhund, *Trial & Error*, p. 308.
20. Oakley, Robert B., interviewed by Charles Stuart Kennedy and Thomas Stern, 7 July 1992, 'Foreign Affairs Oral History Project: Ambassador Robert B. Oakley', The Association for Diplomatic Studies and Training, Arlington, VA, 1999, p. 150.
21. Quoted in Riaz, Bashir (ed.), *Faith in People*, Bhutto Legacy Foundation, Lahore, 2010, p. 86.
22. Bennett-Jones, Owen, *Pakistan: Eye of the Storm*, 1st edition, Yale University Press, New Haven and London, 2002, p. 240.
23. Shaikh, Muhammed Ali, *Benazir Bhutto: A Political Biography*, Oriental Books, Karachi, 2000, p. 200.
24. Bhutto, Benazir, *Speeches and Statements: 2 Dec. 1988–30 April 1989*, Government of Pakistan, Islamabad, 1989, p. 58.
25. Shafqat, Saeed, 'Pakistan under Benazir Bhutto', *Asian Survey*, vol. 36: 7 (July 1996), pp. 655–72.
26. Gargan, Edward A., 'Bhutto Stands by Nuclear Program', *New York Times*, 21 October 1993.
27. Bhatia, Shyam, *Goodbye Shahzadi: A Political Biography of Benazir Bhutto*, Roli Books, New Delhi, 2008.
28. Niaz, Anjum, 'Goodbye Shahzadi (Book Review)', *Dawn*, 27 July 2008.
29. Frantz, Douglas and Collins, Catherine, 'A Tale of Two Bhuttos', *Foreign Policy*, 19 November 2007.
30. Abbas, Hassan, 'Shiism and Sectarian Conflict in Pakistan: Identity Politics, Iranian Influence, and Tit-for-Tat Violence', *Occasional Paper Series*, Combatting Terrorism Center at West Point, 2010, p. 23, www.jstor.org/stable/resrep05604.

31. Reminiscence of a Bombay friend, Ram Lalwani.
32. Abbas, 'Shiism and Sectarian Conflict in Pakistan', p. 24.
33. Author interview with Bashir Riaz, Lahore, February 2019. All the close relatives of Benazir I have spoken to have stated she was Sunni.
34. Omar, Kaleem, 'Huge Crowd At Benazir Wedding', *The Star*, 19 December 1987.
35. Author interview with Sanam Bhutto, London, April 2019.
36. Author interview with Hassan Abbas, London, July 2019.
37. In February 2017 ninety people were killed when violent jihadists attacked the shrine.
38. Shaikh, *Benazir Bhutto*, p. 141.
39. Bhutto, Benazir, *Daughter of the East: An Autobiography*, Pocket Books, London, 2008, p. 142
40. Shah, Syed Mujawar Hussain, 'Bhutto, Zia and Islam', p. 136, available on www.sanipanhwar.com, accessed 13 May 2020.
41. 'Sufi Teachings Can End Hatred Prejudices: PM', *Dawn*, 20 July 1989.
42. Bhutto, Benazir, 'Conference of Asian Political Parties Manila – September 17, 2000', in Panhwar (ed.), *Benazir Bhutto*, p. 326.
43. Akhund, *Tia & Error*, p. 2.
44. 'Benazir's jinxed New York apartment', *The News*, 25 April 2008.
45. *Woman's Own*, 13 September 1986, p. 23. Benazir's sister Sanam has said that she suggested the séance and that Benazir played a minor part in it, only attending as a show of support.
46. Niazi, Kausar, *Last Days of Premier Bhutto*, Jang, Lahore, 1991.
47. Hashmi, Ashraf, 'Bedlam in House on Calling Benazir "Kafir" ', *Dawn*, 10 August 1992.
48. 'I Do Not Accept FSC Supremacy says Benazir', *Dawn*, 12 August 1992.
49. 'I believe in Quran, Sunnah Supremacy', *Dawn*, 12 August 1992.
50. Bhutto, Benazir, *Issues in Pakistan: Selection of Speeches in National Assembly, 1990–1993*, Jang, Lahore, 1993, pp. 5 and 6.
51. Shaikh, *Benazir Bhutto*, p. 143.
52. Bhutto, Benazir, 'A Conversation with Benazir Bhutto – August 15, 2007', in Panhwar (ed.), *Benazir Bhutto*, p. 592.
53. This account is drawn largely from Bennett-Jones, *Pakistan*.
54. Bhutto, Benazir, 'International Leadership Day – November 25, 1997', in Panhwar (ed.), *Benazir Bhutto*.
55. Bhutto, Zulfikar Ali, *My Dearest Daughter: A Letter from the Death Cell*, Classic, Lahore, 1995.
56. Sham, Mahmood, *Larkana to Peking*, National Book Foundation, Islamabad, 2009, p. 136.
57. Smith, Louis J. (ed.), *Foreign Relations of the United States, 1969 –1976*, Volume E-8, Documents on South Asia 1973–1976, Government Printing Office, Washington, D.C., 2005, Document 148: Memo of conversation between Nixon, Bhutto, Kissinger and others, 19 September 1973.
58. Weaver, Mary Anne, 'Bhutto's Fatal Moment', *New Yorker*, 27 September 1993.
59. Raza, Rafi, *Zulfikar Ali Bhutto and Pakistan, 1967–1977*, OUP, Karachi, 1998, p. 14.
60. Author interview with Tariq Islam, London, April 2018.
61. 'Pakistan – Al Zulfikar', 1982, The National Archives of the UK, FCO 37/2920.
62. Author interview with Shyam Bhatia, London, 7 April 2019.
63. Author interview with Ghinwa Bhutto, August 2018.
64. Bhatia, Shyam, 'Bhutto Dynasty's Outcast', *Observer*, 5 February 1989, p. 27.
65. Author interview with Shyam Bhatia, London, April 2019.
66. Author interview with Ghinwa Bhutto, August 2018.
67. Weaver, 'Bhutto's Fatal Moment'.
68. Hussain, Zahid, 'Divided: The House of Bhutto', *Newsline*, August 1993, p. 2.
69. Moore, Molly, 'The Battle of the Bhuttos Threatens to Split Ruling Party in Pakistan', *Washington Post*, 1 February 1994.
70. Author interview with Ghinwa Bhutto, August 2018.

71. Moore, 'The Battle of the Bhuttos Threatens to Split Ruling Party in Pakistan'.
72. Haider, Salahuddin, 'Benazir Nothing Minus Bhutto Trappings', *Dawn*, 23 December 1994.
73. Moore, 'The Battle of the Bhuttos Threatens to Split Ruling Party in Pakistan'.
74. Moore, 'The Battle of the Bhuttos Threatens to Split Ruling Party in Pakistan'.
75. 'Murtaza has to Clarify his Position: Benazir', *Dawn*, 9 September 1993. Lodhi, M.A.K., 'No Basis for Hijacking Case Against Murtaza', *Friday Times*.
76. Bhutto, Mir Murtaza, 'The State of Strife', *The Nation*, 27 August 1996.
77. Bakhtiar, Idrees and Jafri, Hasan Iqbal, 'I am an older member of the party than Benazir: Murtaza Bhutto', *The Herald*, June 1994.
78. Author interview with Ghinwa Bhutto, August 2018.
79. Soomro, Javed, 'Benazir Ready to Bury the Hatchet if Murtaza Buries the Gun', *Dawn*, 31 August 1995.
80. A number of people have mentioned the photograph and one Bhutto family member described hurriedly removing it when they thought Benazir might visit 70 Clifton and see it.
81. The following account comes from an author interview with a friend of Murtaza's, London, August 2018.
82. Author interview with a friend of Murtaza's, London, August 2018.
83. Bakhtiar and Jafri, 'I Am an Older Member of the Party Than'.
84. Quoted in Riaz (ed.), *Faith in People*, p. 91.
85. Bhutto, Fatima, *Songs of Blood and Sword: A Daughter's Memoir*, Vintage, London, 2011, p. 20.
86. Bhutto, Fatima, *Songs of Blood and Sword*, p. 21.
87. Author interview with pathologist Peter Acland, Birmingham, May 2018.
88. Author interview with pathologist Peter Acland, Birmingham, May 2018.
89. LaPorte, Robert Jr, 'Pakistan in 1966: Starting Over Again', *Asian Survey*, vol. 37: 2 (Feb. 1997), pp. 118–25.
90. Fatima says of an occasion when Zardari was near her home where Murtaza was killed: 'here I was, standing where my father was murdered, and the man who I believe was in part responsible for the execution, was across the road from me': Bhutto, Fatima, *Songs of Blood and Sword*, p. 430.
91. Evidence of Ishaq Khan Khakwani to the official tribunal inquiry into the death of Murtaza Bhutto. Panhwar, Sani H., *Murtaza Bhutto*, 'Khakwani Deposes Before Mir Case Tribunal', p. 442, www.sanipanhwar.com, accessed 13 May 2020.
92. Evidence of Benazir Bhutto to the official tribunal inquiry into the death of Murtaza Bhutto. Panhwar, Sani H., *Murtaza Bhutto*, 'Benazir Narrates Events Leading to Shooting', p. 481, www.sanipanhwar.com, accessed 13 May 2020.
93. Author interview with Shoaib Suddle, Islamabad, July 2019.
94. Tanoli, Ishaq, 'All 18 Policemen Acquitted in Murtaza Murder Case', *Dawn*, 6 December 2009.
95. Bhutto, Benazir, *Daughter of the East*, p. 421.
96. Author interview with Ghinwa Bhutto, Karachi, August 2018.
97. Author interview with Shoaib Suddle, Islamabad, July 2019.
98. Author interviews with Justice (Dr) Ghous Mohammad and Justice Nasir Aslam Zahid – two of the three judges on the three-member commission of enquiry panel, Karachi, July 2019.
99. Bhutto, Benazir, 'Is Islam Compatible with the West? – February 20, 2000', in Panhwar (ed.), *Benazir Bhutto Selected Speeches 1989–2007*, p. 301, available on www.sanipanhwar. com, accessed 20 May 2020.
100. Ali, Tariq, 'A Tragedy Born of Military Despotism and Anarchy', *Guardian*, 28 December 2007.
101. On the judicial issue and this journalist opposition to Benazir see LaPorte, 'Pakistan in 1996', pp. 118–21.

102. Author interview with Shafqat Mahmood, Lahore, February 2019.
103. Oakley, interviewed by Kennedy and Stern, 'Foreign Affairs Oral History Project'.
104. Kareem, Abdul, 'Unruly Mob Storms Top Pakistan Court', *Gulf News*, 28 November 1997.
105. Associated Press of Pakistan, 3 March 1999.
106. Author interview with Safdar Abbasi, Islamabad, February 2019.
107. 'A Disgrace Ignored or Forgotten?', *The News*, 6 August 2007.
108. 'A Disgrace Ignored or Forgotten?', *The News*, 6 August 2007.
109. Bennett-Jones, Owen, 'The Monday Documentary, Benazir Bhutto – The Investigation', *BBC World Service*, 28 October 2007.
110. Bhutto, Benazir, 'Accountability or Revenge', Address at Council of Pakistan Affairs, Karachi, 26 November 1988.
111. Burns, John F., 'House of Graft: Tracing the Bhutto Millions – A Special Report', *New York Times*, 9 January 1998.
112. Letter from Swiss embassy to PPP Canada.
113. 'No Evidence to Link Benazir to Surrey House: PPP', *Daily Times*, 8 August 2008.
114. Baabar, Mariana, 'The End of the Affair', *Outlook*, 5 February 2007.
115. 'New Money Laundering Scam Detected Against Benazir', *Dawn*, 2 March 2006.
116. Bhutto, Benazir, *The Nation*, 21 June 2003.
117. Author interview with Mark Siegel, New York, February 2020.
118. Bhutto, Benazir, 'A Conversation with Benazir Bhutto', p. 579.

8. ASSASSINATION

1. See Chapter 5.
2. Bhutto, Benazir, *Daughter of the East: An Autobiography*, Pocket Books, London, 2008, pp. 411–13.
3. Ottaway, David B. and Coll, Steve, 'Retracing the Steps of a Terror Suspect: Accused Bomb Builder Tied to Many Plots', *Washington Post*, 5 June 1995.
4. Dougary, Ginny, 'Destiny's Daughter', *The Times*, 28 April 2007.
5. Author interview with Rehman Malik, December 2017.
6. The best account of the sourcing of this quote is in 'I Have Sent My Men to Welcome Benazir', *Dawn*, 7 August 2012.
7. Wilkinson, Isambard and Holt, Richard, 'Benazir Arrives Back in Pakistan', *Daily Telegraph*, 18 October 2007.
8. Witte, Griffe, 'Benazir, Returning from Exile, Adds to Pakistan's Uncertainty', *Washington Post*, 18 October 2007.
9. The following account is taken from Aitzaz Shah's confession. At a later stage in his trial, he withdrew the confession and was acquitted.
10. Lamb, Christina, 'It Was What We Feared, but Dared Not to Happen', *Sunday Times*, 21 October 2007.
11. Bhutto, Benazir, 'When I Return to Pakistan', *Washington Post*, 20 September 2007.
12. Author's personal archive. I have various versions of the JIT report. Earlier copies have more detail than later copies. The interrogation report of Saifullah Akhtar, for example, has been removed in later versions.
13. Author interview with Saud Mirza, December 2017.
14. JIT report, p. 71, copy in author's personal archive.
15. The quote is only in the first, hardback edition. A lawyer in Islamabad, representing Saifullah Akhtar, threatened the publishers with a libel case if they did not remove the quote from subsequent editions. The publishers complied.
16. These are the arrests referred to in Muñoz, Heraldo, *Getting Away With Murder: Benazir Bhutto's Assassination and the Politics of Pakistan*, Norton, New York, 2014, p. 31.
17. Nelson, Dean and Hasnain, Ghulam, 'Benazir Defies Taliban Threats to Visit Family Shrine', *Sunday Times*, 28 October 2007.

18. Williams, David, 'I was Warned', *Sunday Telegraph*, 21 October 2007.
19. Baker, Aryn, 'A Bloody Welcome for Benazir', *Time Magazine*, 18 October 2007.
20. Associated Press, TV clip, October 1999, copy in author's personal archive.
21. '126768: Benazir Asks Ambassador for Security Assessment Assistance', *The Hindu*, 22 May 2011.
22. Author interview with an adviser to Benazir Bhutto who was present at the meeting, August 2018.
23. The following account is taken from Husnain Gul's confession. Gul later withdrew his confession and was acquitted.
24. 'Benazir Asks International Community to Back Pakistan People', *BBC Monitoring*, quoting *Geo TV*, 3 November 2007.
25. Shah, Saeed, 'Musharraf Sweeps Democracy Aside', *Globe and Mail*, 5 November 2007.
26. 'U.K. Journalists Kicked Out Of Pakistan', *CBS News*, 10 November 2007.
27. 'Pakistan a pressure cooker, journalists expelled', *Reuters*, 10 November 2007.
28. 'Pakistan ex-PM Benazir Call for President's Resignation', *BBC Monitoring*, quoting *Geo TV*, 13 November 2007.
29. Walsh, Declan and Borger, Julian, 'Benazir: I will not serve as PM as long as Musharraf is President', *Guardian*, 3 November 2007.
30. Shah, Saeed, 'Rice's Deputy in Pakistan Makes Effort to Revive Benazir Musharraf Pact', *Globe and Mail*, 17 November 2007.
31. 'Benazir Launches Election Campaign', *Associated Press*, 1 December 2007.
32. The seven tribal agencies in north-west Pakistan, of which Kurram was one, were at the time semi-autonomous territories in which federal law did not apply.
33. Author interview with Mohammad Azhar Chaudhry, July 2017.
34. Zafar, Ziad, 'The Masterminds of the Assassination', *Dawn*, 24 December 2017.
35. The original note was in Arabic. Fragment in author's personal archive.
36. 'Benazir Assassination: Cell Phones of Suspects Recovered', *Express Tribune*, 19 January 2011.
37. Warraich, Sohail, *The Bhutto Blood: An Independent Probe into Benazir Bhutto's Killing*, Sagar, Lahore, 2013, p. 90.
38. Author interview with British police official, London, March 2017.
39. Author interview with Peter Galbraith, London, May 2019.
40. Author interview with Peter Galbraith, Oxford, 26 April 2017.
41. Muñoz, *Getting Away With Murder*, p. 173.
42. 'Pakistan Report Says No Headway in Probe into Killing of Benazir Bhutto', *Dawn*, from *BBC Monitoring*, 8 February 2016.
43. 'Pakistan: "Mastermind" behind Several Karachi Killings Arrested', *BBC Monitoring*, 22 September 2010.
44. Zaffar, Ziad, 'The Slaying of Chaudhry Zulfikar', *Dawn*, 24 December 2017. 'Murder Case of FIA Prosecutor Ch. Zulfiqar Resolved', *Pakistan Today*, 18 September 2013.
45. Zaffar, 'The Slaying of Chaudhry Zulfikar', *Dawn*. 'Murder Case of FIA Prosecutor Ch. Zulfiqar Resolved', *Pakistan Today*.
46. Letter from the Inspector General of Police in Lahore to the Ministry of Interior in Islamabad, copy in author's personal archive.
47. Warraich, *The Bhutto Blood*, pp. 240 and 249.
48. Author interview with a former Pakistani minister, December 2017.
49. Author interview with a former Pakistani minister, December 2017.
50. Author interview with Rehman Malik, 8 December 2017.
51. Cheema, Umar, 'Plotter of Benazir's Death Dead, Amid Growing Mystery', *The News*, 29 May 2010.
52. Author interview with Pervez Musharraf, December 2017.
53. Scott-Clark, Cathy and Levy, Adrian, *The Exile: The Flight of Osama bin Laden*, Bloomsbury, London, 2017.
54. Author interview with an eyewitness, January 2018.

55. Author interview with a former intelligence official, July 2017.
56. Mir, Amir, *The Benazir Murder Trail: From Waziristan to GHQ*, Tranquebar, Chennai, 2010, p. 132.
57. Bhutto, Benazir, Address at Middle East Institute, Washington, 25 September 2007, https://www.c-span.org/video/?201169-1/benazir-Benazirs-final-address-washington-dc-2007.
58. Warraich, *The Bhutto Blood*, p. 43.
59. Author interview with Mark Siegel, June 2018.
60. Author interview with Mark Siegel, October 2017.
61. Author interview with Ron Suskind, June 2017.
62. Author interview with Pervez Musharraf, December 2017.
63. Author interview with Mohammad Azhar Chaudhry, July 2017.

9. THE DYNASTY'S FUTURE

1. Khan, Roedad, *Reflections at 94: Collected Works*, Vol. 1, PanGraphics, Islamabad, 2018, p. 23.
2. These comments were actually made well before Benazir's death. 'Benazir Inherited Cruel Streak of Her Father: Wolpert', *Dawn*, 13 November 1996. Stanley Wolpert, 'History's Hold on Pakistan', *New York Times*, 12 November 1996.
3. Author interview with Ashiq Bhutto, Karachi, June 2019.
4. 'Aamir Made New Sardar of Bhuttos', *The News*, 20 October 2008.
5. Author interview with Sanam Bhutto, London, May 2019.
6. Suvorova, Anna, *Widows and Daughters: Gender, Kinship and Power in South Asia*, OUP, Karachi, 2019, chapters 1 and 2.
7. Bhutto, Benazir, 'Address on 20th Martyrdom Anniversary of Shaheed Z A Bhutto – March 8, 1999', in Sani H. Panhwar (ed.), *Benazir Bhutto: Selected Speeches, 1989–2007*, M.H. Panhwar Trust, Hyderabad, 2009, pp. 235–42.
8. Interview with Benazir Bhutto, interviewed and recorded by Linda Francke for *Daughter of the East*.
9. Author interview with Peter Galbraith, London, May 2019.
10. Allen, Brooke, *Benazir Bhutto: Favored Daughter*, New Harvest, Boston, 2016, p. 56.
11. Hussain, Syeda Abida, *Special Star: Benazir Bhutto's Story*, OUP, Oxford, 2017.
12. Lamb, Christina, 'Bhutto Clan Divided by Zardari's Rise to Power', *Daily Times*, 10 April 2012.
13. Author interview with Husain Haqqani and Farah Isphahani, Washington, July 2017.
14. 'Three Queer Pakistani Artists Explore Identity and Disrupt Borders with their Art', *Hyperallergic*, 8 May 2019.
15. Bhutto, Fatima, 'My Blood Froze when Zardari Became President: Fatima Bhutto', *Hindustan Times*, 3 April 2010.
16. 'Who Are the Senior Bhuttos?', *Dawn*, 24 September 1997.
17. https://www.thenews.com.pk/archive/print/618615-the-many-illnesses-troubling-mr-zardari; Peel, Michael, 'Farhan Bokhari, Doubts Cast on Zardari's Mental Health', *Financial Times*, 25 August 2008.
18. Steele, Jonathan, 'WikiLeaks Cables: Pakistan's Zardari is a "Numbskull"', *Guardian*, 30 November 2010.
19. 'Nato Officials Bewildered by Ill-prepared Zardari', *Dawn*, 21 May 2011.
20. 'Zardari says US behind Taliban Attacks in Pakistan', *The News*, 13 October 2010.
21. Author interview with a US official, London, May 2019.
22. 'Zardari Greatest Obstacle to Pak Progress: King Abdullah', *The News*, 29 November 2010.
23. Small, Andrew, *The China–Pakistan Axis: Asia's New Geopolitics*, Hurst, London, 2015, p. 112.
24. 'Immunity for Musharraf Likely after Zardari's Election as President', 21 August 2008, WikiLeaks, 08ISLAMABAD2802_a.
25. 'Immunity for Musharraf Likely after Zardari's Election as President', WikiLeaks.

26. 'Zardari Makes Top Five of World Losers List', *The News*, 23 March 2009.
27. Farwell, James, *The Pakistan Cauldron: Conspiracy, Assassination & Instability*, Potomac Books, Washington, D.C., 2011, p. 261.
28. 'Zardari Visits French Chateau as Floods Rage', *AFP*, 4 August 2010.
29. Author interview with a Zardari adviser, Washington, 2017.
30. Mir, Amir, *The Bhutto Murder Trail: From Waziristan to GHQ*, Tranquebar, Chennai, 2010.
31. Bhutto, Benazir, 'The Security Apparatus Has Run Amok', *The Nation*, 11 January 2001, available in Bashir Riaz (ed.), *Faith in People*, Bhutto Legacy Foundation, Lahore, 2010, p. 77.
32. Author interview with Tariq Islam, Karachi, February 2019.
33. Author interview with a retired senior civil servant and adviser to Benazir Bhutto, August 2018.
34. 'Profile: PPP Co Chair Asif Zardari', 31 March 2008, WikiLeaks, ISLAMABAD 00001368 003 OF 003.
35. Author interview with Safdar Abbasi, Islamabad, February 2019.
36. Barak, 'How Benazir Let Her Hair Down', *Daily Mail*, 30 December 2007.
37. Raza, Syed Irfan, 'Government Forced to Withdraw ISI decision', *Dawn*, 28 July 2008.
38. Author interview with Peter Galbraith, London, May 2019.
39. 'Pakistan Ready for Nuclear No First Use Offer: Zardari', *Dawn*, 22 November 2008.
40. Raza, Syed Irfan, 'Nuclear Button Handed over to Premier', *Dawn*, 27 November 2009.
41. 'Zardari's Overture to India', *Dawn*, 15 October 2008.
42. Haqqani, Husain, *Magnificent Delusions: Pakistan, the United States, and an Epic History of Misunderstanding*, Public Affairs, New York, 2013, p. 333.
43. 'Zardari Haqqani Tape Against the Army Revealed', *The News*, 28 November 2009.s
44. 'NAB set to Receive Swiss Case Record', *Dawn*, 15 December 2009.
45. Nebehay, Stephanie, 'Swiss Close Case Against Zardari; $60 mln Unfrozen', *Reuters*, 26 August 2008, https://www.reuters.com/article/us-swiss-pakistan-zardari/swiss-close-case-against-zardari-60-mln-unfrozen-idUSLQ17107020080826.
46. 'Ill-Gotten Gains: Bhutto's jewellery to remain in Switzerland', *SWI*, 14 November 2014, http://www.swissinfo.ch/eng/bhutto-s-jewellery-to-remain-in-switzerland/41116270.
47. A facsimile of the memo can be found on http://www.washingtonpost.com/wp-srv/world/documents/secret-pakistan-memo-to-adm-mike-mullen.html.
48. 'Military Takes on PM', *The Nation*, 12 January 2012.
49. Mateen, Amir, 'Aik Zardari, Sub Par Bhari', *The News*, 12 April 2010.
50. Mateen, 'Aik Zardari, Sub Par Bhari'.
51. 'Zardari's Planned Approach to Holbrooke', 9 February 2009, WikiLeaks, 09ISLAMABAD289.
52. 'Why Bilawal Cannot Be Head of the Bhutto and Zardari Clans', *The News*, 31 May 2011.
53. Tunio, Hafeez, 'Dastar Bandi: Zardari Takes Over as Chief of His Own Tribe', *Express Tribune*, 30 December 2014.
54. Bhutto, Bilawal Zardari, 'Zardari's Legacy Will Be Written in Gold, the Best Ever Leader', *The News*, 12 September 2013.
55. Walsh, Declan and Williams, Rachel, 'Unlikely Lad Thrust into the Limelight by Fate', *Guardian*, 31 December 2007.
56. 'Imran Khan Has Had More Failures than Successes: Aseefa Bhutto-Zardari', *India Today*, 3 September 2019.

A NOTE ON SOURCES

1. Balkind, Jeffrey, *Life and Death on a Tarmac – The Hijacking of PK326*, World Bank Group Archives.
2. *Benazir Papers: The State and Government: Democracy, Historical Resistance and Resilience*, Aizaz-ud-Din TBM Publishers, Lahore, 2014.

3. Bhutto, Benazir, *Daughter of the East: An Autobiography*, Pocket Books, 2008.

4. All are available on www.sanipanhwar.com, accessed 13 May 2020

5. Bhutto, Zulfikar Ali, *The Myth of Independence*, OUP, Lahore, 1969.

6. Bhutto, Zulfikar Ali, *The Great Tragedy*, Vision Publications, Karachi, 1971.

7. Bhutto, Zulfikar Ali, *My Dearest Daughter: A Letter from the Death Cell*, Classic, Lahore, 1995.

8. Bhutto, Zulfikar Ali, *If I Am Assassinated*, Vikas, New Delhi, 1979.

9. Bhutto, Benazir, *The Way Out: Interviews, Impressions, Statements, and Messages*, Mahmood Publications, Karachi, 1988.

10. Panhwar, Sani H. (ed.), *Benazir Bhutto: Selected Speeches, 1989–2007*, M.H. Panhwar Trust, Hyderabad, 2009.

11. Bhutto, Benazir, *The Gathering Storm*, Vikas, New Delhi, 1983, p. 78.

12. Mitra, Sumit, '"Pakistan: The Gathering Storm" Raises More than a Storm in India and Abroad', *India Today*, 15 October 1983.

13. Booklet recording contributions to a 'national seminar' held Sunday, 8 March 1998, Hotel Avari Towers, Karachi.

14. Mody, Piloo, *Zulfi My Friend*, Thompson Press, New Delhi, 1973.

15. Junejo, Chakar Ali, *Zulfikar Ali Bhutto: A Memoir*, National Commission on History and Culture, Islamabad, 1996. Shah, Sayid Ghulam Mustafa, *Bhutto: The Man and the Martyr*, Sindhica Academy, Karachi, 1993.

16. Raza, Rafi, *Zulfikar Ali Bhutto and Pakistan, 1966–1977*, OUP, Karachi, 1997.

17. Hassan, Mubashir, *The Mirage of Power: An Inquiry into the Bhutto Years, 1971–1977*, Jumhoori, Lahore, 2016.

18. Niazi, Kausar, *Last Days of Premier Bhutto*, Vikas, New Delhi, 1992.

19. Khan, Gul Hassan, *Memoirs of Lt. Gen. Gul Hassan Khan*, OUP, Karachi, 1993.

20. Arif, K.M., *Working with Zia: Pakistan's Power Politics, 1977–1988*, OUP, Karachi, 1995.

21. Taseer, Salman, *Bhutto: A Political Biography, 1944–2011*, Ithaca, London, 1979.

22. Wolpert, Stanley, *Zulfi Bhutto of Pakistan: His Life and Times*, OUP, New York, 1993.

23. Hameed, Syeda, *Born to be Hanged: Political Biography of Zulfikar Ali Bhutto*, Rupa Publications, New Delhi, 2019.

24. Ahmad, Shamim, *Zulfikar Ali Bhutto: The Psychodynamics of His Rise and Fall*, Paramount Books, 2018.

25. Lodhi, Maleeha, 'Bhutto, the Pakistan People's Party and Political Development in Pakistan: 1967–1977', PhD thesis, London School of Economics and Political Science, 1980, p. 25.

26. Shaikh, Muhammed Ali, *Benazir Bhutto: A Political Biography*, Oriental Books, Karachi, 2000. Akhund, Iqbal, *Tia & Error: The Advent and Eclipse of Benazir Bhutto*, OUP, Karachi, 2000.

27. Allen, Brooke, *Benazir Bhutto: Favored Daughter*, New Harvest, Boston, 2016.

28. Bhatia, Shyam, *Goodbye Shahzadi: A Political Biography of Benazir Bhutto*, Roli Books, New Delhi, 2008.

29. Anwar, Raja, *The Terrorist Prince: The Life and Death of Murtaza Bhutto*, Verso, London, 1997.

30. Bhutto, Fatima, *Songs of Blood and Sword: A Daughter's Memoir*, Vintage, London, 2011.

FURTHER READING

COLONIAL PERIOD

Ansari, Sarah F.D., *Sufi Saints and State Power: The Pirs of Sind, 1843–1947*, Cambridge University Press, Cambridge, 2002.

Cheesman, David, *Landlord Power and Rural Indebtedness in Colonial Sind, 1865–1901*, Curzon Press, Richmond, Surrey, 1997.

ZULFIKAR ALI BHUTTO

Fallaci, Oriana, *Interview with History*, trans. John Shepley, Michael Joseph, London, 1976.

Hassan, Mubashir, *The Mirage of Power: An Inquiry into the Bhutto Years, 1971–1977*, Jumhoori Publications, Lahore, 2016.

Niazi, Kausar, *Zulfikar Ali Bhutto of Pakistan: Last Days*, Vikas Publishing House, New Delhi, 1992.

Raza, Rafi, *Zulfikar Ali Bhutto and Pakistan, 1967–1977*, Oxford University Press, Karachi, 1998.

Taseer, Salmaan, *Zulfikar Ali Bhutto: A Political Biography*, Vikas Publishing House, New Delhi, 1980.

Wolpert, Stanley, *Zulfi Bhutto of Pakistan: His Life and Times*, Oxford University Press, New York, 1993.

BENAZIR BHUTTO AND HER BROTHERS

Akhund, Iqbal, *Trial & Error: The Advent and Eclipse of Benazir Bhutto*, Oxford University Press, Karachi, 2000.

Allen, Brooke, *Benazir Bhutto: Favored Daughter*, New Harvest, Boston, 2016.

Anwar, Raja, *The Terrorist Prince: The Life and Death of Murtaza Bhutto*, Verso, London, 1997.

Bhutto, Benazir, *Daughter of the East: An Autobiography*, Pocket Books, London, 2008.

Bhutto, Fatima, *Songs of Blood and Sword: A Daughter's Memoir*, Vintage, London, 2011.

Shaikh, Muhammed Ali, *Benazir Bhutto: A Political Biography*, Oriental Books, Karachi, 2000.

INDEX

For Pakistani names as far as possible normal inversion has been used in the compilation of this index so individuals are entered under their last or family name. If usage or familiarity suggests otherwise this has been signposted at the entry for the last or family name.

INDEX

INDEX

INDEX

Maududi, Maulana 94, 106
mausoleum 249
May, Philip 124
May, Theresa 124
May Day 78
Mayhew, Colonel Alfred Hercules 18–21, 24, 193
McMurdo, James 11
Mehsud, Lieutenant General Allam Jan 166
Mehsud, Baitullah 218, 228–31, 244
Mehsud, Mohsin 231
Mehsud, Rehmatullah 231
Mehsud tribesmen 230
Menon, V.P. 30
Middle East 80
Middle East Institute 241
MIDNIGHT JACKAL, Operation 169, 170, 216
military *see* army
Military Intelligence 166
Mill, John Stuart 72
Ministry of Commerce 47
Ministry of Defence 157
Ministry of Finance 156
Ministry of Fuel, Power and Natural Resources 47
Ministry of Religious Affairs 193
Ministry of the Interior 229
Mirza, Iskander 45–6, 47
Mirza, Saul 221
Modi, Narendra 266
Modi, Piloo 74, 79, 183
Moghuls 8, 10
Mohajir Quami Movement *see* MQM
Mohajirs 94–5, 97, 101, 160
Mohammed, Dost 126
Mohammed, Khalid Sheikh 216, 237
Mohammed, Prophet 92
Mohammed, Sufi 195
Mohammed, Wali 230
Mohammed, Yar 114
Mohmand Agency 238
Mohmand rifles 237
ul-Momineen, Amir 196
Monde, Le 72
Moscow 48, 73
Mother Eugene 122
Mothercat 58
'Mountains Don't Cry' (*Dawn*) 77
Movement for the Restoration of Democracy (MRD) 131, 150
MQM
  Al Zulfikar and 140
  pressures mount 189
  share of votes 159
  switches sides 169
  violence in Karachi 178–9
MQM Haqiqi 189
Muharrem ceremonies 192
Mukhtar, Chaudry Ahmed 208
Mules, H.C. 24
Mullen, Admiral Michael 262
Mullen, General William F. 258
Multan 98, 102, 165
Mumbai 237, 240, 253, 262 *see also* Bombay
Munir Commission 92
Muñoz, Heraldo 235
Murree 121, 122
Musa, General 51
Musawat (PPP) 127, 142
Musawat-i-Muhammadi 94
Musharraf, General Pervez 6, 208, 214–15
  American support 220
  attempt on life of 237
  Benazir holds back on 223–4
  Bilawal accuses 267
  declares state of emergency 225–7
  investigating of Benazir assassination 233, 239, 241
  involvement in Benazir's death considered 243
  offensive on South Waziristan 240
  seeks alternative leader to Benazir 256
  Taliban and 217
  voters looking for change from 251
  Zardari and PML(N) against 253
Mushtaq, Maulvi 139
Muslim League
  Ayub's faction 48
  ISI opposition alliance 157
  leftist viewpoint of 206
  Murtaza sets out to kill leaders 202
  Raja Anwar 137
  rally cancelled 150
  share of vote 190, 208
  Zulfikar considers faction of 58
Muslims
  a history 59
  conquest of Spain 52
  country dwellers 13
  female leaders and 161, 162–3
  Hindus and 38–9, 76
  in Sindh 10, 26–30
  Pakistan claims leadership 173
  UN, birth control and 164
  University 24
  younger generation 88
  see also Islam

313

INDEX

INDEX